Identity and the Failure of America

of America

From Thomas Jefferson to the War on Terror

JOHN MICHAEL

UNIVERSITY OF MINNESOTA PRESS

MINNEAPOLIS • LONDON

Passages from the Introduction were previously published as "Liberal Justice and Particular Identity: Cavell, Emerson, Rawls," *Arizona Quarterly* 64 (Spring 2008): 27–47. An earlier version of a portion of chapter 5 was published as "Democracy, Aesthetics, Individualism: Emerson as Public Intellectual," in "Ralph Waldo Emerson Bicentenary," special issue, *Studies in Nineteenth-Century Prose* 30 (Spring/Fall 2003): 196–226. An earlier version of the Conclusion was published as "Beyond Us and Them: Identity and Terror from an Arab-American's Perspective," in "Palestine America," special issue, *South Atlantic Quarterly* 102 (Fall 2003): 701–28.

Published by the University of Minnesota Press
111 Third Avenue South, Suite 290
Minneapolis, MN 55401-2520
http://www.upress.umn.edu

Library of Congress Cataloging-in-Publication Data

Michael, John
Identity and the failure of America : from Thomas Jefferson to the War on Terror / John Michael.
p. cm.
Includes bibliographical references and index.
ISBN 978-0-8166-5143-6 (hc : alk. paper) — ISBN 978-0-8166-5144-3 (pb : alk. paper)
1. National characteristics, American. 2. Nationalism—United States—History. 3. Group identity—United States—History. 4. Allegiance—United States—History. 5. Failure (Psychology)—United States—History. 6. Social justice—United States—History. 7. United States—Social conditions. 8. United States—Politics and government. 9. United States—Intellectual life. 10. American literature—History and criticism. I. Title.
E169.1.M597 2008
305.800973—dc22
2008014711

Identity and the Failure
of America

CONTENTS

ACKNOWLEDGMENTS

I began writing what eventually became this book about a month before September 11, 2001, and finished it as the war in Iraq intensified in its fourth year. As the project evolved, it inevitably took on a certain shape under the pressures of these events.

Over the years many, as always, have helped me think through the issues I here address. Thomas DiPiero, Randall Halle, Rachel Ablow, Stephanie Li, Karen Beckman, James Longenbach, Genevieve Guenther, Barry Tharaud, Edgar Dryden, and Mohammed Bamyeh read various chapters, took on various arguments, and forced me to clarify my thinking. That my thinking is not clearer than it is cannot be blamed on them. They tried.

Bette London and Tom Hahn furnished much in the way of food, wine, and intellectual stimulation. Joan Saab, Robert Levine, Grant Farred, Stephen Brauer, Bruce Robbins, Hortense Spillers, Larry Hudson, Jeffrey Tucker, Cilas Kemedjio, and Paul Smith offered encouragement and insights sometimes, I'm sure, without realizing they were doing so. Like anyone who writes on Thomas Jefferson, I owe a debt to my colleague Frank Suffelton. The Frederick Douglass Institute for African and African-American Studies and the Susan B. Anthony Institute for Gender and Women's Studies offered me many occasions for frank and open discussion with generous colleagues. These represent interdisciplinarity at its most challenging and very best.

For his generous belief in this project, I am deeply in Richard Morrison's debt and also for his willingness to share drinks at conferences.

Nancy Sauro and Rebecca Burditt worked unstintingly to prepare the final manuscript.

I would like to remember my father, my mother, and my brother, who make an appearance in the book's conclusion, and my sister's and my family who are still here.

As always I drew lavishly on the formidable resources of Sharon Willis who read every chapter at least once, put up with my testy responses to criticism, and lent me her confidence when my own failed. I couldn't have done this book without her, but there is little in my life about which I couldn't say that. I hope my daughters, Marta and Krystyna, will like this book and that they will live in a world where the failures of America and the claims of identity no longer press so heavily on so many.

The Failure of America and the Claims of Identity

Justice and Identity in Theory, in Practice, and in the United States

Within the university and in the more general public sphere, thoughtful people seem uncertain what to say about identity. Identity, of course, has long been a problem. For several decades considerations of identity—the construction of subjects by particular attributes or positionings related to race, class, or gender—energized research in literature, history, and the social sciences. Differences of culture and perspective rather than the commonalities of national belonging or universal values focused work in women's studies, in African and African-American studies, in postcolonial theory, and in mainstream English, history, and political theory.[1] While the best of such work struggled to avoid easy attributions of essential or authentic contents to the identities it analyzed, the focus on difference posed problems that pundits were quick to point out. In the early 1990s, public critics (usually from the right but occasionally from the left) launched a series of attacks on "multiculturalism," "pluralism," and "relativism" that Dinesh D'Souza, Arthur Schlesinger, and Todd Gitlin (to take three varied examples) described and condemned as politically divisive, inherently racist, and intellectually indefensible.[2] In one form or another each of these critics claimed that linking culture to identity and identity to difference impeached the prerogatives of individuals, made group identities impenetrable or incomprehensible to each other, and made ethical universals and democratic politics more difficult to imagine.

I

More specifically, the field of American studies has also come to be ruled by two powerful, influential, and mutually contradictory visions of identity. On the one hand there is a multicultural or pluralist critique of national identity in general and American identity in particular, a critique that dissolves the implicitly universalizing and abstracting tendencies of the nation into particularities of race, gender, class, and ethnicity. This critique calls the saliency of the nation into question or reduces its existence to little more than an ideological deception occluding specific realities of power, difference, and exploitation. Influential work by, among many others, Hortense Spillers, Dana Nelson, Robyn Wiegman, and Russ Castronovo have helped make this compelling position current.[3] On the other hand, there is a universalizing critique of identity categories that reintroduces universality but rejects the saliency of specifically racial, gender, class, or ethnic particularities. This critique calls identity itself into question by exposing the belief that any prescribed identity (African-American, male or female, gay or straight) has salient characteristics incommensurable to the realities of material existence or the contingencies of individual agency in an increasingly cosmopolitan economic or social world. Recent and powerful work by Walter Benn Michaels, Ross Posnock, Paul Gilroy, and Philip Fisher have advanced this claim, which seems about to become the field's accepted wisdom. After decades of fascination with the ins and outs of identity, "indifference to difference" seems about to become the new watchword in literary and cultural studies.[4]

This argument, which continues in public and academic discourse, represents a neat intellectual and ethical problem. Both sides, as so often happens, have a point. It is remarkably difficult to specify in general terms what the relationship between individual and group identity is. Attempts to reduce the former to the latter, to see individuals primarily as members of groups, tend to lapse into essentialist errors, prescriptions, and even violence and seem to complicate more general appeals to just impartiality. But both history and literature suggest that attempts to deny the salient existence of group identities and allegiances deny as well a crucial part of social and political life both within and beyond the United States. Most recently, a resurgence of interest in cosmopolitanism, linked to the putative decline of the nation-state, and in liberal ideals of individual autonomy and universal justice within the academy promises to further distance American studies from identity questions.[5] Yet, lived experience, the stuff of literature,

politics, and ethics, seems more complex than either embracing or rejecting identity can allow. At this moment many, perhaps most, people experience themselves—voluntarily or not—as individuals situated in the world
through their complex, conflicted, and compelling identifications with, belonging to, or rejection of various and heterogeneous groups. In the United
States and elsewhere, national identity retains a vital and sometimes lam-
entable appeal, though agreement on what might be the actual content of
any identity—national or otherwise—remains elusive.

This book examines historical instances and contemporary articulations
of a crucial aspect of identity in the United States: its intimate if often
conflicted relationship to justice. The concept of identity in the United
States has always been complex and involves two distinct senses. The first
is an inclusive national identity, which in nationalist discourse has based
itself on appeals to a universal and just lawfulness, sometimes called an
American creed. The second involves identities in America that are more
regional or corporeal, identities involving race and ethnicity or class and
gender, for example, borne by peoples who have met injustices and suffered discrimination at the hands of those who, paradoxically, believe they
uphold the nation's fundamental belief in equity, opportunity, and freedom, those abstract idealizations that continue to stir the pride or stimu-
late the yearning of American citizens. In this sense, then, the debates over
whether or not identity exists are not debates over identity in the United
States but arguments within the discursive contours of American identity
itself. In discourse, at least, the United States remains the land of opportunity, the home of the free, the world's greatest democracy. In reality,
the history and legacy of exclusion, oppression, and disenfranchisement of
blacks, women, and the poor indicate the nation's failure to fulfill its promise. The peculiarity of identity in the United States emerges in the contestations between those prescribed identities, the injustices they have borne,
and a national identity promising justice to all.

Frequently the very phrases that identify the nation's ideals have helped
to hide the disenfranchisement, oppression, and injustice suffered by people marked by differences of race or class, gender or sexuality, language or
religion. If as Gunnar Myrdal, who first coined the phrase the "American
Creed" in 1944, put it, "America is continuously struggling for its soul," then
that struggle has most often occurred when those people whose suffering
gives the lie to the nation's self-congratulatory discourse make known their

identities and the injuries they have suffered because of those identities.[6] What seems crucial here is not only the existence of both these senses of identity in America—the abstract universal and the corporeal particular— but also the complex conflicts and interplay between them. In that intricate and ongoing dynamic, both the tragic failures and the persistent appeals of American identities have emerged and continue to change. To put this point differently, identity in the United States has frequently taken shape and shifted in moments of crisis marked by a constitutive conflict between a national promise of justice and those who indicate or embody the injured identities that prove that the nation has failed to make that promise good.

As the title of this book suggests, I see American national identity as marked by failure. The particular identities that sometimes seem to stand arrayed against the nation's claim to universal and impartial inclusiveness bear more potent witness to that failure and its implications than they do to any inherently divisive cultural or racial differences among people. To register the claims of identity in U.S. history and culture requires considering identity's part in the failure of a universalized American ideal of liberty and justice for all to include those whose identities have seemed to place them beyond the nation's pale. In the United States, the claims of identity have most often taken the form not of demands for separation but of accusations that the nation has failed or is about to fail to live up to its own inclusive principles and to fulfill its own just identity.[7]

I do not wish to return American studies to its original foundations in American exceptionalism. I do want to argue that excluding identity questions—including questions of national identifications—from considerations of culture, literature, or politics misses the way literary and political discourse in the United States has worked and also makes understanding the current global situation in which the United States plays such a large and vexed role more difficult. Far from writing as if the United States— even as an ideal—could be successfully reduced to a single universalizing personification and subject, my point is that the peculiar force of appeals to identity in the United States depends on understanding the nation not as merely plural but as multiply contested. American national identity remains the field upon which those contestations of particular identities most frequently occur. Identity in the United States emerges in the dynamic tension between the nation's claims to universalism and the claims of particular identities whose demands for justice remark the nation's failure to realize its principles. Those demands for justice represent both the failure of the nation and the persistent force of its promise.

Neither theoretically nor historically can this dynamic of American national identity be reducible to a discourse that is the sole or primary province of "white men," though at times—as in my readings of Du Bois, Melville, and Douglass—the incoherencies of that category become important. I show in this book that "race men" like Douglass and Du Bois, feminist agitators like Child and Stowe, and even "terrorists" like John Brown and Nat Turner (particularly in his heroic avatar as a black American folk hero) appeal to the same universal claims for justice and to a national discourse obsessed with justice to legitimize their causes and to mobilize their audiences. In those appeals to justice, the specificities of the identities these plaintiffs inhabit or assume remain both existentially and politically important. They cannot be reduced to essentialized racial, gender, or other embodiments, but that is far from saying that they cease to matter.

People in the United States and around the world, for good and for ill, continue to respond to an American creed that associates the nation with justice and to accuse the nation from a variety of aggrieved identity positions of having failed to achieve its self-proclaimed identity. Unless we who attempt to analyze or describe American culture and politics at this crucial juncture assume the task of accounting for this dynamic of identity and justice, we are unlikely either to generate compelling accounts of this nation's failures—accounts, that is, of America's history—or to shed light on the possibility of a less catastrophic future for the United States and the world.

Not the least motive for this book, explored in its conclusion, is my conviction that the beliefs and attitudes here examined—the promises and limitations of American identity and the pressing identity claims that remark its failure—continue in the constitution and the critique of America's imperial policies. Especially in the Middle East and in the increasingly dangerous war on terror, Americans are told they must fight against an enemy who simply hates their values and freedoms. The nation itself, especially the nation's beliefs, somehow seems to be at risk. The invasion of a foreign country seems to serve as an extension of liberty's empire, though how military occupation and civil war might inaugurate democracy was always difficult to explain. For those on the receiving end of the nation's policies both in the homeland and abroad, the irony of a nation intent upon defending its freedoms by threatening human rights and violating international law is readily apparent. For those conversant with the nation's history, this irony seems bitterly familiar. Dominant ways of engaging with and understanding the contemporary world continue the dynamics of failed justice, persistent identity, and fears about the nation's failures that emerged during the formative years of nineteenth-century American ideological, political, and cultural struggle before and after the Civil War.

The point of this book, then, is to revitalize rather than to abandon questions of identity. I believe that dismissing the discursive pull either of a universal national identity identified with allegiance to just principles or of specific particular identities marked for gender or race or class differences denies the lived experiences, past and present, that American literary, cultural, and political discourses record. I believe it remains important to read that record. As Kwame Anthony Appiah puts it, "Identities make ethical claims because—and this is just a fact about the world we human beings have created—we make our lives *as* men and *as* women, *as* gay and *as* straight people, *as* Ghanians and *as* Americans, *as* blacks and *as* whites."[8] However erroneous or fantastic they may be, identities, on all levels, continue to shape realities, determine allegiances, and define conflicts both here and abroad. An American studies that rejects the problem of identity will be unlikely to reach or to move an audience within or beyond the academy for whom identity questions remain the basis of powerfully attractive appeals, threats, and mobilizations—for ill, certainly, but maybe for good as well. Rather than being antithetical to democracy or to the ideals of the United States, identity groups and their claims have long been—for good and bad—a crucial part of democratic deliberations in the United States and of the evolving and shifting ideal of what justice in the United States, that crucial value in the nation's failed creed and unachieved identity, actually means.[9]

IDENTITY AND FAILURE

Histories of racism, sexism, and nativism have determined that identities in the United States have long involved injustices. Plausibly, therefore, some critics believe that the nation's failures might be redeemed by recognizing identity itself as an error. Philip Fisher, to take a compelling example, analyzes how "collapses of democratic space" and the experience of "catastrophic politics" can forge fugitive and polymorphous identifications—the fragmentary and shifting sense of momentary and contingent belonging common in various forms to all subjects—into apparently monumental and univocal identities dividing the nation along racial, gender, or class lines. He claims that these identities, however powerful they may seem, represent mistakes. "It is important to note," he writes, "that it is only in relation to catastrophic politics and apocalyptic conditions that a collapse occurs in which poly-identities disappear into what we might call a single hunted identity, as happened to European Jews from 1930 to 1945. . . . We would make a grave mistake to apply these apocalyptic conditions of regional identity to ordinary social life."[10] But if the experience of identity is a mistake, it cannot be a simple error like an error of fact. To say, as Fisher does, that those who claim single identities, often in relation to the collapse of politics and an experience of outrage, mistake themselves or exaggerate their suffering is always possible—and it is in fact possible to mistake oneself and to exaggerate one's claims—but it is a different order of mistake than those errors associated with the objective world. Errors of identity are errors of feeling and of judgment. In effect, Fisher says, to those who believe themselves to be inhabiting specific identities and confronting the pain of oppression and the terror of injustice, don't exaggerate your suffering.[11] No doubt one woman's catastrophic apocalypse—being compelled by the state to bring an unwanted pregnancy to term, for instance—may be another's tempest in a teapot. In Fisher's opinion, the democratic space has not collapsed and apparently essential particular identities are in reality merely parts of the polymorphous national whole. That, however, may depend on the position from which one surveys the terrain.

The nation's history and the experiences of its peoples indicate that the free, polymorphous associations that Fisher celebrates have been more available to some identities than to others. Moreover, the fear of America's catastrophic collapse as a democratic place has been far more common and far more definitive in the republic's imaginative life than Fisher admits. Mistaken or not, the fear of the nation's catastrophic failure has, from the nation's beginnings, played a determining part in the imaginative life of the republic and its citizens and a definitive part in their experience of identity's persistent importance.

Nonetheless, Fisher, like other critics of identity, has a point. All this concern with identity may, from a theoretical perspective, be an error. This may be true, but attention to identity may still be a practical necessity in a nation self-dedicated to justice. The catastrophic emotions attached to identity, whether we finally believe them to be well motivated or not, make it difficult simply to ignore identity. Fisher's own telling association of identity with catastrophe suggests that identities cannot be adequately imagined as peaceful incorporations of or identifications with others in one's group if one seeks accurately to represent identity as an experience in and of the world. Identity frequently names an experience that is violently reactive, catastrophically incorporative, and terrifyingly abject. These are not issues incidental to identity but processes constitutive of it and outside of which it makes little sense at all. In this light, it seems largely irrelevant to call identity mistaken since—viewed logically—any identity may well be a mistake, but asking someone to accept her view of her own identity as mistaken is a bit like telling a friend that they are wrong about whom they choose to love or hate. It seldom works. One loves or hates or feels injured, often suspecting that there is something wrong in doing so, though that suspicion not only seems to function on a different level from the troublesome sense of connection possessing one's heart but might actually intensify one's experience of the emotion in question.

Identities, as Hume knew, stand not as natural things or objective facts but as imaginative constructs and emotional attachments. Identity plays a crucial part in the agonistic and affective movements of the world. Despite repeated claims from influential writers that the world has entered a post-postmodern period, in which national and corporeal identities no longer much matter, the hopes and fears attached to problems of identity persist. In the United States, identities have always been problematic. Yet the problem of identity does seem recently to have changed and therefore seems to require, especially within the confines of the United States, new attempts at articulation.[12]

IDENTITY AND COSMOPOLITANISM

The self-conception of the United States as a just nation, an empire for liberty (to evoke Jefferson's well-known and deeply unsettling phrase) founded upon lawful networks of association rather than upon brutal impositions of force, participates from the first in a conflicted but inescapable global worldliness. American values persistently enjoin ideals of universal hospitality, expansive belonging, and reliable justice that remain powerful though they have yet to be realized. These ideals—not uniquely but peculiarly

American—entail confrontations or negotiations with "the other," meaning those who may be dispossessed, excluded, or injured, who come from somewhere else and seek to make a home here.[13] Questions of individual, national, and international identity, issues of global civilization and cosmopolitan circulation, have long been at home in the United States.

Cosmopolitanism and globalization are thus unlikely, at least for the foreseeable future, to signal the end of national or regional identities because, especially in the United States, they have been part of both since the beginning.[14] Cosmopolitanism, part of the everyday life and anxiety of American communities, has also been since the Enlightenment a special property of intellectual work. The lives of American intellectuals, from the seventeenth century to the present day, have been, like the lives of their European and non-European contemporaries, determinately international. In Emerson's time, ministerial and academic aspirants pursued advanced degrees in German universities, returning home with philological techniques and rationalist philosophies that were as essential to the emergence of Boston Unitarianism and New England transcendentalism, to take a regional example, as were the local Puritan legacy and the woods around Concord. But of course, Perry Miller's examination of the New England mind long ago established that Puritanism itself was a transatlantic tradition deeply rooted in the intellectual ferment of the European renaissance and the political upheavals of the English revolution. In the nineteenth century, men of letters, like Longfellow—romanticist of the New World and its natives *and* a professor of romance languages who translated Dante—were more commonly polyglot than they are today. American writers like Irving, Cooper, Hawthorne, and Fuller spent long periods of time abroad and brought those experiences to bear in their work. None of this is controversial or unfamiliar. But recently such facts have received renewed attention because they seem to offer a way to leave the question of national identity in American literature behind.

Among students of American literature, Wai Chee Dimock has made the most original and ambitious argument for the ways in which cosmopolitan perspectives dissolve issues of national identity. Dimock argues strenuously against the "logic [that] assumes that there is a seamless correspondence between the temporal and spatial boundaries of the nation and the boundaries of all other expressive domains."[15] The effort that it takes an Americanist to overcome what has admittedly been a founding and limiting assumption of the field—that American literature grows from American soil and obsessively reflects on the problem of American experience and identity—is evident in the rhetorical overstatement that furnishes the hypnotic music of Dimock's lovely prose. "This book," she writes in *Through Other Continents,*

> Is an attempt to rethink the shape of literature against the history and habitat of the human species, against the "deep time" of the planet Earth, as described by two scientific disciplines, geology and astronomy. The former works with a geological record of some 600 million years, and the latter with a record still more staggering, 14 billion light-years. The humanities have no time frame of comparable length. What we do have are written records going back five or six thousand years, and oral, musical, and visual material going back further. (6)

Dimock's project is wholly laudable, and her presentation of it is very striking. But it should not require recourse to the sublime to reintroduce the concept of transnational traditions or the practices of comparative literature to literary studies. This work comes like a proverbial breath of fresh air to a discipline too long locked in a stuffy inwardness and airless historicity. And yet it leaves me dissatisfied as well, as if finally its brilliant rhetorical effects and impressive scope cannot quite sustain the basic claims its author wants to make. For example, the relationships between the Ghitas, Thoreau, Gandhi, and King, are fascinating, and Dimock traces them with truly impressive energy and invention. But when she claims that she has thus traced out "the spatial width of one community of readers, at once nonmilitary and nongovernmental," something drops out of her account (22). Similarly, when she bravely takes on the universalizing aspect of aesthetics in Ezra Pound's fascination with Fascism, a crucial confrontation with the political seems simultaneously announced and avoided (107–22). For in the cases of Thoreau, Gandhi, and King, and the example of Pound, something governmental requires address even if only in their opposition to it, and certainly the least interesting aspect of Pound's situation would seem to be his treason, on which, admittedly, his critics focused. In each case issues of the state and of identity, of the failure of governments to adhere to their own principles, and the identities—racial and national—of those aggrieved by that failure continue to determine the nature of global civil society "both above and below the plane of the nation" (23) and indicate as well that just politics and equitable policies do not flow naturally or inevitably from either identification with or resistance to national identity or state power. Cosmopolitan politics occurs at the place where the limitations of the nation and the challenges of global civility intersect. Dimock's refocusing of her readers' attention on the sublimity of planetary space and deep time threatens, from that elevation, to lose sight of that usually conflicted locality.

When the failure of America occasions sublimity, it comes most often in the form of Burkean terror rather than of Kantian transport. In this book, I am interested in exemplary moments when precisely the nature of the United States as an irreducibly cosmopolitan and essentially conflicted nation comes to the fore. I am interested in the functioning of an assortment of discursive acts—scientific reports, novels, speeches, and essays— that seek to reclaim or challenge the nation's identity with universal justice in the context of conflicted particularities. In an important sense there is nothing extraordinary about this, since it entails the articulation of the particular with the universal that judgment and justice both require. Kant, of course, knew that this articulation occurs in the realm of the aesthetic and the world of experience that belongs to art as much as to ethics or politics. But it brings us to the very limit of what art can do. Dimock notes elsewhere that literature is little suited to elaborations of justice because literature dwells with the particular and justice refers to the universal. For this reason, as she elegantly puts it, in "literary texts . . . we can encounter the idea of justice not as a formal universal, and not as an objective relation among things, but as a provisional dictate, an *incomplete* dictate, haunted always by what it fails to encompass."[16] In the literature that interests me here, it is precisely the productive tension in a society that is practically heterogeneous and in principle cosmopolitan, between assertions of the universal and the claims of the particular. In the United States this tension emerges in a nation committed to justice but failing to achieve it. In that productive tension, issues of identity take and change shape in ways that literature may be best suited to construe. Refusing to forget this American aspect of U.S. identity and American culture recalls a tradition where the promises of American national identity served not only as a sop for the self-satisfied but as a mobilizing rhetoric for those confronting the nation's failure and constrained to demand justice for other sufferers or for themselves.

U.S. national discourse has a deep time of its own, to borrow Dimock's suggestive term from her later work, sedimented into its imaginative life as the image of an American nation that writers, intellectuals, and activists both idealize and seek to reform. At this moment, when so much done in the name of American ideals has gone so badly for so many, reclaiming a discourse of national belonging as a critical tool and reformulating once again the nation's promises and limitations in the light of its glaring failures seem too important a project, too pressing an ethical obligation, for American critics and writers to ignore. Especially in mapping the nation's conflicted place on the planet, it may be well to remember that in the absence of justice, cosmopolitanism may be as much an opportunity for identities to clash and to reassert themselves as an occasion for them to disappear.

Justice in Theory, or Identity and the Liberal Tradition

Despite the passing fashion of identity politics and multiculturalism, the claims of identity have always been difficult for Americans to assess. In the liberal tradition, so long dominant in the United States and recently resurgent in the American academy, the relationship of particular identities to justice is especially and necessarily conflicted. To many Americans—both left and right—justice and identity seem mutually exclusive. Identity, prejudice, and discrimination stand opposed to universality, equity, and freedom. Liberalism—for example, as elaborated by Locke and Kant during the Enlightenment and by John Rawls in the twentieth century—demands that justice dissolve all particularities to enact a universal and equitable lawfulness. The history of the modern world, and the history of the United States in particular, makes clear that such dissolutions of identity accomplish themselves far less often in practice than in theory. Identities and identity claims persist. As Kwame Anthony Appiah, considering the vexatious persistence of identities in liberal political thought puts it, "What's modern is that we conceptualize identity in particular ways. What's age old is that when we are asked—and ask ourselves—*who* we are, we are being asked *what* we are as well."[17] In practice, it would seem, a concern with justice, even when justice gets identified with liberalism, cannot make identity disappear. As long as the question of who we are includes, in our confrontation with our interrogator, what we are—even if that interrogator is ourselves—identity seems less a sign of harmonious belonging than a site of contestation and of potential conflict. Such sites are places where justice, the principled effort of adjudication, would seem to be required.

Interesting tensions emerge when the theory of liberalism is made to reflect on the United States, where liberalism seems most at home, as a site of justice or, as Philip Fisher puts it, a democratic space. In this context, justice and identity may be, in fact, not mutually exclusive but interdependent. In a discursive space deformed by discriminatory prejudices like racism, sexism, and class privilege, doing justice entails not ignoring the other's identity but recognizing what that identity demands in contexts where injustice and identity have been firmly linked. Identity, in these cases, represents both the possible fulfillment and the present failure of liberalism's dream of universality, the dangerous and necessary essence of America's national self-identity. Debates about liberalism usually miss this point. The failure of America has been the failure to do justice to identities and the failure to adequately attend to the demands those prescribed identities represent. In the final analysis, these problems of justice and identity in the United States are neither abstract nor theoretical but concrete and practical, the residuum of a specific history of bigotry and exploitation.

Failures to do justice to people or to groups are, of course, not particularly or especially American, but in the United States they often assume a particular significance. The United States has only its paradoxically universal principles with which to identify its own particularity. The conflicted nature of American inclusiveness has been its most distinctive characteristic.[18] If the United States had ever succeeded in truly becoming a teeming nation of nations, a place where individuals were judged by the content of their character rather than the color of their skin or the weight of their purses, a government truly of (all) the people, for (all) the people, and by (all) the people, a real empire of liberty and justice for all, then identity questions would long ago have ceased to occupy the imagination of its citizens in the pressing, frequently violent ways they still do. Certainly the United States is not exceptional in having failed to achieve these laudable goals, but for no other nation does that failure to negotiate just relationships with diverse identities entail a crisis on the most fundamental level of the national identity itself. The tension between the discourse of justice on which the nation finds itself and the practices of exclusion, violence, and oppression by which it, like so many other nations, has comported itself at home and in the world determines that identity and identity's relationship to justice remain on the U.S. cultural and political agenda.

For these reasons, John Rawls's *A Theory of Justice,* for all its appeals to universal principles, is a particularly American book, one that emerges from and resists the national obsession with identity and with identity's paradoxical entanglements with justice.[19] In surprising ways it looks forward to Walter Benn Michaels's recent attempts to turn attention away from identity and toward redistributive economics.[20] Rawls's theory of liberalism as redistributive justice is a crucial document in the history of American liberalism. Like any good liberal, Rawls attempts to ground principles of judgment in an abstract and universal subject, one that escapes from the limitations of perspective and the biases of judgment associated with identities in the world. *A Theory of Justice* makes evident the difficulties entailed by such an attempt, for identity proves difficult to escape, even theoretically. It remains an imaginative requirement of the lives humans spend together and of their reflections on those lives. For this reason, as we will see, the abstractions of philosophy and the concretizations of literature often speak to each other and sometimes end up speaking a similarly imaginative language.

In fact, Rawls's attempt to free judgment from the vagaries of identity and to found a philosophical practice of justice on universal laws recalls Emerson's transcendentalism. Like Emerson's *Nature, A Theory of Justice* comprises not only an essay on the American subject but a work of imaginative prescription, one that recommends the remedial power of a particular form of imagining as an antidote to the nation's failings. An Emersonian strain of transcendental idealization traverses Rawls's primary theoretical innovation, the "original position," which he imagines as a sort of subjectless common place where deliberative participants become like transparent eyeballs, being nothing themselves and seeing all at once. In the original position, Rawls attempts to realize the abstract and universal subject on which liberalism believes that justice as fairness depends.[21] For Rawls, justice entails fairness in the distribution of goods and services and, crucially, a universal ability to participate in the community's deliberative processes. In this characteristically American effort to separate justice and identity, he fails, though he succeeds in indicating how imagining justice and imagining identity may be related.

The original position, as Rawls imagines it, furnishes a place where "the first principles of justice" may be determined "as themselves the object of an original agreement." What Rawls poetically calls a "veil of ignorance" defines the limits of this place, because the universality of the agreement that emerges depends on imagining "that the parties [to the discussion] do not know certain kinds of particular facts."[22] These facts about which the parties must be or pretend to be ignorant are facts about themselves, those facts that normally determine identity as the mark of the subject's position in the world:

> First of all, no one knows his place in society, his class position or social sta-
> tus; nor does he know his fortune in the distribution of natural assets and
> abilities, his intelligence and strength, and the like. Nor, again, does anyone
> know his conception of the good, the particulars of his rational plan of life,
> or even the special features of his psychology such as his aversion to risk or
> liability to optimism or pessimism. More than this, I assume that the parties
> do not know the particular circumstances of their own society. That is, they
> do not know its economic or political situation, or the level of civilization
> and culture it has been able to achieve. The persons in the original position
> have no information as to which generation they belong. (118)

Behind the veil of ignorance one becomes like Emerson in his moment of transport on the bare commons, "The name of the nearest friend sounds then foreign and accidental: to be brothers, to be acquaintances, master or servant, is then a trifle and disturbance."[23] The determinates of embodied identity—economic situations, political positioning, civilizational and cultural allegiances—recede and the decorporealized universality of the liberal subject emerges.

Yet for Rawls, the original position—unlike Emerson's transport—does not represent a divine influx of transcendental enthusiasm but a "purely hypothetical situation" that "need never take place, although we can by deliberately following the constraints it expresses simulate the reflections of the parties." The original position is thus a commonly accessible and contingent place of constrained feigning and imaginative simulation. Purely hypothetical as it may be, it represents not an extraordinary state but the mode of imagining that parties must accept if the "circumstances of justice" are to be achieved—though parties can always fail to achieve them—in those "normal conditions under which human cooperation is both possible and necessary," those familiar conditions of social life that are "typically marked by a conflict as well as an identity of interests."[24] The veil of ignorance requires, in those familiar situations where conflicts and identities of interest—which so often become conflicts of identity themselves—demand adjudication, that each subject pretends to forget the identities that those very conflicts help constitute. In short, it requires that each person, from his or her partial perspective, imagines him- or herself to be impartial.

To realize the implications of the original position as a commonplace of imaginative dissimulation—one possible description of "a democratic space," like the one that Philip Fisher associates with the success of the United States—is to realize something not only about impartial justice but also about particular identity and the reliance of both on imagination. This is something familiar that often gets forgotten. The simulations of the original position (the feigning to forget, for the sake of impartiality, one's own interests and identity) remain indispensable to justice and expressive of the common desire that deliberation should lead not to a war of each against all but to an equitable resolution of conflicts and a fair redress of grievances. But how may one actually imagine the normal functioning of this commonplace of justice constituted by the constraints of simulated self-ignorance? If the original position be an imaginative trope rather than an abstractly philosophical construct, what does that suggest about justice and identity? A philosophical construct reliant on hypothetical fantasies and constrained simulations is already more richly imaginative than philosophers might care to admit.

The original position makes specific demands on the imagination. The original position (the structural equivalent of the state of nature in Locke and Hobbes) functions as a deliberative meeting of subjects pretending to be dispossessed of all qualities except commonsense reasoning and minimal sociability. These subjects can discover universal principles of justice because the veil of ignorance determines that no subject knows what personal attributes, group affiliations, or social position—in short what identity—any subject has. No subject knows what personal interests or group affiliations will possess it. No subject knows whether he or she will be a man or a woman (the difficulty of finding syntactical and semantic ways of describing such subjects indicates the difficulty of imagining humans without identities), rich or poor, black or white, gay or straight, ambitious or lazy, intelligent or dumb, talented or talentless, normatively abled or putatively disabled, etc. In the original position, behind the veil of ignorance that separates these difficult to imagine "subjects" without identities from embodied social life in historically determined material worlds, all subjects, Rawls imagines, possess and share only an interest in fairness. In this imaginative suspension, deliberative exchange can discover grounding principles of justice as fairness on which all can, in principle, agree. But can one imagine these subjects in this state actually undertaking these deliberations?[25]

Michael Sandel, one of Rawls's most influential critics, uncovers a contradiction close to the core of Rawls's theory. It seems impossible to imagine that the "deontologized" subject Rawls shields behind the veil of ignorance simultaneously does not know the conditions of existence and engages in adjudicating the conflicts of desires and interests that emerge from those conditions.[26] Deontologized subjects have no interests or desires. Moreover, as Amy Gutmann notes, actually existing subjects often receive their desires and their sense of conflict or injury through their identifications as part of, not apart from, their identities.[27] In the world that the theory of justice attempts to address, in the American world where deliberations about justice seem always to be on the nation's agenda, justice and identity frequently emerge inextricably linked.

The veil of ignorance imagines deliberations about justice distanced from demands for justice; and justice, under these constraints, proves difficult to imagine because the veil of ignorance obscures those problems from which the need for justice arises and with which justice must contend. Justice, as Rawls himself specifies, seeks to balance desires and interests among parties in the world who find themselves in conflict. Without acknowledging the social determinants and, very frequently, the particular identities of the embodied world that constitute the experience and the self-understanding of social subjects, without foregrounding precisely that which the original position and the veil of ignorance were invented to obscure, a practical conversation of justice—indeed any conversation or sociability at all—proves difficult to imagine.

This is less a criticism of justice as a fundamental category (as Sandel and other communitarians have argued) than it is a reminder of what conversations about justice in a real world of contending identities and positions, a world like that which U.S. history and the nation's present situation describes, actually require participants to do. It is true that, like Kant's categorical imperative, the original position constrains subjects to think and act not to express their particular and limited individual interests but as if they were universal subjects.[28] But since no one can actually be a universal subject, justice constrains each disputant imaginatively, as Rawls puts it, to "simulate the reflections of the parties." I take this to mean that each participant in a just conversation must read the demands of particular claims in specific situations as if they were his or her own. Because those claims so often come linked to identities owned by those who believe themselves to have suffered injustice because of their identities, identity itself remains crucially part of imaginable conversations of justice, even when the claim made is that identity should not matter at all.[29] Identity remains a practical requirement of the ethical imagination rather than its theoretical grounds.

Rawls's recourse to words like "simulation" and "representation" suggests that the conversation of justice relies on sensible imagination more than on philosophical abstraction. For the conversation of justice to occur, the complaints of those who suffer in the real world must receive a hearing. The experience of that real world has persuaded many of those who suffer that their suffering and their identities are related. What Rawls's veil of ignorance actually requires—perhaps despite the philosopher's wishes—is not the forgetting of identities but the remembering of community and of conflict, the recollection of relationships among people and of the problems of identity and of interest that so often determine them. The conversation of justice in a nation where injustice has frequently entailed prejudice and discrimination requires that each subject simulate amnesia about its own identity. But justice also requires the acknowledgment of and the imaginative identification with demands made from and for identity positions, even when justice may require that identity finally be forgotten. Justice constrains its subjects to shift identities imaginatively rather than simply to forget them; it requires each subject to ask: what would this proposition or situation look like to me if I were, for example, poor or rich, white or black, or male or female, because those demarcate some of the situations of identity and exclusion requiring judgment. The subjunctive voice bespeaks not so much a general ignorance born of some fantastic deontologizing amnesia but rather the common constraint of something akin to what Keats called "negative capability," the imagining of sensible others and the imaginative identification with them. In such capacities one rediscovers not untroubled grounds for judgment (though the grounds for judgment are there) but renewed toleration of the world's uncertainties. In this imaginative area, justice and literature share common ground.

The conversation of justice requires something akin to Keats's negative capability because it requires imaginative and rhetorical representations of those who demand a reckoning. Deliberative subjects must imagine themselves in the position and identity of the plaintive and imagine how the world might appear from that perspective. Negative capability, like the creative reading Emerson recommends in "History," remedies "the defect of our too great nearness to ourselves."[30] As George Kateb has pointed out, such self-distance is integral to Emerson's notion of self-reliance—a sort of original position of Emerson's own—which necessitates (despite common misunderstandings of Emerson) engagement with, not indifference to, other people. For Emerson, as for Rawls, ethical thinking requires the toleration of "uncertainty, mysteries, doubts, without any irritable reaching after fact and reason" that Keats claimed as the essential attributes of poetic sensibility. Keats wrote, "A poet is the most unpoetical of any thing in existence; because he has no Identity—he is continually in for and filling some other Body."[31] Such poetic sensibility, such imaginative placing of oneself in the embodied place of the other, forms justice's essential requirement as well as the poet's essential character, a character Emerson knew all people could share.[32] Justice, as Rawls describes it, requires losing, at least momentarily, the identity of one's self in order to register and represent the identities of others. The transparent eyeball becomes nothing itself in order to better see and to more accurately understand the identities and the demands of those it lives among.

There is nothing portentous or unfamiliar in identifying the requirements of justice with literary sensibility. Literary sensibility, like justice, merely remarks the commonplace necessity of empathy and imagination in our common lives. To deliberate justly, one must imagine—as a novelist asks a reader to imagine—that this is how this situation or proposition would appear to a certain character, perhaps a homosexual who claims a common right to marriage (whether or not "I" happen to be a homosexual or happen to believe in marriage), where to be a homosexual means the following (and what follows is an explanation of that meaning and a narrative account of what such a person would think of such a situation or proposition and what that might entail). Or, more succinctly, this is what "I" understand a gay man to mean when he says that he is the victim of an injustice. His demand for justice, "I" might then conclude and argue for my conclusion, is founded or unfounded for the following reasons, whatever they may be. By such routine and familiar acts of identification, estimation, and elaboration, "we," a collective of subjects with similar and contending interests—a "community," in short—may accept or reject any given accusation of injustice or demand for retribution. Without such imaginative moments of routine identification, such common expressions of negative capability, the requirements of justice go unmet and the conversation about injustice fails to occur. Justice constrains its subjects not to forget identity, but to put identity into play. This requires not merely the power of rational abstraction to universal principles but the force of imaginative identification with concrete particularities, with actual positions, and with the people in them. These identities and relationships literature has long embodied.

Justice seldom discovers the punctuality of self-evident reasons, but usually works, often repeatedly and sometimes endlessly, toward equitable negotiations of rhetorical appeals. Part of these negotiations inevitably involve disputes about identity. Conversations about justice can always and often do go awry. Individuals and communities often fail to do justice or to achieve just conclusions. Such failures are far from rare. The history of the United States—with its particular imaginative investments in justice as the founding creed of its national identity—is famously replete with examples where both empathy and identification have spectacularly failed. The imaginative and deliberative literature considered in the chapters that follow record the experience and analyze the causes of that failure and reveal that when justice has failed in the United States, when America has failed itself, it has often done so because Americans have failed to adequately or honestly imagine the identities of those demanding justice.

The original position thus returns the subject of justice ineluctably and pragmatically to the open-ended and disputatious enactments of identities that the veil of ignorance seemed to forestall. In the absence of these questions and disputations, in the absence of the pressure of difference and identity, no questions of justice are likely to arise. On the other hand, no simple form of identity politics will be adequate to justice's demands. Particular identities cannot be imagined to ground judgment any more than abstract universals. But identity questions must be part of deliberations about justice as long as identities remark and express experiences of interests, inequity, and exclusion. Simply put, questions of fairness do not arise unless there are injustices to be remedied, and in the United States injustice and identity have long been closely related.

The discussion of justice, the national discussion of identity in the United

States (the discussion of a nation whose self-ideal claims justice as its salient attribute), requires the imaginative construction of and contact between at least two positions, victims and victimizers: those who suffer injustice and those who perpetrate it, profit from it, or remain indifferent to it. As Rawls says, "In these remarks I have assumed that it is always those with the lesser liberty who must be compensated. We are always to appraise the situation from their point of view."[33] Rawls might have added that the identity of those with lesser liberty and their ability to partake in just deliberations also remains open to dispute. Slave owners, like Thomas Jefferson, often claimed, for example, to be more encumbered and less free than those they enslaved who, they also claimed, were incapable of full participation in civil life. These surprising assertions do not alter the fact that these primary identities—victims and victimizers, free and not free—constituted within disputes about justice, appear historically and contingently linked to those other, American identities belonging to embodied men and women, especially to those whose identities have legitimated injustices or precluded participation in conversations about justice. These have included and still include Africans and Native Americans, immigrants and the poor, women, Moslems, Jews, and so on and so forth. The concrete, contingent links between identities and injustice determine that in this world, and in a nation self-dedicated to "justice and liberty for all," identity claims remain indispensable to the nation's imaginative and practical discussion of itself.

IDENTITY AND IMAGINATION

Identity's real limitations play as prominent a part as its imaginative power in attempts to grasp relationships between selves and the world. In the United States, the power and the limitations of identity have been aspects of the same problem of justice. Consider the identity claims of the dominant group; long before whiteness studies became an academic discipline, black intellectuals knew that the apparently unmarked position of the white American male constituted an identity of its own. In the middle of his autobiography, W. E. B. Du Bois finds himself constrained to account for "the race concept which has dominated my life."[34] Even the writer whom Ross Posnock identifies as the quintessential antirace race man finds himself shaped by the categories he inhabits and resists.[35] For Du Bois, identity problems—the difficulties of self-dividing consciousnesses—are the province of not only African Americans. At a crucial moment he turns from considering the question of black identity to considering the character and identity of white Americans. The middle-class or affluent American white male lives—Du Bois specifies—according to several overlapping codes that express his sense of who he is or who he should be. These are, specifically, the codes by which he understands and engages the world according to his assorted identities as a Christian, a gentleman, an American, and a white man, the normative type of the dominant national identity. Imagining a hypothetical white friend attempting to explain himself to himself and to his black associate, Du Bois notes the trouble with this white, male, American identity: "When my friend tabulated all of the codes which he at once and apparently simultaneously was to put in action, he found a most astonishing result, and here it is":

Christian	Gentleman	American	White Man
Peace	Justice	Defense	War
Good Will	Manners	Caste	Hate
Golden Rule	Exclusiveness	Propaganda	Suspicion
Liberty	Police	Patriotism	Exploitation
Poverty	Wealth	Power	Empire[36]

The white man suffers from something more complex than double consciousness. The mutual contradictoriness of these assorted codes of identity are, as Du Bois points out, "not only a dilemma, it is almost a quadrilemma." Even if this poor soul had settled on only two of four—becoming a Christian gentleman and forgetting the American white man, there would still be conflicts impossible to reconcile within his concept of himself. To be a Christian white man requires negotiating demands that are diametrically opposed. Is it any wonder that American white men in particular have, since the republic's beginnings, so often found themselves to be violently and obsessively caught between fearing and denying their own failure to embody the identity their own codes prescribe? The nation's dominant identity would seem to be impossible to embody successfully. The white American Christian gentleman, as Du Bois imagines him, finds himself forced to confront the damning inconsistencies of his own identity when he confronts questions posed from the position of one who has experienced American identity only through its failure to embody its own fine-sounding ideals.

Faced with such uncomfortable demands for justice, those who represent the dominant identities in the United States have frequently had recourse to simple and violent exclusions of those who make these demands. They have often attempted to keep blacks, women, and the poor, for example, from the conversations about justice that constitute such an important part of America's national discourse. Thus, the failure of the white American to be a Christian and a gentleman—as Du Bois defines those categories—entails consequences for the identities of those whom the white American, in failing to recognize his own failures, fails to recognize as well.

For Du Bois, the nation's failed justice determines the identities and experiences of those who live within a veil of ignorance different from the veil of ignorance that Rawls describes:

> It is difficult to let others see the full psychological meaning of caste segregation. It is as though one, looking out from a dark cave in a side of an impending mountain, sees the world passing and speaks to it; speaks courteously and persuasively, showing them how these entombed souls are hindered in their natural movement, expression, and development; and how their loosening from prison would be a matter not simply of courtesy, sympathy, and help to them, but aid to all the world.[37]

Here the dwellers entombed in the living death of caste-bound identity demand a just consideration of their plight, making their demands in good Kantian form on the basis of solid, rational principles and explaining how the world looks different from where they are situated. They talk "evenly and logically in this way" only to find that "the passing throng does not even turn its head" (650). A veil—to use Du Bois's famous metaphor for lives constructed and divided by the color line—like "some thick sheet of invisible but horribly tangible plate glass is between them and the world" (650). This is a veil of ignorance, the ignorance of the dominant classes that keeps those stigmatized by caste from occupying a place in the democratic space of the nation or participating in its ongoing conversation. This ignorance ensures not a generous and rational understanding but a mean and terrible misapprehension. "Some of the passing world stop in curiosity; these gesticulations seem so pointless; they laugh and pass on. They still either do not hear at all, or hear but dimly, and even what they hear, they do not understand" (650). With this parable, Du Bois attempts to enliven his readers' sense of the demands of justice and of the nation's failure to meet them. The consequences of justice's failure terrify:

> Then the people within may become hysterical. They may scream and hurl themselves against the barriers, hardly realizing in their bewilderment that they are screaming in a vacuum unheard and that their antics may actually seem funny to those outside looking in. They may even, here and there, break through in blood and disfigurement, and find themselves faced by a horrified, implacable, and quite overwhelming mob of people frightened for their own very existence. (650)

From Du Bois's fable one might draw the moral of this book. On both sides of the color line, the veil of ignorance that marks the failure of justice produces conflicted identities asymmetrically determined by that failure and by the failure to recognize that failure has occurred. This in itself constitutes, for those excluded from the conversation of justice, a catastrophic collapse of the nation as a democratic space, a catastrophic failure of American national identity identified as the practical realization of such a space. Far too often in the United States that denial of justice has culminated in violence committed by or on behalf of white privilege by mobs or legislatures "frightened for their own very existence." In the history of the nation both at "home" and "abroad," the misapprehension, terror, and violence that Du Bois depicts have been far more common an experience than the nation's self-congratulatory self-identification with justice should have allowed. In these circumstances, Du Bois suggests, identity appears and disappears, grounds and evacuates grounds for explanation and communication. Identity appears not as an essential determinant of being, but as part of an interrogative exchange with other selves, an exchange that can always fail to recognize the common humanity of its parties and can never, in itself, capture that humanity whole.

But universalism, that sometimes desperate appeal to that unconflicted wholeness identity always denies, in itself has limitations as well. Not all appeals to universals are just. In reducing his crew to the instrument of his mad quest, Ahab also reduces the particularities of their identities to make them serve his quest for wholeness and for self-transcendence. "My one cogged circle fits into all their various wheels," he says, "and they revolve."[38] The universal citizenship that leaves behind the particularities of differential identities and interests—racial, class, or gendered—does not necessarily make for a more just, a more humane, or a more democratic society. It may, in fact, leave behind humanity, justice, and culture as well. It might leave only the universality of the featureless cog, with no effective check on the mad machinations of its master.

If the United States were ever to succeed in becoming itself, its citizens would have to agree to extend their sense of the universal by honest and painful attempts to imagine the identities they find themselves among, each attempting imaginatively to occupy the position of others, to hear their complaints or explanations, to see the world from the other's position. Emerson expressed a similar idea when he enjoined himself and his readers to "treat the other men and women as if they were real."[39] The imaginative projection of self into other, commonly called negative capability, is an essential literary and aesthetic movement at the heart of political deliberation and moral philosophy. It provides the concrete specificity without which justice remains an empty abstraction. Literary or imaginative sensibility is not only a necessary adjunct to moral and political philosophy but also its paradoxical and fractured ground.[40]

But what does treating other people as if they were real mean in practical terms? Consider, for example, Ishmael's reflections on religion in *Moby Dick*. Queequeg, pagan idolator, hospitably invites Ishmael, good Presbyterian that he is, to join him in worship of his wooden god. Ishmael reverts not to the first and most absolute commandment of the ten engraved in stone for all time. Instead he has recourse to his own imagination and to the dynamic and humane principles of justice as we live it:

> But what is worship?—to do the will of God—*that* is worship. And what is the will of God?—to do to my fellow man what I would have my fellow man to do to me—*that* is the will of God. Now, Queequeg is my fellow man. And what do I wish that this Queequeg would do to me? Why, unite with me in my particular Presbyterian form of worship. Consequently, I must then unite with him in his; ergo I must turn idolater. So I kindled the shavings; helped prop up the innocent little idol; offered him burnt biscuit with Queequeg; salamed before him twice or thrice; kissed his nose; and that done, we undressed and went to bed at peace with our own consciences and all the world. But we did not sleep without some little chat.[41]

How different this is from Ahab's overwhelming ambition to subsume his crew to his own ambitious drive toward wholeness. Here just principles lead to cosmopolitan practices, and Ishmael's crisis of conscience ends in a sociable conversation. Identity does not simply disappear; it is put into a play in a series of reflective relays. Could Ishmael's meditation be a model of the practical workings of justice and imagination and of their necessary interdependence in a just republic and a cosmopolitan community? Ishmael cannot do justice to Queequeg according to the injunctions of the Kantian imperative without descending from that abstract universal to imaginatively construe and momentarily adopt Queequeg's particular identity and thereby complicate his own. Contingency and transcendence, the particular and the universal, the moral universes of communitarian skeptics and universalizing rationalists, Ishmael's world and Ahab's too, here seem not only conjoined but interdependent. The categorical imperative in practice depends as much on the uncertainties and negative capabilities of imaginative projection (imaging what the other wants in both its similarities to and its differences from one's own desires) as it does on the universal application of noncontingent principles or transcendental theories.

Justice emerges, if at all, through the recognition of identity's particularity; justice requires each to assume the other's place to do justice not just to the other but to the difference that the other represents. This justice can only begin when the individuals and the nation, in their self-interrogation and public discourse, confront the threat of their failure that the other's demand embodies. Considering these demands often depends on an aesthetics of negative capability and a poetics of imaginative projection. For this reason literature, so frequently concerned to represent the difference of the other as an object of identification, often becomes a crucial site for just deliberation. This describes not merely a parallel between literature and moral philosophy but the way in which moral philosophy and the ethical republic rely on cultivated imagination and refined sensibility. This identification of literature with justice occurs because of, not despite, the fact that, as Wai Chee Dimock has noted, its insistence on the rich particulars of life make literature antithetical to the promulgation of just principles. Justice, as even Kant recognized, cannot remain a matter of universal principles but must address the judgment of particulars. In the history of the United States, demands for justice have often sought to provoke the imagination and to outrage the sensibility of the republic, frequently producing works of enduring literary power that challenge widely admired and accepted ideas about the nation's sense of itself, its beliefs about community, and its relationship to the world beyond the nation's borders. To consider the questions of identity, justice, national belonging, and cosmopolitan engagement that have shaped the nation's embattled identities and its conflicted cultures requires attention to the imaginative worlds in which Americans actually live and the imaginative works that have struggled with the nation's problems.

ERRORS OF IDENTITY

When thinking about identity, however sympathetically, certain errors seem unavoidable. The attempt to ground ethics and policy in identity and the desire to deny identity altogether both pose problems. Consider Martha Nussbaum's sympathetic effort to grasp the links between culture and identity in order to do justice to others. Because she knows the risks of errors on this difficult terrain, she specifies two fallacies, chauvinism and romanticism, that deform attempts to describe other cultures. Each prejudice distorts judgment and leads to unreflecting condemnations, celebrations, or refusals to judge difference. In her critique of these errors, she commits an error of her own. She assumes that the link between culture and identity is best grasped as an expression of difference, and that the proper ethical response to difference is tolerance.[42] Nussbaum's descriptive errors and evaluative vices are really the same thing. Chauvinists assume that other cultures are invidiously different from ours; romanticists assume that they are ideally different; and relativists (if any actually exist) refuse to judge and seek merely to accept diversity. The assumption of difference structures each position so that each is less a thinking through of difference than a prejudgment regarding it. The question of how different various cultures actually are and how one might understand the differences among them does not get much play on either side of the polemic, nor does the question of when difference should figure in judgment and when it should not.

Such questions of difference and judgment have a special force in the world today when the public sphere is awash with accounts of culture and identity that seek to explain global conflicts as expressions of cultural difference. Nussbaum, sympathetic and humane as she is, comes close to sounding like a more humane version of Samuel Huntington's perniciously influential interpretation of global politics as a "clash of civilizations."[43]

Consider the terms in which she champions the laudable goal of studying other cultures:

> To be ignorant of Islam, of Buddhism and Hinduism, of the traditions and religious practices of China and Japan, is not only to lack an essential prerequisite of international enterprise and political debate. It is also, frequently, to lack the equipment necessary to talk to one's neighbors, to vote with understanding on measures connected with immigration and diversity, to think about the legal issues involved in a Buddhist prisoner's request for sacred books and chapel services, to deliberate well about bringing up an adopted child of Chinese origin, or to understand why author Salman Rushdie faces an edict of death.[44]

As Nussbaum's argument continues, it becomes more puzzling. The longer one looks at the examples she gives, the less important their dependence on cross-culture instruction seems. One requires no special knowledge of Buddhism to consider an incarcerated Buddhist's request for books or public observances, only a decision to treat all religions alike and indifferently within a given institution and a willingness to recognize Buddhism as a religion. Why Anglo-Americans adopting a child from China should find knowledge of China useful certainly requires more thought, unless one believes that culture is innate and that people who look East Asian (assuming this child does) should culturally be East Asian (whatever that means). One can imagine reasons for wishing an adopted child to have an imaginative relationship with the distant homeland or with its biological parents, but those reasons do not seem self-evident or incontrovertible. Most troubling, I find, is the generous-sounding suggestion that knowledge of Islam could explain the criminal idiocy of the cynical fatwa once pronounced against Salman Rushdie. To assume that is to assume that fanaticism is normatively Muslim and that murder is indigenous to Islamic belief, though many Muslim scholars believed this edict to be heretical. Yet, when American Christians harass and murder abortion providers, when they picket the funeral of a murdered gay teenager with signs proclaiming that his death, like AIDS, is God's vengeance, and when they ban the teaching of biological science to American schoolchildren, few describe these cruel and stupid aberrations as expressions of Christianity's essential traditions and beliefs. Why assume that Islam explains the actions of Islamic extremists? Amin

Maalouf, the Lebanese-French writer, questions "the habit that people have got into, both in the North and in the South, and whether they are distant observers or zealous partisans, of classifying everything that happens in a Muslim country as related to Islam, whereas there are many other factors that are much more relevant. You could read a dozen large tomes on the history of Islam from its very beginnings and you still wouldn't understand what's going in Algeria [referring to the Islamicists there]. But read 30 pages on colonization and decolonization and then you'll understand quite a lot."[45] Nussbaum, like Huntington, could have profited from Maalouf's advice.

Martha Nussbaum, more than most contemporary Western writers, struggles with the links between culture and identity. She thinks seriously about Western traditions of denigrating the Orient as "nonrational, superstitious, and amoral" and cites rational traditions of inquiry in Arab, Indian, and other cultures. Moreover, she continuously reminds herself and her readers of something that seems to be very difficult to remember or conceptualize: cultures are permeable to each other, in constant interaction with each other, internally complex, and usually conflicted. In her own attempt to think other cultures as a curricular topic, however, Nussbaum forgets this herself and speaks unreflectingly about a "we" and a "they," an "us" and a "them," as if these identity categories were natural types that exist apart from the conflicts in which they play a part and can therefore simply be respected, with cool detachment and indifferent toleration, as different.

In the moments of conflict this book explores, from the founding of the U.S. republic to the war on terror, questions of identity seldom seem to engender such detached contemplation. Rather, both at home and abroad, identity always seems to entail, on some level, violence and injustice. Considering these questions leads quickly from the issues of politics and culture within the borders of the United States to considerations of America's global situation with which this book in fact ends. As Maalouf points out, identity frequently expresses the violently dislocating force of modernization as an inexorable global process. The trajectory of this book from Thomas Jefferson to the war on terror traces an arc from U.S. history to the contemporary world in which modernity represents a constant pressure. Maalouf, for his part, sees modernity as organically linked to Western identity. He writes, "The more Westerners modernize themselves the more completely in harmony they feel with their culture." For most of the rest of the world, for "all those born in the failed cultures, openness to change and modernity presents itself differently. . . . For the Chinese, Africans, Japanese, Indians and American Indians, as for Greeks, Russians, Iranians, Arabs, Jews and Turks, modernization has constantly meant the abandoning of part of themselves. Even though it has sometimes been embraced with enthusiasm, it has never been adopted without a certain bitterness, without a feeling of humiliation and defection. Without a piercing doubt about the dangers of assimilation. Without a profound identity crisis."[46] He is right about modernity's dislocations, but wrong in assuming that subjects in the West do not suffer from them or from the fear that they too live in a culture that has failed or is about to fail. By contrast, in this book I see the United States as one Western enclave whose residents have often experienced the modernity of their identities as a moment of crisis and as the reality of loss and the threat of failure.

Maalouf, I think, underestimates the extent to which, both historically and contemporaneously, many in the United States and Europe, even those identified with the dominant classes and cultures, have experienced and continue to experience the pressure of modernization, rationalization, massification, and globalization as a threatening loss not just of local agency but of character, culture, and identity as well. For many in the West—members of the non-Western groups Maalouf names or not—modernity, even if it "succeeds," feels like the failure of culture and the loss of identity. Obsession with tradition, religious traditions most obviously, is one of modernity's most characteristic symptoms, one that links, I believe, the Islamic fundamentalist to his born-again Christian counterpart.[47] The failure of modernity's project to found a more rational or just social and political order inclusive of all those subject to modern government—African Americans, Native Americans, women, the poor—has often constituted those identities as challenges to modernity itself. Even, perhaps especially, in the United States, modernity represents a force that few can completely embrace and fewer still can successfully resist. In this light, Maalouf's description of the experience of "failed cultures" may be generalized to crucial aspects of experience within and of the West as well.

For Maalouf, identity emerges not as the organic expression of preexisting traditions and timeless belief (as if there were any such things anywhere), but as a reactive formation to challenges and assaults perceived as external to the self and the group in question. Identity and difference are ineluctably linked expressions of an inherently intercultural and conflicted process, the mark of our often unhappy engagement with rather than a retreat from the world. For Maalouf, identity questions and violent injustice appear so often conjoined because identity emerges as both an expression and a denial of conflict. One frequently experiences a strong affiliation to the aspect of one's identity that seems to be under attack and denies the potentially contingent fluidities of existence in doing so.

Identity is thus personal, but never simply so. It is rather a matter of allegiances with groups or identities larger than any individual. Of course, most people understand themselves to have many different allegiances, and those allegiances often conflict. Such conflicts are not incidental to but essential parts of the question of identity. Crucially, both these allegiances and the conflicts they demark come from experiences of the world and not from the essential being of the self. As Maalouf explains:

> What determines a person's affiliation to a given group is essentially the influence of others: the influence of those about him—relatives, fellow-countrymen, co-religionists—who try to make him one of them; together with the influence of those on the other side, who do their best to exclude him. Each one of us has to make his way while choosing between paths that are urged upon him and those that are forbidden or strewn with obstacles. He is not himself from the outset; nor does he just "grow aware" of what he is; he *becomes* what he is. He doesn't merely grow aware of his identity; he acquires it step by step.[48]

Moreover, that acquisition is one too frequently experienced in moments of physical or symbolic violence and real or imagined injustice. Denigration and oppression both symbolic and material form identity in the crisis of their aftermath:

> It is these wounds that at every stage in life determine not only men's attitudes towards their affiliations but also the hierarchy that decides the relative importance of these ties. When someone has been bullied because of his religion, humiliated or mocked because of the colour of his skin, his accent or his shabby clothes, he will never forget it. Up till now I have stressed the fact that identity is made up of a number of allegiances. But it is just as necessary to emphasise that identity is also singular, something we experience as

a complete whole. A person's identity is not an assemblage of separate affiliations, nor a kind of loose patchwork; it is like a pattern drawn on a tightly
stretched parchment. Touch just one part of it, just one allegiance, and the
whole person will react, the whole drum will sound. (26)

Identity emerges as an inorganic construct. It does not grow naturally nor
does it naturally express anything but the disruptive violence of the individual subject's negotiations with the world. Out of the mass of a person's
contradictory allegiances, an identity emerges at the point where she experiences actual or threatened violence or insult. As Maalouf puts it, "People often see themselves in terms of whichever one of their allegiances is
most under attack" (26). The result of such attacks is the simultaneous
emergence of identity and the desire for vindication or justice. Identity
emerges as a psychosocial construct that is both hysterical and obsessive,
shaky and fractured in its very foundations. For these reasons, if justice is
denied, the claims of identity can become horribly violent.

Those who want to deny identity's importance want to forget the violence in which identity originates. Walter Benn Michaels is no doubt correct when he notes the desirability of leaving identity behind, for identity
is not the cause of injustice but one of its expressions. He has argued forcefully and repeatedly against identity and diversity and for a more universally applicable form of justice. "In an ideal universe," Michaels writes,
"we wouldn't be celebrating diversity at all—we wouldn't even be encouraging it—because in an ideal universe the question of who you wanted to
sleep with would be a matter of concern only to you and to your loved ones
(or unloved) ones. As would your skin color; some people might like it,
some people might not, but it would have no political significance whatsoever."[49] Few would disagree with this characterization of an ideal world
where justice would no longer find itself confused with violent experiences
and expressions of identity. The problem with Michaels's argument—it
seems wrong to call it an error since of course he knows this—originates
in his claim that this ideal universe can become real without continuing
to work through how identity continues to express failures of justice and
the demands for something better.[50]

One of the most interesting moments in Michaels's critique of identity
occurs in *The Trouble with Diversity*, and it illustrates why his claim that
identity no longer matters seems so problematic. It demonstrates, in fact,

how I think identity works. He tells a story of meeting a genteel anti-Semite, a senior faculty member's wife in the department where he was a new assistant professor. She asserts that Jews were ruining the English Department. Michaels, though he neither believes in nor practices Judaism, finds himself constrained to assert his Jewish identity, which causes her no embarrassment whatsoever but, he reports, at least for the moment makes him feel better. This leaves him with an "obvious problem." Because he believes in the invisibility of his Jewishness (though why he assumes this empowered spouse did not know he was Jewish I can't imagine—anti-Semites make it their business to know these things), he is able to pose in terms of pure interiority the question, "When I assert my claim as a Jew, what exactly am I claiming?" (35). And Michaels is perfectly right to say that, based on his own introspective inventory, then neither biology nor culture offers an adequate answer.

In fact, pure interiority, should it exist, offers no answer to such questions at all. Michaels's own experience indicates that these questions do not, for this reason, seem any less pressing at the moments they appear and rearrange the interiors of those who confront them. In this story, the differences in power and identity between the waspish wife of a senior colleague visiting her dislike of Jews upon a junior professor who suddenly finds himself identified with a people who have abruptly become "his," the experience of identity demands consideration of those external considerations that shape this confrontation. These include social and economic class, gender, ethnicity, and the threat of material injustices when a tenure decision will place the assistant professor at the anti-Semite's mercy. Moreover, the answer must involve more nuance than simply calling Michaels's own self-identification under pressure, however momentary or unsatisfying, "a mistake." For if identity is a mistake, and no doubt in many ways it is, it remains a mistake that seems indissolubly part of the lives people live together and in conflict with each other. Michaels is pained, irritated, or angered enough to feel himself constrained to speak, and by making his claim he finds he feels better. His theory of identity attempts to deny such common experiences. In distinguishing identity from subjectivity, Michaels distinguishes it from pain about which, he says, "you can't in principle be mistaken" (37). But identity is often closely linked to pain, as it was for him in his discomfort when that senior colleague's wife either did or did not recognize him as a Jew and made him feel compelled to own an identity that had suddenly become, at least for the moment, "his."

In the discourses that have helped define the United States, identity frequently arrives by way of failures of justice or tact, just as Jewishness comes
to Michaels through his experience of aggression. Identity often comes
associated with pain. It sometimes comes with terror. "Genocides—all hate
crimes—are crimes of identity," Michaels writes, "and we live in a world
that is vigilantly (and given our history, understandably) on guard against
crimes of identity" (61). The United States has since its inception been implicated in various crimes of identity—enslaving blacks, extirpating natives,
oppressing women, suppressing workers, dominating other nations—and
these crimes have ensured that identity has been and remains a central concern for those who study and those who suffer the effects of this nation's
history. Thus when Michaels collectivizes American society and claims that
it has evolved from being a "racist" society to become an "anti-racist society," he forgets for the moment that whether or not American society appears
to be racist has always depended on which segment of that society one is
looking at and who is doing the looking.[51] The woman who—intention-
ally or not—insulted and threatened Michaels when he was an assistant
professor might well not have described herself as racist or anti-Semite. She
offered, from her viewpoint, a simple statement of a natural order violated
and threatened and of social harmony and cultural achievement compromised by the presence of those who do not belong. She might well have
prefaced these remarks with "I have nothing personal against Jews" and
believed it. She might, in this connection, have evoked Thomas Jefferson's
relationship to blacks and immigrants.

In fact, the short narrative Michaels offers may serve as a schematic of
how identity has functioned in the United States. Here one must note both
the viewpoint of the empowered spokesperson, afraid that a cherished
identity—the principles of the republic, the civility of the English department—will fail if the barriers of race, class, or religion do not hold, and
the experience of the unjustly threatened or excluded subject, often a recent
arrival, in whose pain the real failure of principles and civility, the real failure of the republic's principles, registers. As attractive as Michaels's vision
of a world beyond identity may seem, the persisting failure in the United
States and abroad to achieve a situation in which identity and justice might
be uncoupled produces instead a world where identities and identity claims,
however confused and contentious, still matter.[52]

Each chapter of *Identity and the Failure of America* analyzes and relates a discursive moment in the failure of the United States and the claims of identity that that failure provokes and expresses. The tension between cosmopolitan and democratic principles of justice on the one hand and the realities of a conflicted, hierarchical, and frequently iniquitous society on the other informs each chapter.

Part I examines the ideal identification of the nation with virtue—both just principles and democratic ethics. Chapter 1 considers the exemplary affective dimensions of Jefferson's anxious attempts to mediate between the principles of republicanism, with its dreams of harmonious union among virtuous citizens, and the facts of his state where violent displacements, heterogeneous populations, and especially slavery threaten cataclysmic disruptions. It also considers the ways in which Jefferson's embattled image in contemporary critical and popular estimations of him continues to express these conflicts that still haunt the nation, in which the virtuous ideals and the iniquitous practices of the United States collide. In chapter 2, I turn to Melville's magnificent monument to American failure, *Moby Dick*. Captain Ahab's catastrophic leadership and his work to forge his cosmopolitan crew into a signal manifestation of his own madness illustrate the failure both of individual agency (Ahab's dream of perfect independence) and of democratic association (the mysterious complicity of the crew in their own demise). Melville's novel dramatizes the irreducible tension between the masculine assertions of the self-empowered liberal subject and the unavoidable demands of communal association. There can be no reliable grounds for justice without violence in this world, the world of *Moby Dick* suggests, but the conditions of power, its reliance on a politics or ethics of sociability no one can ever wholly control, inevitably structure power's limitations and the possibility, foregone or fulfilled, of resistance. The asymmetrical failures of Ahab to command himself and of his crew to save themselves from him indicate the troublesome failures and identifications, the dreams of power and the lures of identity, of which modern democratic politics consists.

Part II considers failures of sympathy. Sympathy, of course, is a primary virtue in a well-regulated republic and the alternative to violent upheavals on which moral suasion as a strategy of reform depends. Chapter 3 considers how, for those concerned with justice, violence turns out to be easy to criticize but difficult to do without. Lydia Maria Child's evolving political engagements and analyses from *Hobomok* through *A Romance of the*

Republic point up the ways in which alternatives to Ahab's style of aggressive masculinity may fail to realize better versions of the nation's identity that are more generous to those who differ or dissent. *Hobomok,* in this light, is less a sympathetic portrayal of a Native American than a sketch of a cosmopolitan community in conflict in which those who claim to speak for the law and those who seek justice never find a common language and moral suasion itself fails. As her relationship to moral suasion becomes more attenuated, Child becomes more sympathetic to the justice of manly violence when it expresses the demands of specific identities—the enslaved, the immigrant, the poor—for retribution. Violence comes to seem paradoxically necessary for the realization of America's cosmopolitan promise. Here her frequently wonderful "Letters from New York," her intriguing work on world religions, and her much underestimated late romance furnish exemplary instances of her developing thought about sympathy's limits. Chapter 4 focuses on the terrors and legacies of John Brown and Nat Turner and the way in which both have haunted and continue to haunt the nation's white imagination and to divide the nation along racial lines. Brown's example, especially in recent historical and fictional accounts of him, points up both the terrible consequences and the terrifying prospects of successful, sympathetic identifications across racial lines in works ranging from contemporary accounts of his hanging to Robert Penn Warren's vitriolic history *The Making of a Martyr* and Russell Banks's brilliant novel *Cloudsplitter.* Nat Turner's various legacies as a scourge of white America's conscience and a hero of black resistance come into focus around Harriet Beecher's Stowe's *Dred,* which sympathizes with its violent black hero, and William Styron's *The Confessions of Nat Turner,* which fails to do so. Styron's persistent failure to understand what was at stake, in terms of both ethics and aesthetics, in celebrations and criticisms of his novel are of particular interest in gauging how Brown and Turner continue to divide us. These nineteenth-century figures of terror illustrate the continued difficulties imaginative identifications across racial lines still pose when injustice and violence demarcate identities.

Finally, Part III considers the exigencies of judgment and the necessity of self-mortification as necessary aspects of an American citizen's subscription to American principles. Chapter 5 considers Emerson's antislavery activism as an exemplary instance of how the duties of citizenship involve identification with and aversion to the nation's identity and its failures. Emerson attempts to persuade other citizens that both U.S. leadership and democratic culture have failed and that both the republic and their place in it must be reimagined along more equitable and inclusive lines. In doing this he relies on transcendental principles and sympathetic aesthetics and exposes the limitations and even the repugnance of democratic politics in the face of moral atrocities, like slavery, that remain popular. He thereby reveals the promises and limitations of the concerned citizen's necessarily unpopular attempt to make the American people confront their own failures of judgment and to persuade them to reform in accordance with the discomfiting principles of justice in which they claim to believe. In chapter 6, Frederick Douglass's long fight for racial equity and his controversial ministry to Haiti furnish illuminating instances of the viability and the limitations of American principles and their appeals to universality. These moments in Douglass's career illustrate how those principles can furnish a basis of cosmopolitan engagement at home and in the world and how they can help hide the fact that that engagement has failed to occur. The failure, practical and ethical, of Douglass's ministry to Haiti also illustrates the unsettling ways in which belief in those very universal and cosmopolitan principles can blind Americans to the reality of their nation's place in the world. Here Douglass's own embattled ideals and his struggle against his nation's racist fantasies and for vindication of his own manhood all play a role. Douglass's ministry to Haiti illustrates how American imperialism can betray the very principles of democratic equity and self-rule that Americans pretend to advance. As Douglass learns in Haiti, this obfuscation and betrayal ensures that the nation will fail to spread its principles abroad even as it fails to realize them at home.

By way of conclusion, *Identity and the Failure of America* considers how, in the context of America's embattled projects in the contemporary Middle East, cosmopolitan identities, implicit though unrealized from the first in America's best principles, if more fully and justly imagined along lines suggested by the failures this book analyzes, might help in some small way to remedy the long and painful predicaments of the nation's failures at home and abroad.

PART I

FAILED VIRTUES

chapter 1

Jefferson's Headache: Race and the Failure of a Benevolent Republic

Jefferson is one of the great men whom this country has produced, one of the men who has contributed largely to the formation of our national character—to much that is good and to not a little that is evil in our sentiments and manners.

—JOHN QUINCY ADAMS

THE POPULAR JEFFERSON

On the way to writing what has been perhaps the most crucial sentence identifying the American republic with its commitment to equality and justice, Jefferson suffered the first of the migraine headaches that would afflict him throughout his long public career. It delayed his return by several days to the Continental Congress, where he would compose the Declaration of Independence.[1] These headaches suggest Jefferson's conflicted inner life. They bespeak his sense of the problems besetting the virtuous republic he hoped to establish and intimate that the most difficult problems in the way of accomplishment were internal to the state. In his one completed book, *Notes on the State of Virginia,* Jefferson grappled with those problems, primary among them the problem of slavery, for the ideas of racial difference and the system of slavery they helped support represented a headache from which Jefferson found little relief. His struggle with slavery in his *Notes* represents an early failure in the nation's long struggle to live up to its own idea of itself. Tracing Jefferson's conflicted inner life in his account of his native state will reveal not only Jefferson's personal anxieties regarding slavery and race but the role those fears still play in America's obsession with itself.

Perhaps no American figure seems less likely a candidate for a study of failure or fear than Thomas Jefferson. Americans have long loved to imagine the sage of Monticello as the embodiment of the nation's triumph over all that is not reasonable, enlightened, and modern. Washington may be "the father of the nation," but Jefferson is its ego ideal. When Andrew Burstein, seeking to introduce Jefferson's sentimental side, remarks that Americans have an "obsession to know the founding father with the passionate pen," he has in mind primarily the intellectual passions for liberty, equality, and science.[2]

Despite continuing fascination with the sage of Monticello, whose "passionate pen" articulated the most widely revered and most frequently violated of American beliefs in the equality of all "men," Jefferson himself remains something of an enigma. As Joseph Ellis's popular biography would have it, he is the most sphinxlike of all America's founders. Like the Sphinx, Jefferson tends to reflect images of themselves back to those who consider his riddle. As Merrill Peterson put it, "He swiftly becomes a symbol, perhaps many symbols, through which men of different persuasions and at different times seek to comprehend their experiences and state their purposes."[3] In Jefferson all American political persuasions, including Federalists and Democrats, slaveholders and abolitionists, conservatives and liberals, have found reflections of their own beliefs. Just below the polished surface of his image, more recent scholars have found a compromised morality and an ethical complicity that reveal Jefferson to be more than just a mirror of American ideals. He also reflects the material conflicts and ethical incoherence that have always been part of the social, political, and psychological life of the United States and of its citizens. For Jefferson, these conflicts have most frequently and intensely involved relationships among the nation's races.[4]

Despite his burnished image, Jefferson's complexities have long vexed his critics. Since his own time, Americans have struggled to understand how the champion of equality and of republican virtue could own, sell, and live off the labor of slaves. This is more a structuring conflict than a mere contradiction. Tories during the American Revolution frequently noted the irony that the most passionate spokesmen for liberty were Virginia's slaveholders, prominent among whom was the author of the Declaration of Independence. Paradoxically, the subjugation of enslaved laborers made it easier to champion liberty and equality. Racial distinctions made it clear

from the outset that the advent of freedom would not disrupt the economic and social hierarchies on which Virginia planters depended: "Aris-
tocrats could more safely preach equality in a slave society than in a free
one. Slaves did not become leveling mobs, because their owners would see
to it that they had no chance to."[5] Though actual and imaginary slave rebellions haunted Jefferson and other planters, they represented a different order
of threat and a differently structured problem of domination and control
than demands for justice or rights by lower-class whites.

In *Notes on the State of Virginia,* Jefferson articulates many of the founding assumptions of American racism, including the belief that dark skin
could not be beautiful and that black people could not be creative. In pro-
mulgating such ideas, the architect of American freedom and egalitarian-
ism became an apologist for American racism and slavery as well. Slavery
functioned as what Edmond S. Morgan has called "a flying buttress to freedom," one that absorbed much of the stressful weight placed on society by
the "fear and contempt" that propertied men felt for "the inarticulate lower
classes." Slavery could not, however, free the master classes from their fear
of the enslaved nor from their anxiety about what their dependence on slavery meant for themselves and their society.[6] The ways in which he lived and
recorded these anxieties make Jefferson a representative American.

Jefferson believed that slave owning contradicted and undermined his
cherished liberal and republican ideals. Like other members of his class,
Jefferson lived these contradictions daily, and that has become part of his
popular image as well. As so often happens in the American imagination,
sex has served to focus a popular obsession with race. From his own time
to the present, the American public has commonly believed that Jefferson
maintained a long, intimate relationship with Sally Hemings, his deceased
wife's enslaved half sister, and that she bore him several children. Next to
the O. J. Simpson trial, the most widely reported use of DNA evidence in
the 1990s traced Jefferson's genes in Sally Hemings's descendents. At present, scholarly and popular interest in the Jefferson-Hemings relationship
continues unabated.[7]

For some, the possibility that Jefferson's slave bore his children seems to
taint everything he wrote, and this can seem a national crisis. As Roger
Wilkins puts it: "Among the major sources of our identity are the things
that Thomas Jefferson wrote."[8] It is troubling to find that identity polluted
at its source. To remember that Jefferson, in whose words the nation's best

principles took form, was also mired in its worst practices makes him more, not less, important and fascinating. Simply to condemn Jefferson's hypocrisy or to believe that it compromises his or our principles misses the agony through which he and his nation lived their relationship to slavery and to those they enslaved. For him and the nation this agony was, Wilkins says, "the product of the irreconcilable tension between earned guilt and the aspiration to honor" (50). This tension makes Jefferson a primary example of the part failure plays in the making of American identity.

JEFFERSON'S IMAGE AND THE STRUGGLE OVER SLAVERY: THE STRUCTURE OF AMERICAN IDENTITY

Surely both his defenders and detractors exaggerate the role of the Hemings affair in indicating Jefferson's failings. Wilkins writes that Jefferson "was a dizzying mixture of searing brilliance and infuriating self-indulgence, of idealism and base racism, of soaring patriotism and myopic self-involvement. He was America writ small."[9] In this light, the long debate over his relationship to Sally Hemings appears less a search for the keys to Jefferson's character than a symptom itself of a national malaise that demands analysis. Whether or not Jefferson and Hemings had sex or children seems less interesting than the obsessive interest this question still generates. Peterson aptly describes Jefferson's image as "a sensitive reflector, through several generations, of America's troubled search for the image of itself."[10] In this search, Jefferson's putative miscegenation has figured prominently and troubled many. Unhappily, the "discussion" around this "scandal" reflects aspects of white American identity that are all too familiar. As Annette Gordon-Reed explains, the nature of the controversy and the vehemence of the denials reveal more about the disputants than they do about Jefferson: "historians, journalists, and other Jefferson enthusiasts have . . . shamelessly employed every stereotype of black people and distortion of life in the Old South to support their positions."[11] Or as Wilkins even more pointedly observes: "The elements that sustained the white Jefferson family story as *the truth* were that relatively few whites could believe that this American founder could possibly have *debased* himself by lying repeatedly with a person who was even half black. . . . It all adds up to a very complex strategy for removing blacks from the rank of humans."[12] What should most scandalize Americans in the Sally Hemings affair is not the affair but the way in which even scholarly "debate" concerning it reveals a deep current of obsessive denial in the national character—a denial of the humanity, intelligence, and attractiveness of African peoples even when their labor, their skills, and their bodies get regularly exploited for economic gain and sexual pleasure. Moreover, one important participant in that white project to remove blacks from the ranks of the human was, of course, Jefferson himself.

In addition, the very structure of the most characteristic form of denial by Jefferson's "defenders" reveals the precise structure of inversion or reversal that often characterizes American obsessions with race. Consider Gordon-Reed's description of the peculiarities of this "defense": "The horror is not at the thought of the defilement of Sally Hemings but at the thought of Thomas Jefferson defiling himself by lying with Sally Hemings. By doing so, Jefferson would have hurt himself and, by extension, other whites. That particular sin would be unforgiveable."[13] John Chester Miller's rather overstated defense of Jefferson's character, to take only one typical example, manifests precisely the horror that Gordon-Reed describes. He writes:

> To give credence to the Sally Hemings story is, in effect, to question the authenticity of Jefferson's faith in freedom, the rights of man, and the innate controlling faculty of reason and the sense of right and wrong. It is to infer that there were no principles to which he was inviolably committed, that what he acclaimed as morality was no more than a rhetorical façade for self-indulgence, and that he was always prepared to make exceptions in his own case when it suited his purpose. In short, beneath his sanctimonious and sententious exterior lay a thoroughly adaptive and amoral public figure—like so many of those of the present day.[14]

This outburst particularly surprises because it occurs in a book detailing many of Jefferson's noxious attitudes, unprincipled compromises, and exploitative practices as a slaveholder, including his extensively documented use of enforced child labor in his textile and nail factories and his failure, rare among the founding fathers, to manumit any of his slaves. Everything Miller claims the Hemings story would indicate about Jefferson's "character"—especially doubts about the authenticity of his commitment to freedom when that commitment threatened to inconvenience himself or his arrangements at his beloved Monticello—already stands incontrovertibly in the public record, for Jefferson's most troubling violations of his principles resulted from his daily practice as an owner of slaves. That Jefferson, like so many other slave owners (including his father-in-law and his brother Randolph) may have sexually exploited an enslaved woman or even fallen in love with a woman over whom the laws of the state gave him despotic powers may or may not be true. His failure as a slave owner to live up to the ideals of equality and freedom for which he so powerfully spoke hardly depends on his relations with Sally Hemings. Moreover, in the defensiveness that Miller exemplifies, the perpetrator of violence gets represented as its victim.[15] Jefferson, not the woman he held in bondage, suffers from the liaison. Such substitutions of the victimizer for the victim frequently structure America's obsession with race in ways that Jefferson himself clearly exemplifies.

NATURAL HISTORY, THE POLITICAL ORDER, AND JEFFERSON'S SAD STATE

Forms of obsession figure familiarly in Jefferson's story. Endlessly tearing down and rebuilding Monticello, carefully recording diurnal temperatures wherever he went and the annual dates on which vegetables and fruits came to table and ended their seasons, exhaustively cataloging and classifying the flora and fauna of his native state: even by eighteenth-century standards, Jefferson's method seems driven by a rage for order. Fawn Brodie observes, "His orderliness reached such proportions that it can be properly called compulsive." Whether method or madness, Jefferson's record keeping, like much eighteenth-century science, attempted to master his environment. Yet, in his personal life, this method failed to master contingencies or to avert disasters. Brodie notes, "In his fantastically detailed account books . . . Jefferson's orderliness and passion for recording details begin to seem compulsive. Here in these books he listed almost every expenditure of his adult life. Still, this attention to detail did not prevent his going steadily ever deeper in dept." Jefferson could seldom bring himself to tally his totals. But the act of recording itself bespeaks his desire to stabilize a world too evidently marred by strife, conflict, and loss: his own world and the world of the modern nation he helped to found.[16] His avoidance of the bottom line suggests an understandable reluctance to confront a clear indication of his failure to achieve the order he so desired.

Both the methodical recording of data and the ideal of an orderly world shape Jefferson's only book. Leo Marx, among the first to consider *Notes on the State of Virginia* as a literary work, described it as "a cross between a geography text book and a statistical abstract."[17] In comparison to the great natural histories of the eighteenth century, those for example by Jefferson's intellectual heroes Linnaeus and Buffon, *Notes* can seem largely devoid of theoretical speculation or imaginative construction. Jefferson, in fact, deeply distrusted both his own capacity as a theorist and theoretical speculation itself.[18] He knew that theories could lead him, as they led Buffon, into enormities of error. Most of the theories in which Jefferson did indulge now seem quaint. He attempted to explain the presence of shells far removed from existing seas by the organic action of growing rocks. Confronted with the fossilized remains of the mammoth, he argued that the mammoth must still exist because extinction itself was impossible since nature has formed no "link in her great work so weak as to be broken."[19] These theories are also significant. Charles Miller is no doubt right to specify that such errors grew out of Jefferson's deeply held need to believe in an orderly and harmonious living world without violent rifts or cataclysmic ruptures. In a world where nature could produce massive dislocations and catastrophic extinction, a social order founded on natural and universal principles of benevolence and harmony could have no natural place. In a violent natural world, abominations like subjugation and slavery could not simply be dismissed as unnatural and transitory. Above all, Jefferson's *Notes* attempts to produce a harmonious vision of nature on which a happy republic might be founded.[20]

Race undermines Jefferson's attempt to envision an orderly, natural republic from the start. In writing his natural history, he consistently enacts his own identification of whiteness with reason, a quality he determinedly attempts to deny to blacks.[21] Racial identity was Jefferson's national and personal headache, for how could the institutions and practices that enslaved Africans and dispossessed Native Americans be part, even provisionally, of a nation founded in accordance with nature's laws if those laws and the subjects they governed were supposed to be rational and benevolent?[22] Such questions led to Jefferson's most notable and bizarre moments of theoretical speculation in *Notes,* his comments on race. Slavery in Jefferson's imagination was incompatible with the rational, harmonious order he meant to establish, yet the order of his state and his life seemed to depend on the labor of slaves.

Natural histories—the genre of static inventories and timeless taxonomies to which Jefferson's *Notes* largely belongs—tend to fix and stabilize the land they describe.[23] The rhetoric of natural history, as Pamela Regis calls it, tends to remove its objects from the turbulent contingencies of human history. The endless catalogs that make Jefferson's *Notes* sometimes seem like a statistical abstract have themselves a noteworthy aesthetic effect. Read through, the book stages an encounter between the flux of human time and the fixity of the completed catalog or exhaustive inventory. Jefferson's lists of topographical features, of flora and fauna (including enslaved and indigenous peoples), of rivers and streams, of products and manufactures, of notable landscape features and political arrangements seem to leave nothing out. By the time Jefferson gets to the section on "Histories, Memorials, and State-Papers" at the book's end, the state of Virginia appears to have been suspended for a moment out of time and out of space, caught and distanced from the course of human events. But in fact, *Notes* does not wholly succeed in stabilizing the state of Virginia. The strain of the attempt emerges most forcefully at those moments when Jefferson deals with human subjects and conflict, especially with aggrieved Native Americans and enslaved blacks. At these points the stabilizing rhetoric of natural history breaks down.[24]

At the time of his book's composition, Jefferson had excellent reasons to dream of his state as a world apart from the shocks of history and the failures of mortals. The proximity of his work to his catastrophic and humiliating tenure as war governor of Virginia is well known. His protracted mourning over the deaths of his daughter Lucy in April 1781 and his wife in September 1782 are equally familiar. His distracted, Byronic wanderings through the mountains of Virginia, the state he would eventually find some solace in describing, form part of his personal legend.[25] That death and mutability were sadly linked in Jefferson's imagination and experience finds expression in his wife's deathbed inscription for her grieving husband of a passage from Sterne: "Time wastes too fast: every letter I trace tells me with what rapidity life follows my pen. The days and hours of it are flying over our heads like clouds of windy day never to return—more[.] every thing presses on." Jefferson completed this passage, adding "and every time I kiss thy hand to bid adieu, every absence which follows it, are preludes to that eternal separation which we are shortly to make!" For the rest of his life, Jefferson kept this scrap of paper "in the most secret drawer of a private cabinet which he constantly resorted to," along with a lock of his wife's and of his daughter Lucy's hair.[26] For Jefferson, his *Notes* functioned as a sort of pastoral elegy—that essentially hybrid genre of mourning work that contrasts the fragility of human life with the persistence of the natural world while offering sermons on politics and lamentations of corruption.

Jefferson's personal losses may explain the peculiar importance he attaches to reading the remains of the dead, fossilized bones and burial mounds, at several moments in the book. Virginia begins to seem a charnel house. His theoretical excursions address the mysteries of cataclysmic geological upheavals in the state's terrain, of possible mass extinctions among its animals, and of burial mounds replete with the mortal remains of its indigenous people: with fossilized seashells on mountaintops, with mammoth bones in riverbeds, with Indian skeletons in barrows.

Perhaps the most fascinating and saddest moment in *Notes* deals with these last. Jefferson's excavation of the barrow near Monticello coincidentally represents one of the most impressive moments of scientific method in *Notes*. Within the barrow he finds heaped together in various strata the bones of hundreds of Native Americans. These he proceeds to sort and examine, finding among them the remains of children. On these bones he focuses:

> There were some teeth which were judged to be smaller than those of an adult; a scull, which, on a slight view, appeared to be that of an infant, but it fell to pieces on being taken out, so as to prevent satisfactory examination; a rib, and a fragment of the under-jaw of a person about half grown; another rib of an infant; and part of the jaw of a child, which had not yet cut its teeth. This last furnishing the most decisive proof of the burial of children here, I was particular in my attention to it. (105)

Knowing Jefferson's desperate grief at the death of his wife and child just before he began his book, one senses in his fascinated contemplation of the infant's bones a moment when personal tragedy erupts within natural history. "The bones of infants being soft, they probably decay sooner, which might be the cause so few were found here" (105). At this melancholy site, Jefferson's thoughts turn to mortality itself.[27]

Jefferson's methodological innovation, the cross-sectional dissection of the barrow, reveals, frozen into the strata of the natural landscape itself, the passage of human time encoded in successive layers of human bones: "At the bottom, that is on the level of the circumjacent plain, I found bones;

above these a few stones, brought from a cliff a quarter of a mile off, and from the river one-eighth of a mile off; then a large interval of earth, then a stratum of bones, and so on. . . . The bones nearest the surface were least decayed" (105–6). These myriad personal extinctions fixed in the barrow's layers not only the processes of human time as a spatial inventory within the stabilizing orders of natural history but also bespeak, more troublingly, the problem of extinction itself that Jefferson when confronted with other bones seems so intent to deny. For the Indians buried in this barrow have already fulfilled the highest function that Native Americans in Jefferson's republic can fulfill: they have vanished from the earth's face. Like Chief Logan, whose speech Jefferson famously admired, these Native Americans have left few living descendents to obstruct the progress of European civilization that has supplanted them and under whose plows even these monuments "will probably disappear in time" (106).

The function of Native Americans like Logan and these mound builders is not merely to disappear, however, it is—along lines established by James Macpherson's Ossianic poems and Rousseau's melancholy meditations—nobly to embody the disruption and loss that modernity itself entails. Jefferson, like most Americans, most admires the Indian at the point when he vanishes before the inevitable triumph of the new civilization (which Jefferson claims is less a question of conquest than has usually been supposed [102]). These vanishing Indians represent both the triumph of modern civilization and the loss of organic tradition and natural nobility before modernity's onslaught. The barrow forms the centerpiece of Jefferson's commentary on the Indians in his state and prepares the way for his consideration of the European towns, settlements, charters, and conflicts constructed over them that immediately follows. For those towns and that culture must construct themselves on the ruins of a more natural and noble civilization identified with and embodied in the land itself.

Notes on the State of Virginia is, in fact, constructed a bit like the layered composition of Jefferson's barrow. Fundamental details of the natural order provide the deep structure for the culture and the republic Jefferson seeks to found and for the considerations of political history and governmental arrangements that bring the book to the present day. Section by section, Jefferson lays the strata of his state bare. Nature as the static object of the natural historian embodies Jefferson's political hopes. Yet nature, Jefferson also knew, is not so easily stabilized in the imagination or in fact. "Nature," for political philosophers in the eighteenth century, was also an "engine of attack on the authority of tradition" and a monument to the losses and anxieties that this attack entailed.[28] The fate of the Native American, as Jefferson imagined it, was to embody both the Rousseauvian nobility of nature's order as the republic's ground and to represent the violence of nature's disruption as modernity's result.

Jefferson's defense of Native Americans from Buffon's depredations reflects both his sympathy with the losses Native Americans suffered and his complacency concerning their disappearance. His personal grief and the conflicted complexity of his culture's attitudes toward Native Americans resurface in one of the best-known moments in *Notes*. Jefferson attempts to illustrate the Indian's nobility—and to refute Buffon's theory that New World animal life degenerates—by demonstrating their "eminence in oratory" and, not coincidentally, their capacity for manly grief. The example Jefferson puts forward is the speech made by Chief Logan explaining why he has sworn vengeance against the white men who have massacred his family. He represents the old warrior as a New World Ossian, the embodiment of the "joy of grief" for his beholders:[29]

> Such was my love for the whites, that my countrymen pointed as they passed, and said, "Logan is the friend of white men." I had even thought to have lived with you, but for the injuries of one man. Col. Cresap, the last spring, in cold blood, and unprovoked, murdered all the relations of Logan, not sparing even my women and children. There runs not a drop of my blood in the veins of any living creature. This called on me for revenge. I have sought it: I have killed many. . . . Logan . . . will not turn on his heel to save his life. Who is there to mourn for Logan?—Not one. (100)

As Malcolm Kelsall remarks, "Every sentimental reader of Ossianic fiction would shed a tear," and such sentiments were deeply involved in justifying the origins and grounds of modern cultures.[30] Lee Quinby points out that *Notes on the State of Virginia* may be the "inaugural discourse of an American ethics," but Logan's speech reflects poorly on the virtues of Jefferson's people.[31] Logan's noble mourning demonstrates the capacity of the New World to nurture civilizations, but it also suggests that the new civilization may lack the natural nobility Logan exemplifies. European civilization produced Colonel Cresap, and he violated Logan's hospitality and murdered his children. Logan's manly grief may evoke Jefferson's personal losses and the sentimental grounds of his political hopes, but the Indian's just vengeance suggests that the virtuous and benevolent republic Jefferson sought to establish founded itself on the violation of its own principles and the mourning of its own failed promise.

BENEVOLENCE AND CONFLICT IN MODERN SOCIETIES AND THE FEARFUL PSYCHOLOGY OF FAILURE

Jefferson's thought engages elements of a liberal vision traceable to Locke's ideas of individual rights and a republican sense of social virtue based on the communitarian notions of the Scottish philosophy of common sense. Moreover, as Jean Yarborough argues, his view of rights and of virtue must be understood in relation to each other. In particular, the character and role of rights, those prerogatives that belong inalienably to each individual, must be understood within a hierarchy of virtues, of which the broadest and most important are social virtues. The most significant of these is benevolence. "Doing good to others" lies at the heart of human happiness, one of Jefferson's founding principles: "The ground of moral virtue is the unselfish 'love of others, a sense of duty to them, a moral instinct, in short, which prompts us irresistibly to feel and succor their distresses.'"[32] Happiness and virtue coincide in the realization of benevolent impulses, which rely in turn on a capacity to sympathize with and respond to fellow citizens. As Jefferson would put it in a letter to Correa de Serra in 1814, "The order of nature is that individual happiness shall be inseparable from the practice of virtue."[33] Moreover, the pursuit of happiness is the final and most comprehensive "right" that Jefferson lists in the famous Declaration of Independence. Happiness and moral duty, as he explained in his second inaugural address, coincide: "With nations as with individuals, our interests soundly calculated, will ever be found inseparable from our moral duties."[34]

This happy coincidence of virtue, rights, and happiness is an early articulation of the American creed as an American psychology. Yet Jefferson indicates that this creed can be difficult to realize in practice. Rights and virtues did not always seamlessly coincide. In Yarbrough's view, Jefferson, throughout his long career, struggled to mediate the conflict in his own mind between "the classical virtues of wisdom, tranquility, and self-sufficiency and the Scottish emphasis on philanthropy, benevolence, and service to others."[35] The conflict was not merely in his mind, for Jefferson knew that personal benevolence and republican virtue could never flourish in a society where sympathetic mutuality failed to bind the citizens together. A republic in which civil life was based on violence and exploitation could not endure.

For these reasons, difference and identity come to obsess Jefferson in *Notes on the State of Virginia*. Sympathy and benevolence, he believed, could only flourish where peoples and interests harmonize, where differences not only in the wealth and power of citizens but in the cultures and values of people do not conflict. Nature itself, in Jefferson's view, manifests a principle that isolates different populations by geographical limits. Thus, regarding the differences of mammoths (again) and elephants, the "Creator has therefore separated their nature as far as the extent of the scale of animal life allowed to this planet would permit" and identifying them would be "perverse" (47). In the human world, as Jefferson imagined it, both nature and prudence dictate a similar separation of differing populations. Therefore, he argues, immigration to the New World from the old must be strictly curtailed:

> It is for the happiness of those united in society to harmonize as much as possible in matters which they must of necessity transact together. Civil government being the sole object of forming societies, its administration must be conducted by common consent. Every species of government has its specific principles. Ours perhaps are more peculiar than those of any other in the universe. It is a composition of the freest principles of the English constitution, with others derived from natural right and natural reason. To these nothing can be more opposed than the maxims of absolute monarchies. Yet, from such, we are to expect the greatest number of emigrants. They will bring with them the principles of the governments they leave, imbibed in their early youth; or, if able to throw them off, it will be in exchange for an unbounded licentiousness, passing, as is usual, from one extreme to another. It would be a miracle were they to stop percisely *[sic]* at the point of temperate liberty. These principles, with their language, they will transmit to their children. In proportion to their numbers, they will share with us the legislation. They will infuse into it their spirit, warp and bias its direction, and render it a heterogeneous, incoherent, distracted mass. (91)

This is the first passage in *Notes on the State of Virginia* in which Jefferson becomes excited. The importation of foreigners threatens the life of the republic itself, compromising the foundation of the "homogeneous," "peaceable," "durable" state he hopes to create. In Jefferson's imagination, domestic tranquility and lasting stability depend on curtailing those differences in station and identity that would make his state an "incoherent, distracted mass" rather than a harmonious, organic whole.

Jefferson emphasizes homogeneity and harmony as the only reliable basis for an enduring, virtuous republic. Only in such a society can he imagine benevolence flourishing. To protect his hopes for such a society, Jefferson sometimes confuses the location of the republic's enemies as when, in the Declaration of Independence, he blames King George for the slave trade carried on in fact by the colonists themselves. In *Notes* he coins a startling and grotesque phrase to describe the Revolution. In the midst of Query XIII, considering the legitimate power of legislatures to alter constitutions—a discussion, of course, with profound implications for the emergent nation invented by a delegate assembly of questionable legitimacy—Jefferson writes: "True it is, this is no time for deliberating on forms of government. While an enemy is within our bowels, the first object is to expel him" (131). Here the confusion of similarity and difference—is that within our bowel part of us?—yields to a logic of abjection: that which has been within us must be expelled, and having been ejected from the system it must then be recognized, once and for all, as the excrescence of decent government.[36] But the unspoken anxiety here is that the enemy can never be sufficiently purged. As Jefferson remarks not long before the passage cited above, "The time to guard against corruption and tyranny, is before they shall have gotten hold on us. It is better to keep the wolf out of the fold, than to trust to drawing his teeth and talons after he shall have entered" (127). But, of course, the wolf of corruption and tyranny was already within the fold of Jefferson's republic and gnawing at its very entrails. In addition to those subjects who remained loyal to the crown, there was also a class of immigrant laborers, imported in chains and bound for life, lodged within the body politic.

Jefferson's fears that his republic will fail to achieve harmonious composition, benevolence, and happiness provide the crucial context for understanding why the problem of slavery caused him such headaches throughout his life. For Jefferson, slavery was more than just a "wolf by the ears," as he later described it, reverting to his metaphor for corruption itself, which "we can neither hold . . . nor safely let . . . go." It was a breach in the very affective foundations of the republic. It is not simply that "justice is in the

one scale and self-preservation in the other," he continued, but that a republic that must preserve itself by denying both sympathy and benevolence to
people within its borders cannot be harmonious, stable, or just, and its citizens can never be happy.[37]

Jefferson's mixed metaphor, comparing slavery to both a wolf and a scale,
signals his own internal division between terror and judgment, his own
unhappiness at the new nation's prospects. The wolf he holds gnaws at the
country's vitals and corrupts its citizens. In *Notes on the State of Virginia*,
he worried that "the whole commerce between master and slave is a perpetual exercise of the most boisterous passions, the most unremitting despotism on the one part, and degrading submissions on the other." The passions
this subject excites in Jefferson defeat his philosophy, and he throws up his
hands, "It is impossible to be temperate and to pursue this subject through
the various considerations of policy, of morals, of history natural and civil"
(168–69). Rational thought and temperate liberty both seem impossible in
a republic practicing slavery. Slavery renders both the state and its citizens
incoherent and distracted.

Jefferson understood both the social and the psychological dimensions
of this unhappy state. Lord Kames's *Elements of Criticism* was one of Jefferson's favorite books and was not only a work in aesthetics but, like many
such works at this time, an essay in social psychology. Of the mind torn
by conflicting emotions, Kames wrote: "Dissimilar co-existent emotions, as
said above, never fail to distress the mind by the difference of their tones;
from which situation a feeling of harmony never can proceed."[38] The social
and political conflicts attending modernity's emergence made the discords
of the passions as crucial and critical a topic for Kames as it was for Jefferson in their common search for self-evident principles on which to ground
modern societies. In America, a society dependent on slavery violated every
liberal principle and republican hope. The discords between benevolent
ideals and material realities, between a passion for justice and the desire
for self-preservation, tore at the heart of Jefferson's republic and of Jefferson himself.

Such social and psychological discords, as Kames knew, distort the mind.
Where one action or belief condemns another, we tend to deceive ourselves to relieve the tension: "That is a strong tendency in our nature to
justify our passions as well as our actions, not to others only, but even to
ourselves. . . . Objects are magnified or lessened, circumstances supplied

or suppressed, every thing coloured and disguised, to answer the end of justification. Hence the foundation of self-deceit, where a man imposes upon himself innocently and even without suspicion of a bias."[39] Jefferson's attempts at such self-deceit shape the most fearful passages in *Notes on the State of Virginia,* the well-known passages in which he deals with enslaved Africans and with the natural prospects of his native state.[40]

SUBLIMITY AND SOCIETY IN JEFFERSON'S NOTES

The new nation's revolutionary hopes and fears found artistic expression in the New World's broken landscapes, majestic mountains, stirring cataracts, and wild expanses.[41] For Jefferson, the disruption of stasis bespoke the promise of revolution, but it also provoked anxieties concerning the viability and virtue of the natural social order in the new nation he imagined. If *Notes on the State of Virginia* stands as the original instance of America's aesthetics of liberty, as Lee Quinby claims, it also dramatizes in its descriptions of nature the tension between sublimely violent disruption and beautifully harmonious order that expresses both Jefferson's most pressing anxieties and his most cherished desires.

Literary critics discussing *Notes on the State of Virginia* have generally ignored its lists of geography, flora, and fauna (what Leo Marx called a statistical abstract or geography textbook) and focused on set pieces like the descriptions of the Natural Bridge and of the confluence of the Susquehanna and Potomac rivers. Each of these passages manifests a tension between beauty and sublimity that bespeaks both Jefferson's and the emergent nation's inner conflicts. These passages, closely considered, set the stage for Jefferson's comments on race—also ignored by most aesthetic commentary—which may be the most sublime passages in the book.

Like other natural historians in the revolutionary epoch, Jefferson meant *Notes*—as Christopher Looby puts it—to foster a "uniformity of sentiment and conception among the people" through the "overwhelmingly static, synchronic presentation of knowledge." Without such uniformity Jefferson believed a virtuous, harmonious republic to be impossible. Nature's stability grounds republican virtue. A republic torn by conflict and situated in a restless natural world could not be virtuous because change and corruption would beset it. In light of these beliefs, Jefferson's aesthetically charged descriptions of his state bear a social and political burden.[42]

This may seem odd because the descriptions of Natural Bridge and the

confluence of rivers seem devoid of people. But in fact they aren't. The peopling of the terrain in these set pieces of wilderness description occurs, as
it often will in Hudson River School landscapes a half century later, as part
of a distant prospect. The composition in its entirety balances sublimity
and beauty and suggests a historical progression from savagery to civilization. As William J. Scheick explains, describing Jefferson's balancing of the
river's tumultuous confluence against a peaceful, distant prospect:

> The "placid and delightful" distance symbolized for Jefferson the future of
> America; the "small catch of smooth blue horizon, at an infinite distance in
> the plain country" expresses his vision of a future imaginative order, his hope
> for the realization of a "temperate liberty" eventually redeeming men from
> the chaotic "riot and tumult" in which they presently find themselves.[43]

Jefferson's hopes for the future of the nation looked forward to a moment
when, as he put it, "cleared of the present contest" it shall give "perfect freedom to all persons" (180). But those future prospects, in 1780, depended
on the outcome of the revolution and, less easy for Jefferson to imagine,
the end of slavery. Jefferson and his state depended on enslaved Africans,
and slavery violated their most basic principles and compromised their
benevolent promise. Little wonder that Jefferson recurs to the topic of race
with increasing intensity as *Notes on the State of Virginia* proceeds. In doing
so, he makes the nature of his own and his nation's fears and failings clear.

The strain of Jefferson's predicament makes itself felt in his relationship
to the landscape's most impressive features. The well-known paragraphs
describing the Natural Bridge begin, "The *Natural bridge,* the most sublime of Nature's works, though not comprehended under the present head,
must not be pretermitted" (26). The presence of this description of what is
neither a cave nor a cavern in a Query addressed to those topics disrupts the
order of Jefferson's catalog. Jefferson's composition thus mimics the sublimity it describes; it disrupts systematic order and suggests higher purposes
and imperatives.

Cold-blooded statistics compose most of the actual description. These
report both the canyon's and the bridge's dimensions and sketch the arch's
"semi-elliptical form." The sublime emerges when Jefferson evokes the be-
holder's emotional response. Though there are rocky parapets at the bridge's
edges, Jefferson reports that "few men have resolution to walk to them and

look over into the abyss" (26). The word "abyss" cues the reader's reaction. It describes not an objective statistic, but an emotional state, terror. Jefferson moves sentence by sentence from the third person—"few men"—to the second person—"you"—to the first person—"I": "You involuntarily fall on your hands and feet, creep to the parapet and peep over it. Looking down from this height about a minute, gave me a violent head ach [sic]" (26). From impersonal observations to common emotions to his individual reaction, Jefferson's description of Natural Bridge narrows until it focuses the scene's sublimity in his own painful and symptomatic reaction to it.

That Jefferson, who worked intensively on this passage, should focus on his own headache is suggestive. Headaches were Jefferson's characteristic psychosomatic symptom when confronted with public duties he wanted to avoid or demands he found difficult to meet. Jefferson's convulsive pain seems to measure his sympathetic reaction to the "great convulsion" that he believed created the Natural Bridge. He even adds a long footnote refuting a Spanish naturalist who contended that a similar rock formation in South America was formed not by "any convulsion of nature" but by the gradual "wearing of the water that runs through" the chasm (27). That Jefferson should here insist on a natural cataclysm that gives him headaches suggests a conflict in his cosmology. Generally, as in his denial of extinction with reference to the mammoth ("no instance can be produced of her [nature] having permitted any one race of her animals to become extinct; of her having permitted any link in her great work so weak as to be broken" [55]), Jefferson denied the possibility of cataclysmic ruptures in nature. Similarly, when Jefferson entertains theories that might explain the presence of calciferous shells in the schist of North Mountain, he rejects the possibility of catastrophic floods that might engulf mountaintops or shifting land masses that could "heave" ocean floors to a mountain's height (34–35). Though he withholds final judgment, he clearly prefers Voltaire's suggestion that the earth itself had produced the shells by an inorganic-organic process, passing minerals "through the pores of calcareous earths and stones" and growing shells "unattached to animal bodies" (34–35). This "theory" attributes less violence, instability, and profligacy to nature. For if nature be profligate, if it be subject to violent convulsions, ruptures, and revolutions, then the grounding of republics in nature and nature's law becomes a treacherous business.[44] Thus, the imagined cataclysm at the Natural Bridge belies the idea of nature as a harmonious plenitude. It registers

Jefferson's worst fears. His headache registers not only the sublimity of the landscape but the terror associated with the modern political and social order he believes must—but finally cannot—be made to harmonize with nature.

Still, the passage does not end with Jefferson's headache or the sublime but shades off into a more tranquil evocation of beauty:

> If the view from the top be painful and intolerable, that from below is delightful in an equal extreme. It is impossible for the emotions arising from the sublime, to be felt beyond what they are here: so beautiful an arch, so elevated, so light, and springing as it were up to heaven, the rapture of the spectator is really indescribable! The fissure continuing narrow, deep, and straight for a considerable distance above and below the bridge, opens a short but very pleasing view of the North mountain on one side, and Blue ridge on the other, at the distance each of them of about five miles. (26–27)

Harmony is restored through an abrupt shift of perspective that abandons the tumultuous heights for the tranquil valley. Order and harmony restored, the headache disappears. But the beautiful vista requires that Jefferson forget himself in order to compose it. The pleasing view of the distant, tranquil mountains, as Jefferson confessing to his "error of recollection requiring apology" later admits, can be seen only from the bridge's height and not from the valley below. To compose his prospect, Jefferson must forget his place in the landscape at the site where present strife and peaceful prospect fail to coincide. Coming to the brink of a vision in which nature's violence overwhelms any peaceful prospect, Jefferson mitigates a painful realization that his hopes are groundless by drawing back and shifting his approach. To reestablish the beautiful prospect at Natural Bridge requires a faulty, self-deceiving memory that denies that implication of Jefferson's terrible headache and restores his equanimity.

Natural convulsion and cataclysmic disruption also animate Jefferson's description of the confluence of the Susquehanna and Potomac rivers, which Malcolm Kelsall has read as an instance of the Jacobian sublime.[45] Once again the tumult of the sublime, suggestive of cataclysm and war both around and within Jefferson, yields to a hopeful prospect of peaceful and benign order where nature, the self, and the state can regain their self-composure among the nation's bucolic farms. Both these natural scenes so powerfully encode personal, social, and political anxieties that one scene recalls the other. Moreover, what links them in Jefferson's own mind is his contempt for or disappointment in the fellow citizens on whom so much realization of hopes depends. He writes, "This scene is worth a voyage across the Atlantic. Yet here, as in the neighbourhood of the natural bridge, are people who have passed their lives within half a dozen miles, and have never been to survey these monuments of a war between rivers and mountains, which must have shaken the earth itself to its center" (21). Here sublimity and taste, those two closely linked terms in eighteenth-century aesthetic and moral philosophy, separate those few sensitive souls like Jefferson from their neighbors who are insensible to the virtuous prompting of the moral and aesthetic sense. For Jefferson as for Kant, the world divides into those who can appreciate the sublime and those who cannot.[46] The former have the natural moral gifts that furnish a reliable foundation for Jefferson's virtuous republic; the others, manifestly, do not. Kelsall wrote of this passage: "Presumably the 'aristocracy of virtue' of whom Jefferson wrote to John Adams were also an aristocracy of sensibility."[47] That the peaceful farmers on whose sensibility the republic's future depended should be insensible to aesthetic experience suggests to Jefferson a moral coarseness that clearly pained him. To fix his future hopes on the yeomen peopling the nation's valleys, he must forget the actual character and predilections of those among whom he lives, as he forgets the exact topography of Natural Bridge when he adjusts his memory of its prospect. Otherwise, Jefferson might find himself constrained to admit that the foundations of the new nation in principles and in people may be too compromised to support his dream of an organic community as a virtuous republic.

That Jefferson was manifestly alive to both aesthetic and moral senses causes him other problems and pain. For Jefferson knows, even if his neighbors do not, when he and the republic fail their own deepest sympathies and betray their own most basic principles. Jefferson's terrible knowledge, which threatens to darken the nation's prospects, finds expression in his descriptions of race and slavery and his failure to deal adequately with either.

THE TERROR OF RACE AND THE FAILURE OF BENEVOLENCE

Jefferson's attempts to describe both Native Americans and blacks involve failures of memory and perception as well as failures of benevolence. His fears, especially evident in his comments on race, express common anxieties. Frank Shuffelton has found in these passages not only intellectual inconsistencies (the skeptical cultural comparativism of Montesquieu and Turgot enables the celebration of indigenous noble savages but is at odds with the universalizing rational taxonomies of Linnaeus and Buffon that frame the derogation of enslaved Africans) but also a reflection of the new nation's own contradictions and conflicts: "The ideological contradictions of Jefferson's text thus point to a corresponding uncertainty, a repressed anxiety even, in the culture at large when it confronted an ethnic and cultural Other and at the same time tried to be mindful of the Enlightenment ideals of 'true philosophy.'"[48] These repressed anxieties become manifest in Jefferson's attempts to deal with Native Americans and Africans in his natural history of his state.

The most famous passages dealing with these peoples occur for Native Americans in the answer to Query VI in which Jefferson refutes Buffon's theory of New World degeneracy and for blacks in the answers to Queries XIV and XVIII in which he describes his state's laws and manners. Jefferson's book generally moves from nature (Queries I through VII and XI, which deal with physical nature) to society (Queries VIII through X and XII through XXIII). In this progression, Buffon's analytical anatomizing should dominate the earlier natural history and Montesquieu's skeptical relativism should come to the fore in later commentary on social and political culture.[49] Yet, in his comments on Indians, Jefferson disrupts his taxonomies and statistics with an excursion into skeptical relativism celebrating their humanity, and in his discussion of blacks, he disrupts his analysis of laws and manners to categorize their natural inferiority. Thus, both his celebration of Native Americans in the book's first part and his taxonomy of blacks in its second, like the descriptions of Natural Bridge and the confluence of rivers, disrupt Jefferson's orderly elaboration of Virginia's natural history.[50]

Jefferson's comments on enslaved Africans attempt to establish in the starkest terms imaginable their irredeemable primitiveness, while his discussion of Indians means to make them seem (despite, or perhaps because of, their putative lack of sexual ardor) as civilized as possible. Both cases require rhetorical labor. To fashion the Native American as equivalent to a civilized European, Jefferson must domesticate their exotic and wild sublimity, while to represent subjugated, laboring blacks as barely human he must render their everyday familiarity strange, even sublime and terrible. John Chester Miller remarks, "Jefferson did not fear Indians in the way he feared black slaves . . . [yet] the Indians had accounted for the deaths of far more white people than had the black slaves."[51] In both cases, Jefferson's own fears determine what he remembers and what he forgets.

In refuting Buffon's claims that New World degeneracy manifests itself in the generative, emotional, physical, and moral weakness of the continent's native inhabitants, Jefferson speaks of their amative zeal, their bravery in battle, their sense of honor, their love of their children, their grief and stoicism, and claims that their "vivacity and activity of mind is equal to ours in the same situation" (64–65). Throughout this long passage Indians and whites are equated both emotionally and physically, while all differences (for example in the size of families) get attributed to differences in their material condition (the hardship of nomadic life and of recurrent famine [65]). Jefferson drives his point home:

> To form a just estimate of their genius and mental powers, more facts are wanting, and great allowance to be made for those circumstances of their situation which call for a display of particular talents only. This done, we shall probably find that they are formed in mind as well as in body, on the same module with "Homo sapiens Eurpaeus." (66)

To clinch the argument, he presents Chief Logan's rhetorical tour de force, his Ossianic speech previously mentioned. This speech, as Merrill Peterson notes, became a national favorite: "Schoolboys across the land later declaimed this grave lament on the white man's murderous destruction of the chief's family and his proud revenge, closing with the familiar line, 'Who is there to mourn for Logan? Not one.'"[52] Euro-Americans chose to forget that this is a tale not only of noble mourning but of violent revenge provoked by violent settlers. Colonel Cresap's murder of his family, Logan declares, "called on me for revenge. I have sought it: I have killed many: I have fully glutted my vengeance" (68). This violence is here mitigated, however, by the sympathetic recognition of a shared humanity in light of which Logan's sentiments and actions appear just or at least comprehensible. The tendency of the whole passage is to make the vanishing savage less sublimely terrible and more domestically familiar.

This differs in every way from Jefferson's description of blacks. Here no recognition of variations in condition or culture will be permitted to qualify an assertion of absolute and categorical difference, though the difference in material situation between slaves and masters should have been difficult to ignore. As Kames knew, fear and defensiveness make the mind do strange things. And if terror is the emotion of the sublime, then Jefferson's descriptions of enslaved Africans are the most sublime passages in his book.

For Jefferson and for Virginia, the struggle between self-interest and benevolent virtue joined most poignantly in the struggle over slavery that raged around and within him. To understand the intensity of effort Jefferson expended to deny the talents and accomplishments of enslaved Africans, consider the place within *Notes on the State of Virginia* where the most extensive passages on race occur, "Laws and Manners." That this represents something of a climax after what Lewis Simpson called a progression of increasing agitation over the three passages dealing with blacks bespeaks Jefferson's increasing desperation and frustration, his inability to find a place for blacks or for slavery in the current state of things in a just and harmonious republic. By assigning Africans a lowly place on the great chain of beings, Jefferson attempted to forget the effects of their inherently violent subjugation. Remembering this violence might force Jefferson to confront the failure of virtue in his republic and the injustices of the social order from which he benefited. It might force him to admit that no harmonious natural or social order can survive in a state at war with itself.[53] Little wonder then that Jefferson found the topic of race terrifying.

In *Notes,* Jefferson, as he struggles to include the existence of African slaves in his stabilizing account of Virginia's natural and civil state, does not so much reflect on racial distinctions that might ground violent practices as he produces them as a further extension of that violence. The differentiation of races he needs to stabilize the conflict between whites and blacks—to make more palatable the exploitation of Africans by Europeans—is the result of that conflict and offers no grounds for the reestablishment of harmonious order. Jefferson's inability completely to forget these fundamental contradictions in his republic's composition suggests the fears motivating the symptomatic blindness and fervor of his notorious passages on race.

"The first difference which strikes us," as Jefferson says in Query XIV, "is that of colour" (145). Thus begins the longest and most notorious of Jefferson's digressions on race. This one erupts—the word is no exaggeration—in the midst of a fairly dry enumeration of revolutionary Virginia's proposed revisions of the legal code. It follows directly from the following list:

To hire undertakers for keeping the public roads in repair, and indem-
nify individuals through whose lands new roads shall be opened.
To define with precision the rules whereby aliens should become citi-
zens, and citizens make themselves aliens.
To establish religious freedom on the broadest bottom.
To emancipate all slaves born after passing the act. (144)

And while this last proposal was not adopted, it does serve to introduce
the bizarre account of enslaved Africans that runs over the next six pages.

The bulk of those several thousand words are framed as a response to a
query within the Query concerning Jefferson's colonization plans that would
have separated the white and black races after emancipation. "It will probably be asked," he writes, "Why not retain and incorporate the blacks into
the state . . . ?" Which question, self-asked, provokes what follows, which
is of course too well known to require lengthy citation here. Color determines a deficit of physical comeliness and moral sentiment, of affectionate
attachment, and of the capacity for grief. Jefferson speculates that they
"secrete less by the kidneys, and more by the glands of the skin," which,
he notes, "gives them a very strong and disagreeable odour" and renders
them more tolerant of heat but less of cold. They require less sleep and are
brave only through lack of forethought. They have a disposition to sleep,
unless directly employed, which Jefferson takes to indicate a tendency toward sensation rather than reflection (145–46). They are, in other words,
admirably suited by nature to sustain and survive the beastly lot of enforced
labor to which Jefferson's state has assigned them.

There is no need to belabor the mystifications and obtuseness of Jefferson's speculations here. To accuse those forced to endure physical servitude
of the harshest sort who seek amusements when offered and sleep when
possible of lacking the capacity for reflection demonstrates in Jefferson himself an absence of reflection truly remarkable given his usually observant
habits.[54] Such obtuseness in so acute an observer can only be explained by
the distorting pressure of "self-deceit."

But it is in the next series of descriptions that Jefferson's desperate self-
deception makes itself most manifest. Here Jefferson offers the following:
"Comparing them by their faculties of memory, reason, and imagination,
it appears to me, that in memory they are equal to the whites; in reason
much inferior . . . ; and in that of imagination they are dull, tasteless, and

anomalous" (146). No example of a Phyllis Wheatley or an Ignatius Sancho will be allowed to contradict or complicate the naturalist's description. Here, as Frank Shuffelton indicates, Jefferson blinds himself to many examples much closer to home than Wheatley or Sancho. "What in fact astonishes here is Jefferson's blindness to the creativity of the black artisans in his own household who were accomplished cooks, cabinet makers, storytellers, and so on."[55] As Shuffelton also notes, the reasons for Jefferson's blindness are complex, but in the final analysis his blindness blinds him to himself. Again and again the deficiencies Jefferson attributes to the blacks derive from the conditions under which they are held and forced to work, while the triumphs of crafts and expression they manage to produce in such circumstances are either denigrated or ignored. It is as if the full realization of slavery's enormity would cause Jefferson a pain neither he nor his republic could endure. To make the headache of slavery more manageable requires that Jefferson forget the most painful aspects of his own relation to the violence and injustices of slaveholding and attempt to deceive himself concerning the origins and nature of the slave's condition. What Jefferson cannot allow himself to see is not only the character and culture of the slave but the master's presence—his own place—in the landscape. His own identification of reason with whiteness, his own identity as natural master of the land and its people, depends on his denial of reason to those his state brutally subjugates. He cannot allow himself to recognize that his own shadow and the shadow of the institutions from which he benefits and with which he identifies himself darken the terrain he describes and the people in it.

The frequently noted tentativeness with which Jefferson advances these racial theories says less about his enlightened skepticism then it does about his half-realization that he has missed something obvious. Mitchell Breitwieser has noted the occlusion of vision that so often forms part of the prospect in Jefferson's most characteristic works. "The ingenuities at Monticello," he writes,

> presume a slave economy while simultaneously expurgating signs of labor as often as possible: the hidden stairways; the slave passages to the kitchen; laundry and stables hidden . . . beneath the terraces; the dumbwaiters, invisible within the fireplace, that obviate the need to have wine carried into the room; the ladder that folds so that it does not look like a ladder; and the

seeming door that revolves to reveal shelves of hot food, but conceals the
servers. As if there were some sort of shame at work, Jefferson's instrumental
innovations at Monticello are aimed at projecting a *sprezzatura* that denies
that labor that permits Monticello to be: it's a magic place.[56]

Shame seems to be exactly what is involved. The fear of the other's regard,
which, as Kames knew, is also one's own self-regard, distorts Jefferson's prospect, a prospect from which he attempts to elide his own presence and
the results of his own actions. The uncharacteristic intemperateness of Jefferson's omnivorous attack on the slaves whose labor supported him and
whose condition was difficult not to see as a result of his actions represent
an obsessive attempt not merely to place the black population in the state
of Virginia in a timeless taxonomy justifying their bondage but most important an attempt to remove himself and his republic from the historical injustice being perpetrated. Because the conflict between practices and principles
seems impossible to resolve, the responsibility for conflict must be assigned
to the victims of the nation's violence. Slavery may be an unfortunate institution and a danger to the republic, but slavery is also the slave's proper
condition in Jefferson's state.

Shame and fear motivate Jefferson's obsessive denigration of blacks. The
fear that motivates Jefferson's projections in his passages on slavery and race
emerges in the passage on law, but reaches a sublime height in the chapter
on manners, which they completely dominate. When he first introduces
the topic of race in the Query on law, he begins by specifying what he calls
a political reason for the removal of Africans from America to achieve the
necessary separation of the races. He writes:

> Deep rooted prejudices entertained by the whites; ten thousand recollections,
> by the blacks, of the injuries they have sustained; new provocations; the real
> distinctions which nature has made; and many other circumstances, will
> divide us into parties, and produce convulsions which will probably never
> end but in the extermination of the one or the other race. (145)

Here at least he allows blacks a recognizably human desire for retribution.
But the passage approaches sublime terror in its exaggerated paranoia about
violence rebounding on the white population, and Jefferson's final comments
move fully into apocalyptic prophesy and horror:

And can the liberties of a nation be thought secure when we have removed their only firm basis, a conviction in the minds of the people that these liberties are the gift of God? That they are not to be violated but with his wrath? Indeed, I tremble for my country when I reflect that God is just: that his justice cannot sleep for ever: that considering numbers, nature, and natural means only, a revolution of the wheel of fortune, an exchange of situation, is among possible events: that it may become probable by supernatural interference! The Almighty has no attribute which can take side with us in such a contest. (169)

Then, as if realizing that he has become hysterical, he draws back: "It is impossible to be temperate and to pursue this subject." There at the heart of the moral and legal foundations of his happy, benevolent republic, Jefferson finds the misery and violence inflicted by the institutions that support him. But he continues to blind himself to the daily violence perpetrated by the order of his own life as a slaveholder. His physical fear seems exaggerated because it masks the more realistic moral terror in which he lives, the moral terror born of the fact that no taxonomy of nature and no inventory of morals can justify the system with which he and his nation collude and on which his life depends. Slavery was a headache that would not just go away.

Jefferson's fear typified the fears of his class and nation. They also typified the dynamic structure of America's obsessions—a combination of blindness to the self as the origin of violence and a projection of inadequacy on those to whom violence has been done.[57] The obsessive insistence on race as the basis of social order destabilizes the system it is meant to support. Racial difference depends on racial laws and perpetual violence to enforce distinctions that few truly believed were simply natural. If they were natural they would not have required constant policing by vicious legal and extralegal sanctions. This bespeaks a structuring terror that is, fundamentally, the terror of a self-realization denied, the denial of a realization of fundamental principles violated and future hopes betrayed, the realization that the self and the nation thus recognized would be unrecognizably different from their own idealized self-images. This structure of terror and projection, self-blindness and violent attribution, is a characteristic and recurrent structure in America's attempt to realize a national identity. It appears in many segments of American social, political, and cultural life and bespeaks a fear that is often well founded. It appears not only in Jefferson but in Jefferson's admirers in the terms by which they—under the cloak of scholarly objectivity—have denied not so much his intimate relations with one enslaved woman but his far more significant intimate relations with slavery itself. They, in their defense of Jefferson, mask the real violence of slavery and its perpetrators and further victimize those who suffered. In this sense they become like the man they admired.

Jefferson, who did not permit any examples of African genius with which he was presented during his life or the widespread participation of African Americans in the struggle for independence to alter his views on blackness or colonization, might have lived to see some of his fears about race and violence materialize.[58] Jefferson feared that the violence done to slaves would be done by slaves in turn, a fear justified not only in numerous actual rebellions but in the rhetoric of a free African American reacting to American injustice and in response to *Notes on the State of Virginia*. Five years after Jefferson's death, David Walker published his *Appeal to the Coloured Citizens of the World*. Near the end, he makes reference to the same sentimental and moral sense philosophy Jefferson held dear, and whose prompting toward benevolence Jefferson's racist hysteria was meant to resist. Walker writes:

> They [the whites] know well, if we are *men*—and there is a secret monitor in their hearts which tells them we are—they know, I say, if we *are* men, and see them treating us in the manner they do, that there can be nothing in our hearts but death alone, for them, notwithstanding we may appear cheerful, when we see them murdering our dear mothers and wives, because we cannot help ourselves. Man, in all ages and all nations of the earth, is the same.[59]

Walker sounds a bit like Chief Logan himself. His appeal means to apply the natural law of morality, the basis of harmonious human relations and virtuous republics, to himself and his African brethren. His language is both sentimental and sublime, almost Gothic in the horror it evokes: "there can be nothing in our hearts but death alone, for them." If white men put themselves in black men's place, they would feel this terrible truth in their hearts. They already do. Walker thus unmasks the terror behind the white racists' obsessive attempt to stabilize difference and to deny what they already know. He finds Jefferson himself to be a characteristic and egregious instance of this willful blindness and motivated forgetting. Echoing the stirring pledge at the conclusion of the Declaration of Independence, Walker writes, "For I pledge you my sacred word of honour, that Mr. Jefferson's remarks respecting us, have sunk deep into the hearts of millions of the whites, and never will be removed this side of eternity" (30). He might have Jefferson himself in mind when he describes the plight in which whites, self-deceiving and denying, find themselves:

> The whites knowing this, they do not know what to do; they know that they have done us so much injury, they are afraid that we, being men, and not brutes, will retaliate, and woe will be to them; therefore, that dreadful fear, together with an avaricious spirit, and the natural love in them, to be called masters, (which term will yet honour them with to their sorrow) bring them to the resolve that they will keep us in ignorance and wretchedness, as long as they possibly can, and make the best of their time while it lasts. (64)

And he concludes with precisely the threat Jefferson feared, couched in the grotesque metaphors of bodily abjection Jefferson himself might have used:

> Consequently they, themselves, (and not us) render themselves our natural enemies, by treating us so cruel. They keep us miserable now, and call us their property, but some of them will have enough of us by and by—their stomachs shall run over with us; they want us for their slaves, and shall have us to their fill. (64)

Jefferson did not live to see it, but Walker's appeal to his black brethren in its resolute recognition of the violence done by slavery and its responsible perpetrators represented the materialization of his worst fears, the manifestation that what he hoped would be a healthy, just republic for liberty had failed and become instead fevered, distracted, and violent. Walker stands at the origin of a long tradition of black leaders, including Martin Delaney, W. E. B. Du Bois, Malcolm X, and Muhammad Ali, who by reflecting back to their white oppressors an accurate image of white violence have provoked a panicky condemnation by whites who fail to recognize the justice of their claims. Here whites forget that they are themselves the origin of hatred, violence, and exploitation and not its victims. In his undeniably human outrage, Walker concretized the judgment on Jefferson and his class that Jefferson had in some measure already made on himself. The measure of that judgment's force is the fearful energy with which Jefferson tried to deny its implications for the failure of America.

It is no doubt true, as Ferguson says, that the "mystic identification of law and country intrinsic to our national rhetoric" is "probably the most important legacy" of Jefferson's legal expertise manifested in his *Notes*.[60] However, the tension between the ideal of that identification of just laws with a happy land and the reality of the republic's iniquitous practices and violent oppressions stands at the origin and at the conflicted center of America's attempts to realize its own identity. Fear is the symptom of Americans confronting or refusing to confront their own betrayal of their nation's principles. Insofar as Jefferson embodied both those principles and their failure early in the nation's history, violating the promise of equality and the demand for justice that he himself so effectively expressed, he models American identity and its failure for us. The peculiar combination of promise and failure that is American identity is Jefferson's legacy as well. His headache remains our own.

chapter 2

Ahab's Cannibals:
Vicissitudes of Command and the
Failure of Manly Virtue

> The Hero claims to have acted alone in accomplishing the deed.
>
> —SIGMUND FREUD, *Group Psychology and the Analysis of the Ego*

AHAB'S WORLD

Moby Dick stands as a colossal and spectacular monument to American failure and especially to the failure of American identity for American men. Ishmael, Starbuck, Ahab, and Melville all fail brilliantly to find community, to avert disaster, to encompass revenge, to author a popular success. A description of the plot of Melville's novel need not be long. A sailor with an intellectual and garrulous bent who names himself Ishmael tells the story of a whaling voyage he undertook near in time to the presidential election of 1848. As the ship nears the southern whaling grounds, the captain, deprived of his leg on a previous voyage by the great albino sperm whale known in the fishery as Moby Dick, makes a surprising announcement to the crew. This voyage, in violation of both custom and contract, will not pursue whales for profit in the oil market but will hunt the white whale so Ahab can wreak vengeance on it. Against its own interests and over the first mate's protests, the crew agrees to follow Ahab. During the next months, the *Pequod* follows the normal business of whaling with considerable success. But when the captain's comprehensive knowledge of whale migrations and considerable skill in navigation enable the ship to find Moby Dick on the Pacific cruising grounds, they turn from normal business to the Captain's mad errand. On the third day of the final chase the white whale, apparently with intelligence and fell purpose, turns on his pursuers, destroys their boats, sinks the ship, and kills all, save Ishmael, who escapes alone to turn this cat-astrophe into a book.

The comic inadequacy of this summary should be apparent, for the expe-rience of reading *Moby Dick,* as any student knows, involves, most memo-rably, navigating the remarkable detours and digressions of what one critic has aptly called its "errant art."[1] The book, like all of Melville's most chal-lenging work, seems like the wreck of some even larger ambition. It shares the fate of all human attempts to systematize experience or formalize knowl-edge that Ishmael describes at the end of his bibliographic taxonomy of whales: "I now leave my Cetological System standing thus unfinished, even as the great Cathedral of Cologne was left, with the crane still standing on the top of the uncompleted tower. For small erections may be finished by their first architects; grand ones, true ones, ever leave the copestone to pos-terity. God keep me from ever completing anything. This whole book is but a draught—nay, but the draught of a draught. Oh, Time, Strength, Cash, and Patience."[2] Ishmael may not complete his book, but Ishmael's narra-tive voice fills *Moby Dick*'s copious form. Consider, for example, that for all his rhetorical claims to power, Ahab only exists for readers because Ishmael tells his story. Like so many other things that readers recollect—Queequeeg's tattooed visage, the whale's terrifying whiteness, the mates' character traits, and the fishery's routines and risks—maimed Ahab's mad ambition assumes shape and significance in the agile medium of Ishmael's voice. In a book thoroughly obsessed with the captain's power, Ishmael possesses at least the intellectual's power to have the last word; though who, in the final analy-sis, can be said to possesses any power turns out to be a question that *Moby Dick* makes hard to answer.

Ishmael frequently plays at the sort of exhaustive natural history of which this chapter on cetology affords a familiar, playful example. As did Jeffer-son, Ishmael as naturalist dreams of stabilizing identities and ordering the world. Yet his stab at cetology, like his other attempts to measure or depict the whale, makes the failure of this dream apparent. Ishmael knows that nei-ther identity nor knowledge, of whales or of men, can be fixed apart from the terrifying experience of the dangerous power of the whale's flukes or of Ahab's command. The contrast between Ahab and Ishmael, the isolated, tyrannical captain and the garrulous, democratic narrator, has occupied generations of Melville's critics and has often assumed explicitly political overtones. Samuel Otter succinctly sums up the contrast by attempting to fix univocal significance on nature and on men: "Ahab hopes to secure his own identity"; by embracing multiple meanings that "are to be caressed," Ishmael surrenders secure identity to the contingencies of relation.[3] Knowledge and power are for Ahab, as they were in the racist taxonomies that Otter sees Melville challenging, wielded to destroy the other in order to stabilize the self. Ishmael's amiable meanderings promise a different order of knowing both self and world, one in which power yields to association. Yet both Ishmael and Ahab fail. Ishmael embraces Ahab's apocalyptic desire that destroys the community in which he finds himself, and Ahab must depend on the common seamen of his crew, belying the imperious selfhood he proclaims.

Discussions of *Moby Dick* naturally become discussions of masculinity. Ishmael's wit frequently forces manhood on the reader's attention. For example, the passage on his incomplete taxonomy of whales evokes the phallus as do many of his manic puns. His suggestion of erectile dysfunction reminds the reader that this is a book figured as both a dick and a cathedral, a proper seat for the author or "archbishop prick" who seems, like the sailor draped in the skin of the whale's penis and slicing blubber into bible leaves in "The Cassock," vested with the power of a dismembered body and transubstantiating the whale's flesh into fuel for lights and words for reflection (420). Such punning prominently figures among the book's diversions. Still, one might seriously ask, what does a man who cannot stand alone suggest about the embodiment of masculinity? How is authority vested if the vestments of authority must come from a victim's body? The vicissitudes of manly power, an essential component of America's dominant identity, is a topic about which *Moby Dick* has had and continues to have much to say. And as generations of critics have noted, these questions fundamentally involve politics, or to be more precise, the catastrophic failure of the political.

THE POLITICS OF AHAB

In the middle of the twentieth century, those critics largely responsible for the canonization of *Moby Dick* tended to find in Ishmael an authentic American voice for freedom, one in which they recognized an alternative to Ahab's dictatorial demands for total dominance.[4] F. O. Matthiessen, whose assessment of Ahab remains influential, remarked that "even Melville can hardly have been fully aware of how symbolical an American hero he had fashioned in Ahab." In Matthiessen's view, Ahab represented Melville's worst fears about the authoritarian proclivities and vulnerabilities of the American character and the American democratic system to which Matthiessen, like Melville, was deeply, if ambivalently, committed. Matthiessen saw in Ahab and his effect on his crew the tragic results of Emersonian individualism "carried to its furthest extreme" and bringing "disaster both upon itself and upon the group of which it is part."[5] Ahab's power nonetheless remains mysterious; as Ishmael reminds the reader, the captain is neither an emperor nor a king but "only . . . a poor old whale hunter . . . [without] . . . outward majestical trappings and housings" (148). If, as Ahab himself describes his dominance of his crew, "my one cogged circle fits into all their various wheels, and they revolve" (167), what makes power's machinery work?

Fixated on the effects of Ahab's power, few critics have closely considered its reality. Since Matthiessen, politically minded critics have easily identified Ahab with the nation's most distressing tendencies, especially its obsessional rhetoric of victimage and revenge and its tendency to personalize global conflicts and demonize perceived enemies. William Spanos describes it as an "all-too-familiar pattern of American historical practice in crisis, continuing through the Vietnam War to the war against 'Saddam Hussein'": the practice characterized by the American national psyche's reduction of the "threatening" complex "Other . . . to an utterly demonized One."[6] When in the wake of the September 11 attacks on the United States Edward Said demanded a more complex understanding of the world, he naturally described America's fixation on Osama bin Laden in terms borrowed from Melville's novel, remarking the marshalling of "collective passions" into "a drive for war that uncannily resembles Captain Ahab in pursuit of Moby Dick."[7] Said recognized that wounded, blasphemous, monomaniacal Ahab vividly figured wounded America's dangerous mood. Ahab has become a useful caricature for such topical broadsides. But fixed attention on perceived injustices are politically polyvalent. Had Melville's novel had wider public appeal, Ahab would have furnished contemporary pundits an apt analogy for John Brown whose revolutionary abolitionist acts would galvanize the nation only a few years after *Moby Dick* appeared.[8] Moreover, however useful as caricature, Ahab remains an extraordinary accomplishment of characterization, one whose complexities afford insights into the realities of power more subtle than fixations on his madness alone allow.

More spiritually minded critics have bracketed such essentially political questions when reading Melville's novel, but while such readings pursue Ahab's complexities, they cannot evade the political implications of his story. Harold Bloom, who is always interesting, recognizes Ahab as the crucial positive embodiment of the American ideal as a form of embattled Gnosticism: "Ahab's quest is supremely American because its God is identical with the inner self, and not with the outer God who presides over Heaven. . . . Captain Ahab dies as a Gnostic should, still defying the sanctified monster who is ordained to destroy him. . . . It is the exemplary death of the American Religion, in a complex way a kind of atonement for our national pride in the self."[9] Defiance and atonement, fatedness and self-will, such an image of the American self is complicated indeed and politically ambivalent, equally well describing the promethean aspirations of both tyrants and revolutionaries. Both sorts of heroes refuse the deals fate, compromise, and collaboration offer to those more sane or more compliant with actual necessity or apparent common sense. But Gnostic Ahab, however heroic, does not die alone; and the tally of his catastrophe poses questions from which Melville's critics, desiring to follow Melville's novel, should not turn. Ahab's Gnosticism, as Bloom reads it, requires him to turn from the void without to the God within in order to discover more vital meanings than the world seems to offer. But Ahab's world seems to Ahab not devoid of significance. For the wounded captain, Moby Dick heaps his world with meanings that touch him to the heart. In Melville's imagination, Ahab projects his own violence onto the world and then recognizes that forgotten double of himself as both an external threat and a promise of deliverance. Simply put, Ahab starts it. He tries to kill the whale, and in the ensuing struggle the whale dismembers him. Injured in the conflict he himself initiated, Ahab becomes fixated on vengeance and vindication. "Vengeance on a dumb brute . . . that simply smote thee from blindest instinct!" Starbuck sensibly objects. "Madness!" (163–64). This madness seems not quite Gnostic. It involves a turn from a void within Ahab to the peopled world around him. In that turn lies the source of his power and the keys to his mania. Ahab figures a character, an American character, whose traumatized sense of history mistakes or forgets that the violence he has suffered has been violence he provoked.

Ahab turns the story of his own catastrophe, Spanos suggests, into an event of cosmic proportion, a revision of history around a traumatic event that seems more than common in American public discourse. This is, in part, the logic of trauma and obsession and a too familiar aspect of the most hallucinatory of all American obsessions, national history. The commonplace belief that Americans have no sense of history misses the point. Americans are obsessed with history, but they tend to experience it in terms of their own heroic victimage and perpetual peril by British tyranny, by dangerous immigrants, by sneak attacks, by insidious ideologies.[10] Melville's ragged whaling captain remains the single most compelling figure in whose tortured body and soul the traumatized and maddened imagination speaks itself into U.S. history and culture—into America's sense of itself as a nation.

Ishmael's narrative of *Moby Dick,* with its well-known reluctance to fix meanings or conclude arguments, might be expected to blunt Ahab's drive to fix meaning on the world. But if Ishmael survives Ahab, he does not survive unmarked by Ahab's power. Ishmael seems an ineffective alternative to Ahab, for he appears at every moment complicit with or actually produced by the power Ahab wields. Donald Pease, whose reading of Ishmael remains pointed and provocative, puts it most clearly when he sums up his own sense of Ishmael's relentless playfulness:

> When all the world turns out to be invested with the indeterminate interplay of possibility, it does not seem free but replicates what we call boredom (the need for intense action without any action to perform), and what Ishmael called the hypos, the "drizzly November in his soul" that made him feel attracted to Ahab in the first place. . . . Ishmael's form of freedom does not oppose Ahab but compels him to need Ahab—not only as the purification of his style, but as the cure for a boredom verging on despair. . . . Ahab's compulsion to decide compels Ishmael not to decide.[11]

But Pease presses his point too hard. Ishmael may be complicit in and reliant on Ahab's designs, but fixing on his boredom fails to capture the exuberance of his story's language. He may even find in Ahab an alternative to the blank terrors of the charnel house that he suspects the painted harlot of the world actually is and that he describes in "The Whiteness of the Whale." But certainly one possessed of such exuberance and invention might well have found an alternative to Ahab as well.

Ishmael quickly recovers from the "drizzly November in his soul" (and how truly depressed could the man who produced that lovely line be?). Boredom plays little part in his narrative, which is generally characterized by fervent curiosity, probing playfulness, and errant wit. A desire for friendship leads him to embrace Queequeg, a desire to see the world makes him take up whaling, and something close to the dread that he describes in his chapter on the whiteness of the whale spurs him to follow Ahab's quest:

> Is it that by its indefiniteness it shadows forth the heartless voids and immensities of the universe, and thus stabs us from behind with the thought of annihilation, when beholding the white depths of the milky way? . . . And when we consider that other theory of the natural philosophers, that all other earthly hues—every stately or lovely emblazoning—the sweet tinges of sunset skies and woods; yea, the gilded velvets of butterflies, and the butterfly cheeks of young girls; all these are but subtle deceits . . . so that all deified Nature absolutely paints like the harlot, whose allurements cover nothing but the charnel house within. . . . And of all these things the Albino whale was the symbol. Wonder ye then at the fiery hunt? (195)

Whatever mood produces this much sublime verbiage (and there's much more to the passage), it is not boredom. Ishmael may be drawn to the hunt because the whale inspires his revulsion, dread, or terror, but the albino monster doesn't bore him.[12]

The boredom on which Pease's reading depends may be his own and not Ishmael's. In fact, boredom has become something of a critical posture among recent Americanist critics. David Leverenz, brilliantly deploying Ahab and his hysterical rage as part of his critique of American masculinity, claims to be bored by his rhetorical scene chewing.[13] Such readings seem less engaged with *Moby Dick* itself than with a more general critique of American politics, culture, and identity. These readings depend on a negative version of what Pease, following Marvin Meyers's influential work on antebellum rhetoric, calls a "persuasion," a set of shared values and assumptions that at a given moment become rhetorical touchstones. Unlike Meyers's account of "the Jacksonian persuasion," which stressed "equality against privilege; liberty against domination; honest work against idle exploit; natural dignity against factitious superiority; patriotic conservatism against alien innovation; progress against dead precedent," however beleaguered and betrayed in practice those principles might be, accounts by recent critics, in Pease's words, underscore "the fundamental problem for a society which has lost sight of a shared covenant."[14] A vision of American society's failings becomes a covenant of its own. The force of these readings depends on a prior consensus concerning a negative national narrative of American identity and power that debunks the optimistic nationalism of popular celebrations of American freedom and popular complacencies about the nation's virtuous triumph over evil and adversity. If the repeated articulations of the American jeremiad—in Sacvan Bercovitch's celebrated reading—draw their power from a shared sense of higher purpose, of national election or manifest destiny, in order to make projections of American power acceptable to the American public, these critical readings draw their power from a countervailing conviction that the United States may best be understood as the unified agent of insidious force and imperial ambition. In these readings, "America" appears personified as a single, univocal subject, "one very Bad individual stretching across four centuries" retaining "its penchant for exterminating Indians, kidnapping and enslaving Africans, and raping the environment." Ahab emerges as the exemplary antihero of this negative national narrative; he becomes America and the crew become his dupes. These phrases are from Clare Spark, who criticizes New Americanists for failing to consider the nation as a collection of "diverse but educable individuals" and settling instead for wholesale denunciations. Sacvan Bercovitch, whose own work has inspired some of these critics, writes: "We come to feel, in reading these critics, that the American ideology is a system of ideas in the service of evil rather than (like any ideology) a system of ideas wedded for good and evil to a certain social and cultural order."[15] Such uncompromising negativity fails to distinguish laudable principles from official cant, defensible national ideals from traumatized and terrorized versions of history and identity. More specifically, reading *Moby Dick,* such uncompromising negativity fails to capture the chaotic energies and confused idealism figured in both Ahab's character and Ishmael's narrative or to fairly assess the relationship of either to American culture and its beleaguered, persistent, and failed commitments to democracy, justice, freedom, and equality. Uncompromising negativity can become a means to escape ethical and political commitments rather than a way to engage them. *Moby Dick* should have taught its readers that such wishes to escape can never be realized.

Looking at *Moby Dick,* C. L. R. James notes something that most American critics—fixated on the dyadic pairing of Ahab and Ishmael—have missed. The novel dwells on (and many readers enjoy learning about) the labor of the crew, the skills of the common seamen, the courage of the dedicated worker, "the renegades and castaways and savages of the *Pequod . . .* doing what they have to do, facing what they have to face."[16] The crew have usually been the forgotten characters in readings of Melville's novel. Yet Ishmael's telling of their intricately coordinated work, daring, and skill fills the novel with extraordinary descriptions of the ordinarily dangerous business of pursuing, capturing, processing, warehousing, and bringing to market that is the social and communal labor of whaling. Alone among contemporary commentators, William Spanos spends time analyzing the crew, but he reduces them to figures of alienated labor and unreasoning dupes.[17] But to see them thus, "like machines" as Ishmael at one point describes them (536–37), is to adapt Ahab's or the owner's perspective and to miss the pleasures Ishmael attaches to the wondrous descriptions of their varied tasks and undaunted courage. To adapt Ahab's or the owner's perspective is to miss or forget the dignity and even beauty with which Melville, through his narrator, invests these working sailors. Moreover, when Ishmael describes his crew "like machines," just before the novel's final catastrophic action begins, he comments not on the dull round of their activities or his own disgusted boredom—his passionate interest and delight in their activities has sustained his reader over many pages—but the crew's muted, smoldering resistance to "the old man's despotic eye." Before the novel's final action sweeps them along, the men seem far from simply pliant or merely docile. The moment of intense, fantastic identification with the quest that Ahab produced on the quarterdeck has, in fact, failed.

C. L. R. James notes the crew's failure to identify with Ahab's purposes; the skill, courage, and fraternity of their common labors; the legitimacy of rebellion against Ahab's "usurpation" of the enterprise; and the model of rebellion and resistance offered in "The Town-Ho's Story." This tale involves both Ahab's whale and the rebellious Steelkirk, and, as James points out, it is known only to the crew—told by Tashtego, who received it from *Town Ho* whalemen, who kept it from their officers as the Pequod's crew keeps it from theirs as well (242–43). Thus, it forms, as Ishmael puts it, "the secret part of the tragedy about to be narrated," which involves, primarily, Steelkirk's refusal to serve sadistic and incompetent officers (243). In turn, the story poses the reader a question: with these reasons for and models of rebellion, why doesn't the crew rebel? James notes, "Here Melville does a most extraordinary thing. He gives some reasons. . . . But he says frankly that he doesn't know."[18] One partial answer, and this is James's great point, is that the crew goes along because their leaders and intellectuals fail them and abandon them to their fate. The mates can neither take the crew seriously enough nor sufficiently identify with their interests to try to save them. Nor does the crew happen to produce a Steelkirk of their own. Thus they remain, as James explains, "morally enfeebled . . . by the incompetence of mere unaided virtue or right-mindedness in Starbuck, the invulnerable jollity of indifference and recklessness in Stubb, and the pervading mediocrity of Flask."[19] Yet this is only a partial answer. The riddle of the crew's subjugation takes the reader "deeper than Ishmael can go."[20] Eventually Melville's novel will indicate the political and ethical implications any more complete consideration of power must entail.

Power in *Moby Dick* may dominate, but it also—as Marx knew power tends to do—produces the conditions of its own undoing. Those conditions may or may not, for a variety of contingent reasons, lead to action. In Melville's novel they do not. But to note them demonstrates the possibility of contesting power by illustrating power's internal incoherence, power's failure to achieve monumental status. As *Moby Dick* presents the situation, Ahab's crew fails to revolt, but that failure is a contingency of power's particular workings and not the essential expression of power's unanswerable nature. Could Starbuck find some principle more exciting than the Nantucket market, could Ishmael cease his woolgathering, could some Steelkirk-like leader rise up and forge an alternative alliance with which the men might join, then Ahab would quickly find himself denied access to the force and the identity he claims. But Steelkirk's fabled mutiny reminds us that opposition to power and violence entails bids for power and acts of violence as well. As luck (and Melville) would have it, on Ahab's ship only Ahab has a sufficient appetite for dominance and capacity for violence. Ahab also understands that the ability to wield power requires knowing power's nature and its limits. That knowledge and that understanding does not free him but drives him mad.

Power, as Ishmael describes it, determines knowledge but only in indeterminate ways. Near the last of Ishmael's various parodic forays into science and cetology, he makes a skeptical assessment of the whale's skeleton and the grounds of knowledge. When he seems to have gotten at last to the beast's stable core and foundation, whose measurements he says he copies "verbatim from my right arm, where I had them tattooed" (451), it becomes a moment not of triumph but of failure: "How vain and foolish, then, thought I, for timid untravelled man to try to comprehend aright this wondrous whale, by merely poring over his dead attenuated skeleton, stretched in this peaceful wood. No. Only in the heart of quickest perils; only when within the eddyings of his angry flukes; only on the profound unbounded sea, can the fully invested whale be truly and livingly found out" (453–54). Ishmael makes the skin of his body and the skeleton of the whale equivalent. Man and whale, surface and depth, this suggests, are alike incommensurable with adequate representation or fixed identities. Representation cannot capture—though it inevitably reflects—the phenomena of power that compose identity. The second point, a little deeper than the first, more precisely figures the linkages between knowledge and power. These are forged not in the abstract working over of inscriptions but in the concrete work of engagement, work that transforms both those who do it and the world they live in. Consider an earlier passage on a similar theme relating whales to representation: "The great Leviathan is that one creature in the world which must remain unpainted to the last. . . . So there is no earthly way of finding out precisely what the whale really looks like. And the only mode in which you can derive even a tolerable idea of his living contour, is by going a whaling yourself; but by so doing, you run no small risk of being eternally stove and sunk by him" (264). True knowledge does not articulate power and representation but recognizes the gap between them. Knowledge derives from the use of force in the transformative violence of work, like whaling. The subject engages its object in a struggle that risks all and transforms both. Knowledge emerges not primarily from killing the whale but from being nearly killed by it, yet living to tell the tale that itself can never completely impart the knowledge gained.

Power and knowledge are not simple or univocal consolidations of imperial vision or discursive dominance but an always reversible and unpredictable contest akin to the contest Ahab describes when he boasts that he would strike the sun should the sun strike at him, "For could the sun do that, then could I do the other; since there is ever a sort of fair play herein, jealously presiding over all creations" (164). Ahab rejects any impersonal diffusion of power through irresistible matrices of natural forces (the whale as brute beast who struck from merest instinct) or inescapable webs of human conventions (the Nantucket market). A saner human subject, like Starbuck, would, like any avatar of corporate individualism, submit to what seems inevitable. But such submission might be a mistake. Instead, in his madness, Ahab insists on a representation of the world that personifies power and thus makes struggling against subjugation possible.[21] The problem with Ahab resides not in his bid for power itself but in the ends to which he would put the power he demands.

The principle of power's contestability, the principle Ishmael describes when admitting that final description eludes and that Ahab enacts in his challenge to blind, stupid fate, may apply to Ahab's critics as well. To know Ahab's power, it is not enough to contemplate him from afar or grant him inevitable dominion. One must experience Ahab's force to judge it, which means that the critic must put him- or herself at risk of yielding, like Starbuck and the crew, to his power. In this struggle, the lesson of Starbuck's failure to intervene between his captain and catastrophe remains clear: mere right-mindedness saves neither its pious advocate nor those for whom he speaks unless he overcomes both prudence and prudery and risks recklessness and virtue both in the contest.

For Ahab's part, if he announces a universal principle of "fair play," he enacts it as well. From his first appearance on the quarterdeck to the last day of the fatal hunt, Ahab struggles with mates and men to maintain his hold over the *Pequod* and bend it to his will. His mad ends require him to manipulate sane means, which means that in his relationship to his crew, more than in the brute force of the White Whale's flukes, Ahab confronts the real limitations of his power. Most readings of Ahab have fastened on the madness of his ends and have ignored the complexities of tension, identification, and difference that separate Ahab from the crew on which he relies.

C. L. R. James's brilliant reading of the totalitarian intimations of *Moby Dick* brings some of these issues to light. He focuses at one crucial point on the moment in the text just before the white whale breaches on the chase's second day. Here the crew becomes a single body, an organic totality, as James describes them, "one with Nature, master of technology, all personal individuality freely subordinated to the excitement of achieving a common goal. At this moment the crew has achieved a singular community apart from Ahab's monomania, but placed at its service as well":[22]

There were one man, not thirty. For as the ship that held them all; though it was put together of all contrasting things—oak, and maple, and pine wood; iron, and pitch, and hemp—yet all these ran into each other in the one concrete hull, which shot on its way, both balanced and directed by the long central keel; even so, all the individualities of the crew, this man's valor, that man's fear; guilt and guiltlessness, all varieties were welded into oneness, and were all directed to that fatal goal which Ahab their one lord and keel did point to. (557)

Ahab may dream that his power reduces the men to mechanical extensions of himself, his one cog fitting their many wheels, but the liveliness of Ishmael's description of the chase ("the rigging lived") suggests the organic heart at the core of this doomed community, a heart that Ahab's mad manipulations essentially pervert and inevitably destroy but cannot simply conquer. For James this represents the ways in which the best energies of the modern world, especially those energies he observed among the American people, are tragically usurped by ruthless leaders and feckless elites who turn those persistently admirable energies to evil ends.

But Ahab's ends might not be simply insane. Ahab, as James notes, is himself in revolt against the conditions of modern life and embodies "the revulsion of modern man from an intolerable world" whose highest aspirations find expression in the cash nexus of the Nantucket market. Among so many other things, the hunt for the whale emphasizes Ahab's desire for more meaning in life than the tawdry compromises and brokered morality that modern mercantile existence affords. The political question the novel poses is how to separate a reasoned hatred for injustice and a fine contempt for meanness from what James calls "the genuine totalitarian consciousness of injustice, the totalitarian hatred and the totalitarian readiness to destroy the whole world in revenge."[23] In *Moby Dick*, remarkably enough, no one succeeds in making his negative judgment of Ahab's madness stick. The most remarkable thing about Ahab's fell purpose is not its madness but the absence of any effective opposition to it. No one, no officer like pious Starbuck and no intellectual like clever Ishmael, intervenes on the crew's behalf to stop Ahab and his reckless hunt. James may be right to stress that *Moby Dick* is a cautionary tale for disaffected and feckless intellectuals, for whom "there is always Ahab waiting to give them that protection from having to make choices and from the constant struggles of a world that is too much for them."[24] But in a democracy each citizen carries a portion of the intellectual's responsibility to define and contest identity, to adjudicate between sanity and insanity, to choose between justified resistance and maddened violence. In Melville's novel, the officers and crew fail to make this crucial choice.

To consider the failure of rebellion in *Moby Dick* refocuses attention on the figure of Ahab and the difficulties of trying to reduce him to manageable form as either a rebellious hero or a totalitarian despot. As Matthiessen put it, "To a degree even beyond what Melville may have intended, all other personalities, all other human relations became dwarfed before Ahab's purpose."[25] To a large extent this becomes true of Matthiessen's book as well. In the brilliant pages of *American Renaissance* dedicated to reading the structure, rhetoric, and meaning of Melville's novel, Ahab dominates and mesmerizes the critic the way Matthiessen saw him mesmerizing and dominating his crew and Melville himself. For Matthiessen, Ahab presages something dangerous that is emergent in the very character of America itself:

> The strong-willed individuals who seized the land and gutted the forests and built the railroads were no longer troubled with Ahab's obsessive sense of evil, since theology had receded even farther into their backgrounds. But their drives were as relentless as his, and they were to prove like him in many other ways also, as they went on to become the empire builders of the post–Civil war world. They tended to be as dead to enjoyment as he, as blind to everything but their one pursuit, as unmoved by fear or sympathy, as confident in assuming an identification of their will with immutable plan or manifest destiny, as liable to regard other men as merely arms and legs for the fulfillment of their purposes, and, finally, as arid and exhausted in their burnt out souls. (459)

For Matthiessen, in "one of his sublime moments" as William Cain puts it, Ahab comes to symbolize the magnetic promises and the terrible realities of American politics and culture and the terribly destructive contradictions and obsessions at the core of American identity.[26] Donald Pease suggests that "Ahab performs for Matthiessen the same function he performs for Starbuck: because his inner life is an embodiment of compulsion, he releases Matthiessen from the need to find compulsion at work in the doctrine of self-reliance, the Emersonian will to virtue informing the body of his work."[27] But neither Matthiessen nor Melville—not even Emerson himself—were deceived about how fine a line separates destructive monomania like Ahab's from the will to virtuous power any good leader or good citizen must have, or about the difficult necessity of determining on which side of that line one stands.

Ahab, for better and for worse, represents potentialities in the American character and contradictions in American principles. For Lewis Mumford in 1929, he represented both the potential virtues and the real destructiveness of the West itself: "The whole tale of the West, in mind and action, in the moral wrestlings of the Jews, in the philosophy and art of the Greeks, in the organization and technique of the Romans, in the precise skills and unceasing spiritual quests of the modern man, is a tale of this effort to combat the whale—to ward off his blows, to counteract his aimless thrusts to create a purpose that will offset the empty malice of Moby-Dick. . . . But in battling against evil, with power instead of love, Ahab himself . . . becomes the image of the thing he hates: he has lost his humanity in the very act of vindicating it."[28] To understand Ahab's attractions, his triumphs, and his failure, one must remember the difficulty of distinguishing his best from his worst, his monomaniacal madness from his noble will to power, the valuable principles of Western civilization and American identity from their violent perversion of specifying exactly what evil is and where it lodges. These are the political, ethical, and moral questions that *Moby Dick* asks its readers to engage.

AHAB'S POWER

Though Melville does not solve the riddle of power in modern society, C. L. R. James notes that he does offer a compelling portrayal of power's embodiment in "a new individualism, an individualism which," James feared, "would destroy society."[29] The emergence of this individualism in America and its myths of self-reliance and realities of enforced conformity attracted the attention of virtually every foreign visitor to the United States during the Jacksonian era, including Tocqueville, Chevalier, and Brisbane. Ahab, of course, is such an individualist. He dreams a power that might lift his single person above the mass of men and free him from all constraints. Such individuality stood apart, in the thought of European radicals and American reformers, from the individualism of the cowed and conforming masses (the *isolatos* of Ahab's crew, some might say), the herd that seems

everywhere to threaten the superior man.[30] Both those who celebrate Ahab's
rebellious romanticism and those who condemn his imposing authoritar-
ianism recognize him as a radical individualist, antagonistic to economic
calculation, social pressure, and conventional morality. But what emerges
from the quarterdeck ritual that inaugurates Ahab's domination of the crew
is not the unified embodiment of his single triumphant will embodied in
the crew's subjugation but an ad hoc community momentarily forged by
Ahab's stagy and manipulative performance of power. The crew remains a
corporate entity, and its commitment to Ahab's ends must be repeatedly
renegotiated. Nailing his doubloon to the mast, flinging his navigational
instruments into the sea, playing with St. Elmo's fire, Ahab works repeatedly to exert his magnetism over his potentially restive crew. Ahab is not
simply threatened by other men and their desires; his project depends on
them. Ahab lives something more complicated than the conflict between
self-reliance and conformity one might find in Emerson. He confronts not
"an absolute separation of the actual America ([conforming] individualism)
from the ideal ([triumphant] individuality)" (318), as Bercovitch describes
it, but a maddening confusion and interdependence of the two. His glorious romanticism depends, in practice, on his authoritarian manipulation
of his men.

Ahab's self-reliance relies on his crew. His power to redefine the voyage's
goal and accomplish his own end ("this is what ye have shipped for, men!"
[163]) depends on the willingness of his men to associate with him ("What
say ye, men, will ye splice hands on it now?" [163]). Ahab's apotheosis on
the quarterdeck, with its paradoxical combination of command and con-
sent, reveals the complicated and uneven workings of domination that univocal visions of power cannot capture. Ahab's reliance on his crew suggests
that monomania, the single-minded pursuit of masculine agency and individualistic selfhood, is not something Ahab has or is but something he can
only hope to achieve. As Ishmael puts it, "To accomplish his object Ahab
must use tools; and of all tools used in the shadow of the moon, men are the
most apt to get out of order" (211). To achieve his ends—the vengeful killing of the whale as the expression of his personal ascendancy and power—
Ahab's single mind must be concerned with his crew, must blandish them
with grog and bribe them with doubloons, must make his power theatrical and perform it before them. Successful monomania would preclude such
many-mindedness. If, as Ishmael imagines, Ahab might well say to himself

"all my means are sane, my motive and object mad" (186), then one might add that the madness afflicting him lies in the sane means and calculated manipulations on which he must rely to achieve his goal and to become himself. In the contradiction between the monomaniacal dream of self-agency as the single-minded expression of personal power and the practical reality of social labor required to achieve it lies an important key to Ahab's madness.

Ahab's madness, recent critics have claimed, resides in his masculinity, for the individualism whose failure he models is distinctly gendered. This is certainly true. He models a masculinity from its inception doomed to fail because, while it dreams of absolute self-agency, it depends on a prosthetic relation to the world and to other people for whatever compromised power it can realize.[31] Masculinity, as Ahab embodies it, depends on its ability to make other men and women its arms and legs because by himself he has barely any power at all.

The costs of masculine power as Ahab figures them are high. To pursue his quest, to enact his traumatized and distorted sense of himself and his place in the world, he must stifle all sentiments but one, transferring his erotic attachment from his wife, his child, and his community to the one great object of his self-defining drive for vengeance. Thus it is that Ahab, resisting the promptings of his own heart and of Starbuck's attempts to recall him to his humanity just before the fatal final chase begins, briefly softens and says, "It is his noon nap now—the boy vivaciously wakes; sits up in bed; and his mother tells him of me, of cannibal old me," averts his gaze and "like a blighted fruit tree he shook, and cast his last, cindered apple to the soil," but then recommits himself to his single purpose: "What is it, what nameless, inscrutable, unearthly thing is it; what cozening, hidden lord and master, and cruel, remorseless emperor commands me; that against all natural lovings and longings, I so keep pushing, and crowding, and jamming myself on all the time; recklessly making me ready to do what in my own proper, natural heart, I durst not so much as dare? Is Ahab, Ahab? Is it I, God, or who, that lifts this arm?" (544–45). Ahab speaks the costs not only of his pathological state but of the emergent form of normative mas-culinity itself. For the demands of the marketplace forced the nineteenth-century industrial titan and businessman to voyage far from home and hearth, far from the inclinations of sentiment and passion and women and children, to confront remorseless foes in a life-and-death struggle.[32]

David Leverenz demonstrates that during the American renaissance, American men must contend not only with the dangerous, rebellious Ahab in their souls but with the threat of their feminization before and by other men. This threat, of course, was inseparable from a construction of the feminine that associates women with political subjugation and domestic service. As G. J. Barker-Benfield in *The Horrors of the Half-Known Life* puts it, drawing on observations made by Tocqueville, "It was the anxieties generated by American democratic conditions that shaped a common view of women" and, as Leverenz adds, would constitute a common horror of feminization among American men as well.[33] Regarding the driven ambitiousness of men in America, Tocqueville wrote, "Is a man capable of such sacrifices, a cold and insensible being? Ought not one, on the contrary, to recognize in him one of the mental passions, so burning, so tenacious, so implacable?"[34] Tocqueville, of course, could well be describing Ahab, but he could also be describing any of the men aboard the *Pequod*.

Melville chose well when he chose a whaling ship as the stage for his dramatization of masculinity's perils. Among nineteenth-century Americans, whaling men epitomized manliness. Barker-Benfield observes, "Whalemen were, perhaps, the apotheosis of the insensible, haphazard, self-righteous, extreme, ruthless expression of male energies," and Ahab was their quintessence.[35] When Ahab describes the life he has led in pursuit of whales, he is describing, one imagines, the lives his men lead as well:

> Aye and yes, Starbuck, out of these forty years I have not spent three ashore. . . . —when I think of all this; only half-suspected, not so keenly known to me before—and how for forty years I have fed upon dry salted fare—fit emblem of the dry nourishment of my soul!—when the poorest landsman has had fresh fruit to his daily hand, and broken the world's fresh bread, to my mouldy crusts—away, whole oceans away, from that young girl-wife I wedded past fifty, and sailed for Cape Horn the next day, leaving but one dent in my marriage pillow—wife? wife?—rather a widow with her husband alive! Aye, I widowed that poor girl when I married her, Starbuck; and then, the madness, the frenzy, the boiling blood and the smoking brow, with which for a thousand lowerings old Ahab has furiously, foamingly chased his prey— more a demon than a man!—aye, aye! what a forty years fool—fool—old fool, has old Ahab been. (543–44)

Ahab seeks to dominate men who are driven by furies similar to his own. The economy of obsession that denies the subject's normal exchanges with the world is essential to a model of masculinity for which work absorbs all life's energy and time, leaving a man dead to the intimacies of relationship but free to wreak violence on the world. Monomania is the mental passion of men willing to depart from sociable and family life for three to four years to engage in the vastly dangerous and endlessly filthy business of getting money by hunting whales. This is the norm for Ahab and his men as it is to a degree for the landsmen onshore whom Ahab envies. This is the masculine norm for the nineteenth-century, democratic, American male who was, as a contemporary physician claimed, more prone to insanity than his counterparts in more traditional, stable, patriarchal societies.[36] If Ahab has been recognized as an incarnation of a whole assortment of nineteenth-century figures from Calhoun to Clay to Webster, it is because he incarnates the fundamentally obsessive structure of American masculinity in the ruthless pursuit of its own ends. Achieving those ends in the world, however, complicates a man's individuality, his gender, and his relationship to power, the very things it was supposed to reaffirm.

Moby Dick represents a world in which gendered relations of power construct all human interactions, homo- as well as heterosocial, and those gendered relations of power also mark the limits of Ahab's manly self-reliance. Monomania, the pathological form of self-reliance, is a social disease, what nineteenth-century pathologists called a moral insanity.[37] If Ahab's domination of the crew determines his triumph, it predetermines his failure as well, for self-reliance may turn out to be the maddest and the most maddening end of all.

Leverenz has written most effectively of the normative masculinity that achieves hegemony during the antebellum period, constituted by a desire for dominance, an embrace of competitiveness, and a rejection of sentiment. But, he adds, confused within this type of manhood are both rebellion against authority and submission to power.[38] In Ahab's doomed infatuation with the white whale, rebellion and submission, the desire for revenge and the desire for punishment are nearly indistinguishable. Confronting the lightning fire on his masts near the end of his quest, Ahab says, "I now know thee, thou clear spirit, and I now know that thy right worship is defiance . . . the queenly personality lives in me, and feels her royal rights" (507). As Leverenz, in his intricate reading of this episode, puts it, in this "startling line" announcing Ahab's transgendering, "Defiance has become exposed as a pasteboard mask for slavish adoration."[39] This, in the United States, may be what it means to be a man; masculine rebelliousness and feminine submission each masquerade as the other. Leverenz traces in *Moby Dick* the clearest expression of the ambivalent dynamics of power and subjugation at masculinity's core. As he explains it, echoing and transforming Freud's analysis of masochistic desire in "A Child Is Being Beaten": "Ahab participates wholeheartedly in the underlying dynamic of the new capitalist class: the one-against-the-universe struggle for dominance. He *has* been possessed, by a drive that turns against himself. Ahab's imperial self is an imploding star . . . sucking every human feeling into the black hole of manhood."[40] To claim, as Leverenz does, that Ahab has no self is not to debunk his monomania but to uncover its hysterical roots in his doomed struggle personally to challenge the power of Moby Dick by assuming the desires of his crew and making them his own.

Consider the practical origin of Ahab's power. When Ahab asks, "Is Ahab, Ahab? Is it I, God, or who, that lifts this arm?" the reader recalls that he depends on his crew to be his arms and legs. The "little lower layer" of the question's meaning might be parsed: can Ahab maintain himself apart from other men and their desires? The problem with Ahab resides not alone in Ahab's bid for power and is not so easily discerned as critics attacking his totalitarian impositions or celebrating his heroic resistance have sometimes made it seem. The most interesting aspect of Ahab's problem lies in his necessary relationship with his crew. Here the useful Freudian reference would not be the fairly clear hierarchies of power in "A Child Is Being Beaten" but the more complex analyses of identification and incorporation in *Group Psychology and the Analysis of the Ego* (1921) and *Totem and Taboo* (1913). Attention to the group dynamics (so to speak) of Melville's novel reveals the cooperative bargain or social contract between Ahab and his crew, the paradoxes of domination and empowerment, of obsessive fixity and hysterical incoherence, within Ahab's self-projection and the identities it produces or fails to produce for himself and his men. The problem with Ahab is not power itself, not even the power Ahab assumes to define identities and forge community. Though Melville lays the rhetorical and political workings of power and identity bare, he is too honest a writer to suggest that there are alternatives to some form of power in actual human relations. That Ahab's power depends on his crew is a problem for Ahab. His men have problems of their own. The political and ethical problem that *Moby Dick* explores is not the problem of power itself but the means Ahab attempts in order to make his power serve. To recognize and oppose mad ends may require powerful acts of judgment and violent acts of opposition to save men from catastrophe. In *Moby Dick,* the crew fails to oppose Ahab and to save itself.

AHAB'S POLITICS, OR "CANNIBAL ME"

In *Moby Dick,* cannibals occupy center stage. Queequeg, not Ishmael, may offer the most telling foil to Ahab's character, one in which a gendered dynamic also plays a part. Queequeg, as Geoffrey Sanborn puts it, represents a form of masculinity embodying the "virtues of inconsistency, irreverence, and gameness" and antithetical to the excesses of "consistency, reverence, and heedlessness" represented by Ahab, Starbuck, and Stubb. "There can be little doubt," Sanborn says, "that at least part of the reason Melville rearticulates 'humanity' with the image of the male savage is that he is uncomfortable with the conventional linkage between 'humanity' and the image of the white, Christian female . . . in the service of an unmistakably antifeminine assault on the liberal-Christian model of humanism that was dominant in its day."[41] Femininity, or at least the white, Christian female, haunts Sanborn's account of Ahab's men just as feminization haunts Leverenz's account of Ahab's manliness. Queequeg offers an alternative masculinity, an alternative to femininization, and an alternative to civilization as Melville knew it.

Yet, the figure of Queequeg may be the most conventional creation in Melville's novel. The cannibal has long served Western culture both as a self-affirming foil for civilization and as self-reflective criticism of civilization's failures. Montaigne's well-known essay—the inaugural essay on savagery for the West and an important inspiration for Melville's treatment of his harpooner—makes cannibals serve both these ends. The project Montaigne undertakes in "Of Cannibals" is not simply to identify one group as civilized and the other as savage, and invert the accepted hierarchy by praising the latter in order to criticize the former. It is to call such distinctions between self and other, "us and them," into question. Clearly Melville learned a lot about identity and difference from Montaigne. Ishmael's skeptical meanderings owe both their tone and their form to the *Essais.*[42]

Montaigne's essay on cannibals begins with the comment of Greek King

Pyrrhus upon seeing the Roman army. As reported by Plutarch, he said, "'I know not . . . what kind of barbarians [for so the Greeks called all other nations] these may be; but the disposition of this army, that I see, has nothing of barbarism in it'" (207). The lesson Montaigne draws from this text is the lesson of skepticism itself: "By which it appears how cautious men ought to be of taking things upon trust from vulgar opinion, and that we are to judge by the eye of reason, and not from common report. . . . Everyone gives the title of barbarism to everything that is not in use in his own country" (207, 210). Barbarism appears less to be a quality of the savage observed than it is a projection of the civilized observer. Moreover, for Montaigne such a view of others, predicated on an inability to see one's self, is not a fault to be corrected but an inevitable condition of judgment and perception, for "we have no other level of truth and reason, than the example and idea of the opinions and customs of the place wherein we live" (210). In the absence of external and universal categories of judgment, each person constructs the world according to his own and his civilization's limitations. That includes particularly the judgment of who is barbaric and who is civilized.

Considering the question of barbarism by the light of reason, Montaigne questions the accepted hierarchy of civilization and savagery, doubting even the saliency of the distinction between them. This is a profoundly unsettling project and one similar to Melville's in both *Typee* and *Moby Dick*. What Montaigne records in this early encounter between "civilized" European Christians and "savage" New World cannibals is his own civilization's encounter with a fearsome double, an uncanny relationship between the "civilized" self and the "savage" other. The similarities with Tommo's experiences in the Marquesans among the Typee and Ishmael's in New Bedford with Queequeg should be clear. The implications of this encounter call into question not only the distinction between civilization and savagery, as commentators have often noted, but the distinction of self and other on which depend questions of individual identity, agency and power, so crucial to modernity and to *Moby Dick*.

While "Of Cannibals" constructs a negative space of skeptical doubt within the modern subject, it also explores the absence of a neutral space from which to make objective judgments that might resolve those doubts. The warfare of the West, of which the contemporary wars of religion in France furnished Montaigne examples as shockingly cruel as the exploits

of missionary agents in the Marquesan Islands did Melville, leaves no
morally elevated position from which civilized people might judge the cannibal's conduct. Reporting that the cannibals do not roast and eat their enemies for nourishment but rather as an extreme form of revenge, Montaigne
comments:

> I am not sorry that we should here take notice of the barbarous horror of so
> cruel an action, but that, seeing so clearly into their faults, we should be so
> blind to our own. I conceive there is more barbarity in eating a man alive,
> than when he is dead; in tearing a body limb from limb by racks and tor-
> ments, that is yet in perfect sense; in roasting it by degrees; in causing it to
> be bitten and worried by dogs and swine (as we have not only read, but lately
> seen, not among inveterate and mortal enemies, but among neighbors and
> fellow-citizens, and, which is worse, under color of piety and religion), than
> to roast and eat him after he is dead. (216)

Montaigne does not mean to exculpate cannibals from charges of barbarity but to use them, like the doubloon nailed to the *Pequod*'s mast, as "a
magician's glass," which "to each and every man in turn but mirrors back
his own mysterious self" (431). Queequeg serves as just such a glass in *Moby
Dick*. In the figure of the Cannibal, "civilized" man recognizes his own
savagery. Moreover, the ultimate source of this savagery lies not in the differences dividing peoples but in the difficulties of maintaining distinctions
and hierarchies. Cannibalism is a fitting emblem for the propensity of like-
ness, not difference, to breed violence.

This, as Geoffrey Sanborn demonstrates, is to recognize something other
than a humanizing, cultural relativity in Ishmael's relation to Queequeg.[43]
What both Ishmael and Melville realize about the cannibal is that the failure to find in the cannibal a figure of absolute difference both expresses and
disappoints the violent specularity of the observer's narcissistic attempt to
stabilize his own identity. As Sanborn puts it, "The complete narrative of
Ishmael's shifting perception of Queequeg goes something like this: After
pushing past the representation of the cannibal as a sight and the dream of
intersubjective touch, he arrives at an insight into the ideality of savagery;
but even as he promotes that insight, he asks us to see that the truest form
of looseness requires the recognition that all such visions are in fact after-
sights, provisional resolutions of an unresolved field" (168–69). Aftersight

projects meaning onto the blank screen of the world like a magician's glass (remember the doubloon), a painted harlot (remember "The Whiteness of the Whale"), or Ahab's ascription of agency to what Starbuck calls a dumb brute. To recognize the world as one's own projection means, as Montaigne knew, that no other can be other enough to fix the meaning of the self. No other, not even the cannibal, can stand apart objectively from the subject who assumes the power to imagine him. "Cannibals?" Ishmael exclaims, "who is not a cannibal?" (300). But what does being a cannibal mean?

Montaigne's inaugural exploration of cannibalism demonstrates, as does Melville, that the working through of these questions of identity and power entails more violent confrontation than philosophical contemplation. When Montaigne arrives at his demonstration of the artfulness of his cannibals, he describes their ethos as consisting of only two injunctions: "valor toward their enemies and love toward their wives" (214). They prosecute their endless wars for no other reason but to achieve glory. Glory, the expression of their valor and prowess, depends on what seems an ultimate act in which the victim is annihilated and only the victor remains. They eat their vanquished enemies so that the victims become part of the victors' bodies and of the group of which the individual forms a part. Despite these endless wars, these groups, Montaigne reports, are virtually indistinguishable.

The song of a captive awaiting execution and dismemberment in order to furnish with his body the ritual meal by which his captors celebrate victory and vengeance demonstrates the indistinguishableness of these groups on a very deep level. He denies, in fact, the possibility of either victory or vengeance because the incorporation of the victim has always already happened. He demonstrates that stable identities and hierarchies of power are historical and structural impossibilities. The captive invites his enemies to "come all, and dine upon him, and welcome, for they shall withal eat their own fathers and grandfathers, whose flesh has served to feed and nourish him. 'These muscles,' says he, 'this flesh and these veins, are your own: poor silly souls as you are, you little think that the substance of your ancestors' limbs is here yet; notice what you eat, and you will find in it the taste of your own flesh.'" In the captive's performance, Montaigne judges, "nothing relishes *[ne sent aucunement]* of the barbarian" (219). The cannibal taunts his captors not only with his indifference to their power but with his lack of difference from them. When Montaigne suggests that this "Invention . . . ne sent aucunement la barbarie," he also remembers that these cruel rituals that seem so strange seem uncannily similar to the barbarity he witnesses among the civilized who pride themselves on their difference from and superiority to these cannibals. Identity as an expression of power that depends on a hierarchical distinction between self and other, civilized and savage, trembles and threatens to disappear. The taste of victory smacks of the conquerors' own abjection. The victor cannot simply complete his triumph by eating the other's body because he finds himself already incorporated there, and the gesture always remains equivocal, reversible, reversed before it even takes place. Fixing power and finalizing triumph in a cannibal feast seeks to deny this knowledge, but the victim can always become an uncanny reminder that identity and power always remain part of an irresolvable field of contestation.

In such a field, violence often establishes identity more than it expresses differences.[44] When Ishmael asks "Who is not a cannibal?" he echoes his earlier question, "Who ain't a slave?" (6) and implicates all men in problems of dominance, power, and identity. For it is not, as Sanborn puts it, that "objectivity—nature and nature's God—necessarily disappoints our expectations."[45] Objectivity, like ultimate power, eludes men. The unavoidable and conflicted relationships of men and women to the world around them, the willful and doomed denial of what the magic mirror of the world and its differences might tell them about their own compromised being, can drive them mad. But at what precise point might one say that this psychological or existential problem becomes a political question? This is the question *Moby Dick* tries to draw from its readers.

Among Western thinkers, Freud most closely links the figure of the cannibal to the question of politics. Freud's cannibals in eating their father recreate the savage horde as a political entity, a civilized band of brothers who commemorate their act and identity in totemic feasts and rituals (see *Totem and Taboo*). Cannibals and ritual also make an appearance in *Group Psychology and the Analysis of the Ego,* where Freud attempts to unravel the madness and savagery of World War I, until that time the most profound political catastrophe the world had witnessed. Here he develops an important discussion not of identity as a thing but of identification as a process, one no less fraught with ambivalence than cannibalism itself:

Identification, in fact, is ambivalent from the very first; it can turn into an expression of tenderness as easily as into a wish for someone's removal. It behaves as a derivative of the first, *oral* phase of the organization of the libido, in which the object that we long for and prize is assimilated by eating and is in that way annihilated as such. The cannibal, as we know, has remained at this standpoint; he has a devouring affection for his enemies and only devours people of whom he is fond.[46]

Freud's joke about "devouring affection" points to his serious project here, which is to explain how political groups form and how men abject themselves and renounce freedom to join them. Freud does this by reference to a sort of imaginative cannibalism in which the other is incorporated into the self, and groups, once formed, cement their internal solidarity by fatal acts of external aggression toward other groups (32–34).[47] The analogies to Montaigne's essay on cannibals should be obvious.

Ahab seems just the sort of dangerously charismatic leader Freud feared. His effect on his crew and on his readers is nothing short of hypnotic. In the quarterdeck scene, the crew Ahab calls "unrecking and unworshipping things" stand like Starbuck and the officers "enchanted" by the old man's theatrics (165). For the moment, Ahab's characterization of his men seems apt. As Leverenz remarks, this scene, like Ahab's tricks with the compass needle and with electrical charges in the tempest (518) smacks of conjuring tricks.[48] These tricks, however, have real effects. Despite Leverenz's resistant claim that he finds them boring, their efficacy on crew and critics requires analysis. During the quarterdeck scene, Ahab forges the *isolatos* of his crew into agents of his vengeance by performing a totemic ritual, commemorating his "fishermen fathers" before him and transforming the men into a profane rather than a celestial group identity. The ritual drinking of the grog from the ship's measure and from the mates' and harpooners' upturned irons makes Melville's liturgical intentions plain. Parodying the Christian rite of communion at this crucial moment, Melville—and Ahab—create a cannibalistic ritual whose aim is the incorporation of the men not into the body of the Church but into prosthetic extensions of Ahab's will. Shifting this sacred rite into a profane register, substituting the ungodly whaler and his doomed, vengeful quest for the holy intercessor and his limitless love, Melville does not alter the basic mechanism of ingestion and incorporation, and the basic desire for deliverance from human vicissitudes, that he and Freud found to be the base for both group and individual identity. Proper and unholy ends remain difficult to distinguish, as do group and individual identities.

For Freud, the primacy of individual or group either logically or tempo-rally remains impossible to determine. As Freud put it in a crucial passage in *Group Psychology and the Analysis of the Ego,* "Individual psychology must . . . be just as old as group psychology, for from the first there were two kinds of psychologies, that of the individual members of the group and that of the father, chief, or leader" (55). And from the first each is implicated in the other. Such a coincidence of apparently opposed phenomena suggests more than just a structural confusion, it suggests a mutual constituency and reversibility. If the crew become themselves under Ahab's command, he becomes himself as they empower him. The answer to Ahab's bewildered query "Is Ahab, Ahab?" may be yes, but Ahab cannot be Ahab without Ahab's crew to man his ship.

In Freud's account of the group's formation, each member of the group submits to the group's leader by incorporating him or his desire into his sense of himself, especially as the commanding and censoring part of the self that shapes the individual's identity. Ties and conflicts between the group members and their leader are essentially erotic. But here as well a sort of reciprocity or exchange, a version of the fair play Ahab posits as the world's order, works as well. Each individual becomes a member of the group at the moment when he recognizes part of his sense of himself to be the domi-natingly masculine figure of the group's leader. He finds himself to be thereby the feminized object of his leader's internalized gaze and a manly subject in his own right. That internalized gaze not only subjugates but empowers those who yield to it. For the leader to emerge, he must become objectified before the group's desire. Thus each member of the group, leader and follower alike, achieves a conversion of their isolating and self-destructive hostility into an empowered identity as part of an aggressive communal order. If the primal father is the "group ideal, which governs the ego in the place of the ego ideal," that governance depends on the leader's becoming not a subject but an object before the group's desiring eyes.[49] In light of this discussion, to describe Ahab's role as simple dominance or the crew's place as simple submission would be to miss the fluidity and insta-bility of the relationship's power as a political problem. Politics in this sense becomes another name for the human condition. Men and women, as Freud well knew, exist nowhere but in groups, and therefore no self is imagin-able apart from these gendered dynamics of incorporation and possession for men and women both. In Melville's novel as well, no man's ego can simply be his own ("who ain't a slave?"). No one can escape the cannibal feast of the crew's incorporation ("who ain't a cannibal?"). And no power can exist uncompromised by its own articulation.

These instabilities of power take Freud in a direction he does not want to follow. Melville, however, through Ahab, presses the analysis onward. Freud cannot accept a world in which some form of order cannot be at least momentarily stabilized. He thought the identity of men apart from groups and power to be unthinkable, but he also believed that the leader represented a different order of being, one who stands apart and without relation, a figure of manly self-reliance. Freud contrasted the members of the group to their leader: "members of the group stand in need of the illusion that they are equally and justly loved by their leader; but the leader himself need love no one else, he may be of a masterful nature, absolutely narcissistic, self-confident, and independent."[50] At this moment, Freud accepts the ideal of masculinity itself that Ahab emulates when he stands before Starbuck and the crew and cries, "Who's over me? Truth hath no confines" (164). Melville, by contrast, recognizes that ideal's impossibility. Ahab, for all his expansive boasting, shrinks before the other's regard, a regard on which he knows his power depends. "Who's over me?" yields immediately to a peevish demand to disapproving Starbuck, "Take off thine eye! more intolerable than fiends' glarings is a doltish stare!" (164). And there in a nutshell is Ahab's problem and the secret of his power.

When Ahab cries, "Truth hath no confines," he claims, of course, that his power to arbitrate that truth is unconfined as well. Like the Gnostic hero Harold Bloom so admires, he challenges and defies the deity and mortality itself. But he bears the mark of that mortality on his own dismembered body. Ahab's wounded narcissism as the origin of his madness has occupied generations of masculine critics, both men and women, but the particular form of that narcissistic wound requires comment. It is not primarily the removal of the leg—that too literal moment of castration—that moves Ahab to madness. Consider Ishmael's diagnosis:

It is not probable that this monomania in him took its instant rise at the precise time of his bodily dismemberment. Then, in darting at the monster, knife in hand, he had but given loose to a sudden, passionate, corporeal animosity; and when he received the stroke that tore him, he probably but felt the agonizing bodily laceration, but nothing more. Yet, when by this collision forced to turn towards home, and for long months of days and weeks, Ahab and anguish lay stretched together in one hammock, rounding in mid winter that dreary, howling Patagonian Cape; then it was, that his torn body and gashed soul bled into one another; and so interfusing made him mad. (184–85)

Body and soul, will and materiality, mingling they drive the old man mad. Upon arising from his bed, Ahab will cannibalize a whale to supply his missing part. Paradoxically, his lost leg thus represents an access of power—only with his terrible wound does Ahab begin to become Ahab. But the power Ahab needs to make him Ahab cannot simply be his own. More than whalebone he needs his crew to be his arms and legs.

At the novel's climactic moment, at the height of Ahab's maddened quest during the fatal chase's second day, the captain seems as much the crew's instrument as their motivating agent, their "one lord" but their "keel" as well. Recall again the passage:

> There were one man, not thirty. For as the ship that held them all; though it was put together of all contrasting things—oak, and maple, and pine wood; iron, and pitch, and hemp—yet all these ran into each other in the one concrete hull, which shot on its way, both balanced and directed by the long central keel; even so, all the individualities of the crew, this man's valor, that man's fear; guilt and guiltlessness, all varieties were welded into oneness, and were all directed to that fatal goal which Ahab their one lord and keel did point to. (557)

As lord and keel he is both superior commander and bottommost timber. His madness grows not from dismemberment but from the reminder that he must remember to member himself. His power must be incorporated. He moves through the world only upon the prosthetic instrumentality of other men's wills and bodies. Ahab depends on the enthrallment of his crew and their incorporation in his purposes for whatever agency he may be said to possess. As Christopher Newfield puts it, "Self-reliance . . . involves not the refusal but the incorporation of the other into the self."[51] But this incorporated other, as in Montaigne's cannibal's song, can never be submissive enough. In the reliance of power on incorporation lies the possibility of resistance, and that possibility, though never realized in *Moby*

Dick, is everywhere and repeatedly remarked. This reminder to hysterical Ahab that he cannot be monomaniacal drives him onward in the destructive madness of his hunt for Moby Dick and the impossible apotheosis of his own power, the impossible desire to cannibalize only himself.

Ahab, despite his kingly name, is no old testament king. He is, as Ishmael says, "only . . . a poor old whale-hunter" without "majestic trappings, and housings" (148). From where does his power come? How is it, as Ishmael says, "plucked from the skies, and dived for in the deep, and featured in the unbodied air!" (148)? Ahab's power comes not from within but from without or from a confusion of inner and outer that he begins to realize with the wound that brings his madness to life. Ahab's problem is not that his power is featured in the unbodied air but that the air about him is too necessarily bodied to sustain his ambition to stand on his own. For Ahab to be Ahab would mean to be truly his own man, to cannibalize only his own force, but he must instead incorporate his crew and keep his mind tuned to his crew's mood just as he says he keeps his magnet fixed to Starbuck's skull. He must be as much corporate manager as tragic hero.

When Ahab needs to visit the ship's carpenter for a new leg—maintaining the prosthetics of his cannibalized self, his identity as "cannibal me," and his command of his crew who serve him not just as men but as his arms and legs—he speaks a truth that is not without confines but is in fact a truth of the confinement of his situation: "Oh, Life! Here I am, proud as a Greek god, and yet standing debtor to this block head for a bone to stand on! Cursed be that mortal inter-indebtedness which will not do away with ledgers. I would be free as air; and I'm down in the whole world's books. I am so rich, I could have bid for bid with the wealthiest Praetorians at the auction of the Roman empire (which was the world's); and yet I owe for the flesh in the tongue I brag with" (471–72). Ahab's ivory leg is not the sign of his debility as much as it is the token of the inevitable debts his empowerment entails. He fantasizes ordering one complete prosthetic man, "no heart at all, brass forehead, and about a quarter of an acre of fine brains" (470). But he cannot produce his own prosthetics, and he cannot be himself. Far from being simply above his crew in a position of command, he forms one of his crew because his ego ideal is, paradoxically, the same as theirs. His ideal is the impossible image of his own self-empowerment. His power depends on his ability to incorporate with his men in an act of mutual cannibalization in which the limits of desire and power are from moment to moment defined and effaced. Ahab's limit is not his inability to assume the heavenly fire above him but his absolute dependence on the world and on the men in the world around him. They, not his own will alone, are the source of and limit to his grandeur. If he is the cog that fits their various wheels and makes them revolve, he must also be a cogged wheel as well in order to engage them. They represent to him his failure to achieve what Sharon Cameron called an identity "not constrained by bodies."[52]

But what of the crew that Ahab's obsession leads to destruction? In *Moby Dick* they remain as mystified as Ahab's dream and more in the dark than Ahab about the nature of Ahab's power, about, that is to say, the real conditions of their life in the world. No one has represented it to them and so, apart from Ahab, they remain ill-defined. No one represents themselves to themselves. Within Melville's novel's world, that failure belongs most pointedly to Ishmael the narrator, the skater on surfaces, the schoolmaster, the philosopher of fast fish and loose, the character C. L. R. James recognized as a type of the failed intellectual. But those intellectuals today who criticize Ahab for his traffic in the discourse of manly self-reliance should know that for Ishmael to emulate Steelkirk and to raise his voice against a madness that he and his fellows seem too easily to accept would require more manhood, more individuality, more power, more violence—not less.

Ishmael, as James suggested, may be taken to represent an American intellectual more usefully than he can be labeled the embodiment of an abstraction like American freedom. This makes his situation concrete and specific but in such a way that it has implications for the universal. Should he commit his words and visions to Ahab's quest or to the crew's interests? Can he distinguish between the two? Should he commit himself to dangerous acts of persuasion that might capture the crew's attention and lead them to recognize their interests as divergent from and not identical to Ahab's hunt? Most important, having realized that in this life the difference between a fast fish and a loose fish is always a matter of the inescapable play of power and of relationship and that no man escapes the fields of force and resistance however much he may try to stand alone, should he give up the apparent freedom of his own wandering imagination? Should he seek incorporation with the crew on a different basis than Ahab offers, a different understanding of their identity, their power, and their mission, a different manner to confront the painted harlot of the world? Should he attempt to persuade the crew that other sorts of group identity—other kinds of incorporation, more democratic, more egalitarian, based not on an eroticized father but on an attachment to principles of equality, justice, compassion—might be formed or forged to link them together and acknowledge rather than attempt to deny the affectivity and primacy of their common bonds? Could he do this without assuming the father's eroticized place? This is a version of self-reliance and a use of power that might really save itself and the crew from catastrophe without deceiving itself about the necessity and nature of power or the nature and justice of its relationship to the world. But is it in practice possible? *Moby Dick* leaves its readers with these questions.

Ahab's madness results not from masculinity's triumph but from its impossibility, its always frustrated desire. Power becomes maddening when it becomes an illusory end rather than a useful means. That is not to say that the effects of Ahab's power are not real and are not rendered more deadly by the frustrated energy of his narcissistic projection and his dramatic denials. Ahab's version of American masculinity, of American identity on a mission in the world, can succeed only as it destroys itself and those with whom it incorporates its power. The crew and its intellectuals fail to save themselves and maybe even Ahab from himself because no one takes upon himself the power to distinguish between the sane use of power and Ahab's insane ends. To understand this may help a contemporary observer understand how, on the world stage, the United States, despite its principles, has so often played the part of madness maddened while its citizens have failed to resist leaders and policies whose ends entail moral and political catastrophes that the nation has failed to avoid.

PART II

Failed Sympathies

chapter 3

Lydia Maria Child's Romance: Cosmopolitan Imagination and the Failure of Gender Reform

COSMOPOLITAN DREAMS AND THE ROOTS OF TERROR

Lydia Maria Child's advocacy for Native Americans, enslaved Africans, and oppressed women has made her at times the standard-bearer for canon revisionists who find her unambiguous political commitments an attractive alternative to such masculine ironists as Hawthorne, Poe, and Melville. If Melville's Ahab represents the maddening impossibility of actually being a man and the dangerous tendencies of those who try to become men through mastering self and others, Child explored alternatives to Ahab in her fiction and essays throughout her long career. In Child, "antipatriachalism" takes the place of "irony as the elixir of legitimacy."[1] But these same revisionists often find Child to be only the most sympathetic among nineteenth-century America's many figures of political failure. She is sympathetic because she struggled to revise and expand narrow nativist or racist constructions of the United States, unfailingly standing on the just side of all these issues. Moreover, her political positions and beliefs not only rested on a legalistic adherence to negative freedoms but demanded a positive expansion of affection and identification, a cosmopolitan embrace of "hybridity."[2] She was among the most self-consciously modern thinkers of her time and one of the few who dared to argue that the United States was not a white nation that needed legal and social protections from its own heterogeneity but a multiracial and multiethnic society that would be made more perfectly and justly itself by realizing its own universalist principles through a sociable and sexual intermingling of races and cultures. Unlike Jefferson, she had no apparent fears of the fevered state in the republic that such a mingling of peoples could produce. Instead she offers a vision of a cosmopolitan future that might eventually be better and stronger than the violence and oppression of the disordered state in which she actually lived.

But in imaging a reformed republic, as her best critics have pointed out, she often fails to go far enough.[3] Certainly she remains indebted to familiar middle-class pieties and committed to traditional republican virtues, vexed by Eurocentric identity questions and incapable of vividly imagining the multiethnic, gender-liberated, and harmoniously multicultural and just future she clearly desires. Each of these criticisms is valid. Nonetheless Child remains compelling because her determined attempts to work at and through the problems of particular identity and universal justice in America exemplify the ways in which an unqualified, successful balance of justice and identity in the United States remains difficult to imagine. Moreover, her work suggests that doing without the violent prerogatives of American manhood may finally be as dangerous as trying to live with them. It all depends on the identity of the man in question.

While Child's work does, in fact, fail to fully imagine the cosmopolitan melding of peoples and cultures to which she dedicated the political energies and literary labors of her long career, critics have misunderstood the sources and significance of that failure. These lie not in Child's own imagination, especially not in its residual indebtedness to religious transcendentalism or to liberal ideals of justice, but in the problems posed—both imaginatively and politically—by cosmopolitan sociability itself. Child has difficulty imagining equitable cross-racial and cross-cultural mixings in a heterogeneous and violent nineteenth-century United States because injustice in cosmopolitan America makes peaceable sociability an empty promise. Justice and community may, in fact, be at odds, for justice may require recourse to terrifying violence, and such violence represents the failure of community and not its achievement.

Especially in her romances *Hobomok* and *A Romance of the Republic* and her innovative journalistic essays, such as "Letters from New York," Child realizes the tension between the desire for cosmopolitan community and the necessity for trenchant, even violent, opposition to oppression.[4] Both the imaginative requirements of sympathetic identification and the terrible threat of retributive justice balance uneasily in her work. For this reason, her career remains instructive and disturbing a century and a half later, precisely because she finally failed to imagine an American utopia but compellingly succeeded in staging the conflicts of American identity—the drama of America's failure. Child's work reminds readers that while cosmopolitanism seems to offer alternatives to violence, it can often be at the root of violence as well. Moreover, since gender problems and gendered identities figure largely in her schemes, if violence remains a necessity, then reforming masculinity—projecting a more feminine alternative to the manhood that Ahab, for example, modeled—may not be the best way to reform the status quo.

The First Modern Woman of the Republic, or Managing the American Male

In her first novel, *Hobomok,* Child does attempt to imagine a reformation of aggressive masculinity, a manly but sociable, nonviolent opponent to Puritan patriarchy and a harbinger of a more generous vision of national destiny. Hobomok models an alternative to the dominant paradigm of manhood, an alternative on which a better social order—one not founded on and threatened by violent conflict—might be grounded. But the complications of the romance end by undermining these hopes. Haltingly, and despite its author's intentions, the novel explores the role of violence in a disordered society where cosmopolitanism may be an aspect of the problem of America's failure rather than its solution.

Hobomok's refusal to struggle for possession of Mary and their child, proffered by the novel as the hallmark of his moral superiority over the contentious white men around him, is not incidental to, but actually entails the novel's final failure to realize the cosmopolitan romance of a more mixed and open nation. The hero of reformed manhood that Child imagines could be a poster boy for male masochism—understood as self-abnegation and the renunciation of sadistic patterns of patriarchal power—which has been, from Child's day to the present, inherent in many attempts to imagine men differently. But the political value of masochism, like the political values of manliness or violence, may depend on the identities and conflicts requiring negotiation. In a heterogeneous society, where questions of identity and problems of justice press for solutions, an ethos of renunciation may be inadequate to the imaginative and ethical requirements of a better, more equitable, and inclusive future. Child's failure to imagine that future in her first novel succeeds in illustrating this valuable lesson.

Child's dream of a reformed masculinity expresses her hope that justice might not require violence and that retribution and resistance might need to claim no victims of their own. But *Hobomok* suggests that hopes for non-violent alternatives to violent dialectics of power and imposition are hard to imagine without considering the relative positions of the identities involved. The social utility of self-abnegation in the cause of justice depends on whose self gets abnegated and under whose power the masochist places himself. By virtue of their very self-renunciations, masochistic men risk furthering society's injustices and supporting the ideological fictions that make those injustices palatable. Racial oppression in America has often depended on the fiction of dark-skinned men who, because of too much or too little masculine development, fail to be properly manly.[5] The figure of the masochistic warrior can reinforce an insidious version of Indian identity in which the brave's renunciations rhyme discomfortingly with dominant beliefs that Indians will simply and naturally, because of want of ardor or energy, disappear.

In *Hobomok,* Child attempts to imagine an alternative to received ideas about gender and race by making two difficult-to-reconcile revisions: she offers her Indian hero as a type of reformed or improved male, an embodiment of noble savagery as masochistic self-renunciation; and she imagines the nation as racially mixed, an alternative to the racist delusions about blood and purity that legitimated so many of the injustices and abuses that she witnessed in America. Child, as many commentators have noted, attempted to imagine a more peacefully cosmopolitan and fundamentally just version of community, one founded on a more accommodating, less aggressive version of manhood. But *Hobomok*'s end suggests that such a reconciliation of manhood reformed and injustices redressed may be difficult to realize.

The American historical novel, for Child as for James Fenimore Cooper, inevitably reflects the fractures, fissures, and conflicts that are constitutive of the national identity it attempts to forge. As Carolyn Karcher points out, "The American historical novel inevitably exhibited the same central contradiction as American history itself—the contradiction between an ideology based on the premise that all men are created equal and a political structure based on the assumption that people of color and white women do not fall under the rubric 'men.'"[6] Child begins *Hobomok* with a formal invocation of both Scott and Cooper and a modest disclaimer of her own

inability to share the "proud summit" these national novelists had gained
(3). Thus, of course, she announces her ambition not only to occupy these
heights but to alter the view of the nation available from them. In the New
World especially, the historical romance involves the attempt not only to
codify a national narrative as a common past but to project a national future
as well. In *Hobomok,* Child's narrator pointedly begins—through the conventional device of the found manuscript—by looking back to seventeenth-
century Salem from the nineteenth-century nation whose subjects and
citizens were only just beginning to learn to regard the New England settlers as a national beginning.

When Child's narrator looks back, she sees the early landscape differently
from what those myths of origin involving Puritan founding fathers suggest, and she thereby projects different possibilities for understanding the
American present and imagining the nation's future:

> I never view the thriving villages of New England, which speak so forcibly
> to the heart, of happiness and prosperity, without feeling a glow of national
> pride, as I say, "this is my own, my native land." . . . In most nations the path
> of antiquity is shrouded in darkness, rendered more visible by the wild, fan-
> tastic light of fable; but with us, the vista of times is luminous to its remotest
> point. Each succeeding year has left its footsteps distinct upon the soil, and
> the cold dew of our chilling dawn is still visible beneath the mid-day sun. (5)

So far, Child follows the rhetorical patterns and flourishes rapidly becoming familiar aspects of nationalist rhetoric and that remain familiar to this
day. The "us" in this passage implies the belonging of Americans who trace
their descent from those English settlers who left their early footsteps on
the soil at the nation's chill dawning. But as the passage continues, Child
expands the province of this "us" in ways that confuse the most common
Eurocentric expectations. She continues:

> Two centuries only have elapsed, since our most beautiful villages reposed
> in the undisturbed grandeur of nature;—when the scenes now rendered clas-
> sic by literary associations, or resounding with the din of commerce, echoed
> nought but the song of the hunter, or the fleet tread of the wild deer. God was
> here in his holy temple, and the whole earth kept silence before him! But the
> voice of prayer was soon to be heard in the desert. The sun, which for ages

beyond the memory of man had gazed on the strange, fearful worship of the Great Spirit of the wilderness, was soon to shed its splendor upon the altars of the living God. (5–6)

Child's version of a national narrative moves back before the advent of the English to a moment before their arrival when "our most beautiful villages" (as opposed to the "six miserable hovels" that "constituted the whole settlement" where the Puritans would later live [7]) reposed in nature and were inhabited by Indians. "Our most beautiful villages" refers to a time before the construction of the settler's wretched huts. "We" must include not only "our" European ancestors but the Native inhabitants of the soil as well. The beautiful villages existed before the European settlers came, bringing their conflicts and prejudices to construct a community on principles as intolerant and unaccommodating as the barren clearings and wretched hovels in which they would live. Moreover, Child's sly transformation of historical memory involves a cosmopolitan pantheon of deities—she invokes the sun, the Great Spirit, and the living God—who seem, as she imagines them, to enjoy a rough sort of equality among themselves.[7]

In *Hobomok,* the narrator's relationship to the manuscript she discovers—a bundle of letters by a long-dead ancestor—foregrounds the imaginative work of history that can seek to transform the familiar outline of the nation's story. The narrator warns her readers at the beginning that she "shall . . . take the liberty of substituting my own expressions for [her ancestor's] antiquated and almost unintelligible style," thus modernizing the tale and making its applicability more readily apparent (7). The space she makes for imaginative identification in retelling and recasting the facts of history allows for the attempted revision of national origins to include the peoples the nation has excluded as an attempt to reform and expand the "us"—the limits of national identification—and to constitute a more cosmopolitan United States in the present and for the future.

The tension between Child's cosmopolitan expansions and America's parochial narrowness—a Puritan legacy of bigotry she seeks to change by revising the ancestral text she inherits—informs the whole novel. In nineteenth-century attempts to reform the republic, reconsiderations of the Puritans frequently play a significant part. As Philip Gould remarks, this seems especially true in historical fiction by women: "Virtually everyone recognizes the 'antipatriarchal' nature of women's historical fiction. Yet this theme is made even more significant when recast as part of a larger gendered struggle over the nature of the republic, a struggle, I would argue, taking place in part through the medium of Puritan history. The transitional nature of the early republic, with all of its cultural and rhetorical instability, made such a struggle particularly resonant."[8] In Gould's view, the conflicts and complexities of Puritan history made it a useful distant mirror for the conflicts and complexities of an American republic still searching for acceptable representations of itself.

But to note the importance of Puritan conflicts and complexities in the novel alters the twenty-first-century reader's sense of the novel's significance as well. Child's feminist cosmopolitanism first attracted the scholars and critics who rescued *Hobomok* from obscurity in the 1980s. Because of their desire to emphasize Child's criticisms of masculinity and racism, contemporary critical commentary has focused on the relationship between the brown-skinned Hobomok and the white woman Mary Conant. But in fact this relationship occupies relatively little space in the novel, and Child's representation of it, as critics early and late have noted, lacks detail and conviction.[9] Child spends most of her novel depicting the Puritan community not in terms of its smoothly functioning articulations of patriarchal power but as a polity in a perpetual state of internal crisis. In *Hobomok,* of course, a young Puritan woman, in rebellion against her father and the entire Puritan community, does pledge her love to an Episcopalian royalist and, upon his exile from New England and reported death, she does "marry" a Wampanoag and bear his child. But Mary's acts of defiance, when considered in the context of the entire novel, seem more an expression of her community with its perpetual conflicts and recurrent anxieties than an alternative to it.

The interestingly disheveled state of the Puritan community, troubled as the novel tells us by "Antinomians, Anabaptists, and sundry other sects" (28), has largely escaped notice because, for recent critics, the figuration of female rebellion and racial mixing has seemed to promise a different and better version of Child's and our own nation's story. In such readings, the Anglican and the Indian coincide as occasions for Mary's defiance of her father and the patriarchy he represents.[10] But emphasis on Mary's defiance of Puritanism masks the extent to which Child imagines that the community is not only threatened from without but divided within. In such a community, Mary's defiance seems more an expression of the group's embattled identity than an alternative to it.

In the found manuscript, the bundle of letters Child's narrator discovers, Mr. Conant and his daughter Mary first appear when the letter's author lands from England. Mary asks after the friends and pastimes of her childhood home in England, from which her father, a "rigid Calvinist" (8), has led her into the wilderness. Mr. Conant, seeing the effect of her beauty and vivacity on the rough sailors, upbraids his daughter: "Wherefore, Mary, do you ask about those, who bow the knee to Baal, and utter the mummery of common prayer? Methinks it is enough that the hawk has already brought hither a sprig from their tree of corruption, wherewithal to beguile your silly heart" (9). Continuing his diatribe, Mr. Conant soon mentions an "idle follower of Mr. Morton," another Anglican, who was drowned in the bay as a divine judgment on all such "sprigs of corruption." In fact, Morton of Merry Mount gets mentioned at nearly every turn in the novel's first chapters, though less for his religious fripperies and sexual promiscuity than for selling the Indians "rifles" and teaching them "to take a steady and quick-sighted aim" and thereby threatening the always precarious security of the settlement (29). Thus, in terms more materially troublesome than a young woman's unruly desire or the Puritan's repressive prudery, the novel at its outset marks the association of heretical Anglicans and armed Indians as something truly dangerous.

But most of the Puritans' struggles seem to be internecine. The two patriarchs in the novel, Mr. Conant and Mr. Oldham, disagree about religious decorum, about the relationship of the colony to the crown, and about the status of the covenant itself. Child's narrator makes clear that dissension is so common and so repetitive in the community that it barely needs chronicling when she announces that she skips over many passages of disputations in her manuscript: "The manuscript mentions numerous controversies between Mr. Higginson, Mr. Conant, Mr. Oldham, and Mr. Graves; but their character is so similar to those I have already quoted, that I forbear to repeat them. One maintained justification by faith, and another by works; and the light within-enthusiast, from the Isle of Wight, continued to defend his doctrine of the inward outpouring of prayer, and eventually become one of the most celebrated among the Familists" (57). Familism, one of the heresies by which Anne Hutchinson would provoke and split the colony a few years after *Hobomok*'s time, reminds the reader that a theoretical love for all humanity (a Familist tenet) does not ensure civil harmony.

Moreover, as the comments of young Sally Oldham make clear, religious piety and a desire for pure theology does not even ensure minimally proper everyday conduct or rectitude. Faced with the unctuous attentions of the hypocritically pious Mr. Graves, Sally offers the following confidence to her friend Mary, "A plague on all such sanctified looking folks. There was Mr. Lyford, (I don't care if he was a minister) he was always talking about faith and righteousness, and the falling-off of the Plymouth elders, and yet many a sly look and word he'd give me, when his good-woman was out of the way" (18–19). Sally's favors will eventually become the object of a three-way legal suit between Mr. Hopkins, another Communicant, and Mr. Collier, who will finally win her hand. The contentiousness over marriage with this young woman, like the discord among the patriarchs over every tenet of belief and principle of policy, bespeaks the general level of discord in a community more varied and heterogeneous than emphasis on its patriarchal power suggests. When the elders, sitting in judgment of Sally's suitors proclaim, "We do fear that the daughter hath much of the corrupt leaven of the father" (56), they suggest that Mr. Oldham himself may be less a commanding patriarch than another wayward soul threatening to escape the community's control. For the Puritans, both men and women threaten the settlement with discord and rebellion.

In light of the Puritan community's internal strife, the Anglican Mary loves and the Indian she marries seem markedly less equal as expressions of her rebellion. Differences in situation and character make Hobomok and Charles Brown unlikely doubles. For while both find themselves excluded from the community of saints, differences in the identities that injustice and exclusion here construct make them different from each other as well. Brown may represent the cultural heritage and youthful comforts of England that Mary longs to regain, but he also represents an Anglican religiopolitical order—patristic and patriarchal—that he absolutely refuses to relinquish. Moreover, he wholeheartedly endorses Anglican opposition to religious dissent through oppressive deployments of class privilege and violent exercises of military power. In his confrontation with the Puritans, he is even more dogmatic than they are. Questioned by Governor Endicott, Mr. Conant, and the Salem elders regarding his adherence to the rites and the prerogatives of the Anglican church and the English crown, Brown replies:

> "I have said . . . that 'Religio docenda est, no coercenda,' was a bad maxim of state policy; and that 'Haeresis dedocenda est, non permittenda,' was far

> better. If by the first-born daughter of Rome, you mean that church descended
> in a direct line from Jesus Christ and his Apostles, a church at the feet of which
> the most sacred and virtuous Elizabeth bowed down her majestic head, and
> beneath the shelter of whose mighty arm the learned King James, and our liege
> prince Charles, have reposed their triple diadem—if you mean this church,
> I do say, her sublime ritual should be enforced, till every fibre of the king's
> dominions yields a response thereto. . . . And I would rather," continued he,
> raising the tones of his fine, manly voice, "I would rather give my limbs to the
> wolves of your desert, than see her scepter broken by men like yourselves." (71)

Brown refuses to relinquish the authority of his patristic Church or to
renounce the claims he makes for himself, his dogmas, or his king on its
behalf. His fine manliness, which the narrator so admires, expresses itself
in the same mode as the manliness of those Puritans he opposes. In fact,
Brown's comments precisely echo Mr. Conant's sentiments when the latter
declares, "To my mind there is more danger of Satan's killing us with the
rat's-bane of toleration than the Lord's taking us off with Indian arrows"
(37). Their differing religious dogmas, not their different manners of being
men or claiming dominance, separates these contestants. One is as willing
to resort to violence and to oppression as the other. Each is equally willing to exclude the other from earthly and heavenly community.

When Brown ends his exile and captivity and returns to Salem, he encounters Hobomok—now living with Mary and his child—and says to the
Indian, "Hobomok . . . I am a man like yourself." But in this novel the
Indian and the Anglican are not alike. Hobomok never has a fine, "manly"
moment of spirited defiance like Brown's. Not defying the Europeans seems
to be his special function in the novel, because Child assigns to the racially
marked man the particular burden of reforming masculinity. Hobomok
achieves definition through his renunciation of claims for himself and his
people not only by relinquishing Mary when Brown returns but by earlier
abandoning his people in their struggle for justice. He betrays their military
strategies and political aspirations to the white settlers, just as he betrays
himself by leaving wife and child and vanishing into the woods. His conduct, at this point, does offer a foil to the Puritan men who have struggled
over Sally and to the Puritan community that struggles over everything.
Thus, to the familiar fantasy that Indians will obligingly disappear before
civilization's advances, Child adds another: the vanishing Indian represents

a better, less aggressive and violent form of manhood. Before he disappears, Child makes Hobomok a model of an improved masculinity, the basis for a better republic, for the white settlers who dispossess him.

This is Hobomok's true function in the novel. Child makes him a more effective model of alternative manhood than an object of Mary's desire. In fact, it seems doubtful that Mary actually wants the Indian at all. For her he represents not a fulfillment of sexual desire but an expression of erotic despair. For Mary can only accept Hobomok at a moment when the death of her sympathetic mother and the loss of her English lover have reduced her to near madness:

> There was a chaos in Mary's mind;—a dim twilight, which had at first made all objects shadowy, and which was rapidly darkening into misery, almost insensible of its source. The sudden stroke which had dashed from her lips the long promised cup of joy, had almost hurled reason from his throne. What now had life to offer? If she went to England, those for whom she most wished to return, were dead. If she remained in America, what communion could she have with those around her? Even Hobomok, whose language was brief, figurative, and poetic, and whose nature was unwarped by the artifices of civilized life, was far preferable to them. She remembered the idolatry he had always paid her, . . . In the midst of this whirlwind of thoughts and passions, she turned suddenly toward the Indian, as she said, "I will be your wife, Hobomok, if you love me." (121)

At the moment she runs to Hobomok, she prays to Brown, "If thy pure spirit is looking down upon this action, forgive me, I own that I do but submit to my fate" (123). Her fate, however, while not quite worse than death, is an expression of her deadened life and blighted hopes within her own male-dominated community and has no positive terms of address to the Indian.[11]

But Hobomok, after all, is really not an Indian. He is a figuration of an alternative to the aggressive, self-assertive men of modern culture. As such, he is an unlikely hero. His Native American foil, Chief Corbitant, "possessed of a mind more penetrating and temper even more implacable than most of his brethren," who "foresaw the destruction of his countrymen, and from his inmost soul . . . hated the usurpers," might have been a more plausible hero had Child wanted to portray a Native American man. But his anger and truculence disqualify him for Child's purpose, which is not to represent an Indian but to offer an alternative form of manhood. There is no union between a white woman and an Indian because in Mary's self-obsession, the narrative's persistent focal point at these moments, there is no place for Hobomok's desire to appear to her or to Child's readers except insofar as it furthers Mary's and her author's purposes. In this sense, both Child and Mary seem as self-obsessed and unsympathetic as the Puritan men they both resist.

Corbitant has a point when he accuses Hobomok of disregard for his people's sufferings while he "counts his beaver for the white man's squaw" and "saves his tears for the white-faced daughter of Conant" (30–31). The inequities of power between the Euro-Americans and Native Americans determine that when a Native American assumes a feminized position and denies claims on his own or his people's behalf, desire for the other becomes betrayal of one's own. Because he loves Mary, Hobomok betrays Corbitant's military plans and helps to further the projects of the English settlers, becoming thereby an enemy to and an outcast from his own people and an instrument of the society that oppresses them. Cross-racial desire, then, in Child's imagination, often threatens the crucial social, economic, and sexual economies of the societies in which it appears. This may help to reform a racist and unjust dominant society, but it may have disastrous effects for the society of the oppressed.

In Hobomok, Child produces the fantasy of a masculinity divested of aggression and of violence, one with only the power of renunciation to call its own, one driven to embrace its own abnegation. As Hobomok explains his situation to the returning Brown at the moment of his ultimate renunciation: "For Mary's sake I have borne the hatred of the Yengees, the scorn of my tribe, and insults of my enemy. And now, I will be buried among strangers, and none shall black their faces for the unknown chief. . . . Ask Mary to pray for me—that when I die, I may go to the Englishman's God, where I may hunt beaver with little Hobomok, and count my beavers for Mary" (140). As a model for reforming men, Hobomok fulfills a certain dream of feminine subversion, a dream of subverting the dominant society's construction of normative masculinity, but this subversion actually perpetuates existing structures of power, not only between the races but also within the Puritan community. Ultimately, a reformation of manhood is what the Puritans need.

Hobomok's example finds its true intended audience among the European men whom Child imagines emulating his abnegation and among the white women whom she imagines will encourage them to do so.[12] In response to Mr. Collier's incredulous question, "Is it possible you have met Hobomok alone, and yet live to tell thereof?" Brown responds, "I have a story to tell of that savage, which might make the best of us blush at our inferiority, Christians as we are" (145). Thus, Hobomok, Native American other, is comfortably reinscribed within the strictures of moral exempla for Christian males, men for whom the exigencies of life in an individualistic and competitive civil society increasingly—in both the seventeenth and the nineteenth centuries—led to denials in practice of the communal Christian virtues they espoused in theory. Hobomok stands, before the letter, as a counterexample to Ahab's overbearing dominance and violent impositions. He also stands as a character who makes no claims and on whose behalf no claims need be made, denuded as he is of violence and power both and therefore of the power to resist imposition or to demand justice. He offers a model of masculinity that might make the community of saints not more cosmopolitan and just but more efficiently free from internal discord and strife. In *Hobomok,* Child fantasizes a purer, more easily managed American future, but she fails to confront the violent origins and inequitable conflicts of American cosmopolitanism that violate the nation's principles and perpetuate its problems.

At those moments when Child tries hardest to associate her attack on racism with her critique of masculinity, she ends up being drawn back into the disciplinary structures of the unjust patriarchal order that violates the principles of equity and inclusiveness she seeks to champion. Unhappily, effective opposition to violent impositions often requires violent opposition. Masochism may be the just portion for the oppressor, but for the oppressed it can only mean accepting the pain society inflicts. That the other has legitimate demands for retribution or vengeance may be inimical to the nation's interests as commonly understood and may be difficult, even terrifying, to acknowledge. But without such an acknowledgment, no rectification of American principles, no justice, and no truly cosmopolitan American society can be imagined. Child's first romance fails to imagine a future freed from the oppressions based on gender and race that violate American principles, but it offers a fascinating object lesson in the continuing importance of particular identities in imagining how those universal principles might be realized.

After Hobomok, or The Imaginative Requirements of Cosmopolitanism

Hobomok only begins Child's long career, which is marked throughout by a persistent commitment to justice and a suggestive ambivalence toward violent resistance. A commitment to transcendental and universal principles also figures in her engagements. In this commitment she was hardly alone among nineteenth-century intellectuals and reformers. Carolyn Karcher sees Child's transcendentalism as a falling off from radical politics.[13] But Child's universal or transcendental principles ground rather than blunt her politics and allow her to engage rather than evade the nation whose inequities she struggled to reform. A lifelong committed activist and agitator, Child was never overly interested in the metaphysical vagaries of philosophers or in ethics philosophically considered. And yet, at crucial moments in her work and in her confrontations with her nation, she finds recourse to something in the nature of an absolute to be necessary. How that absolute functions reveals interesting aspects of Child's imaginative relationship to ethics and politics.

Consider, for example, the relationship between imaginative ethics and transcendental values in "The Black Saxons," a story Child published in 1841 as part of her long crusade against slavery. During the War of 1812, the story goes, a group of rebellious slaves "in the vicinity of Charleston, South Carolina," feign religious fervor to beg night passes so that they can escape and join the British forces then menacing their owners. Mr. Duncan, a kindly but benighted slave owner, sits in his "elegantly furnished parlor" reading Theirry's *History of the Norman Conquest* and finds himself moved by the lot of the conquered and enslaved Saxons. Those, like Robin Hood, who took up arms against "the robbers who had beggared them" particularly stir a sympathetic response. Such violent resistance, bred and determined by the violence of oppression, leads the slave owner to reflect that "troubled must be the sleep of those who rule a conquered nation!"[14] As he reads, one after another his slaves come to beg passes to hear "Tom" preach at a Methodist meeting. Kindly Mr. Duncan, who does not at this point apply the Saxon lesson to himself, grants each request. Finally, the remarkable and sudden fervor gripping his slaves makes him suspicious that these meetings may cover more seditious purposes. Disguising himself in "negro clothes" and wearing a "black mask well-fitted to his face," he follows along to the next revival meeting to find his own and his community's worst fears realized. The enslaved Africans not only plan to flee to the British invaders, they are deliberating whether or not to kill their masters before they go. "A tall, sinewy mulatto . . . exclaiming, with fierce gestures" argues that such violence would be just retribution: "Ravish wives and daughters before their eyes, as they have done to *us!* Hunt them with hounds, as they have hunted *us!* Shoot them down with rifles, as they have shot *us!* Throw their carcasses to the crows, they have fattened on *our* bones; and then let the Devil take them where they never rake up fire o' nights. Who talks of *mercy* to our masters?" (187; emphasis in original). Though several of the slaves plead mercy for the masters, none discount the bitter justice of this angry indictment. Prudently, the plotters reject this perilous plan and reject violent retribution, for the point of Child's narrative is not the rebellion itself but the education of Mr. Duncan and her readers.

This occurs in a cosmopolitan framework, one in which the long, transcendent expanses of what Wai Chi Dimock has called "planetary time" have a more local significance than either cosmopolitanism or universal history are usually allowed. Transcendent principles here enable not an abstraction from the conflicts of the present but an identification between discrete identities separated by racist belief and violent injustice. Of course, Mr. Duncan now sees with new eyes not only his own situation and surroundings but his own point of identification with the Saxon history he has been reading and also with the men and women he enslaves:

> Mr. Duncan again found himself in the open field, alone with the stars. Their glorious beauty seemed to him, that night, clothed in new and awful power. . . . Again he recurred to Saxon history, and remembered how he had thought that troubled must be the sleep of those who rule a conquered people. A new significance seemed given to Wat Tyler's address to the insurgent labourers of *his* day; an emphatic, and most unwelcome application of *his* indignant question why serfs should toil unpaid, in wind and sun, that lords might sleep on down, and embroider their garments with pearl.[15]

Moreover, as Mr. Duncan ruminates, he considers not only the applicability of the past, but the potentialities of the future, for these Black Saxons may, like their English counterparts, become foreparents of new strains of freedom however doomed in the present moment they might seem to be, for "who shall calculate what even such hopeless endeavors may do for the future freedom of this down-trodden race?" (191). Duncan both finds himself to be an oppressor and identifies himself with the oppressed.

While Duncan's self-realization of an identity between him and those he has enslaved—achieved by literally putting himself in their place and applying a transcendental principle to their condition—does not lead to immediate acts of emancipation, it does prevent him from informing on their incipient insurrection despite "a painful conflict between contending feelings and duties."[16] He accepts the violence of the oppressed, even when it is terrifyingly directed at himself, because he recognizes his own complicity in the violence to which they respond and that his own violation of a universal principle makes the violence as just for them as it would be for himself in their place. Child has moved far beyond her position in her first novel, for Duncan's renunciation of his own interests differs from Hobomok's. Unlike Hobomok's betrayal of Corbitant's plot, Duncan's keeping of the slave rebellion's secret furthers the cause of justice. In this brief story, cosmopolitan consciousness, historical knowledge, and transcendental identification prove to be the interdependent and interrelated grounds of justice, however terrifying that justice may be.

Child's belief that the principles of justice can transcend time and place figures crucially in her brief essay on internecine conflicts within the abolitionist movement. In "To Abolitionists" (1841) she considers the conflict between those opponents to slavery who accepted violent resistance and those who did not, between those who saw the cause of abolition globally linked to other liberation causes and those who did not. Like Emerson, Child sees in all human affairs a tendency toward dualism rooted in the double nature of the human soul and entailing a perpetual conflict between "conservative" and "reform" parties, the parties of "stop there" and "go ahead," between—she specifies—those abolitionists who were willing to countenance revolutionary violence by the enslaved and those who were not.[17] Child resorts to universal principles and strongly suggests that no double standard can be valid that separates us and them, "white" from "black" Americans. The early abolitionists, she wrote,

> warmly . . . took the ground that slaves *ought* to wait quietly for their emancipation to be effected by the exertion of moral power; that to murder their

masters would be contrary to the Gospel of Christ. All classes of minds united in this; for all shuddered at being the cause, however remotely, of a civil war. But minds of a conservative cast, with their usual passivity, saw just so much as applied to negro slaves, and no more. . . . The question arose, "Then what right had *we* to fight at Bunker Hill? What right had we to promote insurrection among the *Poles,* by sending them standards and flaming addresses?" . . . There was no escape from one of two alternatives; the principle, if true, made all war a violation of the gospel; if not, it should no longer be repeated to screen abolitionists from a painful accusation; nay, if it were not true, might it not some day become a *duty* to send swords and standards to *black* Poles? A very few boldly and honestly took this ground. (196; emphasis in original)

This is, as Child well knew, a terrifying passage. But her identification of enslaved Africans with the national narrative of Euro-Americans on the one hand and with the struggle of oppressed Europeans on the other essentially identifies them with an unbounded and common humanity and makes both the enormity of the violence practiced against them and the justice of violent resistance to it palpable.

Moreover, Child attempts to put these terrors in perspective. Inevitably, she argues, given the nature of the universe, one truth about politics or justice enchains many others: "Every truth is infinite in its relations; and this is a law of the universe. . . . Earnestly pleading for one great truth, they, by reason of this law, and quite unconsciously to themselves, rouse into action many other truths involved therein. These are received or rejected, praised or scorned, according to the temperament and character of various individuals. Some love them, some hate them, but more fear them, as they do a path through an intricate forest, to which there seems no end."[18] Like Emerson, Child encourages her readers not to be dismayed by what are only apparent disagreements but to follow the truth as their own vision allows them to understand the truth and to "fear nothing, but be strong, and of good cheer. The planets will keep their places. No one will fly out of its sphere, or be swallowed by the sun" (199). There is, she suggests, a remedy for violence, but it requires courageous acknowledgment of where violence originates and just measures to redress the injustices of power by whatever means may be necessary.

The interdependence of Child's cosmopolitanism and her transcendentalist principles are most in evidence in her popular column "Letters from

New York" in the *National Anti-Slavery Standard*. As Carolyn Karcher describes these free-ranging communiqués, they "integrated abolitionism into a comprehensive philanthropy that connected slavery with other social problems; urban poverty, an unjust prison system, capital punishment, the oppression of women, prostitution, alcoholism, and prejudice against Jews, Catholics, Irish, and Indians.[19] Child's progress, from her early difficulties thinking different forms of gender and racial oppression together in *Hobomok* to her later persuasion that various forms of injustice were in principle the same, finds expression in these letters. While they cannot be reduced to a single idea, they share with Emerson's work the attempt to scrutinize a nearly inscrutable presence behind and uniting the varied phenomena of the perceptible world, the world of politics and suffering, injustice and redress.

Writing in her first letter of the plethora of perceptions received during a city walk, Child offers the following: "There *was* a time when all these things would have passed by me like the flitting figures of the magic lantern, or the changing scenery of a theatre, sufficient for the amusement of an hour. But now, I have lost the power of looking merely on the surface. Every thing seems to me to come from the Infinite, to be filled with the Infinite, to be tending toward the Infinite."[20] Child's precision of a "little lower layer" beneath the pasteboard mask of appearances seems a more benevolent version of Ahab's obsession because it focuses not on the figure of man alone but on the idea of society: "Do I see crowds of men hastening to extinguish a fire? I see not merely uncouth garbs, and fantastic flickering lights of lurid hue, like a tramping troop of gnomes,—but straightway my mind is filled with thoughts about mutual helpfulness, human sympathy, the common bond of brotherhood, and the mysteriously deep foundations on which society rests; or rather, on which it now reels and totters" (303). The difference in ethical tendency between Ahab's monomania and Child's sociability lies not in the implications of transcendentalism itself but in the judgment and desire of the thinker. On such tenuous threads politics and ethics ultimately hang. For Child, without some such reference to the transcendent, without some access to interpretations rooted in some principled feeling other than the empirically perceptible, no justice and no amelioration of society are possible. But as Scott Pratt argues, such transcendent categories for Child in these "Letters from New York" are determinately situated in the particular. For Child, "truth is a disposition to recognize one's own place in relation to others in a changing world. In this sense, truth is a way of characterizing what one finds '*within* a landscape.'"[21] For Child, what one finds within a landscape are the invigorating forms of human difference and the challenges to sympathy and justice that accompany them, as well as the reeling and tottering of her nation as it fails to meet these challenges.

In one letter, Child somewhat fancifully claimed that the "organ of justice" was "unusually developed" in her head, and the exercise of that organ requires her to find the deeper layers of significance in the phenomena she sees.[22] Thus, during a walk along the battery during which she encounters wretched examples of the city's poorer people, she penetrates beyond the mere wrenching spectacle of a bedraggled urchin selling papers to imagine—as in a novel by Dickens—the sordid details of his life: the "miserable cellar" with its "bed of dirty straw," the drunken parents, the beatings; and of his future: the seduction by criminals, the apprehension by the police and the arrival "in the police-office, surrounded by hard faces," and the evolution of the ruined boy, for absence of love and instruction, into society's enemy, the victim of violence himself in the form of "the slow murder of a human soul" (315). To extrapolate all this from the sight of one poor boy may seem an exercise in sentimental extravagance, but the principle that Child extracts from her melodramatic imaginings is stunning in its simplicity and essential to her appeal: "When, O when, will men learn that society makes and cherishes the very crimes it so fiercely punishes, and *in* punishing reproduces."[23] Such a principle represents transcendentalism with a political point and indicates that, for Child, without this transcendentalism politics would be difficult to imagine. The universalism of Child's transcendental politics frames and gives sense to her vision of society's and the nation's failures.

Failure, in fact, seems much on Child's mind in her "Letters from New York." As she gazes at the paupers' burying ground with its "predominance of foreign epitaphs," Child feels deeply the gap between the reality of these poor graves and the imagined aspirations of those who have ended all but beyond the reach of human sympathy:

> Who could now tell with what high hopes those departed ones had left the heart-homes of Germany, the sunny hills of Spain, the laughing skies of Italy, or the wild beauty of Switzerland? Would not the friends they had left in their childhood's home, weep scalding tears to find them in a pauper's grave,

with their initials rudely carved on a fragile shingle? Some had not even these frail memorials. It seemed there was none to care whether they lived or died. A wide deep trench was open; and there I could see piles of unpainted coffins heaped one upon the other, left uncovered with earth, till the yawning cavity was filled with its hundred tenants.[24]

The pauper's ground marks the limits of a failed dream, an indictment of a nation likewise on the brink of failure that an imagination that relates the perceived to the principled—the imagination of an intellectual like Child—can see and make visible to others.

To imagine a structural link between society and the outcast becomes, for Child, a way of imagining links between the outcast and herself. In letter 29, written after she visited the prison at Blackwell's Island, she reports:

I have not been happy since that visit to Blackwell's Island. There is something painful, yea, terrific, in feeling myself involved in the great wheel of society, which goes whirling on, crushing thousands at every turn. This relation of the individual to the mass is the sternest and most frightful of all the conflicts between necessity and free will. Yet here, too, conflict *should* be harmony, and *will* be so. Put far away from thy soul all desire of retaliation, all angry thoughts, all disposition to overcome or humiliate an adversary, and be assured thou has done much to abolish gallows, chains, and prisons, though thou hast never written or spoken a word on the criminal code.[25]

This is Hobomok's renunciation again but with a difference. Here, like Hobomok, Child renounces the violent forms of apparent justice. But unlike Hobomok, she does so from the position of power and privilege, and therefore her renunciation of the obsessive fixation on the prerogatives of the social order becomes a fuller realization of society's potentials, not an abdication of its future. For the privileged, implicated in an unjust social order, judgment requires such acts of renunciation and identification—an imaginative placing of oneself in the other's place—and justice only finds itself when those acts have been accomplished. Self-renunciation may be a pious principle, but its political and ethical implications differ greatly according to the identity and situation of the self that is renounced.

For Child, national identity depends not on blood but on principle, and she imagines the nation not in terms of fidelity to clan but of allegiance to just principles. These principles are, for Child, ultimately secular, even when they find expression through religion. Her reasons for attempting a global history of religion, put forth in the preface to *The Progress of Religious Ideas,* are exemplary and typical of her later work:

> While my mind was yet in its youth, I was offended by the manner in which Christian writers usually describe other religions; for I observed that they habitually covered apparent contradictions and absurdities, in Jewish or Christian writings, with a veil of allegories and mystical interpretation, while the records of all other religions were unscrupulously analyzed or contemptuously described as "childish fables" or "filthy superstitions.". . . The one-sidedness of the representation troubled my strong sense of justice. I recollect wishing, long ago, that I could become acquainted with some good, intelligent Bramin, or Mohammedan, that I might learn, in some degree, how their religions appear to *them.*[26]

Child responds to the injustice of Christian misrepresentations of other religions and their adherents by undertaking to treat religion from the "novelty" of a different "point of view." She adopts the Kantian strategy of representational justice that attempts to place the writer and her readers in the place of the other, already in evidence in her "Letters from New York," and tries to imagine how the world appears to adherents of other faiths. She fully realizes that such a gesture is tentative and imaginative and impossible ultimately to accomplish, but she recognizes the necessity of the effort nonetheless:

> I have treated all religions with reverence, and shown no more favour to one than to another. I have exhibited each one in the light of its own Sacred Books; and in giving quotations, I have aimed in every case to present impartially the beauties and the blemishes. . . . I have tried to place each form of worship in its own light; that is, as it appeared to those who sincerely believed it to be of divine origin. But even this candid method must necessarily produce a very imperfect picture, drawn as it is by a modern mind so foreign to ancient habits of thought, and separated from them by the lapse of ages. (1: vii–viii)

There are many things one might say about this remarkable passage. Critically, one must note the bias of modernity suggested by the book's title and figured here—what we now would call the Judeo-Christian tradition appears on the side of modernity while the religions of intelligent Moslems or Hindus appear separated from the modern mind by the lapse of ages. Nonetheless, Child's method bespeaks an intellectual openness to identification with the other and a commitment to an attempt to imagine the other's viewpoint that suggests a generosity still too often absent among Westerners in their considerations of other religions, especially, of course, Islam.

Emphasized again and again in Child's account, especially of the "earlier" religions, is the interrelation and transmission, cross-identification, and identity between and among different and frequently opposed religious groups. Thus Hindus and Buddhists and Seikhs, Egyptians and Chaldeans and Greeks, all share remarkably similar deities. They sometimes seem, for all their differences, like familial inflections on a small handful of eternal or at least persistent archetypes. Thus, without resorting to the abstractions of universal mythologies or transcendental analyses, Child urges her readers to consider the historically rooted commonalities and cosmopolitan affinities that run beneath the surface and within the confines of the most violent differences that seem to divide the world.

Following a strain of archaeological speculation widespread in her own day and resurgent in ours, Child cheerfully asserts the links of tradition and association that bind Europe and Africa:

> Athens was founded by a colony from Egypt, and the intercourse between that country and Greece was always frequent. The effect of this on their religion and philosophy is very obvious. But in the Grecian atmosphere of thought and feeling all things were tinged with more cheerful and poetic colours. Egyptian reverence for stability and power was here changed to worship of freedom and beauty. Strong, active, and vivacious themselves, the Grecians invested their deities with the same characteristics. They did not conceive of them as dwelling apart in passionless majesty, like Egyptian gods, with a solemn veil of obscurity around them. They were in the midst of things, just like human beings, from whom they differed mainly in more enlarged powers. . . . Gay, imaginative, pliable, and free, the Grecians received religious ideas from every source, and wove them all together in a mythological web of fancy, confused and wavering in its patterns but full of golden threads. (1: 284–85)

The Hegelian happy childhood of the Greeks clearly attracts Child with its free and innocent physicality, but she also remains mindful that its origins—as always with human artifacts like religion—lay elsewhere and with others and that the distinctiveness of Greek inflections should not obscure Europe's commonality with the non-European cultural roots on which it grafts itself. These express themselves in those aspects of Greek and Roman religious devotion most indebted to mystery cults like Isis and in such beliefs as the immortality and universality of the soul that Christians receive from these pagan sources.[27] Transcendental identifications and cosmopolitan cross-fertilizations do not make identity or conflict disappear, but they undermine attempts to confidently ground absolute differences in the absolute. For Child, heterogeneity and conflict may be the irreducible situation of the nation, but without just principles no worthily diverse society or desirable cosmopolitan future is possible, for these require the power to discriminate and to judge as well as the capacity to sympathize and to understand. For Child, identification and sympathy, rooted in principles, make understanding and judgment possible. Only through such a complex articulation of particulars with universals can something other than the failure of America be imagined.

A ROMANCE OF THE REPUBLIC, OR IDENTIFICATION AND FAILURE AFTER THE CIVIL WAR

As Carolyn Karcher notes, *A Romance of the Republic* (1867), written during a period that—in its narrator's words—"was supposed to be peace" (431), sets its action "against the backdrop of betrayal . . . of all the promises the war had seemingly endorsed—genuine emancipation for African Americans; recognition of the indispensable role they had played as soldiers, spies, and auxiliaries; and their incorporation as equal citizens into a truly reconstructed Union." The book, Karcher continues, "insistently rehearses the history that its white audience was so rapidly forgetting," to which one must add that in Child's romance the incorporation of Africans into the fabric of U.S. life and identity had already occurred and could only be "forgotten" by violent acts of repression.[28]

Child imagines a national identity constructed on passionate principles and enacted through sympathetic identifications. In *A Romance of the Republic,* the ethical and material success of each character—his or her progress through dispossession and loss toward recuperation and restitution in the familiar pattern of the romance plot—depends on that character's success or failure in identifying with men and women who are subject to injustice and in meeting the demands revealed by those identifications. The book thus offers one of the most compelling and one of the truest—in an importantly ideal sense—visions of American identity ever produced.[29]

The story begins in the Deep South in the 1830s, although its crucial action will occur in the North among respectable men and women who support slavery. Child thereby reminds her readers—who were already forgetting these facts—that the crime of slavery and the problem of its aftermath was a national and not a southern problem. The curtain rises on a domestic idyll on the plantation of Mr. Royal, a wealthy New Orleans widower and the doting father of two beautiful and accomplished daughters. The son of his old friend, a Mr. King of Boston, pays a visit and meets Royal's young daughters, Rosa (called Rosabella) and Flora (called Floracita). They call their father "Papasito"; he calls them *mignonnes*. The first of many dramatic ironies (that familiar and favored trope of the romance) momentarily disrupts this happily polyglot hodgepodge of affection, for when Gerald Fitzgerald from Savannah joins the group, coming to court Rosa, Flora to tease her sister begins to sing:

> Un petit blanc, que j'aime,
> En ces lieux est venu,
> Oui! Oui! c'est lui même
> C'est lui! je l'ai vue!
>> Petit blanc! mon bon frère!
>> Ha! ha! petit blanc si doux![30]

Mr. Royal, suddenly irate, admonishes Flora, 'Don't sing that foolish song, Mignonne!" This irony is not particularly subtle. The "apricot" complexion of the girls and their "Spanish" mother signals the experienced readers of American romances that these girls are "black" even before the interracial flirtation of Flora's song provokes her father's outburst. The young women, cultured and accomplished offspring of wealth and privilege in the slave-owning South, will, of course, themselves be subjected to enslavement, like their mother before them. Despite their improvident and unlucky father's love and their own virtues, each will be bought and sold several times before the story ends.

Child handles these romantic and melodramatic materials with great skill, intensifying them and sharpening their point by mounting key moments in the book's action around dramatic ironies and deceitful performances, recurrent tropes of terrible misrecognition and moods of mysterious menace. The romantic world of Child's fiction reminds her readers that in reality slavery depended on obscured self-knowledge and blunted sensitivities to others, ablating identification, vitiating understanding, and disabling just sentiment. Flora unknowingly assumes an identity proximate to the identity that the legal fictions of her society would assign her; voicing a black girl's desire for a white boy, she also exemplifies the distorting pressures of slavery on all human identities.[31] A system that forces some people to pretend to be property and encourages other people to assume their ownership perverts all human relations and makes it more difficult for anyone to really know who in fact he or she might be.

Gerald, who is as handsome as an Italian tenor, will be for most of the novel the perfidious embodiment of the slave system's greatest evils and most deceitful practices. At first he seems to be the novel's hero. He pretends to rescue the girls from slavery after their father's unexpected death and debts reveal them to be not persons but property, he pretends to marry Rosa in order to hide both sisters on his country estate, and he attempts to satisfy his lust with both of them.[32] In Child's romance, slavery depends on and consists of such treacherous and surprising deceits and misrecognitions of both self and others. The work of *A Romance of the Republic* will be to imagine displacing these insidious distortions with truer representations of identities that are more compassionate and just.

Throughout the novel, as in the opening scene, Child structures her dramatic ironies and revelations around scenes involving musical and theatrical performance. The novel's entire plot is itself rather like Italian opera and too beautifully baroque to summarize adequately.[33] For readers unfamiliar with this book, a summary of its main points will be useful. Mr. Royal's mysterious failure to manumit either his daughters or their mother places them, after his death, at the mercy of his creditors. Flora and Rosa realize their altered state and "true" identities when they find themselves humiliated and terrified by being evaluated for sale with the estate's other property. Gerald "saves" them by "marrying" Rosa—whom he actually seems to love—and then hiding her and Flora away until he can purchase and free them. Corrupted by his unlimited power over both these beautiful women, he cannot bring himself to relinquish his ownership of either and, while pretending to be Rosa's loving husband (she conceives his child) begins to pursue Flora as well. Flora, unwilling to disillusion her sister about Gerald's character, escapes with the help of Mrs. Delano—a grand lady of Boston, resident in the South—who befriends her and spirits her away to Europe. Rosa and Gerald believe Flora has drowned. Alone now with her husband and still hidden in the Georgia woods, Rosa realizes his real character and her true situation when he returns from one of his long and increasingly frequent absences and installs a legitimate "white" wife—a Miss Bell from Boston—in the big house while keeping Rosa unwed and hidden in the woods. Both Rosa and Miss Bell give birth to male children. Shortly thereafter, Rosa escapes to Europe with some abolitionist friends and, with many misgivings, leaves her child behind to follow with a faithful retainer. Meanwhile Flora, living in Europe with Mrs. Delano, learns that the ship on which Rosa and her friends booked passage sank at sea with all on board. She does not know that Rosa actually took a different ship. In Europe, Rosa—who has learned that the child she left with her friend died in a fever epidemic—begins a career in opera. Eventually she marries Mr. King, who briefly appeared in the novel's first scene. Mr. King does not merely overlook her African blood, he becomes an abolitionist. At the same time, back in the United States, Flora falls in love with Mr. Blumenthal, an honest but poor German immigrant, whom she weds with the assistance of Mrs. Delano, her adopted mother. Each sister continues to mourn the other's death. Gerald hunts both for a while, especially persecuting Rosa in Europe where he has no legal power over her. Eventually he dies having squandered his resources and his life. His legal wife and child return to Boston to live with her father, Mr. Bell, a wealthy Boston merchant with financial interests in the slave trade. The two Royal sisters come tantalizingly close to meeting several times, but remain apart for nineteen years. Eventually, as readers of romances know they will, Rosa and Flora reunite. This occurs after Rosa, hearing of Gerald's death, returns to the United States, and Flora overhears Rosa singing. Here, in contrast to the novel's first scene, which obfuscated the identities Flora's singing revealed, the sisters recognize each other through Rosa's song. Their reunited, happy households are determinately multilingual and cosmopolitan. Spanish, Anglo-Saxon, and German cultures, languages, and music shape and fill their daily lives. Notably absent, of course, is the cultural presence of

Africa, which Child, like most other Americans both black and white, regarded as too primitive to add to the cultural mix. There seems to be no structural reason for Child why African culture, once recognized, as well as African peoples, could not form part of this American amalgamation. In Child's imagination, promiscuous mixture, cultural as well as racial, is essential to American identity. All of this happens before the novel's first half ends.

The novel's second half revolves around the unraveling of another ironic confusion of identities that slavery entailed. This action begins when Gerald's son begins to court Rosa's daughter, Eulalia. This crisis forces Rosa to reveal—first to her husband, later to Fitzgerald's son and widow—the shocking news (which experienced readers of romance will have expected) that Eulalia and young Fitzgerald are brother and sister. Driven to despair by the ignominy of slavery and the perfidiousness of Gerald, and unwilling that her son should share her lot, she had switched the two nearly identical babies before her escape. Young Fitzgerald was actually her son, actually of mixed racial parentage, and—under the exigencies of the Fugitive Slave Law and Dred Scott Decisions, actually a slave. Believing that Gerald's son had died when she received confused reports about the fever epidemic, Rosa returned to the United States confident that all conflicts from the past had been resolved. But when she realizes that young Fitzgerald is actually her lost son and realizes as well that he has fallen in love with his own sister, she finds herself trammeled again in the welter of misidentifications, misprisions, and false relationships that slavery entails. As they will in Faulkner, miscegenation and incest stalk each other and substitute one for the other, baffling any capacity for honest relationship. The romance of the republic is, from first to last, a terrifying family romance—with all the weight of identity and misidentification that the family romance entails.

When Rosa reveals her son's "true" identity to him, he does not—like Tom Chambers in *Pudd'nhead Wilson* or Henry Sutpen in *Absalom! Absalom!*—suffer an existential crisis of altered identity. Her son, realizing his lineage, begins to explore what the meaning of his altered identity might be and to identify with those enslaved African Americans he has considered simply other than himself. Young Gerald, born subject to slavery but switched at birth and raised as a wealthy white man, when his origins are discovered to him links his freedom to this realization of his "actual" identity by saying that he is now "free to become familiar with my new self"

(380). His new identity becomes a project in exploration and education, of expanded sensibilities and demystified sentiments, rather than a revelation of essential being. Thus, Child's romance refuses to traffic in the already too familiar commonplaces of the tragic mulatto, even as it everywhere evokes them. Only those characters like Mr. Bell and Mrs. Fitzgerald, obsessed with race as a marker of essential difference, experience the romance's late revelations of mixed identity as tragic reversals.[34] Others find these revelations to be an occasion for expanded sympathies and new self-explorations.

At this point in the story, actual history in the form of John Brown's raid on Harpers Ferry and the commencement of the Civil War punctuate the narrative. Posted to the front, young Fitzgerald discovers his half brother, an escaped slave, though he is white and nearly his twin, fighting like him for the Union. Young Fitzgerald dies in the war; his emancipated half brother survives and becomes part of the extended, cosmopolitan King-Blumenthal family (all the King-Blumenthal men take part in the great struggle). This family embodies the promise or the romance of the republic and its ideals that Child dares to dream and that slavery and all the injustices attendant on it and its aftermath betrayed. A realistic estimation of the scope of that betrayal emerges in King's decision that the emancipated slave, though he be white, should go to Europe to assimilate to his new condition away from the racial prejudices and tensions that inhibited the advancement of ex-slaves in the United States. There is, Child suggests, a considerable way to go before the romance of the republic can successfully be realized.

That the realization of racial identity is, for Child's characters, not in itself a tragic moment of self-realization but an occasion for cross-racial identification and transformative self-imagining bespeaks the central component of her belief that the nation is and should be a place of cosmopolitan amalgamation and equitable relationship. Child's dream of amalgamation as a benefit determines the course of the second half of *A Romance of the Republic*. For example, when the narrator recapitulates, at the beginning of part 2, what nineteen years of association between Flora, the escaped slave, and Mrs. Delano, the Boston aristocrat who adopts her, has wrought, she writes: "The bond between her and her adopted mother strengthened with time, because their influence on each other was mutually improving to their character" (297). Certainly her representation of Flora partakes of racial stereotypes about African descent in its natural and uneducable vigor—so different from Rosa's easy culture. Here, as in *Uncle Tom's Cabin,* a type of domesticity becomes a model of sociability, but Child imagines a domestic space far more commodious and cosmopolitan than Stowe's Quaker matriarchies or middle-class hearth sides, one more accommodating to invigorating forms of difference. Flora's character represents only one difference among many. The household reconstituted at the novel's end in Boston differs in many ways from the household with which the novel began. It remains determinately polyglot and promiscuously heterogeneous, but its racial mixings, the repressed secret of the Royal family romance, are no longer secret. The affinity and desire that have always made racial mixture racism's dirty secret freely express themselves not as bondage but as love.

Flora and Rose and their children have pride of place, and the bonds of elective sympathy and identification nearly supplant ties of blood in the little community that meets to celebrate the vindication of the Republic after the bloody Civil War:

> Under festoons of the American flag, surmounted by the eagle, stood Eulalie, in ribbons of red, white, and blue, with a circle of stars around her head. One hand upheld the shield of the Union, and in the other the scales of Justice were evenly poised. By her side stood Rosen Blumen, holding in one hand a gilded pole surmounted by a liberty-cap, while her other hand rested protectingly on the head of Tulee's Benny, who was kneeling and looking upward in thanksgiving. (440)

Karcher notes the reinscription of color hierarchy here—the dark-skinned Benny kneeling in a too familiar posture of obsequious gratitude to the fairer "black" daughters of Rosa and Flora—but in a novel so much committed to recording the contributions of black solders and rebellious slaves to the Union cause, the refreshing force of Benny's offering thanks to those identified with his own race should not be underestimated. Moreover, the scales of justice point us toward Child's insight that a cosmopolitan society requires a just romance, one that recognizes hierarchies of color and culture in order to make them tremble in the balance and eventually disappear.

In the imaginative economy of Child's remarkable romance, identification seems to lie at the basis not only of justice but of identity itself. Consider the following argument between Mr. Bell, the Boston Brahmin deeply implicated in the slave trade, and Mr. Percival and Francis Jackson, the abolitionists who had earlier befriended Flora and who here plead for the fate of several fugitive slaves who have been recaptured from Mr. Bell's ship *King Cotton*. Departing from the letter of the law and the vagaries of the Constitution, they make a strong appeal to Bell's imagination and to the ways in which imagination determines justice in a republic. They urge: "If your grandson should be claimed as a slave, I rather think you would consider the writ of *habeus corpus* a wise and just provision. . . . I take it for granted . . . that you do not wish for a state of things that would make every man and woman in Massachusetts liable to be carried off as slaves, without a chance to prove their right to freedom" (315–16). These characters offer a timely lesson: where injustice is tolerated, no one may be beyond its reach; in a nation that tolerates slavery or oppression, no one can really be free. The irony that one of these escaped slaves will in fact turn out to be Fitzgerald's lost son and Bell's enslaved grandchild scarcely adds to the force of the lesson, one that requires only the imaginative power of identification, the power required to enjoy a romance, to receive.

Again and again, as the novel's second half unmasks the mistaken identities and remedies the missed encounters of the first half, Child's narrator and her characters return to the issue of identification as the basis of justice and as the root of identity. Consider, for example, Joe Bright, the stalwart artisan and abolitionist, in his own account of how he became an abolitionist:

> One winter, I thought I should like to run away from Jack Frost, and I looked in the Southern papers to see if any of 'em advertised for a singing-master. The first thing my eye lighted on was this advertisement:—"Run away from the subscriber a stout mulatto slave, named Joe; has light sandy hair, blue eyes, and ruddy complexion; is intelligent, and will pass himself for a white man. I will give one hundred dollars' reward to whoever will size him and put him in jail."
>
> "By George!" said I, "that's a description of *me*. I didn't know before that I was a mulatto. It'll never do for me to go *there*." So I went to Vermont to teach. I told 'em I was a runaway slave, and showed 'em the advertisement that described me. Some of 'em believed me, till I told 'em it was a joke. Well, it is just as bad for those poor black fellows as it would have been for me; but that blue-eyed Joe seemed to bring the matter home to me. It set me thinking about slavery, and I have kept thinking ever since. (322; emphasis in original)

Of course one wishes that Joe's imagination had not required the prop of physical resemblance to make this leap into identification, but one should also note that once made the identification generalizes to all those enslaved, not only those whose complexion resembles his own. Similarly, the entire melodramatic plot machinery of switched babies, one slave and one free, so familiar and so effective, here serves to bring home the terrifying logic of identification and identity itself. Rose says,

> I was still half frantic with misery and fear. A wild, dark storm was raging in my soul. I looked at the two babes, and thought how one was born to be indulged and honored, while the other was born a slave, liable to be sold by his unfeeling father or by his father's creditors. Mine was only a week the oldest, and was no larger than his brother. They were so exactly alike that I could distinguish them only by their dress. I exchanged the dresses . . . ; and while I did it, I laughed to think that, if Mr. Fitzgerald should capture me and the little one, and make us over to Mr. Bruteman, he would sell the child of his Lily Bell. It was not like me to have such feelings. I hope I was insane. (352)

Rosa's madness is also a moment of illumination, the core of which involves identity, the logic of which the narrative finally does not disavow. That logic determines that any one may find him- or herself in the place of the oppressed and that justice is not an abstract or an abstruse concept. Justice is an existential requirement in the ethical life of a republic. Citizens deny this with whatever obsessive energy they can summon to stabilize the identities that injustice both produces and disturbs, but they do so at their own peril.

Rosa, in a self-reflexive moment, says, "Judging by my own experience . . . I should say that the most fertile imagination could invent nothing more strange and romantic than many of the incidents which grow out of slavery" (361). Slavery generates romantic stories because it means, at its core, that neither justice nor identity can be recognized and that romantic misrecognition (of self and other) and melodramatic injustice (toward one's self and others) are the everyday order of things. This romance of the republic and all its misdirection are founded on the fundamental misidentification of humans as slaves or of people as property that in turn relies on a failure of identification, a failure to recognize the other as human as oneself. "I should consider my birth and position great misfortunes, if they blinded me to the plainest principles of truth and justice," Mr. Percival chides a Southern sympathizer at one point (274), but the romance's point is that such blindness is precisely what slavery and racism engenders and relies on, engendering as well, thereby, a blindness and insensitivity to the true meaning of national belonging and national identity in the United States. From that evil, as Mr. King says, all the other evils and the twisted but logical windings of this romance's plot and of the republic's tortured history derive.

When Mr. Bell, by contrast, who makes money from the slave trade, finds himself doubly subjected to the ironies of mistaken identity and systematic injustice, when he finds out that the grandson he has assumed to be free is actually subject to sale while the slave on his ship is his actual heir, he finds no expansive freedom in this knowledge because he lacks the imaginative capacity for either identification or justice. The novel hammers this point rather hard. When the abolitionist Francis Jackson, repulsed by Mr. Bell's hardened conscience with regard to an escaped slave who will, in the fullness of narrative time, prove to be his actual grandson, utters the following uncharitable sentiment—"It's a pity that dark-complexioned grandson of his couldn't be carried off as a slave. That might, perhaps, bring him to a realizing sense of the state of things" (318)—the novel offers its readers the baldest of dramatic ironies, one that they can enjoy but Mr. Bell cannot. He lacks the imaginative capacity to read or the romantic nature to join the republic. He will never succeed in identifying himself or members of his family with the victims of injustice, never be able to imagine they might be in that place. Mr. Perceval, who accompanied Mr. Jackson on that failed visit to ask consideration for the escaped slave aboard *King Cotton,* remarks, "We hear a good deal about poetical justice . . . but one rarely sees it meted out in this world" (387). Because irony brings no moral illumination to the old man, who refuses to acknowledge his Anglo-Saxon heir because the slave has married a "mulatto" (392–93), this poetic justice is less than satisfying for the reader and useless to the republic's unfolding romance: "A pretty dilemma you have placed me in, sir," Mr. Bell complains, "My property, it seems, must either go to Gerald, who you say has negro blood in his veins, or to this other fellow, who is a slave with a negro wife" (394). This irony kills the old man and he exits the narrative having failed to learn its lessons or let it expand his imaginative and sympathetic scope. Insofar as Mr. Bell represents a realistic rather than romantic character, typical of the racial ideas and policies shaping the nation after the Civil War, no more stinging or despairing indictment of the republic's failure, whose imaginative limits this romance hoped to expand, may be imagined.

But the romance does maintain a vision, however utopian, of other possibilities. Otherwise, what is a romance for? The other characters fare, morally and materially, much better than Mr. Bell. Despite the grim harbinger of John Brown's raid and execution and the dreadful carnage of the Civil War, the novel ends with a vision of human community and cosmopolitan association that offers an effectively better version of national identity and cosmopolitan justice than America had yet realized. As Blumenthal says, contemplating the marriage of the cousins Alfred and Eulalia, "nations and races have been pretty thoroughly mixed up in the ancestry of our children. What with African and French, Spanish, American, and German, I think the dangers of too close relationship are safely diminished" (432). Here miscegenation seems to remove the threat of incest, rather than incest, as it so often does in American fiction, intensifying the threat of racial mixing. "They are a good-looking set, between you and I *[sic]*," said Flora; "though they *are* oddly mixed up" (432; emphasis in original). Intrafamily marriage becomes the final romance of the republic because within the family of the nation already move all the differences that more obsessional versions of identity wish to repress and to project to the exterior of these United States. This too-little-read novel both grips and entertains; it moves and perplexes its sensitive reader even today with a sense that the United States, as a republic, still fails to realize the true romance Child began to imagine.

chapter 4

John Brown's Identities:
Nat Turner and the Fear of Just Deserts

The nineteenth was the first century of human sympathy,—the age when half
wonderingly we began to descry in others that transfigured spark of divinity
which we call Myself; when clodhoppers and peasants, and tramps and thieves,
and millionaires and—sometimes—Negroes, became throbbing souls whose
warm pulsing life touched us so nearly that we half gasped with surprise.

—W. E. B. DU BOIS, *The Souls of Black Folk*

JOHN BROWN AND NAT TURNER

In 1859, John Brown was lying wounded and in the custody of the State
of Virginia after his failed raid on Harpers Ferry. Lydia Maria Child wrote
an open letter to Governor Wise asking his permission to nurse the wounded
insurgent. This permission was denied her, but what ensued was a series
of letters from Child to Governor Wise and to Mrs. Mason, a Southern
woman who publicly doubted Child's Christianity, on the topics of slavery, virtue, and violence. Mrs. Mason's letter to Child had opened with the
following salvo: "Do you read your Bible, Mrs. Child? If you do, read there,
'Woe unto you, hypocrites,' and take to yourself with two-fold damnation
that terrible sentence." In her reply, Child argues that Christian hypocrisy
is not among the faults of the abolitionists and goes on to threaten her
accuser with damnation from the laws of history and the force of human
agency rather than from divine intervention. Evoking both Thomas Jefferson and John Randolph as critics of slavery from Virginia, she drives her
point home:

Your letter to me is published in Northern papers, as well as Southern; but my reply will not be allowed to appear in any Southern paper. The despotic measures you take to silence investigation, and shut out the light from your own population, prove how little reliance you have on the strength of your cause. In this enlightened age, all despotisms *ought* to come to an end by the agency of moral and rational means. But if they resist such agencies, it is in the order of Providence that they *must* come to an end by violence. History is full of such lessons.[1]

Child doesn't shrink from public debate or the threat of violence. In fact, as her final paragraph indicates, she imagines the work intellectuals do in opposition to slavery as a kind of violence in its own right:

The genius of Mrs. Stowe carried the outworks of your institution at one dash, and left the citadel open to besiegers, who are pouring in amain. In the church, on the ultra-liberal side, it is assailed by the powerful battering-ram of Theodore Parker's eloquence. On the extreme orthodox side is set a huge fire, kindled by the burning words of Dr. Cheever. Between them is Henry Ward Beecher, sending a shower of keen arrows into your entrenchments; and with him ride a troop of sharp shooters from all sects. . . . The fact is, the whole civilized world proclaims Slavery an outlaw, and the best intellect of the age is active in hunting it down. (253)

Child's rhetoric here makes the work of persuasion itself a presage of the topsy-turvy violence of war, a violence that threatens the slave owner with the same treatment he visits on the slaves, which would only be, as Child suggests, the slaver's just deserts. The "civilized world" itself proclaims the slave owner an outlaw and hunts him down as an expression of civilized sentiment. In her rhetoric, Child not only accepts violence, she, conceptually at least, practices it.

John Brown was perhaps the most terrifying, real-life embodiment of the potential violence of just deserts during the antebellum period and of the threats both material and ideological that such violence entails. As David Blight puts it, "Revolutionary violence has never found a stable place in the mainstream of American memory."[2] A nation self-dedicated to justice and liberty should never require the violent overthrow of oppression to achieve equity. The revolutionary violence Brown came to represent was especially troublesome. He drew his justifications from the deep ideological wells of the nation's ideals and identity, and he threatened the United States with the most concrete and terrible specter of deserved retribution imaginable, the revolt of American slaves.

In his "Preamble" to his revolutionary manifesto, the "Provisional Constitution and Ordinances for the People of the United States," Brown made the justification for his revolt clear:

> Slavery, throughout its entire existence in the United States, is none other than a most barbaric, unprovoked, and unjustifiable war of one portion of its citizens upon another portion—the only conditions of which are perpetual imprisonment and hopeless servitude or absolute extermination—in utter disregard and violation of those eternal and self-evident truths set forth in our Declaration of Independence.[3]

Not only Jefferson's declaration but also Locke's *Second Treatise of Government,* that urtext of liberal republicanism, ground Brown's apologia for the overthrow of the failed republic of the United States and the establishment of a provisional government, a truly American government, in its place. Like Locke and Jefferson, Brown recognized slavery as the perpetuation of a state of war inimical to justice and democratic society in a successful republic. Brown's revolution meant to realize the nation's principles that the practice of human servitude had violated. Because his attack went to the very foundations of American identity, he provoked fears and hopes disproportionate to the threat his botched attack on Harpers Ferry realistically posed to the state. His justification of revolutionary violence in terms of the nation's failure to honor its own principles pressed on the public consciousness of many Americans, for and against slavery, and called the significance of their national identity into question.

John Brown as a figure, whether demonic or prophetic, has challenged the national conscience ever since. Perhaps the most famous image of Brown, John Steuart Curry's mural *Tragic Prelude* (1937–42) stands opposite the governor's office in the Kansas State Capitol. Brown's cruciform figure dominates a panel structured of allegorical figures suggesting the causes of the Civil War and the expanding nation that emerged from it.[4] Between Brown's glaring eyes and beetled brows and his enormous white beard swept up toward his right shoulder, the open, oblong mouth holds the viewer's eye.

Depending on one's predilections, one might imagine prophetic words or a lunatic's scream to emanate from that dark space. In his outstretched right hand Brown brandishes a Sharps rifle—his preferred weapon along with the machete during the Kansas border war—over the figures representing the Union cause; in his left he holds an open Bible, an alpha and omega traced in red on the pages, over some Confederate soldiers. Curry recognizes in Brown's legend the materials of Mosaic prophecy, Christian martyrdom, and the Last Judgment. But the gape-mouthed insurrectionist seems the harbinger of horrible violence rather than deliverance. Curry places Brown's left foot on the back of a fallen Confederate soldier and arranges by Brown's right side a Union battle corpse with an armed black man standing just behind it. The black man faces front with head and eyes turned to his left, his rifle and gaze fixed on an armed Southern soldier standing on the opposite side of Brown's body with his back to the spectator. The gray-clad expanse of the Southerner's back dominates a small grouping of terrified slaves in calico shifts and faded head rags beneath Brown's left arm, a group that Curry balances against a small portrait of abolitionist Henry Ward Beecher (a leader among the abolitionists who made weapons and money available to Brown and other Free-Soilers during the Kansas war) on Brown's right. To Brown's left Curry arranges a Confederate battle flag and to his right the Stars and Stripes. Brown's large figure with the smaller groupings beneath his arms fills the picture's front central plane. In the rear middle ground an ox-drawn wagon train crosses the picture from left to right, a citation of Curry's *Westward Movement* mural (1937), while in the distant background two terrible expressions of natural force rage—a tornado to Brown's left and a prairie fire to his right. These evocations of nature raging across the plain create a sense of movement, an evocation of national destiny along with sublime weather, that echoes the wind-whipped beard framing Brown's open mouth.

The longer one looks at *Tragic Prelude,* the more disturbing it becomes. The pioneer wagons and the sublime weather do not quite reinscribe the painting's evocations of the madness, violence, and terror in American history within the national narrative's familiar parameters of providence and progress. *Tragic Prelude* remains a troubling composition and therefore appropriate to its subject, for John Brown remains the most troublingly ambiguous shape in the national imaginary. Like the figure who dominates Curry's mural, he may be a demented lunatic or an inspired prophet, a megalomaniacal charlatan or the American Moses, the peaceful nation's most terrifying enemy or its sacred principles' most ardent defender. Curry captures not only the tragic violence in the nation's history but the irreducible terror of that history as well. Curry's title may refer to the tragedy of the Civil War, which Brown's raid on Harpers Ferry was credited with hastening, or it may refer to the tragic nature of the modern nation itself, which has its origins in violence and in demands for justice and in which both violence and injustice continue to play far too large a part.[5]

Curry's mural also suggests that the terror John Brown brought to the nation at Harpers Ferry in 1859 was the terror of black insurrection, the terror associated for nineteenth-century Americans most closely with the name and figure of Nat Turner. Turner was the embodiment of the South's worst fears and an important inspiration for Brown's plan.[6] Curry represents the potential violence of black demands for justice in the figure of the stalwart, armed black man who stands face forward on Brown's right. Whether or not Curry actually meant this figure to recall Nat Turner—he does not wear Turner's headscarf or saber—it is Nat Turner's terror that the figure evokes, and it is that terror that Brown assumed and that made his raid on the Federal Arsenal terrible in the imaginations of most white men and women.

Brown's ability to identify himself with Nat Turner suggests the deepest sources of the terrors he provoked. For an American, Brown was remarkably able to identify across color lines and to recognize the injustices of slavery as a challenge to his own humanity. As Lerone Bennett put it, writing in the 1960s and adopting Brown's figure as a precursor for black power, "John Brown *was* a Negro."[7] Even in the 1960s, Brown's black identification could challenge America's dominant and indefensible sense of itself as a white nation because Brown's revolutionary gesture rested on the acknowledged foundation of liberalism's claims to universal justice. Thus, Brown remains compelling because he embodies the nation's contradictions. He became and remains a focus for its hopes and terrors. His type of American identity is a trope of America's failure. And behind Brown, energizing the terror and the promise of his actions, stands the figure of black insurrection, the figure of Nat Turner.

Like Brown, Nat Turner himself remains an ambiguous character, assuming different shapes depending on who tells his story. Harriet Beecher Stowe was also able to identify across the color line to recognize the justice of his cause. In her brilliant reworking of Turner into the pivotal character of her aptly titled romance *Dred* (1856), Stowe struggles to realize the terrible figure of domestic terror as a harbinger of just deserts.[8] To do so requires that she explore the limits of sympathetic identification and right feeling on which both the popular romance and the politics of moral suasion depend and with which she is, since *Uncle Tom's Cabin,* most closely associated. Doing justice to the terrible figures of John Brown and Nat Turner requires confronting terrors that should make right feeling impossible.

Harriet Beecher Stowe's *Dred:* The Failure of Sympathy and the Novel Use of Terror

Like *Uncle Tom's Cabin, Dred: A Tale of the Great Dismal Swamp* offers a critical revision of dominant versions of masculinity in favor of a more feminine sentimentality. But it goes considerably beyond the comforting appeals of moral suasion and emotive sympathy with which the earlier novel ends. When Stowe urges the mothers of America to look to their feelings, self-assured that proper sentiment will lead white women to oppose slavery and create an aura of sympathetic influence favorable to abolition, she imagines sympathy to be a pleasant circuit of positive self-regard. If each mother makes sure that she feels right, she becomes an inspiration for others to do the same, and feeling right will refute the hollow sophistries of slavery's defenders. In *Dred* she explores more painful modes of cross-racial identification. Between *Uncle Tom* and *Dred,* Stowe had learned to listen to African-American demands for liberation and to sympathize with Nat Turner.[9] Stowe realizes that feeling right too easily leaves the other's feelings out of account. Feeling right may as frequently be a symptom of sympathy's failure as a result of its success.[10] She comes to suspect that black rebellion may be a racist republic's just desert and that justice may require that white Americans forgo the comfortable self-affirmations of feeling right or good. Violence aimed against a slave republic might be a fair response to the violence that those enslaved have suffered. To confront these terrible possibilities requires going beyond the aesthetics of right feeling and might even require an ethics of masochism.[11]

Dred, in fact, offers few occasions for right feeling. The novel seems preoccupied with sympathy's abject failures and offers little to support optimism regarding its promises.[12] Nonetheless, in *Dred,* Stowe expands rather than abandons the moral universe of sentimental fiction. Like Childs in *Hobomok,* Stowe sometimes portrays a feminized, nonwhite male in positive contrast to dominant versions of white masculinity that dull men's moral sensibilities. For example, she stages the death of a poor white woman, Mrs. Cripps, wife of a minor slaveholder in the novel, not only to rehearse familiar pieties concerning the good death (as in the famous scene depicting Little Eva's death in *Uncle Tom's Cabin*) but also to pillory the insensibility of the typical white male to such moral examples.

Stowe makes Tiff, a faithful slave much attached to his dying mistress, a foil for the crass insensibility of Mr. Cripps and, like Uncle Tom before him, the affective and juridical center of the novel in which he appears. Of Tiff's relationship to his mistress, the narrator tells us, "The idea that she could actually die, and go anywhere, without him to take care of her, seemed never to have occurred to him."[13] The staging of the deathbed scene emphasizes Tiff's striking combination of personal abjection and moral authority. Mrs. Cripps dies while her oblivious husband sleeps next to her and Tiff keeps vigil holding her hand: "'Tiff,' she gasped, speaking with difficulty, ' . . . I've seen all why I've suffered so much. He—He—He is going to take me! Tell the children about Him!' There was [a] fluttering sigh, and a slight shiver, and the lids fell over her eyes for ever" (98). Tiff, whose strange presence at the marital bedside seems to require no explanation, informs Mr. Cripps that she has died and adds that this death, in his estimation, represents a delivery from the bonds not only of her life but of her marriage: "See how you look now! Good Shepherd hearn you abusing de poor lamb, and he's done took her whar you'll never see her again!" (99). Stowe writes: "Cripps had, like coarse, animal men generally, a stupid and senseless horror of death;—he recoiled from the lifeless form, and sprang from the bed with an expression of horror. . . . 'Well, now, who would have thought it?' he said. 'That I should be in bed with a corpse! I hadn't the least idea'" (99). In Mr. Cripps's reaction to this news and his failure to react to Tiff's admonishment, Stowe suggests the limitations of right feeling among white folks; for Cripps, above all, wants to feel right and feeling right requires that he reject fine examples and painful accusations. In the case of a coarse male animal like Mr. Cripps, the appeal to right feeling poses obvious problems. Mr. Cripps's right feeling regards only his own comfort and therefore prevents rather than provokes a more sympathetic understanding of the other and a more vivid identification with the other's sufferings.

Tiff's career diverges from Uncle Tom's example after this point. After Mr. Cripps marries Polly Skinflint, a low, cruel white woman who turns his poor cabin into a "low grog shop," Tiff schemes to save the master's abused white children and take them to Canada with the slaves Dred leads. Neither Stowe's equation of rum and slavery, nor her fantasy of a sympathetic black man redeeming slavery's white victims, is very creditable or subtle. But unlike Uncle Tom, Tiff's concern for the children does not express his Christian forbearance of slavery's trials; it becomes a final provocation for his rebellion. To save these children, he steals them and joins Dred in the dismal swamp, thereby establishing the moral authority of the escaped slaves and condemning the white community for failure to protect its own offspring. Moreover, Cripps does not only act, he passes judgment: "Of all the pizen critters dat I knows on," he tells Dred, "dese yer mean white women is de pizinest! Dey an't got no manners, and no bringing up. Dey doesn't begin to know how tings ought fur do be done 'mong 'specable people" (412). Tiff, in ways Uncle Tom never would, voices the novel's condemnation of Mr. Cripps and Polly as types of the failed men and women slavery produces. He also remedies the deficiencies of both. He substitutes for the Cripps children's dead mother and also for their morally insensible father not only because he is the better man but because he is a better woman as well, a lively and sympathetic feminine sensibility coupled with a trenchant and judicial masculine agency that marks the efficacy of both his expansive sympathy and his trenchant judgments.[14]

The abuses slavery breeds, as depicted in *Dred,* require more than right feeling and expansive sentiment to reform them. In fact, the novel's central insight involves the fundamental antipathy of slavery to any ethos based on sympathy and therefore to any standard of common humanity as well. Judge Clayton, the father of the novel's white hero, finds himself constrained to explain and uphold the foundational logic of the slave system, which allows no latitude for right feeling or justice. As a judge, Clayton must overturn a lower court's conviction of a master who assaulted his old and faithful slave, Aunt Milly, thus overruling his own son (Milly's lawyer) and doing violence to his own sentiments. The judge makes clear that slavery must be inimical to both sentiment and justice because slavery affords no basis for social relations. It is a perpetual state of war that pits one class of persons against another and is, therefore, for both master and slave, beyond common morality altogether. Slavery, the judge asserts, differs from any other hierarchical human relation, for unlike parent and child, tutor and pupil, or master and apprentice, slavery offers those it subjects nothing but servitude:

What moral considerations shall be addressed to such a being, to convince him what it is impossible but that the most stupid must feel and know can never be true,—that he is thus to labor upon a principle of natural duty, or for the sake of his own personal happiness. Such services can only be expected from one who has no will of his own; who surrenders his will in implicit obedience to that of another. Such obedience is the consequence only of uncontrolled authority over the body. There is nothing else which can operate to produce that effect. THE POWER OF THE MASTER MUST BE ABSOLUTE, TO RENDER THE SUBMISSION OF THE SLAVER PERFECT. (353; emphasis in original)

Slavery, then, is not and cannot be made a system based on moral law or human justice. It is, as John Brown knew it was, a perpetual state of war in which the master, by essentially violent means, attempts to subjugate and exploit the slave. Such a system must violate any moral feeling. Judge Clayton continues:

I most freely confess my sense of the harshness of this proposition. I feel it as deeply as any man can. And, as a principle of moral right, every person in his retirement may repudiate it. But, in the actual condition of things, it must be so. There is no remedy. This discipline belongs to the state of slavery. They cannot be disunited without abrogating at once the rights of the master, and absolving the slave from his subjection. It constitutes the curse of slavery to both the bond and free portions of our population. But it is *inherent in the relation* of master and slave. (354; emphasis in original)

In the actual condition of things, "the value of the slaves," "the security of the master," and "the public tranquility" depend on the slave's perfect submission and abrogate any principle of Kantian reciprocity that might give sympathy play or realize justice (355). Ultimately the violence the law here sanctions expresses the essential nature of slavery and the necessary terror it entails: that the systematic violence of slavery would, as Jefferson feared it must, become general mayhem.[15]

Stowe's largely impotent white hero, Judge Clayton's son Edward, is less able than his father to realize the system's fundamental inequity. His belief that he can defend Milly is predicated on his inability to recognize that slavery has placed his fellow citizens beyond the reach of justice. As the narrator explains, "It was the fault of Clayton, and is the fault of all such men, that he judged mankind by himself. He could not believe that any-thing, except ignorance and inattention, could make men upholders of deliberate injustice." A belief in Kantian universals under such a system becomes not a virtue but a fault. Unlike his father, who knows that terror and self-interest distort humanity, young Edward believes enlightenment alone can reform slavery and that challenges to the system can be made on the basis of right feeling. "He thought all that was necessary was the enlight-ening of the public mind, the direction of general attention to the subject" (392). In the violent world in which he lives, such optimism is ill-founded and irresponsible. This is *Dred*'s discomfiting message.

Edward Clayton can never accept the knowledge his father and the world he lives in thrust before him. Much of the novel's action revolves around the sufferings endured by Harry, a light-skinned, well-educated slave who manages the plantation for his beloved white sister, Nina, and endures the aggressions of his white brother, Tom. The injustices Harry suffers multiply when his black sister, Cora Gordon, murders her children to save them from slavery and Tom threatens to rape Harry's wife. At this crucial point Edward, sympathetic to Harry's "rights" and the "oppression" and "injus-tice" that Harry and his people suffer, can do no better than advise Harry "to be patient" so that he might not "embitter the white race against them, and destroy that sympathy which many are beginning to feel for their oppressed condition" (442). But the very energy Stowe's own narrative re-leases, the stark implacability of the injustices and outrages visited on the enslaved, make Clayton's advice seem unequal to Harry's situation—even to Clayton himself who admits that it "seems very unfeeling" to counsel patience to one who is "oppressed and suffering." Stowe's reader feels the tragic inadequacy of patience in the face of such injustice because of slav-ery's essentially abusive nature (as Judge Clayton explains it) and because Stowe peoples her novel with characters who not only suffer injustice but also pass judgment on it and take on themselves resistance to it by what-ever means necessary.

Stowe thus represents the violence of the slave system and the justice of violent resistance to it. She thereby implies not only that the masters have reason to be afraid but that what they fear may be no more than their just deserts. The very aesthetic resources of the novel, its polyphonic capacity to voice different views, assists her in maintaining this point. She explains:

There is no study in human nature more interesting than the aspects of the same subject seen in the points of view of different characters. One might almost imagine that there were no such thing as absolute truth, since a change of situation or temperament is capable of changing the whole force of an argument. We have been accustomed, even those of us who feel most, to look on the arguments for and against the system of slavery with the eyes of those who are at ease. We do not even know how fair is freedom, for we were always free. We shall never have all the materials for absolute truth on this subject, till we take into account, with our own views and reasonings, the views and reasonings of those who have bowed down to the yoke, and felt the iron enter into their souls. We all console ourselves too easily for the sorrows of others. We talk and reason coolly of that which, did we feel it ourselves, would take away all power of composure and self-control. We have seen how the masters feel and reason; how good men feel and reason, whose public opinion and Christian fellowship support the master, and give him confidence in his position. We must add, also, to our estimate, the feelings and reasonings of the slave. (445)

Stowe's emphasis is not on feeling for the other but on imagining what the other's feelings might be. The form of the novel, with its capacity to offer space for imaginative attempts to realize a variety of visions of the world, becomes an engine in a revolution of feeling that cannot be, for a white reader, altogether pleasant. In *Dred,* Stowe works toward achieving this revolution of feeling most assiduously through her depiction of the novel's eponymous hero and the witness his voice bears to his judgment of the world.

Consider Dred's introduction to the reader, which Stowe delays until the last part of the first volume.[16] Harry Gordon, met and whipped by his brother Tom while returning to the plantation, must also listen to salacious threats against his wife. Tom departs, and the narrator says: "This last taunt flew like a Parthian arrow backward, and struck into the soul of the bond-man with even a keener power than the degrading blow. The sting of it seemed to rankle more bitterly as he rode along, till at last he dropped the reins on his horse's neck, and burst into a transport of bitter cursing" (197–98). As if materialized from Tom's violence and Harry's outrage, as if summoned by Harry's bitter cursing, Dred makes his first appearance. The narrative first notes a "deep voice," speaking from the "swampy thicket" by the roadside: "Aha! Aha! it has come nigh *thee,* and thou faintest!" (198; emphasis in original). The narrator then embodies this remarkable voice in a description worth quoting at length:

> He was a tall black man, of magnificent stature and proportions. His skin was intensely black, and polished like marble. A loose shirt of red flannel, which opened very wide at the breast, gave a display of a neck and chest of Herculean strength. The sleeves of the shirt, rolled up nearly to the shoulders, showed the muscles of a gladiator. The head, which rose with an imperial air from the broad shoulders, was large and massive, and developed with equal force both in the reflective and perceptive department. The perceptive organs jutted like dark ridges over the eyes, while that part of the head which phrenologists attribute to the moral and intellectual sentiments, rose like an ample dome above them. The large eyes had that peculiar and solemn effect of unfathomable blackness and darkness which is often a striking characteristic of the African eye. But there burned in them, like tongues of flame in a black pool of naphtha, a subtle and restless fire, that betokened habitual excitement to the verge of insanity. If any organs were predominant in the head, they were those of ideality, wonder, veneration, and firmness, and the whole combination was such as might have formed one of the wild old warrior prophets of the heroic ages. (198)

Certainly Stowe here fetishizes the black man's body. But she also manifests, by means of phrenology, his intellectual capacities—ideality, wonder, veneration, firmness, and ample endowments of moral and mental abilities. As a direct reply to racist science, like Morton's measurements of cranial capacity, Stowe's construction of a powerfully human interiority based on her reading of Dred's skull makes its polemical point with inspired efficiency.[17] When she places a red turban on that formidable head, she links her hero unmistakably with Nat Turner's terrifying figure of black revolt, and she offers justification for such violence from the slave's point of view and judgment.

Dred makes his point of view and judgment manifest in his varied and remarkable verbal performances. For while he often speaks in the prophetic vein with which he here begins, mining the rich veins of the American jeremiad to denounce the inequities and failures of principle he witnesses and experiences, Dred can shift codes. For example, his encounter with Harry continues at first in the high-flown diction with which he began as he chides

Harry for accepting privileges as plantation manager that blind him to his true position as a slave and to the real character of the system his labor helps support:

> Hast thou not eaten the fat and drunk the sweet with the oppressor, and hid thine eyes from the oppression of thy people? Have not *our* wives been for a prey, and thou has not regarded? Hath not our cheek been given to the smiter? Have we not been counted as sheep for the slaughter? But thou saidst, Lo! I knew it not, and didst hide thine eyes! Therefore, the curse of Meroz is upon thee, saith the Lord. And *thou* shalt bow down to the oppressor, and his rod shall be upon thee; and *thy* wife shall be for a prey! (199; emphasis in original)

When Harry protests that Dred is "raising the very devil in me!" Dred continues the attack in a more colloquial and ironic vein. "Dropping from the high tone he at first used to that of common conversation, and speaking in bitter irony," Dred goes on to mock not only the slave owner's Christianity but the ethos of patient moral suasion as well:

> "Did your master strike you? It's sweet to kiss the rod, isn't it? Bend your neck and ask to be struck again!—won't you? Be meek and lowly; that's the religion for you! You are a *slave,* and you wear broadcloth, and sleep soft. By and by he will give you a fip to buy salve for those cuts! Don't fret about your wife! Women always like the master better than the slave! Why wouldn't they? When a man licks his master's foot, his wife scorns him,—serves him right. Take it meekly, my boy! 'Servants obey your masters.' . . . Go! *you* are a slave! But, as for me," he said, drawing up his head, and throwing back his shoulders with a deep inspiration, "*I* am a free man! Free by this," holding out his rifle. (199; emphasis in original)

These are, for a white author, amazing imaginings. What's more, they have, despite the codifications of melodramatic diction and staging, a remarkable air of truth about them. Here is a black man who is master of his situation and master of his language. Here is an escaped slave who is armed, angry, dangerous, and right to be so. Moreover, he can explain for himself and for others the rectitude of this stance in language that cannot but be familiar to those reasonable Americans inclined to accept the common blandishments and insidious compromises of paternalistic morality and conventional Christian piety. He demands and is prepared to take justice in both word and act into his own hands. Dred is a creation of remarkable depth, power, and achievement, a triumph of identification that leads the reader far beyond the simple comforts of self-reflective sympathy to contemplate a dangerous encounter with one justly enraged by the injustices he suffers.

Dred describes those injustices in language terrifyingly familiar to his American audience. He is the avenging voice not only of God but of democracy. When he appears before a revival meeting and addresses the slaveholders who have come to indulge in the sort of easy, enthusiastic Christianity that helped make slavery palatable, he speaks "with a deep sonorous power in the voice . . . and the words fell pealing down through the air like the vibrations of some mighty bell." It is the voice of an American prophet who speaks these frightening words:

> Take away from me the noise of thy songs, and the melody of thy viols; for I will not hear them, saith the Lord. I hate and despise your feast days! I will not smell in your solemn assemblies; for your hands are defiled with blood, and your fingers are greedy for violence! Will ye kill, and steal, and commit adultery, and swear falsely, and come and stand before *me,* saith the Lord? Ye oppress the poor and needy, and hunt the stranger; also in thy skirts is found the blood of poor innocents! And yet ye say, Because I am clean shall his anger pass from me! Hear this, ye that swallow up the needy, and make the poor land to fail, saying, When will the noon moon be gone, that we may sell corn? that we may buy the poor for silver, and the needy for a pair of shoes? The Lord hath sworn, saying, I will never forget their works. I will surely visit you! (262; emphasis in original)

Drawing on the Hebrew prophets—on Joel (2:1–2), Amos (5:18), and Moses himself (Exodus 13:10)—Dred goes beyond the limits of the jeremiad and does not merely interpret God's will but actually speaks in God's words.[18] He not only performs a deeply impressive interiority, he also assumes a dimension of transcendent authority. But Dred's impersonation of the deity does more to explain man to himself than it does to explain God to man. Dred's imprecations of inequity point up the violation by these men and women not merely of God's will but of their own professed values. That is the democratic meaning of these strong words from an enraged black man. He speaks in the voice of God, but he speaks of the people's outrage. As Nina herself reminds us, in a democracy the "voice of the people is the voice of God" (255). Dred's democratic jeremiad, his appropriation of the republic's and not the church's values, makes him the moral center of this novel and a terrifying embodiment and realization of his nation's fears. Stowe demands that her readers confront their own inequity in the right-eous anger of a black man who speaks from his own inner conviction and condemns them.

Where Edward Clayton could only advise patience, Dred, like Nat Turner, foments rebellion, slave terror in resistance to the terrors of slavery, even if such a rebellion should fail, even if it mean inevitable death:

> "Let us die, then!" said Dred. "What if we do die? What great matter is that? If they bruise our head, we can sting their heels! Nat Turner—they killed him; but the fear of him almost drove them to set free their slaves! Yes, it was argued among them. They came within two or three votes of it in their assembly. A little more fear, and they would have done it. If my father had succeeded, the slaves in Carolina would be free to-day. Die?—Why not die? Christ was crucified! Has everything dropped out of you that can't die— that you'll crawl like worms, for the sake of living?" (341)

Dred's appropriation of both Nat Turner and Christ models not a femi-nized ability to suffer but a manly resolve to meet violence with violence and visit justice on the perpetrators. Stowe means Dred to terrify her readers not to comfort them.

Though his rebellion fails, Dred succeeds in reflecting the terrible vio-lence of slavery back on its real perpetrators. Their own violence indicates that they continue to misrecognize both him and themselves. And yet when he comes to die, Stowe offers his death as yet another variation on the theme of the good death. Dred's death before he can lead his threatened rebellion allows Stowe to avoid tipping the scales of sympathy and terror too definitely against the justice of her hero's cause. Nonetheless, instead of focusing on the sentimental appreciation of the reward to come at the moment of his passing, Dred—who receives his mortal wound while attempting to rescue a slave from a drunken lynch mob—enjoins this world, "O, earth, earth, earth! Cover thou not my blood!" (513). Dred demands that his death be remembered not as a token of eternal reward but as a sign of continuing

injustices. He demands that he become an example of violent resistance
and redemptive manhood, like Nat Turner, for those who will follow and,
in turn, terrorize their oppressors. Their violence will be no more than the
just deserts of an unjust nation.[19]

NAT TURNER AND THE MIRROR OF THE OTHER, OR REPRESENTING TERROR

Remembering Nat Turner has been more difficult than Dred hoped. This
became most interestingly evident during the controversy provoked by
William Styron's novel, *The Confessions of Nat Turner,* which appeared in
1967 and reintroduced twentieth-century white audiences to the black revolutionary. The controversy was more interesting than the novel itself. For
Styron and for the mostly white critics who championed his book, Nat
Turner, who had been largely forgotten by the dominant culture, provided
an opportunity to air their problematic ideas about an increasingly restive
and threatening African-American presence in the nation's imagination.[20]
For many African-American readers and critics, for whom Nat Turner had
remained a popular folk hero, Styron and his apologists failed to do Turner
justice, and that failure became an occasion for them to address America's
persistent failure to deal equitably with race. This controversy over Styron's
novel resumed the struggle over Nat Turner's memory that began with
Thomas Gray's publication of the original *Confessions of Nat Turner* in 1831.

Styron's self-proclaimed desire "to *know* the Negro" and thereby fulfill
"the moral imperative of every white Southerner," may be taken seriously.[21]
To attribute motives and to explore psychology has long been the province
of novelists, and Styron wants to feel right about having imaginatively
crossed the color line in the interests of more universal forms of understanding. Sometimes, as with *Dred,* such efforts do culminate in triumphs
of narrative imagination with serious moral implications. But Styron's response to the controversy his novel provoked, more than the controversy
itself, indicates that this desire to know the "Negro" can also result in baf-
flement and defeat. Sympathetic identification, while necessary, remains
treacherous.

Styron's Nat Turner has it exactly right when he says, on the evening of
that murderous raid, that everything depends "on how you view what came
to pass in Jerusalem."[22] Whether or not one views Turner's rebellion as a
blow for freedom by oppressed slaves or an outbreak of senseless savagery

by brutal fanatics—ultimately whether or not one views slavery itself as benign paternalism or violent oppression—makes all the difference in the type of interiority one can imaginatively construct for the rebellion's leader and for the "Negro" one wants, like Styron, to know. In one way or another Styron's angry black critics attempt to make him aware of a different perspective on Turner and slavery that separates the white Southerner's viewpoint from their own. Unfortunately, Styron, despite his desire to "know the Negro," seems incapable of hearing what black people say. This becomes interesting to the extent that Styron's personal incapacity duplicates what has too often been a national failure.

No one, of course, can really listen to Nat Turner. Recent commentary, ranging from Eric J. Sundquist's influential study of the *Confessions* to Charles Burnett's documentary film reenactment, *Nat Turner: A Troublesome Property* (2003), makes abundantly clear that there is no discernable Nat Turner apart from the troubled and troubling repetitions of "his" legend.[23] Accounts of what happened that summer night begin with the odd and tendentious "confessions" themselves, "taken down" and reworked by the imprisoned leader's court-appointed counsel. Gray's desire to correct the "thousand idle, exaggerated and mischievous reports" about the rebellion that had "greatly excited the public mind" controls his presentation of Turner. The slave's confession, Gray explains, "reads an awful, and it is hoped, a useful lesson, as to the operations of a mind like his, endeavoring to grapple with things beyond its reach. How it first became bewildered and confounded, and finally corrupted and led to the conception and perpetration of the most atrocious and heart-rending deeds."[24] Gray invents an interior dimension for Turner that reduces the black rebel's recognizable humanity in order to quell white Southern panic. More generous forms of identification remain beyond the lawyer's reach, too much for the operations of a mind like his to grapple with.

For Gray, and for his readers, Turner and his rebellion cannot signify violence met by violence, the resistance of identifiable human subjects to an inhuman situation, a state of war provoking warlike acts that will continue to threaten white society until the injustices motivating them are rectified. Instead, the terrible violence Turner and his confederates unleashed on Southampton County, Virginia, on August 23, 1831, must confirm the unfathomable difference and darkness of Turner's mind.[25] Like others of his race, Gray suggests, Turner has been befuddled by learning what he cannot understand, bedazzled rather than enlightened by religious zeal and the ability to read. Gray reduces the rebellion's demand for freedom and retribution to the result of confusion and misunderstanding, a demonstration that men like Turner never can and never should be free.

Thus, the moral Gray points up in Turner's tale proves the wisdom and necessity of stern reprisals and more stringent oppressions:

> [Nat's story] is calculated also to demonstrate the policy of our laws in restraint of this class of our population, and to induce all those entrusted with their execution, as well as our citizens generally, to see that they are strictly and rigidly enforced. . . . [The rebellion] was not instigated by motives of revenge or sudden anger, but the results of long deliberation, and a settled purpose of mind. The offspring of gloomy fanaticism, acting upon materials but too well prepared for such impressions. It will be long remembered in the annals of our country, and many a mother as she presses her infant darling to her bosom, will shudder at the recollection of Nat Turner, and his band of ferocious miscreants.[26]

To characterize Turner's motivations as gloomy fanaticism allays the even starker terrors attached to recognizing the alternative possibility, that the violence of slavery breeds the violence of the resistance to it and justifies that violence as well. It is this terror, the terror Jefferson experienced when considering that injustices borne by the slave must eventually rebound on the masters, that Gray seeks to assuage "by removing doubts and conjectures from the public mind which otherwise must have remained" (42). Turner's name may continue to make white women and their children shudder, but for Gray the implications of the slave's revolt will remain carefully contained by the slave's propensity toward gloomy fanaticism and mad savagery. This version of Nat's story simultaneously reinforces the apparently contradictory beliefs that on the one hand slavery is benign and paternalistic and on the other that slave society requires increasingly oppressive laws to prevent further outbreaks of violence.

In assuming Gray's title, Stryon also assumes Gray's view of his subject as a gloomy and savage fanatic.[27] He seems no more capable of imagining a legitimate justification for black insurrection than was Turner's first redactor. Instead, Styron gives Turner a bruised and damaged psyche, a mind beset by smothered resentments and frustrated sexual desires that occasionally find expression in homosexual acts and eventually lead to murder. Styron gives Turner's murderous savagery more complex motivations than Gray's fanatic required. He invents a thoroughly modern antihero (that familiar ornament of postwar American popular culture), a nearly neurasthenic hysteric who actually fails to lead the rebellion he starts. In Styron's novel, Turner commits his only successful act of violence when he bludgeons to death the young white woman whose unavailable pink flesh, more than slavery's injustices, provokes him to rebel.

Sexual frustration becomes the central motivation in the novel and the determining factor in Turner's life. Styron's *Confessions* reads more like *Portnoy's Complaint* or *Rebel without a Cause*—despite its obvious borrowings from *Native Son*—than the story of the most terrifying black figure in American history. In a nation reeling from political assassinations and urban insurrections, the novel was, of course, an instant critical and popular success. Like Thomas Gray, Styron made the threat of black rebellion comprehensible as pathology and distanced it from politics and ethics. As Albert Stone puts it, Styron's Turner encouraged "white readers to feel at home inside . . . black consciousness."[28] But in a moment of African-American resurgence, Styron found himself constrained to confront the angry criticism of black intellectuals and writers who failed to recognize Styron's Nat Turner as their own and who felt themselves dispossessed by the consciousness the novelist imagined. In their anger, Styron confronted the possibility that his sympathies and his belief in his own right feelings may have led him astray. *The Confessions of Nat Turner* becomes a case study of sympathetic identification gone desperately wrong, an imaginative failure that successfully raises important questions about history and identity in the United States, the implications of which should convince any reader that right feeling is seldom to be trusted.

John Henrik Clarke borrowed words from Herbert Aptheker to frame the collection of essays that became the controversy's key text, *William Styron's Nat Turner: Ten Black Writers Respond*. "History's potency is mighty," Aptheker wrote. "The oppressed need it for identity and inspiration: oppressors for justification, rationalization, and legitimacy. Nothing illustrates this more clearly than the history writing on the American Negro people."[29] In the relationship of history and identity lies the reason for the anger and dismay Styron's novel generated among black intellectuals and readers. Far from being something new, Styron's vision of Nat Turner seemed like just more of the same brutalizing and demoralizing history writing on American blacks, another example of white Americans failing to hear or understand what black Americans had to say. By challenging Styron's appropriation of Nat Turner, the black writers Clarke collected attempted to regain possession of themselves. Without understanding the dynamic relation of history and identity, this contestation of representations and of selves, no one can understand why Nat Turner remains so troubling a figure. Styron did not have this aspect of history in mind when he described his novel in its preface as a "meditation on history."[30]

Ernest Kaiser, one of John Clarke's "ten black writers," offered an annotated guide to the many fawning reviews that Styron's volume garnered.[31] He makes two crucial points applicable to the novelist and his champions: first, that "having rejected the Negro people's history, Styron cannot see Turner as the hero he was and as the Negro people see him; as a *slave* who led a heroic rebellion against the dehumanization of chattel slavery"; and second, that "reviewers of Styron's *The Confessions* have seized upon this book as pointing up the current Negro ghetto uprisings as led by mad Negroes, as futile, stupid rebellions which should be put down ruthlessly." For Kaiser, Styron's meditation on history seems all too active an intervention into a contemporary crisis. Ultimately, he charges, Styron has failed to learn anything about black Americans from his own historical moment, one marked by "twelve years of the Negro social revolution and struggle in the U.S." This contemporary failure to understand black Americans precludes his ability to understand the history he presumes to narrate.[32] The failure to identify with black people and their struggles in the present vitiates the novelist's ability to identify with a black hero who resisted injustice in the past.

As Loyle Hairston in the same volume puts it, this failure to identify becomes a novelistic and aesthetic failure to create a believable character: "Nat Turner, the literary creation, suffers the same fate as his real-life namesake: he is enslaved. He is not allowed to speak his own piece, to give expression to sentiments and passions which are born of the slave's tragic experience."[33] Charles V. Hamilton follows this line of reasoning, observing that Styron's novel fails not because the author fails to register difference but because he does not recognize the universal humanity possessed by black as well as white Americans: "The important thing is that the desire for human freedom resides in the black breast as well as in any other. . . . Man—black or white or yellow or red—moves to maximize his freedom: THAT is the lesson of

Nat Turner that Styron did not deal with."[34] That lesson of history links identity and universality, bridging the different understandings of those positioned differently in the world. Styron's novel fails because he fails to imagine adequately both the nature of the differences actually dividing white and black subjects and the principled demand for justice that should unite them.

Mike Thelwell specifies that Styron's novel disappoints not because it is historically wrong but because the story it tells fails to be novel enough: "This is not to say that it had no basis in reality, but that there were other realities which are not shown."[35] Styron fails to realize the novel's capacity to consider other points of view and to explore what those other realities might mean. For all the heated rhetoric that sometimes agitates the black critical response to *The Confessions of Nat Turner,* all these complaints seem reasonable enough. They demand not simply a vindication of an essential identity before the bar of historical judgment but an effort to correct or at least to expand America's story and its contemporary imagination, especially where these have most notably failed when confronted by the subject of race. Any white, Northern or Southern, really interested in learning about "Negroes" might have listened to what these black intellectuals had to say.

Albert Murray, whose piece on Styron appeared in the *New Leader* of December 1967, before Clarke's volume was published, may have best expressed what most of these black writers were saying. He faults Styron not for his racism or ill will but for the failure of his imagination, a failure to do justice to Nat Turner. This failure, Murray suggests, is particularly Styron's but is a characteristic of the "white American writer" who "is either unable or unwilling to bring himself to make a truly intimate and personal identification with his chosen black protagonist." This seems especially true, Murray continues, when it is a matter of "a storybook hero." Then the writer seems compelled "to equate the strongest Negroes with the most helpless."[36] As Murray makes clear, there was already a version of Nat Turner forming part of America's national narrative, at least for many African Americans. Southern black children during "Negro History Week" celebrated Nat Turner as "a magnificent forefather enshrined in the National Pantheon beside the greatest heroes of the Republic." This Nat Turner was an American "epic hero," "a special breed of man who had given his last full measure of devotion to liberation and dignity" (18–19). Murray describes the black revolutionary in phrases borrowed from the nation's richly idealized history of resistance and rebellion. He even goes that history one better, for where Patrick Henry and Tom Paine thought and wrote revolutionary words, Nat actually embodied revolutionary principles in terrible deeds. Murray's account of Turner as a black American hero suggests some reasons why the black leader has remained difficult for white Americans to accept. He not only challenges white complacencies, he tends to turn the national narrative inside out.[37]

For Murray, the problem is emphatically not reducible to cross-racial identification; it is caused by Styron's failure to imagine Turner, the black insurgent, adequately. Murray claims that barbershop commentators, black intellectuals, and even black nationalists looked forward to the novelty of a celebrated white novelist taking a black hero as his subject. But Styron's version of Turner remains too irredeemable, too much the result of white fantasies and fears.[38] This is a particular shame, Murray concludes, because the black version of Turner was already so perfectly attuned to literary adaptation. Murray implies, though he doesn't quite specify, the reason for Styron's failure to realize the potential of his own materials: a typical white inability to confront the existence of principled and justified black violence, violence justified by precisely the principles of freedom and the justice that America has failed to embody. Murray's final point is not that cross-racial identification is impossible or undesirable. His point is that Styron's novel fails aesthetically and imaginatively because Styron fails to confront his own identity and fears in the face of what Nat Turner might tell him about himself, his region, and his nation.

In the face of this controversy, Styron understandably assumed a defensive posture of aggrieved virtue and baffled good intentions. His own account of the novel's reception ultimately reveals much more about his motives and desires than the author probably intended. These make the representative character of his failure in *The Confessions of Nat Turner* more painfully apparent. In a fascinating afterword to the 1992 reissue of his novel, Styron tells how in November 1967 he found himself at Wilberforce University, a historically black institution in Ohio, to receive an honorary degree: "There was no hint of the gathering storm. The angry word had not yet gone out. In a sea of smiling black and brown people I was greeted with good will, thanks, praise." Styron associates this moment with "Martin Luther King, Jr.'s grand and impossible dream" and restates his own belief that "an increased awareness of the history of the Negro [he notes

the historical provenance of this term] . . . especially of Negro slavery, would
allow people of both races to come to terms with the often inexplicable turmoil of the present." His own inability to come to terms with the turmoil
his novel provoked passes without comment here. For the moment he basks
in the waves of good feeling originating in this undifferentiated mass of positive regard, a sea of smiling black and brown faces that beam their approval
but do not talk back. The possibility that he might have, in the estimation
of any of these faces, misunderstood the history he has attempted to narrate seems impossibly remote. Recalling that they all sang "The Battle Hymn
of the Republic," Styron reflects back on that now difficult to imagine and
impossibly brief era of good feeling in which the "grand and impossible
dream" of racial justice and the beaming faces of black gratitude seemed
to be parts of the same harmonious moment. Then the storm of black protest and criticism broke in on him and shattered his hopes:

> Standing in that auditorium, I was moved by a feeling of oneness with these
> people. I felt gratitude at their acceptance of me and, somehow more impor-
> tantly, at my acceptance of them, as if my literary labors and my plunge into
> history had helped dissolve many of my preconceptions about race, which
> had been my birthright as a Southerner and allowed me to better understand
> the forces that had shaped our common destiny. For me it was a moment
> of intense warmth and brotherhood. It would have been inconceivable to
> me that within a short time I would experience almost total alienation from
> black people, be stung by their rage, having unwittingly created one of the
> first politically incorrect texts of our time.[39]

It is difficult not to be moved and baffled by the piety and the perversity
of Styron's hopes and by the peculiar mixture of good intention and blind-
ing narcissism in this passage: the rush of warmth and brotherhood, Styron's sense that his self-regard has been confirmed by this black audience's
reception of his work. Though he gives no black face an actual voice, Styron feels that he has not only crossed but actually erased the color line. He
feels himself buoyed by generous sentiments and sustained by a sea of mute
black admiration. Most miraculously, in a bizarre orgy of self-congratulation,
he notes the broad sympathies that allow him, as a Southerner, to accept—
and be grateful for—this association with black Americans. But the good
feeling cannot last. Styron's self-regard meets with bitter disappointment

and an "almost total alienation" from "black people." Remarkably, even after black artists and writers articulated their criticisms of his work, "black people" seem to remain, in Styron's imagination, an undifferentiated mass, a sea of faces primarily defined by their acceptance or rejection of him. For Styron, the attempt to understand "the Negro" by attempting to understand the history of Nat Turner is not about the Negro or history at all but about himself and that sea of black faces in which he admires his own achievement. Like some sentimental readers, since Styron is certain that he himself feels right, he cannot imagine why anyone should feel differently. Not only Styron's novelistic imagination but his sense of what justice entails seem sadly inadequate to the subject of race and the history of the United States.

Styron's defense of his novel manifests precisely the projective narcissism that so many black critics found vitiated in his attempt to portray a black folk hero. The fracas over *The Confessions of Nat Turner* seems in Styron's imagination to be only about his own dreams, hopes, and terrors and not really about any other subject at all. As John Oliver Killens put it, this is as much a failure to understand the differences in perspective entailed by positioning along the color line as it is a failure to project oneself imaginatively across that color line:

> I don't say that William Styron is dishonest. I imagine he is as honest as he can be, granted his racial backwardness. I'm saying that it is impossible for the slavemaster's grandson to see the revolutionary black man in the sense that Gabriel saw himself, as the "George Washington" of his people, ready to lay down his life for their liberation. I repeat: What we have in this new novel is not the confessions of Nat Turner, but rather the confessions (unintentional to be sure) of Master William Styron, White Anglo-Saxon Southern Protestant. Moreover they are confessions which reveal that Styron has progressed but a very short distance from the attitudes of his grandfather. He is still in desperate need of emancipation from his slavemaster's psychology. He remains until this very day an unreconstructed southern rebel.[40]

This stings and is no doubt meant to. But Styron's patronizing characterization of the "intellectual squalor" of his black critics and his dismissing of their "major complaint" against him ("how dare a white man write so intimately of the black experience, even *presuming* to become Nat Turner by speaking in the first person?") suggests that he continues to miss the point that his critics repeatedly made.[41] The problem wasn't his presuming to imagine a black character but of having failed to do so adequately and in a way that repeated rather than challenged the most perniciously received ideas about black identity in the United States. Again and again, in a variety of ways and with a range of rhetorical intensities, the complaint is not that this is primarily a "malicious book" but that it is an artistic and therefore—given its historical subject matter and its author's expressed desire to understand the Negro—a moral and political failure. As Mike Thelwell summarizes his argument and the argument of many of Styron's critics:

> If this book is important, it is so not because it tells much about Negro experience during slavery but because of the manner in which it demonstrates the persistence of white southern myths, racial stereotypes, and literary clichés even in the best intentioned and most enlightened minds. Their largely uncritical acceptance in literary circles shows us how far we still have to go. The real "history" of Nat Turner, and indeed of black people, remains to be written.[42]

Styron's book misses the real problem with history itself: as Stowe knew, the facts of history depend desperately on who is telling the story and on his or her willingness to entertain identifications that may reflect poorly on his or her own identity. For Styron's black critics, the novel does not represent the failure of a white imagination to encompass what Styron himself calls the "exotic territory" of the black experience.[43] Repeatedly they indicate the familiar desires for freedom and justice that might help map the terrain. But *The Confessions of Nat Turner* attempts to tell the story of a black folk hero from the limited perspective of a white man's fears and therefore botches the job. That Styron believed he could understand black Americans without attempting to understand their hopes and aspirations and anger, without learning to listen to the stories that they themselves might have to tell, may be the most remarkable aspect of this telling episode of literary history as literary failure.

Consider the striking terms in which Styron, twenty-five years after the publication of *The Confessions of Nat Turner* and decades after the controversies it had provoked, reflected on his own motivations for writing the novel:

Although of course I was an outsider, I fell under the spell of *negritude,* fascinated by black people and their folkways, their labor and religion and especially their music, their raunchy blues and ragtime and their spirituals that reached for, and often attained, the sublime. Like some young boys who are troubled by the "unnatural" sexual longings, I felt a similar anxiety about my secret passion for blackness; in my closet I was fearful lest any of my conventionally racist young friends discover that I was an unabashed enthusiast of the despised Negro. I don't claim a special innocence. Most white people were, and are, racist to some degree but at least my racism was not conventional; I wanted to confront and understand blackness.[44]

Styron continues to defend his right to right feeling, the very complacency that blunts his ability to effectively imagine the threats and promises of insurgent violence in the United States that Nat Turner embodied. Like any passage of self-consciousness, Styron's account of himself comes easily apart into evasions, misrecognitions, and revelations. The disclaimer as to special innocence is, of course, disingenuous. There is nothing special about the sort of fetishization that characterizes Styron's fascination with blackness. The cultural and historical record of these United States makes clear that this is no alternative to conventional racism but one of its most familiar characteristics. To fetishize the other is, of course, to avoid a living encounter with the other and to make the understanding that Styron believes he desires to further impossible to achieve.

Most revealing here, and the passage's real surprise, is the analogy Styron makes between his fascination with black culture (in itself this requires no explanation) and unspecified but "unnatural" sexual longings. By these the reader must understand a reference to the closet that appears in the paragraph's very next line. Styron's only real identification with Nat Turner might have come during the notorious scene when he imagines Nat's one achieved sexual act as a homosexual coupling. Moreover, and more interesting, the novel's central obsession with Margaret Whitehead's death may represent considerably more than a familiar retailing of racist fears about black rapists. Nat recognizes that the white girl might actually want him to desire her. In this moment, Styron creates a more poignant point of identification for himself within his story than the black leader whose internal life he never really gets. Like her author, Margaret may well harbor an "unnatural" longing that a black man should love her. Styron, perhaps unwittingly and perhaps anxiously, identifies himself with his young white woman victimized by the big black man whose rage she never anticipated and can't understand. In her prattling on about her own concerns she fails to imagine—and the prattling functions to make this imagining impossible—what her desire suggests she already knows, that Nat Turner is in fact a man.

When Styron finds himself attacked, even reviled, by the black men whose love he desired, he might have taken the occasion to confront the meaning of his own desires and to recognize in them something more than the fetishized distortion of his own demand for love and commendation. The failure to recognize his own place in his attempts to imagine the other, the failure to recognize that it is not his place to feel right as he undertakes this task, entails Styron's failure to do justice to Nat Turner or the history he represents. It is a common failure in imaginings and identifications across the terrible chasm of the color line that still divides American society and that still demands that Americans undertake the difficult and dangerous task of doing justice to each other. Neither Nat Turner nor the nation that failed him can be understood without renewed and discomfiting attempts to accomplish this realization.

JOHN BROWN: NATIONAL IDENTIFICATION AND HISTORICAL JUSTICE IN A CONTEMPORARY NOVEL

The nineteenth-century man who most effectively evoked and assumed the terrifying tradition of black insurgency was white. John Brown not only studied Nat Turner's rebellion, he identified with its leader. A century and a half later, in a nation still fascinated by the color line, Brown's cross-racial identification has made his career an object of scholarly attempts by literary historians like John Stauffer and David Reynolds to rethink questions of race, identity, and justice in America. But perhaps the most compelling essay in this line exploits the aesthetics of identification central to the traditional novel's appeal in precisely those ways that Stryon's treatment of Turner failed to do. Russell Banks's *Cloudsplitter* (1998), like Child's and Stowe's novels before him, reaffirms the role a novelist can play in questioning the nature and disrupting the limitations of America's social imagination and national identity. *Cloudsplitter,* like its nineteenth-century precursors, revolves around problems of sympathetic identification and racial identity and deploys the aesthetics of the novel to interrogate requirements of justice.

Banks invents an elderly Owen Brown as his novel's narrator. The sole surviving son of the terrorist, Owen continuously worries over the meaning of the past, reconsidering the terrible deeds in which he played a fatal part and reanalyzing the problematic identifications and troublesome identities that urged his father and brothers onward. Writing to Miss Mayo, a research assistant to John Villard who, decades after Harpers Ferry, is writing his father's first scholarly biography, Owen struggles to understand himself and his father and to do justice to both their high ideals and the low acts those ideals seemed to require. Owen's haunted, self-reflective narrative gives the novel its psychological urgency and moral drama. For example, remarking on his family's transformation from angry activists to cold-blooded killers, Owen repeatedly reworks his statements and in doing so uncovers a gap between identity and identification wherein he locates their motivation: "We were," Owen says, "becoming like Negroes, or wanted to become like them. Or, to be honest and exact, we were becoming the kind of men and women that we wanted Negroes themselves to be."[45] Thus, Brown and sons play the part and assume the aspirations of intellectuals of no very organic type. By identifying themselves with black men, they hope not simply to become black but to remake and reform the identities with which they identify.

John Brown becomes, to borrow Owen's insight, the violently rebellious black man he wants black men to become. The identification is sincere and troubling. Owen suspects that "at bottom" his father believed that "he himself" along with the entire family "was a Negro." "He seemed to believe that his white skin—and the skins of his children, too, and of his wife, and the skin of anyone who would cleave to him in his enterprise—was black underneath." Owen makes his father's belief seem ridiculous in ways Banks's readers must find discomfiting. "As if," Owen continues, "his old-fashioned, pointy, New England Yankee face, that long narrow hooked nose, grim slash of a mouth, and large red ears, were a mask hiding an African nose, mouth, and ears" (415). The minstrel masks in white and black that Owen imagines defining his father's multilayered sense of himself are caricatures but establish an important point. The promiscuity of the white man's cross-racial identification may be—as John Stauffer and David Reynolds suggest—a transformative moment in the history of race.[46] But it's hard to simply feel good about what this entails. Brown's masks reveal an underlying and persistent gap that makes any identity, however serious and indispensable, faintly ridiculous as well. Brown's identification indicates how friable and fungible identity is and how crucially important it remains to the changing ways in which one grasps one's place in the world and one's obligations toward justice. The identities that Owen explores depend not only on contingent identifications with other people but also on a transcendental identification with a principle of justice. They are, that is to say, ridiculous caricatures and serious delimitations of American identities at one and the same time.

Whatever the errors of fetishization or misunderstandings involved in John Brown's adaptations of black identity, they enact the imaginative ability to put oneself in the other's place that any realization of justice requires. Owen's father first came to know "that Negroes were as human as" himself when, as a child of twelve, he saw an enslaved boy being beaten and realized that "it was as if I myself were being insulted and beaten" (420). The masochistic urgency and the ethical burden of such sympathetic exchanges of identity seem endlessly complex. Who can explain why some white men and women identify with the sadistic master rather than the suffering slave? It is on such erotic and narrative contingencies, such identifications and failures to identify, that morality, ethics, and politics find their shifting and unstable foundations.

Owen finds no way of imagining himself in his world and in relation to the issues of his day that does not require recognizing the contingencies and exigencies of race. His father, Owen explains, "took race to be the central and inescapable fact of American life and character, and thus he did not apologize for its being the central fact of his own life and character" (421). Race in Owen's America is inescapable because denying its saliency, as much as asserting its centrality, only reaffirms its importance. Consider Owen's comments on white Americans who believe themselves capable of escaping the color of their skin:

> Amongst Negroes, a white man is always white; they cannot forget it, and therefore neither can he. It's only amongst whites that he suddenly turns colorless, is privileged to forget his skin, is allowed to move inside it, as it were. But beware, because if he does forget his skin, he becomes like them— he becomes another, specially privileged white man, a man who thinks the word "colored" does not apply to him. No, in America, whites are as much stuck with their skin color and bannered by it as the Negroes, and the Indians and Orientals, too. We may be a society founded on racial differences,

a society poisoned at the root, perhaps, but we also aspire to be a democracy. Thus, until we have truly become a democracy, every American, white as much as black, red, or yellow, lives not in his skin but on it. (423)

Owen recognizes that the continued failure of America determines the continued importance of race. For the Browns as for their nation, injustice proceeds and determines identity. Americans, like John Brown, may forge their own identities but, as with history, no American can do so just as he pleases.

For a white person, Owen argues, justice requires forgoing the privilege of invisibility that whiteness confers and thus identifying with the suffering of those African slavery marks for bondage. "Paradoxically, then," Owen writes, "it is when a white person *resists* the privilege of turning colorless that he frees himself, at least partially, from the sickness of racialism" (423; emphasis in the original). The cost of such identifications is to assume the perpetual ironic distance of the disengaged analyst or the omniscient narrator: "He has to separate himself from the luxurious unconsciousness that characterizes his own race, without claiming as his own the historical experience of the other. There is a price, though. He pays with cold loneliness, an itching inner solitude, a permanent feeling of separation from his tribe. He has to be willing to lose his own history without gaining another" (424). Such a person must realize that no race or history or people are ever simply or organically his own. That realization becomes not the liberation of the individual from identity but the recognition that each individual finds himself constrained to act up or through his identifications and disidentifications with the identities around him. "Feeling right," if it were possible for a such a person, could never be an adequate guide for these ethical reflections. None of this introspection and analysis, none of this identification with higher principles and ethical imperatives, protects anyone from the possibility that their identifications and judgments might lead to errors. Owen believes his father has led him astray, causing him to do things that could be "wholly evil" (446). Not only the failed raid on Harpers Ferry but the cold-blooded murder of five proslavery farmers in Kansas—pragmatically justifiable in light of the justice of Brown's struggle against slavery—keep Owen's mind and his narrative voice disturbed. He does not so much fear his just deserts as he cannot be certain what that justice might be.

Behind Banks's portrait of Brown's high principles and doomed leadership stands not only Curry's *Tragic Prelude* and Nat Turner's terrors, but Melville's magnificent failure, Captain Ahab. The last words in *Moby Dick* furnish *Cloudsplitter*'s epigraph: "And I alone am escaped to tell thee."[47] Like Ishmael, Owen finds that his endless self-questionings and skeptical reserve cannot save him or his brothers from his father's terrible end, the end that defines his place in American history by martyring him to American principles in their most terrible and uncompromising form. It is Owen, therefore, who most closely represents for the reader what it is like to live and act in the nation that John Brown exemplified and terrorized, to have to choose sides in a desperate struggle where terrible means and laudable ends seem to clash in any determined effort to redeem the nation's failure.

Brown's legend links his attempts to redeem American principles to his repulsively violent crimes. His principles and the nation's avowed ideals were identical. Consider, as Owen Banks reports it, the oath his father asks him to compose for the League of Gileadites, an armed band of Massachusetts whites and blacks sworn to resist, by force if necessary, slave catchers and the civil authorities who supported them: "As legitimate citizens of the United States of America, trusting in a just and merciful God, whose spirit and all-powerful aid we humbly implore, we pledge that we will ever be true to the flag of our beloved country, always acting under it" (440). To resist the country in the country's defense, to recall the nation to its own best self, this is the work of an American prophet, a democratic Jeremiah armed with civic rhetoric and a loaded rifle and determined to secure "the enjoyment of our inalienable rights" for all (439). As Owen listens to his father read his composition of these national themes aloud, the words return him to himself. But that self, like the nation with which he identifies, turns out to be morally compromised and irreducibly complex:

> To hear my words spoken in his resonating, public-hall voice by Father to a sober-faced audience of people who, because of those words, were made ready to take up arms and slay the enemy was wonderfully thrilling to me, and I felt the blood course up and down my arms and could scarcely repress a smile from my lips. I trembled with joy, as much for the meaning of the words and the pictures they painted in my own mind of making quick and bloody work of my enemies, as for the occasion of hearing Father speak them. (439)

Owen finds himself caught up in a morally dangerous conflation of filial sentiment and righteous rage. His narration of these events reveals the questionable bases on which he makes necessary judgments and the uncomfortable truth that justice may require acts that justice cannot redeem. This is John Brown's truth as Owen knows it, "the truth about Father and why he did the great, good things and the bad, and why so much of what he did was, at bottom, horrendous, shocking, was wholly evil" (446). He only upheld the values of justice and liberty for all people that the republic he attacked demanded its citizens to uphold. If that republic violated its own most fundamental principles, its sole legitimate reason for being, did not justice itself require its destruction of any just man be he black or white? But justice, for Owen, becomes mingled with patricidal impulses and oedipal urges, a horrific transport intensified for Owen by hearing his own call for rebellion against his fatherland in his own father's voice. Does such a vortex of emotions and motives leave any room for right judgment or right feeling? *Cloudsplitter* intensifies the terrors that make the figure of domestic insurgency, the figure that John Brown and Nat Turner embodied, impossible for America's national narrative to contain.

Near the midpoint of his novel, Banks stages a fantasy meeting aboard a ship in midsea. Traveling to England with his father, Owen wrestles with seasickness and moral dread born of his inability to share his father's zealous certitude. He momentarily befriends a young woman, pregnant out of wedlock and fleeing to Europe to escape scandal. Their brief encounter occurs on deck one wind-tossed night during which these two tormented individuals exchange their stories. The reader soon realizes that the woman is not only Nathaniel Hawthorne's sister-in-law but that she carries Hawthorne's child. When Owen—trying to be sympathetic—remarks on the shameful price she finds herself constrained to pay, she replies:

"Yes, I must pay the price. At least publicly. There's your 'shame,' Owen. *My* shame. Although it must also be my child's. But *he* [Hawthorne] pays another way. In secret. He knows everything that I know, naturally, but he can never say it, can never stand forth in public and accept responsibility for his sins. He can never be publicly accountable. . . . No, he will have to live with his guilt instead," Sarah said. And because it is a secret guilt, it would be compounded for the rest of his life. His sin was like the pearl of great price purchased with borrowed money, which he would never be able to pay back. . . . "[H]is guilt will grow and grow. No one can ever forgive him, not even he himself, and he can never forget me. For as long as he lives, whether I live or die, I'll remain the emblem of his sin. I know him well, Owen Brown. He's a brilliantly sensitive man, and he makes all the finest moral distinctions. He's practically famous for it." (350–51; emphasis in original)

Banks, of course, interpolates the plot of *The Scarlet Letter* into his modern reworking of *Moby Dick* as John Brown's legend. The affinity Banks feels for Hawthorne's victim and John Brown's son has something to do with their status as modern subjects. For what Sarah and Owen recognize in each other, and what Owen's shipboard illness and historical doubts represent in *Cloudsplitter,* is the failure of adequate grounds for judgments that might redeem modernity's failure. For Hawthorne, as for Melville and Banks, this is the meaning of modernity and of being modern. Speaking of Sarah Peabody's situation, Owen muses that

[her parents'] generation had abandoned the Calvinist theology in their youth, but had kept the morality. She, on the other hand, having been encouraged by her elders since her nursery days to forsake the old Puritan forms of religion, had retained none of the Puritans' moral uprightness and rigor. She was a sinner, she said. A sinner without the comfort of prayer and with no possibility of redemption.

"I wonder, Owen Brown, do you think that this is what it means to be all modern and up-to-date?" (347)

Her situation, Owen imagines, is precisely like his and different from the fervent and enabling beliefs of his untroubled father, the preacher-warrior and Puritan, John Brown.[48] Faced with the secular sophistication of the other modern subjects on board their ship, Father Brown complains to his son, "But regardless of their stance on slavery . . . they all split the Bible off from the Declaration and the Laws, and in that way they mis-read both. Consequently, every one of them gets away with feeling smug and above it all. I don't understand these people. It's the Holy Bible that impels us to action, and it's the Declaration and the Laws that show us precisely where to act. What's the problem with these people?" (341). The problem with these people, of course, is that they have become all modern and up-to-date. Uncertainty haunts them and—to give their smugness the most generous interpretation—the fear of error makes them reluctant to adopt extreme measures or desperate remedies. This may be wise skepticism or complacency in crime. But John Brown the fundamentalist, blinded by his own belief that the Bible's light illuminates the nation's path, cannot see this. Owen, the reader's surrogate, tormented by the memory of terrible deeds, knowing that sympathetic identification can destroy as well as preserve, uncertain that his father's high-minded principles have survived the mayhem wrought in their name, not only understands his fellow passengers, he identifies with them.

To be all modern and up-to-date is to be cast out into the cold world of godless ethics and secular confusion. Modern readers, of course, are expected to recognize themselves in these two baffled people who meet at sea. Even here, though, differences pertain. Owen searches for just grounds of action on behalf of others while the young woman looks for some way to survive the injustice she suffers herself. Owen's sympathies fail to provide a moral compass in the terrible territory of his father's vengeance; Sarah's moral sense fails to rectify her relation to the world. Neither gets what he or she deserves. Sarah chooses suicide and Owen chooses murder and both remain sinners beyond hope of redemption. Are unjust acts in a just cause better than a fastidious inaction that commits no crime itself but fails to stop the crimes of others or to succor their victims? Why does the terrorist kill innocents to preserve principles that should make murder impossible? How can the morally sensitive influence a world that makes morality itself ridiculous? Owen Brown cannot answer these questions, yet he finds himself forced to confront them and to struggle to live through their contradictions. No one should expect that he could possibly feel right while doing so.

PART III

Failed Judgment

chapter 5

Emerson's Activism: The Trials and Tribulations of an American Citizen

Paradise is under the shadow of swords.

> —attributed to Mohammed by Emerson in "Heroism"

It is not possible to extricate oneself from the questions in which your age is involved.

> —EMERSON, "The Fugitive Slave Law"

THE CITIZEN AS THE DUPE OF HOPE

Robert Penn Warren's first book was an essay on the prehistory of the Civil War. *John Brown: The Making of a Martyr* (1929) defends the South and its peculiar institutions in the Jim Crow era of the twentieth century and blames the North for a misguided and unjust war of aggression. For Warren, Northern reformers, especially Ralph Waldo Emerson, who failed to distinguish high-sounding principles from practical realities, who championed abolition and made Brown its martyr, bear a large part of the blame. Like Thomas Dixon's *The Clansman* (*The Making of a Martyr* boasts a chapter titled "The Birth of a Nation" in honor of D. W. Griffith's 1915 adaptation), Warren's history identifies the white Southerner as the victim of an imperialistic North intent on elevating false ideas of universal right over the prerogatives of popular sovereignty and the sustaining force of organic traditions. Emerson, like many Northern idealists, failed to recognize John Brown as a dangerous charlatan and a confidence artist and made him a hero, thereby ensuring that America would fail and the South would fall.

No one, in Warren's estimation, could have been right thinking and moved to do what Brown did.[1] When Emerson left off woolgathering in his study to champion abolitionism, he committed a colossal failure of judgment and advanced not freedom for the slaves but oppression of the South. Warren's Southern version of populist history, whether or not one agrees with his specific charges against Emerson, does pinpoint and highlight the difficult decisions American citizens must make when confronted with what they believe to be the failure of America. For while Warren and Emerson both may be said to recognize the Civil War as a catastrophic instance of the nation's failure, their understanding of the nature of that failure and its implications stand diametrically opposed. That two concerned citizens could so fundamentally disagree on such a basic issue indicates the difficulties that citizens frequently face and the courage that the public performance of the American citizen's role requires.

In Warren's view regional autonomy, customary usages, and respect for the legality of democratic processes trump the moral concerns of slavery's opponents. In the 1850s advocates for slavery found such a position easy to maintain for their control of the federal government, and their increasing hold on nascent states seemed sure to legitimate slavery and protect its expansion. But for one convinced that slavery itself was an act of war, a "barbaric, unprovoked, and unjustifiable war of one portion of . . . [American] citizens upon another portion . . . —in utter disregard and violation of those eternal and self-evident truths set forth in our Declaration of Independence," as John Brown described it, such procedural legitimacy and legal sanctions could never seem just.[2] For many abolitionists by the 1850s, including Emerson, slavery violated principles of justice more fundamental than any law a government could pass. Warren has little use for idealists who believe in universal laws or principles of justice or for any transcendent truths that might condemn more local allegiances and identifications. For him, a susceptibility to such ideals represents a failure to which idealistic reformers, like Emerson, are particularly prone.

Warren's irony becomes most corrosive when he describes the shortcomings of Brown's Yankee sympathizers and idealistic supporters, especially Emerson and his cronies, who accepted "[Brown's] definition of himself" and, blinded by utopian hopes, failed to detect his fundamental falseness. These are the true villains of Warren's piece. They made the confidence man a martyr, providing his misguided cause with an aura of sanctity much more valuable than money. Warren reserves his most bitter contempt and most biting condescension for Emerson:

> Emerson possessed a set of ideas which have been given the interesting name of Transcendentalism; he spent his life trying to find something in man or nature which would correspond to the fine ideas and the big word. In John Brown, Emerson thought that he had found his man. "For himself, Brown is so transparent that all men see him through. . . . He joins that perfect Puritan faith which brought his ancestor to Plymouth Rock, with his grand-father's ardor in the Revolution. He believes in two articles—two instruments, shall I say?—the Golden Rule and the Declaration of Independence; and he used this expression in a conversation here concerning them: 'Better that a whole generation of men, women, and children should pass away by a violent death, than that one word of either should be violated in this country.'"[3]

To this last, admittedly shocking, sentiment, Warren offers the riposte by which solid common sense frequently seeks to challenge the reformer's dangerous zeal: "That is a big value to place on a 'word,' but Emerson was a man who lived in words, big words, and not in facts" (245). The language of reform and the language of the golden rule, the language that requires men and women not only to recognize but to identify with the victims of injustice and to respond as their humanity then dictates, requires the big words Warren mocks Emerson for valuing. Despite Warren's cautions, such big words are the language of American citizenship itself. Without them no representative politics may be possible, for these are the words that stir audiences, provoke responses, and forge identifications. These are the very language, the very big words, that give the United States the only actual identity it has ever had. It is precisely that national demand for identification with those struggling against bondage that Warren's unrepentant Southern regionalism wishes it could reject. "One intention of the Constitution," he asserts, "was to check that very aspect of especial horror, and ruthless dispatch which characterizes a racial struggle" (281). When Warren invokes the Constitution to forestall racial struggle—be it that which led to Harpers Ferry or that which became the civil rights movement—he himself fails to consider that slavery and segregation might actually be the root cause of the conflict, a preexisting violence to which the violent idealism of reformers responds.

Warren mocks Emerson as the dupe of hope in fine-sounding principles that are only empty words and that disable the realism required to discern necessary evils and impossible virtues, inevitable violence and impracticable justice. He condescends to grant the misguided Northerner's good intentions: "It is only natural that once or twice when he tried to deal with matters of fact words made him a common demagogue. And it is only natural, that Emerson, in his extraordinary innocence, should have understood nothing, nothing in the world, about a man like John Brown to whom vocabulary was simply a very useful instrument."[4] But the issue of vocabulary, the ways that words can be used as instruments of enlightenment as well as tools of seduction, cannot so easily be settled, and no one was less innocent or more uneasy about words and their ambivalent powers than Emerson himself.

Warren's suggestion that radical abolitionist vocabulary in general and Brown's words in particular were, as Emerson might have said, merely counterfeits circulating with no bullion in the vault reveals much about Warren's attitudes at this time. While he criticizes Emerson's inability to imagine that Brown and his cause are fraudulent, Warren's own positions make the Southerner's failures of imagination, his intellectual and moral failures, equally apparent. Warren cannot imagine that Brown's profound identification with the sufferings of those black men and women held in bondage is sincere. The sympathetic vocabulary of human rights, the basic currency of political discourse in the United States, when applied to African Americans can only, for Warren, be a manipulative instrument of demagoguery.

Thus Emerson's lofty ideals of humanity and justice make him not only a dupe, but also—most terrifying failure for an American, a failing tragically familiar in the nation's long and tragic history—a successful shill for murder and terror masked by fine-sounding words and noble sentiments. Emerson, as Warren sees it, should have understood the South and its peculiar institutions more clearly. He failed to respect the expressed democratic will of the Southern states and to uphold local community and popular sovereignty against a tyrannical state apparatus. But Warren's sneer cannot disguise the uncomfortable position in which the Southern citizen finds himself. When he advocates for regionalism, community, and common sense, he not only limits the appeal of national identity but risks blunting ethical sense and common decency as well, for it was frequently on the basis of ethical sense and common decency, the debt each human owes another, that Emerson and the abolitionists attacked slavery. When it seems that the nation's values—those universal values for which self-evidence may be claimed—require breaking the nation's laws and attacking its citizens, the choice that Americans face becomes troubling indeed. This is the choice with which Emerson struggled. That his antislavery positions could still provoke a Southern apologist over fifty years after the Civil War suggests that, while he may have failed democracy (or it may have failed him), his appeal to transcendent principles successfully touched particular American nerves.

Those nerves, one suspects, might have been painful because Warren suspects that he, not Emerson, has failed; that he, not Emerson, has been the dupe of fine words and mistaken judgments. Slavery was unjust, though a majority of the nation's citizens South and North supported it. There are limits to popular sovereignty and to common sense when these countenance crimes, as dangerous as this principle may be. Emerson at least believed this to be true. What if Emerson stands as an example not of a reformer gone terribly wrong but of the terrible choices conscientious citizens must face in terrible times, choices that make simple distinctions between justice and violence difficult to credit? The nation's failures and the failures of its citizens at such moments become difficult to discriminate. These choices remain terrible because those who must make them (each conscientious citizen and thus, one assumes, Warren and Emerson both) must feel their exposure to terrible errors and abject failures. Emerson might then exemplify the challenges citizens must face if politics is to have any relationship to principle at all, if, that is, something like a U.S. national identity—that identity based on a belief, however forlorn, in just principles— can ever hope to be realized. That realization requires that each citizen, in the frequent moments of the nation's crises, function not only as an individual judge but as a public intellectual, attempting to save the republic from its own failures by appealing to fellow citizens to reform. But Emerson's example also demonstrates that the role of public intellectual the American citizen must assume possesses problems and paradoxes difficult for any democratically minded citizen to successfully resolve.

The Citizen as Intellectual, or Emerson's Amateur Hour

On August 1, 1844, Emerson, with some reluctance, gave "An Address . . . on . . . the Emancipation of the Negroes in the British West Indies," making his first public statement in support of the unpopular cause of abolition.

Emerson's lecture and his speeches against slavery over the next fifteen years make him an early and representative public intellectual in America, what Peter S. Field has called an emergent "democratic intellectual."[5] But the very notion of a democratic intellectual is rife with contradictions, as Emerson's reluctance to assume the role suggests.

As a private citizen who finds himself constrained to speak against slavery, Emerson confronts problems that distinguish his interventions from the speeches made by professional abolitionists like Garrison, Phillips, or Child for whom opposition to slavery was a true vocation; from the sermons of Channing or Parker for whom furnishing moral guidance on contemporary issues was part of a ministerial portfolio; and from the testimony of Frederick Douglass or Sojourner Truth for whom the lived experience of slavery furnished something akin to an authorizing credential.[6] Emerson had no such profession to authorize his position and no personal experience of oppression to represent for his public. As he himself put it in his 1854 address on "The Fugitive Slave Law," "I have lived all my life without suffering any known inconvenience from American slavery. I never saw it; never heard the whip; I never felt the check on my free speech and action."[7] He could only speak as a concerned citizen hoping to persuade other citizens to share his concerns with the morally repellant practices the state asked its citizens to countenance. Such hopeful appeals to a shared sense of moral outrage by one private citizen to others in his or her community could be any citizen's task in a democratic society. However, any citizen undertaking this task must know that such appeals are unlikely to succeed.[8] If outrage among the citizenry had not already failed to appear, then the concerned citizen would not feel constrained to speak to the nation about its failure. The tensions between identification with the nation's ideals and alienation from the state's failures, affection for America's promises and repugnance at American short comings, make the citizen intellectual's role difficult to perform and unlikely to succeed. Habermas remarks that since the time of Dreyfuss, intellectuals in the public sphere have enjoyed and suffered the liberties and stigmas of their amateur status, hovering between "the irresponsibility of the political dilettante" and "responsibility for the whole without official jurisdiction."[9] To be simultaneously an irresponsible political dilettante and to presume to speak for the whole without official jurisdiction—this is precisely the difficult position in which Emerson as a concerned American citizen finds himself. Given the nature of these difficulties, Emerson's failures as a democratic intellectual need occasion no surprise.

The most interesting recent criticisms of Emerson's political activism have focused on three linked failings: his elitism and his failure to become an organic representative of the American people's culture and values; his aesthetical ethics and his failure to find a more materially concrete grounds for his position; his commitment to transcendental principles and his failure to embrace more locally rooted forms of liberation.[10] Emerson often testified to his sense of unfitness for the political work he had taken on, but he remained committed to its importance. For a decade and a half he dedicated himself to opposing his community's popular will, to finding terms that might persuade others to join the opposition, and to making explicit the grounds of his position. He did this knowing both the importance and the impotence of idealism in the world of practical politics and material interests. In his antislavery speeches Emerson stands not so much as the representative of "man thinking" as he does of a thinking man acting as a critical citizen in a public sphere where American identity continues to play a crucial part and announcing to his fellow citizens that the nation has failed.

Democratic Dissent

Emerson's reluctance to assume a leading role in the cause of abolition grows in part from his sense that he is no expert in the complexities of slavery's insidious intertwining with virtually all aspects of American life. It grows also from the difficulty that one who is professionally habituated to critical detachment and discriminating reflection experiences when circumstances demand he consort with zealots, even when he finds their cause to be just. He notes at the beginning of his 1844 address:

> I might well hesitate, coming from other studies, and without the smallest claim to be a special laborer in this work of humanity, to undertake to set this matter before you; which ought rather to be done by a strict cooperation of many well-advised persons; but I shall not apologize for my weakness. In this cause, no man's weakness is any prejudice; it has a thousand sons; if one man cannot speak, ten others can; and whether by the wisdom of its friends, or by the folly of its adversaries; by speech and by silence; by doing and by omitting to do, it goes forward. Therefore I will speak,—or, not I, but the might of liberty in my weakness. (7)

Much has been made of Emerson's reluctance. Cornel West, for example, in his brilliant and productive analysis of the strengths and limitations of Emerson's example as a cultural critic, writes extensively of the essayist's "perceptions of the impotence of his criticisms" in the world of action; and John Carlos Rowe, in his critique of the political tendencies of transcendentalism, says that throughout his engagement with abolition Emerson "felt the anxiety and defensiveness of the intellectual whose commitments to political causes are often likely to appear publicly less substantial than judges' laws or soldiers' acts."[11] This anxiety about his own inadequacy was well founded. Armed only with words and without any institutional authority to give those words force, setting himself against both governmental power and popular policy, Emerson's fear of failure, indeed failure itself, seems practically inevitable. Only by appealing to putative belief in commonly held principles—the nation's values of democratic justice, freedom, and equality—can Emerson, as a citizen, license himself to speak, but he finds those principles to be already violated and the efficacy of appeals made to them questionable in advance.

Still, it is the violation of those American principles, the manifest proof that they are not commonly held beliefs, that constrains Emerson as a citizen to speak. In the opening of "Address to the Citizens of Concord" (May 3, 1851), Emerson says: "I accept your invitation to speak to you on the great question of these days, with very little consideration of what I might have to offer; for there seems to be no option. The last year has forced us all into politics, and made it a paramount duty to seek what it is often a duty to shun" (53). And yet once more, and most notoriously, the remarkable sentences that begin his March 7, 1854, address, "The Fugitive Slave Law":

> I do not often speak to public questions. They are odious and hurtful and it seems like meddling or leaving your work. I have my own spirits in prison,— spirits in deeper prisons, whom no man visits, if I do not. And then I see what havoc it makes with any good mind this dissipated philanthropy. The one thing not to be forgiven to intellectual persons is not to know their own task, or to take their ideas from others and believe in the ideas of others. . . . —They say, what they would have you believe, but which they do not quite know. (73)

Much has been made of Emerson's spiritual prisoners. The important fact is that he leaves these metaphorical captives, however reluctantly, because the nation has failed to confront the plight of those it holds in bondage.

In each of these Emerson suggests that events constrain him to speak what he does not quite know, to speak in a way that does not flow organically from his own inclinations and expertise, to speak because the nation's proper representatives have failed to speak: "To what purpose," Emerson asks, "have we clothed each of those representatives with the power of seventy thousand persons, and each senator with near half a million, if they are to sit dumb at their desks, and see their constituents captured and sold;—perhaps to gentlemen sitting by them in the hall?" (25). Emerson similarly denounces his community's leaders in the aftermath of Webster's apostasy:

> One intellectual benefit we owe to the late disgraces. The crisis had the illuminating power of a sheet of lightning at midnight. It showed truth. It ended a good deal of nonsense we had been wont to hear and to repeat, on the 19th April, the 17th June, and the 4th July. It showed the slightness and unreliableness of our social fabric. . . . It showed the shallowness of leaders; the divergence of parties from their alleged grounds; showed that men would not stick to what they had said: that the resolutions of public bodies, or the pledges never so often given and put on record of public men, will not bind them. (55)

This failure of representation in the government constrains the private citizen to attempt the task of representing the whole. He does so knowingly without any ultimate authority to represent anyone other than himself or any interests other than his own but with the desire to do both. He must hope that his hearers can be brought to see what he sees, to judge as he judges, and to feel as he feels, but he must know that he is likely to fail.

Emerson knows that this failure of representation is democracy's failure and the nation's fault. He also knows that too few of his fellow citizens share his outrage and his indignation at this self-betrayal. Widespread racism obscures the criminal violence of enslavement and oppression, blunts popular indignation, and licenses both the complacency of citizens and the complicity of legislators. Armed only with words, Emerson knows that he must confront this racism as well. But racism's power to dehumanize and desensitize already corrupts the words he must use. As Emerson wrote in his journals: "What arguments, what eloquence can avail against the power of that one word *niggers*? The man of the world annihilates the whole combined force of all the antislavery societies of the world by pronouncing it." West cites this passage, nearly without commentary, as part of his clear-sighted analysis of Emerson's own ambivalence about race.[12] Emerson's journal makes clear his sense of the overwhelmingly difficult task he faces as he sets himself against the prevalent wisdom and worldliness of his day, a task that involves attempts to persuade in the language that worldliness itself controls.

For these reasons Emerson must often speak against the democratic consensus of the community he seeks to represent and in a form antagonistic to that community's common sense. One task for the abolitionist, Emerson knew, must be to overcome the dehumanization in language that racist speech entails and to encourage an identification across the boundaries that racism in language helps construct and maintain. That he should find such a task daunting should surprise no one. West specifies the limitations of Emerson's political engagements at the beginning of his critique of American philosophy:

> Emerson's ability to exercise moral and intellectual leadership over a small yet crucial fraction of the educated middle classes and enlightened business elites of his day principally rests upon his articulation of a refined perspective that highlights individual conscience along with political impotence, moral transgression devoid of fundamental social transformation, power without empowering the lower classes, provocation and stimulation bereft of regulated markets, and human personality disjoined from communal action. Emerson is neither a liberal nor a conservative and certainly not a socialist or even civic republican. Rather he is a petit bourgeois libertarian, with at times anarchist tendencies and limited yet genuine democratic sentiments.[13]

Whether or not West's characterization of Emerson accurately describes the nature and extent of his political engagements, the assumptions that underlie and enable West's criticism of Emerson's commitments to individualism and abstraction over community and democracy point up the general problem that Emerson faced in addressing America's failure. For when popular errors and communal crimes become the public intellectual's target, it is difficult to see how he can remain popular. If he does not remain popular, it is difficult to see how he can succeed.

No one can completely exonerate Emerson from West's indictment: his tendency to address elites and depend on a hierarchical conception of value and society when assessing people, policies, and positions; his reliance on high-sounding abstractions and universalized principles that often seem airy and insubstantial; his manifest impatience with the demands of public, political performance that take him from his ruminations on the infinitude of the private man he always felt was his real work. In sum, West charges Emerson with his manifest failure to become an organic intellectual of the American underclasses, however sincere his limited democratic tendencies might have been. But these failings represent not personal but positional limitations, the limitations of a critically minded citizen in a democratic society who judges that his fellow citizens are failing to honor justice itself and their nation's self-identity with it.

In the failure of America, Emerson confronts a failure not only of representation but of democracy itself. Empowering the "lower classes" in the years before the Civil War, the first epoch of mass politics in the United States, would not likely have furthered the cause of justice or ended the crime of slavery. Jacksonian democracy, which remade American politics in the first half of the nineteenth century, bred at least as much vicious demagoguery as progressive enlightenment. In the light of the fugitive slave bill and the public's reaction to it, Emerson—whose antipathies to the Jacksonian persuasion are well known—unflinchingly reads this desolate fact:

> The levity of the public mind has been shown in the past year by the most extravagant actions. Who could have believed it, if foretold, that a hundred guns would be fired in Boston on the passage of the Fugitive Slave bill? Nothing proves the want of all thought, the absence of standard in men's minds more than the dominion of party. Here are humane people who have tears for misery, an open purse for want, who should have been the defenders of the poor man, are found his embittered enemies, rejoicing in his rendition,—merely from party ties. I thought none that was not ready to go on all fours, would back this law. (56)[14]

Like Lydia Maria Child, Emerson finds himself disheartened by an "entire absence of a moral sense" regarding slavery and race among the nation's people.[15] Faced with such moral and national apostasy, Emerson must often sound like a modern Jeremiah and confront Jeremiah's proverbial failure to be popular. He must judge for himself, must distinguish for himself, must take it on himself to denounce iniquities where they appear even if they appear among the people he hopes to represent. Emerson may hope to represent the American citizen because a common allegiance to the nation entails, ideally, an allegiance to the very values he accuses the populace and the state of having betrayed. But he also knows that the American people are unlikely to thank him for telling them they have failed their nation and themselves.

For this reason, Emerson knows that democracy must be the American citizen's watchword but never his grounding principle. A certain elitism inheres in the democratic citizen's role. After Preston Brooks, a proslavery congressman from South Carolina, beat Massachusett's abolitionist Senator Charles Sumner with a cane in the U.S. Senate Chamber, Emerson put the matter bluntly: "The whole State of South Carolina does not now offer any one or any number of persons who are to be weighed for a moment in the scale with such a person as the meanest of them all has now struck down" (108). Robert Penn Warren found these sentences especially objectionable, but any citizen in a republic must sometimes make blunt judgments as well as fine discriminations. Emerson knows that he may well, perhaps must, fail to be popular when he champions moral principles against the weight of popular opinion. The concerned citizen, like the critical intellectual, often finds himself between identification with democratic principles and alienation from the popular will. Surveying the corruption and despair engendered in the polity, Emerson contemplates the conditions of his likely failure. Reform and democracy, principles and the people, the nation's ideals and the nation's policies are often at odds. Yet the democratic will remains the only real measure of the citizen's success, and persuasion the only test of the reformer's power.

Emerson wrote words in "New England Reformers" that aptly describe the reformer's plight, the potential powerlessness of those who seek to speak truth to both institutional and popular power: "The reason why anyone refuses his assent to your opinion or his aid to your benevolent design, is in you: he refuses to accept you as a bringer of truth, because though you think you have it, he feels that you have it not. You have not given him the authentic sign."[16] T. Gregory Garvey claims that Emerson here focuses on the forms of language but also confronts the pragmatics of democratic persuasion. The difference is subtle but crucial. In Garvey's account, Emerson's phrase "the authentic sign" bespeaks his "confidence that language can serve as a perfect medium of truth" and close "the gap between the values for which reformers speak and the language through which they promote their causes."[17] To focus on the power of the words themselves misses the pragmatic criteria by which Emerson measures language's authenticity: not in its formal attributes but in its persuasive power, its power to move and change its hearers. The audience poses urgent questions to the speaker's thought ("though you think you have it, he feels you have it not"). This shifts the burden of the message from the content of the words to the context of their reception.[18] Such pragmatic criteria make the empowerment of the speaker by a vision of the truth and an allegiance to principle and his powerlessness to meet the audience's challenge two moods or moments in Emerson's work that differ but cannot be made distinct.[19] Emerson knows very well that he may affect indifference to democracy's brute force, but he cannot ignore its importance. He must work toward the enlightenment of that force if he hopes not to fail.

For all his well-founded if elitist suspicions of the popular will, Emerson bases his appeals to the American public on his paradoxically democratic belief that the audience can be made to correspond to his representation of them. For all of its dream of power, this is an essentially democratic faith. As Emerson put it in *Representative Men,* the book most closely related to his experiences as a public intellectual, "The constituency determines the vote of the representative. He is not only representative, but participant. . . . Their quality makes his career; and he can variously publish their virtues, because they compose him."[20] George Kateb observes that the preponderance of writers and thinkers in *Representative Men* "makes it hard for us to believe that Emerson appreciates the typical activities of ordinary persons in the world."[21] Yet, as Kateb also knows, Emerson's democratic faith was such that he believed that all people at times act as intellectuals, making judgments and discriminations, just as he believed that all people are potentially self-reliant. Self-reliance is the fundamental basis for critical activity and the fundamental requirement for concerned citizenship. Kateb says: "He preaches self-reliance because he thinks that all people already have self-reliant moments and could more successfully become self-reliant if they tried. Self-reliance is thus not a doctrine of superiority to average humanity. Rather it is a doctrine urging the elevation of democracy to its full height, free of the aristocratic, but also free of the demotic" (18). To elevate democracy by speaking as a critical citizen to the higher potentials in each citizen is the democratic reformer's most crucial function. It lies between the extremes of elitist or professional entitlement and populist or popular demagoguery. This is an uncomfortable position, but it is one that the concerned American citizen, the aspiring representative of a democratic will that he hopes to help (re)form, must occupy. Anxiety and defensiveness come with the territory.

AESTHETIC APPEAL

To think about the politics of aesthetics in the abstract is notoriously difficult and perhaps futile. Aesthetics is by definition the theory and practice of the bodily and the concrete, yet at least since Kant, aesthetics has also held out a promise to realize the abstract and the universal. Aesthetics appeals to sensation, to the immediacy of feeling, and that felt immediacy is both its power and its limitation. Emerson, of course, was persuaded throughout his life by romantic aesthetic theories, shaped and influenced by Kantian philosophy, that linked beauty and virtue, moral rectitude and right feeling, the embodiment of moral law with the realization of rhetorical power. Yet, in ways that John Carlos Rowe has made abundantly clear, in Emerson's political practice from 1844 to the Civil War these theories fail to explain the positions he feels himself constrained to take.[22] Criticizing both Emerson and the potentialities of "liberal dissent" that Sacvan Bercovitch analyzes in *Rites of Assent,* Rowe identifies "an internal contradictoriness between the anticommunal, ahistorical aspects of his philosophy and the demand he placed upon that philosophy to effect social reform" (40). Emerson's philosophy, based on moral sense, was essentially aesthetic. Unlike Bercovitch, Rowe does not find these moments of contradictoriness to be "enabling paradoxes" but rather "disabling contradictions" in both Emerson and the traditions of American thought with which Emerson is associated (41). Rowe puts the case strongly: "The 'critical imperative' that Bercovitch reminds us is also our inheritance from 'the Emersonian legacy' has too often served false gods or made Americans appear tolerant of differences when in fact they are intent on maintaining the same old powers."[23] Thus Rowe finds Emerson to be a founding instance of an American tradition in which an "aesthetic ideology" works "to support the very social forces it overtly criticizes" (22–23), forces that perpetuate narrow nationalist ideologies and racist imperialist policies. Aesthetic ideology certainly has played this part in the

American tradition, but aesthetic appeals to a higher law, one that in principle is available to all, may also oppose the simple maintenance of these provincial powers. However confused they may be, U.S. citizens often respond viscerally—which is to say aesthetically—to the fine-sounding, but unreliable, principles of liberty and justice that they claim as their nation's own. And as Emerson knew, no one practicing politics in a democratic society can dispense with the power of visceral appeals if he hopes to successfully move an audience to action.

In theory, Rowe is perfectly justified in his suspicions of the aesthetic. A belief in a beautiful lawfulness and a moral sense corresponding to it offers no reliable grounds for actual politics. The problem, however, may have less to do with shortcomings in either transcendentalism or aesthetics than it does with the absence of identifiable and reliable grounds for judgment and action. Nonetheless, the failure of aesthetics as a grounding discourse should not preclude a practical appreciation of aesthetics as a political tool. For Emerson in his political speeches, searching to find or create common ground on which to meet and win over a potentially hostile audience, aestheticized appeals to individual feelings, and personal sentiments is a necessary weapon in his persuasive arsenal.

Emerson hopes to galvanize his audience's resistance to slavery and to persuade new recruits to abolition's cause. As a citizen he assumes what Andrew Ross has called the intellectual's "habitually recruitist or instructional postures in the field of popular correction" and what Habermas refers to as the process of democratic will formation.[24] To do so he recurs repeatedly to his transcendentalist association of aesthetics and virtue and the venerable traditions of moral sense philosophy of which Kant is a part. But then again, what else would one expect a literary professional to do? To cite Habermas once more, he "makes use of the means of his profession outside the sphere of his profession—that is, in the political public sphere."[25] And he does so to excellent effect.

Emerson relies on knowledge as well as affect. He has researched his topic to find materials with which to work. In particular, he read James A. Thome and J. Horace Kimball's *Emancipation in the West Indies: A Six Months' Tour in Antigua, Barbadoes, and Jamaica, in the Year 1837* and Thomas Clarkson's *The History of the Rise, Progress, and Accomplishment of the Abolition of the African Slave Trade by the British Parliament.*[26] Unlike Frederick Douglass, whose brilliantly disciplined recitations on the platform and in his 1845 narrative sought primarily to put the horrors he had witnessed and suffered as a slave on record with little rhetorical intensification or appeal, Emerson focuses on the affective responses such horrors elicit or should elicit in those who only witness and suffer vicariously:

> If we saw the whip applied to old men, to tender women; and, undeniably, though I shrink to say so,—pregnant women set in the treadmill for refusing to work, when, not they, but the eternal law of animal nature refused to work;—if we saw men's backs flayed with cowhides, and "hot rum poured on, superinduced with brine or pickle, rubbed in with a cornhusk, in a scorching heat of the sun;"—if we saw the runaways hunted with blood hounds into swamps and hills; and, in cases of passion, a planter throwing his negro into a copper of boiling cane juice;—if we saw these things with eyes, we too should wince. They are not pleasant sights. The blood is moral; the blood is anti-slavery: it runs cold in the veins: the stomach rises with disgust, and curses slavery. (10)

The blood and the body are moral because they rise with disgust—visceral, aesthetic disgust—at slavery's spectacle. But "we," Emerson and his audience, have not actually seen these things. "We" have heard or read about them thanks to the testimony of those like Douglass and Clarke and Thome and Kimball who have reported what they have suffered and seen. Emerson continues, "Well, so it happened; a good man or woman, a country-boy or girl, it would so fall out, once in while saw these injuries and had the indiscretion to tell of them. The horrid story ran and flew; the winds blew it all over the world" (10). And the movement to abolish slavery took shape in the horror and nausea of moral and aesthetic revulsion that these stories provoked.

Emerson manages to remind his readers of a fair number of slavery's actual outrages, including the atrocities of the Middle Passage (9). But aesthetic revulsion, his own visceral reaction to these accounts, and his assumption that his audience will share it anchor this passage and ground his appeal. To ground this passage and the opposition to slavery in such a response is to ground a political position in an aestheticized rhetoric that seeks to find or create a common engagement with and judgment of the world.

During the same year that Emerson took up the public cause of abolition, he also noted the lesson he learned from two well-known aestheticians:

"We are impressed by a Burke or a Schiller who believes in embodying in practice ideas; because literary men, for the most part who are cognizant of ideas, have a settled despair as to the realization of ideas in their own times."[27] Emerson might well have added Shaftesbury and Kant to the list of literary men who looked to aesthetics as a way of realizing ideas in the world through the persuasive force of their affective embodiment. In the philosophical and political tradition that reacted to the problematic emergence of a capitalistic, democratic, middle-class culture and society, aesthetics played a central and crucial role. Terry Eagleton explains that as power shifts "its location from centralized institutions to the silent, invisible depths of subject itself," aesthetics becomes the locus of both the crisis and the promise of modernity itself:[28]

> Once the bourgeoisie has dismantled the centralizing political apparatus of absolutism, either in fantasy or reality, it finds itself bereft of some of the institutions which had previously organized social life as a whole. The question therefore arises as to where it is to locate a sense of unity powerful enough to reproduce itself by. In economic life, individuals are structurally isolated and antagonistic; at the political level there would seem nothing but abstract rights to link one subject to the other. This is one reason why the "aesthetic" realm of sentiments, affections and spontaneous bodily habits comes to assume the significance it does. (23)

The turn to aesthetics may help furnish a conservative basis for society's reproduction, but it may also offer a practical basis for crucial reforms.

Thus, when Harriet Beecher Stowe searches at the end of *Uncle Tom's Cabin* for a principle that might guide her readers' opinions and protect them against the sophistries of worldly practicalities, she famously hits on sentiment, the aesthetics of feeling right, as the basis for resistance. "But, what can any individual do? Of that, every individual can judge. There is one thing that every individual can do,—they can see to it that *they feel right*."[29] Right feeling for Stowe, the bodily aesthetics of sentiment, grounds moral virtue and political judgment in a place removed from the sophistries of common sense that urge the denial of right feeling in the interests of practical calculation. As Jane Tompkins and others have pointed out, the appeal to feeling elevates feminine sentiment over manly reason.[30] For Emerson as well as for Stowe, the aesthetic appeal to feeling transgenders sympathy in ways that few of Emerson's critics have noticed. Of John Brown's terrible appeal he writes: "All women are drawn to him by the predominance of sentiment. All gentlemen, of course, are on his side. I do not mean by 'gentlemen,' people of scented hair and perfumed handkerchiefs, but men of gentle blood and generosity" (123). This transgendering depends not on effeminacy but on the manly possession of feminine sympathies. Those sympathies can become, as they did for John Brown, the basis for powerful identifications across the color line, which can in turn lead to terrible acts of violence. In judging those acts, as well as in provoking them, sentiment will prove a necessary but inadequate guide.

Emerson's engagement with the opposition to slavery originates, by his account, with his own sensitive reaction to distortions in his world of feeling. "We do not breathe well," he said in 1851. "There is infamy in the air." Continuing the paragraph, Emerson makes clear the degree to which his sensibilities are afflicted by the ugliness of slavery and its effects on his political and emotional state:

> I wake in the morning with a painful sensation, which I carry about all day, and which, when traced home, is the odious remembrance of that ignominy which has fallen on Massachusetts, which robs the landscape of beauty, and takes the sunshine out of every hour. I have lived all my life in this State, and never had any experience of personal inconvenience from the laws, until now. They never came near me to my discomfort before. I find the like sensibility in my neighbors. And in that class who take no interest in the ordinary questions of party politics. There are men who are as sure indexes of the equity of legislation and of the sane state of public feeling, as the barometer is of the weight of the air; and it is a bad sign when these are discontented. (53)

To be one of these sentimental barometers, a sensitive instrument attuned to the aesthetic pressure of political infamy, is a responsible citizen's obligation. The citizen who suffers these discontents must hope that giving voice to his moral discomfort will encourage the more insensible general populace to share it. "The whole population," Emerson hopes, "will in a short time be as painfully affected" (53–54). Or they will be, he might have added, once he communicates his sense of oppression and dishonor to them, playing on the sympathies of the men and women who hear him and may come to feel as he does.

Like Stowe, Emerson depends on the power of sentiment, the power of the aesthetic, to urge opposition to the vested interests and perverted reasoning of powerful institutional and ideological forces set to protect and perpetuate the evil practices of human bondage. He draws on what Eagleton describes as the subversive potential of aesthetics that appeals to "a new kind of human subject—sensitive, passionate, individualistic—[and] poses an ideological challenge to the ruling order, elaborating new dimensions of feeling beyond its narrow scope."[31] But, Rowe warns, aesthetics furnishes no reliable grounds for political judgment or action. The politics of right feeling can be and was powerfully evoked by conforming church men and creative artists to sentimentalize slaves and to mask slavery's violence. Eagleton notes the radical ambivalence in aesthetic appeals that can equally well win hearts and minds to a noble cause or furnish a conservative consensus that functions as "an insidious force which binds subjects to the law" (27). Like any rhetoric, the rhetoric of feeling furnishes a political tool rather than an ethical ground. It remains, however, the crucial means by which the critical citizen, confronted with the necessity of political action in a democratic sphere, performs his persuasive task.

John Carlos Rowe's criticism of Emerson's aesthetic dissent is not so much a criticism or celebration of aesthetics as it is the wish for a position beyond politics altogether, for a grounding of positions that could not be controverted. But Emerson knew that "there is no other world" here among the vagaries of politics, representation, and feeling.[32] Where reason never functions alone or simply masters the discursive field, aesthetics describes the world in which subjects and citizens must live and judge and act. Is aesthetics an essentially democratic or an essentially authoritarian discourse? Is it reforming or reactionary? Nativist or cosmopolitan? It has tendencies in both directions. When Walter Benjamin balanced the possibilities of a liberating politics of aesthetics against the oppressive threat of an aestheticized political practice, he described the full and inescapable range of political and aesthetic possibilities in a modern democratic state.[33] That the alert citizen must constantly judge and choose between these alternatives without absolute grounds in aesthetics or reason for the choice and without guarantees of political success is no reason for despair. Rather, it is the condition for democratic action in a democratic society. Emerson's choice of aesthetics is essentially pragmatic. The same might be said for his self-identification as an American—his politics determine his understanding of this identity and the hopes he lodges in its promises—however dismayed he might have been at his nation's actual apostasy and errors.

INDIVIDUAL JUDGMENT AND THE FAILURE OF AMERICA

Emerson's critics have frequently in recent years found his emphasis on individualism to be both antidemocratic and apolitical. They have also found it to be the most objectionable aspect of his national identification. Among those critics, Christopher Newfield develops the most complex and challenging view of Emersonian individualism and its relationship to principles that are ultimately identified with national values.[34] Newfield analyzes the movement of Emerson's thought as a socially dynamic, three-step process: first, the statement of the individual's radical priority; second, the attempt to "define the free self through equitable relations to others"; and third, a surprisingly conformist submission disguised as "transcendental destiny."[35] The third step, in Newfield's view, accepts current authorities and hierarchies, surrenders agency and resistance, and vitiates resistance and reform. It does not simply harmonize the moments of radical individualism and social negotiation that precede it; it changes their meaning and alters their tendency. Submission to a transcendental destiny shifts the very grounds of imaginable social being, from the liberal-democratic association of critical individuals in search of equitable principles to a massed, corporate society where the moral center resides no longer in the individual's judgment but in the laws to which all individuals must submit. In such a massed, corporate society, whose prophet Newfield's Emerson becomes, power cannot be figured as personal and contestable because it appears to be impersonal and absolute, part of the fated order of things. In Newfield's estimation, it becomes part of the structure of conformity that furnishes to U.S. national identity its salient characteristic.

Emerson's positions, with regard to power, relation, and authority—especially authority, that troublesome third step—do follow the stages Newfield indicates, but Emerson's enactment of those stages may be more nuanced and productive than Newfield believes and the problems inherent in transcendentalism may be more intractable than he supposes.[36] The third step, the appeal to law, does not reverse the tendency of radical individualism and the search for equitable relationship; it is, for Emerson, their necessary ground. Emerson's appeal to law—also an appeal to the nation's sense of itself—is a rhetorical ground for his appeals to the individual and his calls for more equitable relations. Nonetheless, Emerson's vision of the law does not in the final analysis transcend either.[37] For Emerson the law may only be realized through the negotiations of individuals and the amelioration of social relations, even when he claims that the law masters the individual and prescribes his conduct. The proof of the law lies in its appeal, its persuasive power. The law cannot be contemplated; it must be enacted and tested through the pragmatic venture of rhetorical performance. And that performance can always fail and almost always does. Thus Emerson after 1850 focuses his philosophical attention ever more closely on the pragmatic requirements of rhetoric, persuasion, and power.

The essays that compose *Representative Men* stand as a watershed in Emerson's development as an American intellectual, though none of the men he writes about are Americans. Essays such as "The Uses of Great Men," "Plato, or The Philosopher," "Montaigne, or The Skeptic," "Napoleon, or The Man of the World" look back to *Nature,* "The Poet" and "History," and forward to *The Conduct of Life* and even *Society and Solitude.*[38] But where the earlier work famously celebrates lawful power in language and thought, the latter Emerson seems less sanguine that law and power ultimately coincide. In particular, Garvey has emphasized the moral ambiguity, the authority without ethical guarantees, that characterizes the representative generally and the prime example of Napoleon particularly. This moral and ethical ambiguity sets the historical figures in *Representative Men* apart from earlier, more abstract, avatars of representativeness like the Poet or the Scholar in the earlier essays and addresses.[39] This shift in emphasis may be due less to Emerson's waning faith, or to his experience of Daniel Webster's perfidy, than to his increasing focus on practical power over theoretical abstraction, a focus sharpened by his experience as a public speaker in the service of universal laws in the context of American politics. Garvey remarks, "Emerson's idea of the relationship between the representative and his society also more closely resembles the form of Emerson's own participation in the antislavery movement from 1844 onward" (28). Yet, the form of that participation and Emerson's doubts about the law's efficacy were implicit in his work from the very beginning of his career.

For the literary man who becomes a public intellectual, adapting his professional skills to new tasks in the public sphere, the links between language, principles, and reform seem especially essential. In a democratic society, language possesses special importance and is especially easy to corrupt. Emerson always imagined the reclamation and purification of language to be the poet's task. In *Nature* he wrote of language's degradation when "duplicity and falsehood take place of simplicity and truth . . . [and] old words are perverted to stand for things which are not."[40] It is the poet's task to pierce this rotten diction and renew both language and thought. Addressing the Kansas Relief Meeting in 1856, Emerson applied the lessons of *Nature* to the politics of abolition and American rhetoric. "Language," he said, "has lost its meaning in the universal cant. *Representative Government* is really misrepresentative; *Union* is a conspiracy against the Northern States which the Northern States are to have the privilege of paying for; the *adding of Cuba and Central America* to the slave marts is *enlarging the area of Freedom. Manifest Destiny, Democracy, Freedom,* fine names for an ugly thing. They call it otto of rose and lavender,—I call it bilge water" (113–14; emphases in original). Emerson despairs that such language so easily misleads his fellow citizens: "But this is Union, and this is Democracy; and our poor people, led by the nose by these fine words, dance and sing, ring bells and fire cannon, with every new link of the chain which is forged for their limbs by the plotters in the Capitol" (114). Emerson, as an opponent of American slavery, finds it necessary to appeal to the judgment of individuals in the very language of value and judgment, freedom and democracy, that has already been corrupted by the opposition. The perversion of the nation's privileged terms, rather than the lost universality of law and justice to which those terms refer, is what deprives Emerson's Americans of their self-reliance. But if the law cannot be reliably uttered, of what earthly use can it be?

To combat the corruption of the nation's language, to reinvigorate the tools of national judgment, Emerson seeks to revalue the words and principles that official cant has falsified. He works to persuade his audience that those who stand accused of treason because they defy the nation's laws are in fact the patriots truest to the nation's common principles that demand opposition to the state, even with violence, rather than submission to unjust and immoral demands. Emerson says, in his 1855 "Lecture on Slavery" in which he also criticized the "fathers" for the "fatal blunder" of a flawed constitution, "Patriotism, public opinion, have a real meaning, though there is so much counterfeit rag money abroad under it, that the name is apt to disgust" (103). The citizen's task, then, must be to distinguish the counterfeit from the real patriotism and to reclaim that term and the values with which it is associated from the vandals and forgers who degrade them. To do so requires not only appealing to the higher laws of a common principle, but attempting to reconstitute the interpretation of those laws and the nature of the national identity to which they refer. In the contest of representations in which Emerson engages, the limits of the political arena get defined and shifted by evocations of justice, fairness, and freedom. Without these words, Emerson knows, no successful American politics, no modern politics at all, can well be imagined.[41]

Emerson attempts to alter the terms of American political discourse by changing the meaning of its most potent word, *patriotism*. In a passage in "To Aid John Brown's Family," he characterizes Brown, the condemned traitor and terrorist, as the man truest to his nation's principles. This passage could still jar Robert Penn Warren's nerves over fifty years later, not only for its Jacobean fervor but for its rejection of the popular will. Emerson, for all his verbal commitment to democracy, remains clear that democracy cannot finally arbitrate morality or justice. "The end of all political struggle, is, to establish morality as the basis of all legislation. 'Tis not free institutions, 'tis not a republic, 'tis not democracy, that is the end,—no, but only the means: morality is the object of government" (153). And morality can only be judged for each individual according to the golden rule. There is this limit to the conformist strain in Emerson's thinking. Fidelity to a higher law or principle becomes the basis of dissent when the meaning of that law or principle becomes the object of contention. Emerson saw that democracy and morality, patriotism and justice, might not coincide. To make them coincide constitutes the citizen's critical task. To make them coincide may require contemplating the terrible truths contained within an honest identification with justice that sets both national policy and narrow self-interest aside.

Emerson's well-known speech on the fugitive slave law is largely a disquisition on the failure of Daniel Webster as an American citizen, his failure to believe in the golden rule and the Declaration of Independence, and the disastrous consequences of that failure for the nation and its peoples. Emerson writes, "Now it is a law of our nature that great thoughts come from the heart. It was for this reason I may here say as I have said elsewhere that the moral is the occult fountain of genius,—the sterility of thought, the want of generalization in [Webster's] speeches, and the curious fact, that, with a general ability that impresses all the world, there is not a single general remark, not an observation on life and manners, not a single valuable aphorism that can pass into literature from his writings." These, Emerson specifies, are the "defects of this great man's mind" that the "history of this country has given such a disastrous importance" (77). The failure to utter the generally applicable as a challenge to the specifically convenient becomes a disaster when, at a particular moment, the nation loses track of the fundamental principles that give its union meaning. At that moment, the citizen's intellectual function becomes immediately essential. For Emerson, here as elsewhere, the immediate defines the transcendent and not vice versa.

Webster's intellectual failings become the moral failures of the American people. He values "dexterity too much and honor too little" (77), Emerson charges. The political amateur criticizes the professional politician for the amoral efficacy of his very professionalization. For Emerson, Webster's compliance with evil is a "ghastly result of all those years of experience in affairs" (78). Such amoral efficiency is the hallmark of modern political and social organization. It makes otherwise unthinkable outrages like slavery possible precisely because it is no one's particular job to undertake the painful and frightening task of thinking about iniquity in terms of general laws rather than under the pressures of more limited requirements of regional interests, constitutional qualifications, and party votes. No one, that is, but the private citizen seeking to bespeak a higher law, an amateur free from limiting practicalities and enabled to recall that by tolerating injustices, even to save itself, the nation risks its own failure. As Emerson puts it a little later in this speech, "I suppose, in general, this is allowed; that, if you have nice question of right and wrong, you would not go with it to Louis Napoleon; or to a political hack; or to a slave-driver. The habit of mind of traders in power would not be esteemed favorable to delicate moral perception" (85). Delicate moral perception is the work of the private citizen seeking to speak for the whole. As Emerson well knew, such work is seldom popular because it seeks to correct rather than to conform to the popular will.

Faced with public jubilation at the passage of the fugitive slave law, Emerson said, "I wish to see the instructed or illuminated class know their own flag, and not stand for the kingdom of darkness. . . . It is an immense support and ally to a brave man standing single or with a few for the right, to know, when, outvoted and discountenanced and ostracized in that hour

and place, yet better men in other parts of the country appreciate the service, and will rightly report him to his own age and posterity" (87). How
to estimate a sour face, as Emerson put it in "Self-Reliance," how to resist
society's power to ostracize and condemn and embrace a higher standard
of judgment than conformity to common sense or material expediency,
that is the citizen's task and burden.[42] Sometimes, in the presence of apparent failure, he may read the signs of a truer success. Sometimes success and
failure can be difficult to distinguish.

Finally, as Emerson's researches into legal theory taught him, "an immoral
law cannot be valid" (78–79). Morality, not statute or expediency, must
finally tip the balances of judgment and force, as in Emerson's estimation
of John Brown, a reconsideration of even the most terrible implications of
injustice. In the name of morality the private citizen may have more authority than the professional politician to speak for "the power of rectitude
[which] is apt to be forgotten in politics" (79). Finally, the problem with
the law is the problem of interpretation: "The law was right; excellent law
for the lambs. But what if, unhappily, the judges were chosen from the
wolves? and give to all the law a wolfish interpretation?" (82). What happens when a private citizen judges that society's legal authorities have abetted criminals and persuades others that he is right. Who then violates the
law? Who is to judge? What is true of statute is true of religious belief as
well. In the actual world it guarantees nothing. "For one would have said,"
Emerson writes, "that a Christian would not keep slaves, but the Christians keep slaves. . . . They quote the bible, and Christ, and Paul to maintain slavery" (83). For democratic citizens, finally it is not the law that judges
but the law that must be judged. Even without John Brown's terrible figure casting its appalling light on the landscape, this is a terrible prospect.
Emerson clinches his point and points up the inescapably political nature
of such principled deliberations: "These things show that no forms, neither Constitutions nor laws nor covenants nor churches nor bibles, are of
any use in themselves; the devil nestles comfortably into them all. There
is no help but in the head and heart and hamstrings of a man. . . . Why
have the minority no influence? because they have not a real minority of
one" (83). Emerson's stance as a critical citizen, however alienated from popular sentiment, does not stand apart from the nation's identity but addresses
and hopes, at last, to redefine or reawaken American citizens to the higher
angels of their better nature.

Emerson dreams that if he speaks as a minority of one, as a passionate amateur of a just cause and a right understanding of principle, then not only will he influence the people but he will change the nation's politics. He imagines the politician saying, "I am as you see a man virtuously inclined and only corrupted by my profession of politics. I should prefer the right side. You gentlemen of these literary and scientific schools have the power to make your verdict clear and prevailing. Had you done so, you would have found me its glad organ and champion. . . . But you have not done it. You have not spoken out. You have failed to arm me. I can only deal with the masses as I find them. Abstractions are not for me" (88). Emerson's citizen must struggle to make those abstractions concrete, to make them part of "parties and opinions" that furnish the servants of power a "working apparatus." To do so he must evoke and rely on the power that the national ideal gives to the identification of the nation with principles of freedom, democracy, and justice, however compromised that power may be. This may be the citizen's best hope of success, however slim, and of saving the nation from failing itself and becoming an agent of violent terror and lawless power.

chapter 6

Douglass's Cosmopolitanism: American Empire and the Failure of Diplomatic Representation

DOUGLASS: PARTICULAR IDENTITIES AND UNIVERSAL PRINCIPLES

Frederick Douglass made his literary career and fashioned his public identity by championing the universality of America's abstract principles against the specificity of its racist failings. Throughout a long career, during which he enthusiastically embraced the role of public intellectual that Emerson found so burdensome, he repeatedly staged the question of his own identity and his conflicted identifications with "his" race and nation to advance the cause of justice. That he in fact became the representative colored man in the United States and that he identified with American culture and values has earned him both praise and blame.[1] Douglass's self-identification with the dominant culture's vision of masculinity has come in for particular commentary and criticism. For example, bell hooks writes that "Douglass and other black male activists allied themselves with white male patriarchs on the basis of shared sexism," and Deborah McDowell has noted that electing Douglass as "'representative man' . . . reproduces the omission of women from view."[2] Doubtless Douglass in his autobiographies and public statements embraced, exemplified, and attempted to embody the masterful and aggressive masculinity that since the nineteenth century has been associated with American universalism. Moreover, the conflicts and struggles that Douglass thereby assumed—more than any unproblematic notion of identity or power—make him not only America's representative "colored" man but a fair representative of American masculinity itself and an excellent example of the promises and problems of American identity as it presents itself to the world. These promises and problems become evident in the contrast between Douglass's earlier and later career, his familiar early struggles for racial justice and, by contrast, his less well-known later support for American imperialism. In both instances, masculinity plays a crucial part, for Douglass understands himself to be an agent of the universal values of equity and democracy that define his nation's sense of itself and of its increasingly aggressive claim on the world. His very belief in American values blinds him, during his final post as minister to Haiti, to the failure of his nation to honor its own principles, and in that failure of self-recognition—both Douglass's and the nation's—the predominance of American manliness plays an important part.

Because Douglass championed universal values, he has recently become the representative man of the post-identity movement as well. Ross Posnock, for example, in *Color and Culture* enlists Douglass as an early and prime example of the "anti-race race man," one who rejects what Posnock considers the narrow prescriptions of blackness in order to embrace a broader, more fluid, more self-fashioned cosmopolitanism:

> Like David Walker before him and Du Bois and his cohort after him, Douglass has ceased being merely a problem to be patronized or a freak to be exhibited. Rather, as a thinking black subject he could be said to initiate a crisis in established ways of making sense. As such, he is someone "we do not know what to do with . . . If he breaks our sociological and sentimental image of him we are panic-stricken and we feel ourselves betrayed" . . . I have borrowed James Baldwin's words that describe white reaction when a black individual emerges from the "jungle of statistics" and is revealed not as a "problem or a fantasy" but as a "person." When that person is a black intellectual, anxiety is heightened.[3]

In Posnock's vision of Douglass's career, race becomes an impediment to the writer's progress, a "jungle" of attributions and estimations from which the black man emerges as fully human and black no more, saved from the racist attributions (as opposed to attributes) that would keep him in the jungle—as Baldwin called it—forever. For Posnock, race must be overcome so that the false, essentialized primitive can become the true, self-fashioned cosmopolitan. In Douglass, Posnock suggests, you will see how the slave becomes a cosmopolite.

Of course, Posnock well knows that things are not so simple and that while men may make their own identities they never create them just as they please. His own description of Douglass's staging of black identity reveals Douglass's situation as a black man to be central to his self-fashioning:

> As a black intellectual Douglass inevitably challenges the way a white supremacist culture understands black identity. More precisely, he contests the ideology of authenticity, which is grounded in the absolutist metaphysics of rationalist and intellectualist thought. Pervading these discourses is a rhetoric of the natural, of origins, of organicism, and of immutable identity. These essentialist tenets provided the intellectual armature of white Anglo-Saxon supremacy and its instruments of nationalism and imperialism. . . . What emerged from the crisis of authenticity was the modern notion of intellectuals.[4]

The crucial moment in Posnock's argument is contained in the last sentence of this passage. For Posnock, this moment in which the authentic idea of identity based on group affiliation, the authentic idea of an identity rooted in race, for example, gets challenged marks the emergence of the modern intellectual as a representative of the universal and the enemy of particularity itself. But the modern intellectual can never be as disidentified and rootless as Posnock or the intellectual himself might wish. Douglass's effective challenge to racist assumptions and essentialist ontology depends, as Posnock cannot help noting, on his own identity as a member of the prescribed group. He challenges white supremacy because he makes his claims on culture as a black man representing himself and his race, contesting their exclusion from the property and propriety of whites. Posnock's single-minded focus on the universalism of Douglass's claims blurs the particularities of identity that give those claims force. An irreducible and pressing particularity, his experience of racial injustice in the United States shapes and determines Douglass's appeals to universal principles and conditions his claims on cosmopolitan identity.

Posnock's challenging and important reading of Douglass as a modern intellectual blunts an important point in his appeals for justice and reform. Douglass, as well as Hegel, understood the paradoxical truth that any access to the universal can only be had through the particular, a paradox especially true for oppressed peoples and their complex and conflicted relationships to the identities inscribed within the culture that the dominant claims. As a dissident participant in that culture, Douglass challenges the injustices it perpetuates by working through the identities it prescribes. This differs from denying identity altogether. Thus, to take one example, Douglass appeals to the very ties of blood and identity that Posnock wants the intellectual to leave behind:

> By every consideration which binds you to your enslaved fellow country-men, and the peace and welfare of your country; by every aspiration which you cherish for the freedom and equality of yourselves and your children; by all the ties of blood and identity which make us one with brave black men, now fighting our battles in Louisiana, in South Carolina, I urge you to fly to arms, and smite with death the power that would bury the Government and your Liberty in the same hopeless grave.[5]

To link black identity to blood is, as much as Alexander Crummel's pan-Africanism, to find in a putatively organic conception of race a basis for solidarity in authentic belonging to a distinct and particular group. This is more than an opportunist strategic essentialism on Douglass's part; it is a persistent trope and a necessary theme in his exploration of his place not only as a black man in American society but as a black intellectual on the American scene.

Douglass, of course, has many moods, or many moves, in pursuing his public work of criticism and recruitment. When not attempting to enlist black Americans beneath the banner of racial solidarity, he can, as Posnock so well demonstrates, attack white supremacists by mounting masterful attacks on the prescriptive idea of racial identity itself. But even here, the persistence of distinct and particular identities fascinates Douglass and not merely as a primitive impediment to modern man's emergence into a more civilized and cosmopolitan space. In fact, Douglass imagines that social evolution requires the enlivening tangles and complicating thickets of differ-ence and identity, contact and conflict, to proceed.

For example, in his attack on the theory of polygenesis, America's unique contribution to nineteenth-century social science, Douglass refers to the equal humanity and the essential identity between the European and the African, for "the whole argument in defense of slavery, becomes utterly worthless the moment the African is proved to be equally a man with the

Anglo-Saxon."[6] The emphasis on equality between African and Anglo-Saxon here suggests that indifference to difference that post-identitarians like Posnock and Walter Benn Michaels might well celebrate. But Douglass does not conclude with this point. He argues for the nation as a site where both identity and difference emerge through invigorating confrontation. Near the end of his presentation, having canvassed the Egyptian origins of European civilization, the pejorative biases of accounts and representation of Africans, and the circular logic of appeals to separate racial origins, Douglass offers the following: "A powerful argument in favor of the oneness of the human family, is afforded in the fact that nations, however dissimilar, may be united in one social state, not only without detriment to each other, but, most clearly to the advancement of human welfare, happiness and perfection. While it is clearly proved, on the other hand, that those nations freest from foreign elements present the most evident marks of deterioration" (2: 522). Douglass continues to hold this position after the Civil War when he championed Asian and German immigration in "Our Composite Nationality" (1867). He possessed a vision of cosmopolitanism to be sure, but one in which social and cultural vitality depends on an invigorating heterogeneity of identities—the active presence of foreign elements within the nation as the condition of the nation's advancement. Progress, that quintessentially modern ideal, requires not only that Americans recognize the unity of the human family but that they also admit the differentiation of identities. Identity constitutes a complex, positive force in society and not a simple impediment to the individual's emergence.

Douglass's positive orientation toward the particularities of identity may be obscured by overemphasizing his antipathy to racist essentialisms. For Douglass, cosmopolitanism—which he calls composite identity—does not clear the jungle of identities within the nation but shifts the tensions and conflicts among identities to a more invigorating and edifying level, the only level on which a full expression of the human and of the individual is possible. Identity may be continuously challenged and shifted, its limits and the forms of belonging and exclusion it entails repeatedly interrogated, but the nation's composition and its investment in justice require that Americans—and other aspiring citizens of the modern world—continue to respect identity's force in social and individual life. This means remaining mindful of the challenges to universal principles of justice and freedom that the injustices and exploitation of particular identities so often pose.

DOUGLASS AND THE SCARS OF IDENTITY

Douglass struggled with the problems of identity and the promises of universalism throughout his long career. The struggle itself, more than any final accomplishment of an identity, make Douglass a representative figure and a representative of American manliness as well. In his introduction to Douglass's second writing of his life, *My Bondage and My Freedom,* James M'Cune Smith—the radical black abolitionist—nominates Douglass a representative American man and marks Douglass's aspirations toward self-possession and his traumatic origins that make self-possession difficult to imagine. "When a man raises himself from the lowest condition in society to the highest," he begins, and he points to Douglass's career as "an example of self-elevation."[7] The recursiveness of self-reflexive verbs becomes a symptomatic tic in Smith's remarks. He notes Douglass's fidelity to his "self-pledged word" (127), his "self-relying and independent character" (129), and his struggle to "carve out for himself a path" toward "self-elevation" (131) to support his central claim that Douglass had "raised himself by his own efforts" (132) and especially through his literary achievements, for, Smith asserts, "The style is the man" (135). Yet, in this celebration of masculine self-reliance as manly self-authorship, a Byronic melancholy colors the representative's identity and both impels and vitiates the gendered gesture of Douglass's self-creation. Smith describes Douglass's "will" as "an unfaltering energy and determination to obtain what his soul pronounced desirable; a majestic self-hood . . . [and] determined courage" born of a "fiery indignation at his injured self-hood . . . [and] the scars which slavery and semi-slavery had inflicted upon his body and soul" (126–28). The majestic self-hood that emerges in Douglass's career as a "born orator" (128) responds to and compensates for his injured soul and scarred body, both of which bear the marks of slavery, the experience of the self's abjection at the hands of an other. In these passages, Douglass sounds less like a self-possessed man of letters and more like a wounded, brooding Ahab attempting to strike through the mask of a hostile world toward the malign heart of the society that has wounded and unmanned him. Smith suggests that in his wounds Douglass possesses the "secret of his power" as a "representative American man—a type of his country men," one who "bears upon his person and upon his soul every thing that is American" (132). On his soul, as Smith indicates, Douglass bears the scars of self-possession's failure—perhaps of its final impossibility, the failure of American masculinity as the dream of self-possession to authorize itself. Not just America's failure to be just and equitable marks Douglass as an individual and as a representative; the impossible requirement that American masculinity achieve a majestic self-hood of independent agency leaves its trace as well.

As he took up his pen, Douglass faced problems that were also opportunities particular to his identity as a black intellectual. He confronted not only generic expectations encoded within previous slave narratives but also stereotypical preformulations of black masculinity (and femininity as well) established in antebellum literature and culture. As Francis Smith Foster puts it: "Ante-bellum literature featured five black character types: the wretched freedman, the clown, the contented slave, the victim, and composite of the later three."[8] To create and possess himself, Douglass must evoke and transgress each of these emasculated racial stereotypes and manipulate the highly conventionalized genre of the slave narrative itself. Moreover, to achieve individuality as a black man, Douglass must also avoid sympathetic appropriation by condescending abolitionist sympathizers. Only through such identifications by "disidentificatory means" can a black man in nineteenth-century America achieve an individualized self.[9] Only through specific negations of attributed identity can Douglass participate in a universal humanity. He continues to bear the scars of slavery, the wounds of particularity that enable and condition his self-making and identity and mark the place he achieves in his nation's history. In this complex and conflicted sense, Douglass's *My Bondage and My Freedom* is, as Smith says it is, "an American book for Americans."[10] It records a telling instance of American failure as it shapes an American identity that remains structurally and strategically reliant on what it sets itself against.

Throughout Douglass's career he realizes that his body itself plays a crucial part in the continuous war of interpretation and signification that constitutes his identity. This may be clearest in his critique of the polygenic theory of racial origins that attempted to make a scientific case for the inferiority of black bodies and the black minds within them. In his 1854 speech, "The Claims of the Negro Ethnologically Considered," Douglass argues that the case for polygenesis depends significantly on a trick of representation, for if "a phrenologist or naturalist undertakes to represent in portraits, the differences between the two races—the negro and the European—he will invariably present the highest type of the European, and the lowest type of the negro." He continues, "The European face is drawn in harmony with the highest ideas of beauty, dignity and intellect. Features regular and brow after the Websterian mold. The negro, on the other hand, appears with features distorted, lips exaggerated, forehead depressed—and the whole expression of the countenance made to harmonize with the popular idea of negro imbecility and degradation" (510–11). Douglass here identifies the problem with identity. Racist scientists maintain a vision of identity that becomes a procrustean scheme determinedly cropping reality to fit their preconceptions. To maintain these identities, white and black, they rigorously maintain repressions and exclusions from representations of Africans and African Americans that might trouble the integrity of their categories and hierarchies. Never, Douglass points out, do these "scientists" present an image of a Garnet, Ward, Remond, Wilson, Pennington, Gaines, or Delaney (Douglass asserts that he could mention "hundreds of others"). They miss, he argues, not simply the truth of black identity but the range and variety of black possibilities. "While it must be admitted that there are negroes answering the description given by the American ethnologists and others, of the negro race, I contend that there is every description of head among them, ranging from the highest Indoo Caucasian downward. If the very best type of the European is always presented, I insist that *justice,* in all such works, demands that the very best type of the negro should also be taken" (513–14; emphasis in original).

Douglass maintains a complicated and conflicted position on identity, even beyond his troubling references to high Caucasian and low negro types. On the one hand, he gestures toward the sort of universality—a common human identity and belonging—that transcends race. On the other hand, he continuously reminds his audience that he himself embodies the particularities expressed by and the injustices perpetrated on black bodies by a slave system defending itself through "a denial of the negro's manhood" (501). He points out for his white audience that the legitimacy of slavery depends on the maintenance of rigidly schematized identities that distinguish blacks from whites. He cites an argument from the proslavery *Richmond Examiner* in which the author claims that "if the negro has the same right to his liberty and the pursuit of his own happiness that the white man has, then we commit the greatest wrong and robbery to hold him a slave—an act at which the sentiment of justice must revolt in every heart— and negro slavery is an institution which that sentiment must sooner or later blot from the earth." However, Douglass continues, "After the stating the question thus, the *Examiner* boldly asserts that the negro has no such right—BECAUSE HE IS NOT A MAN!" (501; emphasis in original). For the United States as a slaveholding society, the recognition of black humanity generally and black masculinity in particular entails a perceptual shift of apocalyptic proportions, one that would destroy both American slavery and the racial distinctions on which slavery depends.

That Frederick Douglass could effectively speak to these issues depends to a large extent on his identity as a black man and an escaped slave. There is a double sense, of course, to Douglass's meaning when he responds to the *Examiner*'s assertion by coolly noting that "I feel myself somewhat on trial" (501). In these circumstances, to inhabit the identity that is being contested is both a trial and a tribulation. To defend the claims of the negro to common humanity, Douglass finds himself constrained to claim and embody the black identity in question and to transform the meaning of that identity through his own identification with the dominant forms of masculinity being denied to him. This is Douglass's response to abusive characterizations of black men and his own self-defense against threats to his own masculinity. What is at stake is, of course, a certain form of cosmopolitan universality, but one experienced through the wounds of a particular identity. Douglass describes it in the most heatedly rhetorical passage of the essay on ethnography:

> It is somewhat remarkable, that, at a time when knowledge is so generally diffused, when the geography of the world is so well understood—when time and space, in the intercourse of nations, are almost annihilated—when oceans have become bridges—the earth a magnificent ball—the hollow sky a dome—under which a common humanity can meet in friendly conclave—when nationalities are being swallowed up—and the ends of the earth brought together—I say it is remarkable—nay, it is strange that there should arise a phalanx of learned men—speaking in the name of *science*—to forbid the magnificent reunion of mankind in one brotherhood. A mortifying proof is here given, that the moral growth of a nation, or an age, does not always keep pace with the increase of knowledge, and suggests the necessity of means to increase human love with human learning. (503–4; emphasis in original)

Douglass experiences his own identity as a black man and as an American under the sign of this mortifying proof of his nation's failure. His identity emerges in the failure of more universal identifications, the failure of a greater expansion of love and brotherhood and enlightenment. Douglass's intellectual courage enables him to confront this mortification, but America's failure raises a further question. Can an increase of love and enlightenment ever succeed in making a black man just a man? What does it mean that for Douglass to make a claim on universal brotherhood requires that he perform the particularity of black identity? More generally, what kind of manhood finds itself constrained to perform its own self-mastery before a hostile audience?

In "The Claims of the Negro Ethnologically Considered," Douglass performs as a learned black man, one who masters himself and seeks to master his audience by mastering the subject in question. In this effort, his own black identity furnishes crucial evidence for his argument. "The subject is before you," he concludes, referring to both his topic and himself. "I speak as unto wisemen, I stand as in the presence of Scholars. . . . Whatsoever things are true, whatsoever things are honest, whatsoever things are just, whatsoever things are of good report, if there be any virtue, and if there be any praise, think on these things" (525). Douglass, like Emerson in "The American Scholar," inveighs against intellectual sloth as a moral failing of the American mind. Large questions of humanity and justice depend on scholarship that seeks a fresh encounter with the world. Both Emerson and Douglass appeal to a lost human wholeness that the scholar must seek to repair, but such similarities make the differences in these performances visible, and these differences express the different identities of the speakers. Emerson includes himself in his discourse by identifying with his audience of scholars in his unself-conscious use of "we." "We are met," he intones at the beginning of his address, confident that no one will contest his right to call himself a scholar. Douglass, for his part, while gesturing always toward common interests as members of a human and a national collectivity, eschews the inclusiveness of the first person plural, identifying himself rhetorically not with scholars but with the object of study. To claim a common humanity for blacks, Douglass must perform his black identity before this white audience. However scholarly he may be, he remains in the complex and mortifying position of being at once the masterful subject of knowledge and the proffered object for study.

In his argument against polygenesis, Douglass considers and dismisses three "superficial" points drawn from Charles Hamilton Smith's *Natural*

History of the Human Species: First, that the "negro" head is round and dense to facilitate the carrying of burdens. (He notes that German, Irish, and Oriental societies also carry burdens "upon the same vertical extremity.") Second, that "the voice of the negroes is feeble and hoarse in the male sex." (Douglass—no doubt drawing on his own credentials as an expert witness to subjugation, replies, "An oppressed people, in addressing their superiors—perhaps I ought to say their oppressors—usually assume a minor tone, as less likely to provoke the charge of intrusiveness.") And third and most important, Smith's repetition of the oft-made clam that Africans are inferior because they "have never discovered an alphabet [or] framed a grammatical language." To this last accusation Douglass replies:

> Now, the man is still living, (or was but a few years since), among the Mandingoes of the Western coast of Africa, who has framed an alphabet; and while Mr. Smith may be pardoned for his ignorance of that fact, as an ethnologist, he is inexcusable for not knowing that the Mpongwe language, spoken on both sides of the of the Gaboon River, at Cape Lopez, Cape St. Catherine, and in the interior, to the distance of two or three hundred miles, is as truly a grammatically framed language as any extant [referring here to the published grammar of that language by then president of Rochester University M. B. Anderson]. (518–19)

In each of these cases, Douglass demonstrates either that the attribution in question is not unique to Africans or that its manifestation is the result of nurture not nature. That is to say, he substitutes material history for racial essentialism. "A man is worked upon what he works on," as he puts it. On this basis he refutes the arguments of polygenesists and advances the claims of the Negro to be included in "the oneness of the human family" (522). In this clear sense, Douglass may be claimed, as Posnock claims him, as a spokesperson for the universal and the cosmopolitan, as an antirace race man who, like Walter Michaels, advocates indifference to difference.

But once again, Douglass is not indifferent to difference. Within the oneness of the human family, difference promises health. He writes, "It is clearly proved . . . that those nations freest from foreign elements present the most evident marks of deterioration. Dr. JAMES MCCUNE SMITH, himself a colored man, a gentleman and a scholar, alleges—and not without excellent reason—that this, our own great nation, so distinguished for industry and enterprise, is largely indebted to its composite character" (522–23; emphasis in original). Douglass alters the assumption, common since before Jefferson, that harmonious nations require homogeneous populations. For him healthy union becomes a function of conflicted compositeness. Far from being indifferent to difference, modernity itself depends on repeated and perhaps violent confrontations with difference in order to generate the invigorating complexity of composite, which is to say cosmopolitan, identity. In this sense, the United States promises to become the most advanced because it is the most internally conflicted of nations—but only if the United States learns to confront the challenges and dangers associated with the differences it contains. The failure to do so, the sheltering of the unjust status quo behind bad arguments and poor scholarship, scars the nation's body politic and constitutes the reality of American identity as Douglass, so painfully, experiences it.

Douglass ends with an a fortiori argument shifting the dispute's grounds and ending its to and fro by adducing himself and assuming to himself the burden of difference. He makes the negro's claims in his own person by baring the scars that formed his own identity in its confrontation with difference. "Now, gentlemen, I have done," Douglass concludes, "The subject is before you."

> I shall not undertake to make the application. I speak as unto wise men. I stand in the presence of Scholars. We have met here to-day from vastly different points in the world's condition. I have reached here—if you will pardon the egotism—by little short of a miracle. At any rate, by dint of some application and perseverance. Born, as I was, in obscurity, a stranger to the halls of learning, environed by ignorance, degradation, and their concomitants, from birth to manhood, I do not feel at liberty to mark out, with any degree of confidence, or dogmatism, what is the precise vocation of the Scholar. (525)

The scars of Douglass's identity, the imperfectly healed tissue of his own subjugation, become the origin of his empowerment and the force behind his voice. His modesty concerning the scholar's vocation may color these concluding remarks, his different origin—not biological but situational—entitles him to denounce America's inequities and to prophesy terror: "There is but one safe road for nations or for individuals. The fate of a wicked man and of a wicked nation is the same. The flaming sword of offended justice falls as certainly upon the nation as upon the man" (525). Speaking as a black man, embodying a vital form of difference within the human family's universal community, standing not only as an American scholar but, as he puts it, "as a denizen of the world, and as a citizen of a country rolling in the sin and shame of Slavery, the most flagrant and scandalous that ever saw the sun" (529), Douglass performs the saliency of his own identity, in the field of justice and of the national challenge of composition to which, he reminds Americans, they can never be indifferent. He ends by offering his rhetorical ascendency and his black body as the final examples in his argument against essentialized identity. He refutes the difference ascribed to him as an African by pseudotheories like polygenesis, but he defends difference as the distinguishing feature of advanced societies. If "human rights stand upon a common basis" (523), then a nation, claiming to be founded on "inalienable and universal rights," will be judged as it meets the challenge of justice, or of common decency, that difference entails. Douglass bears the scars of the nation's failure to meet that challenge and testifies to the narrowed prospects that failure entails.

DOUGLASS'S COMPOSITE IDENTITY

In Douglass's account of himself he registers not an essentialized racial identity but the pressure and power of a racist society.[11] In Douglass's experiences, American principles promise that a slave can be made a man, but the realities of American racism determine that the nature of that man's identity will always be in question. Consider the difference between Douglass's description of his emergence on the public stage in his first and second narratives. At the end of his 1845 *Narrative* he describes his first public address as a tribulation and a triumph. "It was a severe cross, and I took it up reluctantly. The truth was, I felt myself a slave, and the idea of speaking to white people weighed me down. I spoke but a few moments, when I felt a degree of freedom, and said what I desired with considerable ease."[12] Thus culminates the struggle in which "a slave was made a man," accomplished by his emergence in the public sphere. But retelling this story ten years later in the middle of *My Bondage and My Freedom,* Douglass drops the phrase "a degree of freedom" and rewrites this passage to read: "'Who or what,' thought I, 'can withstand a cause so good, so holy, so indescribably glorious. . . . Now let the truth be spoken, and a nation will start forth at the sound!' In this enthusiastic spirit, I dropped into the ranks of freedom's friends, and went forth to battle. For a time I was made to forget that my skin was dark and my hair crisped" (366). Here Douglass describes himself in a series of oddly passive constructions, "let the truth be spoken" and "I was made to forget." His freedom appears conditioned by unnamed forces exterior to himself. Even his assumption of abolition seems oddly attenuated, "I dropped into the ranks of freedom's friends." And "for a time" suggests that what once seemed an apotheosis had become a disappointment. Those who made him feel like a man, for a time, soon made him realize that saying what he desired and taking possession of himself might be more difficult than he had supposed. The ironies of the latter passage elaborate the nearly tacit reservation already registered by the "degree of freedom" reported in the first account. If Douglass's naive enthusiasm for or his seduction by his newfound abolitionist friends leads him to believe he can participate in and possess himself through the universalized virtues of American identity and "forget" the racial particularities of his corporeal self, he soon recognizes his error.

In the very next paragraph of *My Bondage and My Freedom,* Douglass reports that the proprietary conduct of the very abolitionists with whom he is supposedly working for freedom constrains him to remember what he has momentarily been "made" to forget. The community he addresses demands that he remain bound to the identity he first fashioned. "Many came, no doubt, from curiosity to hear what a negro could say in his own cause. I was generally introduced as a 'chattel'—a 'thing'—a piece of southern 'property'—the chairman assuring the audience that it could speak."[13] While these abolitionists meant to be ironic, Douglass experiences their irony as a constraint. Being described as "a graduate from the peculiar institution with my diploma written on my back!" meant that Douglass himself was not free to read the meaning that his suffering had inscribed (365). "Give us the facts," John A. Collins, general agent of the Massachusetts Anti-Slavery Society tells him, "we will take care of the philosophy," a task Douglass found to be "too mechanical" for his nature (367). The abolitionists ironically replicated the division of labor and of profits in the slave economy Douglass thought he had escaped. His body and his labor were still not his own. To have dark skin and crisped hair meant being denied the power of self-representation associated with full manhood rights. The power to represent the self and the nation remained the power of white

men. The young Douglass nearly forgot the particular identity that circum-
scribed his life (his crisped hair and dark skin), but he does so at the very
moment when he finds himself called on to perform blackness for the community's edification. The older Douglass realizes that he may never forget
who he is as he attempts to own himself in the public eye. The young
Douglass may have momentarily forgotten his race, but the older man who
reports this forgetting in *My Bondage and My Freedom* does so to remind
his audience that he now remembers it.[14]

Douglass assumes the complexities of his identity to signify the nation's
failure to embody its universalist ideals. Consider, for example, his account
of those Americans—both white and black—who felt free to plague him
with questions, which he calls American questions, concerning color and
the mysteries of his own composition:

> There is no disguising the fact that the American people are much inter-
> ested and mystified about the mere matter of color as connected with man-
> hood. It seems to them that color has some moral or immoral qualities and
> especially the latter. They do not feel quite reconciled to the idea that a man
> of different color from themselves should have all the human rights claimed
> by themselves. When an unknown man is spoken of in their presence, the
> first question that arises in the average American mind concerning him and
> which must be answered is, Of what color is he? and he rises or falls in esti-
> mation by the answer given. . . . Hence I have often been bluntly and some-
> times very rudely asked, of what color my mother was, and of what color
> was my father? In what proportion does the blood of the various races min-
> gle in my veins, especially how much white blood and how much black blood
> entered into my composition? . . . Whether I considered myself more African
> than Caucasian, or the reverse? Whether I derived my intelligence from my
> father, or from my mother, from my white, or from my black blood? . . .
> Why did I marry a person of my father's complexion instead of marrying
> one of my mother's complexion?[15]

Such questions shaped the significance of the life Douglass found himself
constrained to live. Being subject to such questions compromises the un-
questionable manhood he attempted to embody.

Douglass, by the time he came to write *My Bondage and My Freedom* in
1855, had developed a definite answer to one of these questions, one that

both bespoke the origins of his power and its always compromised nature. In response, no doubt, to racist assumptions about the linkage of blood and talent (some of which he sometimes gave evidence of sharing), Douglass reconceived the story of his mother and her relationship to him.[16] His brief, dry mention of her and his loss of her in the *Narrative* is here expanded to include not only a record of his sentiments regarding her loss ("The side view of her face is imaged on my memory, and I take few steps in life, without feeling her presence; but the image is mute, and I have no striking words of her's [sic] treasured up")[17] but also a striking modification of her muteness. She becomes for him not only a figure of sentimental attachment but a prefiguration of his own voice and power, which he receives from her along with the "complexion" that identifies him. He writes:

> I learned, after my mother's death, that she could read, and that she was the only one of all the slaves and colored people in Tuckahoe who enjoyed that advantage. . . . I can, therefore, fondly and proudly ascribe to her an earnest love of knowledge. That a "field hand" should learn to read, in any slave state, is remarkable; but the achievement of my mother, considering the place, was very extraordinary; and, in view of that fact, I am quite willing, and even happy, to attribute any love of letters I possess, and for which I have got— despite of prejudices—only too much credit, not to my admitted Anglo-Saxon paternity, but to the native genius of my sable, unprotected, and uncultivated mother—a woman, who belonged to a race whose mental endowments it is, at present, fashionable to hold in disparagement and contempt. (155–56)[18]

Continuing his self-affiliation with his mother, Douglass recounts how he finds in Prichard's *Natural History of Man* (a volume he was probably using in his polemics against racist polygenesis theories about this time) "the head of a figure—on page 157—the features of which so resemble those of my mother, that I often recur to it with something of the feeling which I suppose others experience when looking upon the pictures of dear departed ones" (52).[19] That picture, as James M'Cune Smith tells us in his preface to the book, "is copied from the statue of Ramses the Great, an Egyptian king of the nineteenth dynasty" (136). Complexly overdetermined in race and gender, Douglass here digs deeper into his personal history and the cultural and racial history of the West. He insists not only on his own identification with his mother's black identity but his continued indebtedness to her condition that makes her achievement (as much as his) remarkable. The origin of Douglass's literacy and power stems not from his Anglo-Saxon patrimony but from his enslaved mother and the "mixed" culture she comes to represent for him. While it would be overstating the case to claim that through this readoption of his mother Douglass acknowledges the inevitably feminized component of the masterful masculine identity to which he aspires, his portrait of his mother as a model for his own achievement at least suggests his awareness that the promises of self-agency and self-possession must be qualified by an awareness, first, that the conditions of identity persist as the grounds of any effort to transcend them, and second, that his bondage and his freedom may remain implicated each in the other and difficult at times to distinguish.

The complexity of Douglass's cross-gendered affiliation with black identity through his reidentification with his enslaved mother illustrates his simultaneous insistence on identity's importance and his refusal to essentialize its differences. In collapsing his parentage into the single figure of his African mother as represented by the silent statue of an Egyptian pharaoh, Douglass not only displaces the racist slave owners in his own personal story but gestures toward an empowering cultural genesis in an ancient civilization, one that was at the center of ethnological arguments about cultural and racial origins in the middle of the nineteenth century (as it is today).[20] But Douglass's invention of these origins remains complex and conflicted, marked by the scars of slavery and injustice that qualify the claims of power even as they emerge as the basis of his identity. As Jenny Franchot has noted, "As a primary Christian symbol of racial and religious oppression, the pharaoh, after all, is a dual figure: Douglass's selection of 'him' to impersonate 'her' reimposes the slaveholder on the figure of the mother. The recovery of origin would always speak of duplicity rather than union."[21] Given the constitutive role of the struggle for and with identity within Douglass himself, it is not surprising that his return to his mother finally fails to free him from the problems of identity or the demands of masculinity with which he continues to contend throughout the rest of his long career.

Douglass refuses to essentialize culture or identity, but he does not thereby free himself from the questions his own culture attaches to race. During his visit to Egypt in 1887, a trip he described as having "an ethnological purpose," Douglass made the following entry in his diary: "I do not know of what color and features the ancient Egyptians were . . . but the great mass of the people I have yet seen would in America be classed with Negroes. . . . This would not be a scientific description, but an American description."[22] Race remains for Douglass a political, moral, and national issue not because race in itself signifies but because racist significations legitimate injustices that perpetuate and provoke violence. By tracing his own and his cultures' origins back to the point where the African continent and its cultures touched on and influenced, mixed with and helped determine the origins and character of the West, including the technologies of writing and reason, Douglass hoped to further his attempts to alter the significance of race and culture in America. He hoped to undo the white nationalist legitimation of Euro-American hegemony by revealing that, in its origin as in its present life, identity, like all identities and like Douglass himself, was composite.

In his speech on "Our Composite Nationality," which deals with the controversy over restricting Chinese as well as German immigration to the United States, restrictions that Douglass himself strongly opposed, he wrote the following:

> A knowledge of the character, resources and proceedings of other nations, affords us the means of comparison and criticism, without which progress would be feeble, tardy, and perhaps, impossible. It is by comparing one nation with another, and one learning from another, each competing with all, and all competing with each, that hurtful errors are exposed, great social truths discovered, and the wheels of civilization whirled onward. . . . The voice of civilization speaks an unmistakable language against the isolation of families, nations and races, and pleads for composite nationality as essential to her triumphs. . . . Those races of men who have maintained the most distinct and separate existence for the longest periods of time; which have had the least intercourse with other races of men are a standing confirmation of the folly of isolation. The very soil of the national mind becomes in such cases barren, and can only be resuscitated by assistance from without.[23]

Douglass works to guarantee, in his own person, that his audience will remember the multifarious composition of the nation's identity so that the iconography of the nation cannot remain forever a white-faced sham.

Through his own composite identity, U.S. citizen and member of a pre-scribed race, he attempts to think for himself this paradoxical identity and represent it for the nation. This is the manner in which he unites his own conflicted subjectivity and the conflicted subject of the nation. It is a diffi-cult position to occupy and a difficult role to play.

The language of competition and strife in which Douglass couches these observations is the language of competitive and aggressive manliness that comes to be the masculine ideal for nineteenth-century American men. The virtues that composition or cosmopolitanism brings to the fore are the competitive virtues of self-command and courage, the capacity to win a fight, even against all odds. These become healthy signs of vigor and virility, the hallmark of men in a healthy and growing society. Douglass tries to maintain a difficult balance between struggle and conquest on the one hand and respect and reciprocity on the other, but his argument for the creative tension between nationalities and cultures within a composite nation re-quires the persistence of individual identities and a continuing play of and for power among the men who compose it.

This is the nonutopian aspect of Douglass's embattled discursive practice, and it frames and determines the significance of both the more utopian universalism of his cultural aspirations and the determinately masculine aggressiveness of his bid for self-possession. He provokes Americans to remember that the potentially productive tensions within their composite national identity involve inextricably intertwined differences. These make the republic's universalizing languages inevitably ironic and put its various identities into tense, agonistic play. To register those ironies, to realize the truth of the republic's character, requires remembering the exclusions, the violence, and the inequities that have scarred U.S. society and marked the identities that compose it. Without this difficult remembering, what passes for universality in American national identity, and what passes for the end of identity itself, will require that Americans forget themselves and their situations and forgo opposition to the nation's failure.

DOUGLASS AND HAITI

Frantz Fanon noted that to be a black intellectual is to be "forever in com-bat with [one's] own image." Ross Posnock argues that Fanon and other black public figures have often tried, therefore, to reject racial identity and to opt for the "universal."[24] Douglass engaged in this self-reflexive struggle throughout his long career. In classic speeches like "What to the Slave Is the Fourth of July," "Our Composite National Identity," and "The Claims of the Negro Ethnographically Considered," he appealed for racial liberation by opting for the universal in the form of those principles of equality and justice that are especially dear to Americans and peculiarly central to the nation's identity. These universal principles offer no defensible grounds for exclusion or privilege and should make the inequities of the color line and of imperialism unacceptable to America and its peoples. But later in his career, Douglass also exemplifies the dangers inherent in the universal promise of those extraordinarily appealing Enlightenment ideals that Americans love to claim as their own. Given the difficulty of his position and the complexities of identity as Douglass experienced and understood them, his failure always to successfully embody the American virtues he championed should surprise no one. Even his failures remain instructive. Liberal universalism, when assorted with national identity, can, as the rest of the world long has known, be made an excuse for imperial domination. At his worst moments, Douglass perhaps does no worse than to remain a representative American man. When Douglass failed to condemn—or arguably even to recognize—America's imperialistic designs on Haiti during his consulship there, he manifested America's more general and characteristic failure to accurately recognize itself or its true place in the world. Douglass's failure in Haiti illustrates the especially occluded nature of the American empire and the dangerous proximity of the promise of human liberation to the extension of imperialist dominion in the American imagination. The ease with which Americans confuse liberty and empire projects the nation's domestic problems with identity and justice abroad. However, Douglass's failure in Haiti does not so much disprove the efficacy of universal principles themselves, or even the promises of American identity they subtend, as it demonstrates the careful moral calculus and political calculation required to live up to either. This more careful moral calculus may require remembering rather than rejecting the importance of racial, gendered, and national identity.

The story of Douglass's ministry to Haiti will seem, to those distressed by today's events, depressingly familiar. American interests, mercantile and imperialist, having fomented a rebellion against an uncooperative foreign government in Haiti, found themselves unable to control the subsequent course of events. The rebellion was led by two black generals, François D. Légitime and Florvil Hyppolite, who then fought over leadership of the new government. Légitime, supported by the French, initially won control and grudging recognition from President Harrison's government. Hyppolite, however, mobilized support among "black" Haitians whom the "mulattos" in Légitime's government had turned against. Despite the U.S. president's recognition, the American navy, fronting for powerful New York shipping and mercantile interests connected to the secretary of the navy, Benjamin Franklin Tracey, backed Hyppolite's insurgency, and using the Atlantic fleet of irascible Admiral Ghirardi, broke a blockade, resupplied Hyppolite's forces, and assisted them in seizing control of Haiti. In exchange, these U.S. interests believed they deserved special terms for doing business in Haitian ports, and American imperialists wanted an indefinite lease on the Haitian harbor at Mole St. Nicolas for a coaling station that would improve America's position in the international competition to build and maintain access to a Central American canal. Haiti, on its tiny half island, thus occupied, for a moment, a key position in U.S. strategies of empire as it had long occupied a key position in the American imaginary about race.[25] However, Hyppolite, once installed, proved difficult to control. The Haitian people for their part demonstrated surprising unity against compromising Haiti's fragile sovereignty, especially when threatened by Admiral Ghirardi's Atlantic fleet. Thus, as minister to Haiti, Douglass immediately found himself caught up in the maneuvers and machinations of ruthless, aggressive private interests, a willful, rebellious military, and a weak, pliable chief executive. This describes the situation on the American side.[26]

The failure of any diplomatic mission to Haiti was probably predetermined from the outset by the militaristic temper of those imperially fevered times. As an index to that time, metonymic juxtaposition becomes interpretively informative. Alongside Douglass's apologia for his failure to gain title to the Haitian coaling station in the fall 1891 issue of the *North American Review* may be found an article by Admiral Luce, "The Benefits of War," on the invigorating effects of war on cultures and peoples, which, as Douglass biographer William McFeely says, bespeaks "an ominous line of thinking essentially new to America."[27] Yet another article in the same issue, by an Admiral Porter, brings Luce's lesson home. War builds certain kinds of characters and demands certain virtues, especially for men, and Porter describes these as he tells the story of a celebrated "hero of the [Civil] war," William Barker Cushing, who sank the Confederate ironclad *Albemarle*.

The story merits retelling here. Responding in print to a request for information from General James Grant Wilson regarding "the Young Heroes, Cushing and Custer," Porter, who was Cushing's commanding officer at the time of the *Albemarle* adventure, tells how the brash lieutenant surprised the rebels and destroyed their ship on the night of October 27, 1864.[28] This "gallant and successful" enterprise of a "dashing" youthful volunteer began inauspiciously enough with the loss of two of Cushing's three torpedo launches before he ever got near the enemy. But in this tale the man's intrepid character trumps his doubtful competence. Porter's account might furnish an appropriate scenario for a John Wayne movie, though as the history of a military engagement or a model for manly conduct in command it should pose problems. Romantic heroes tend toward insubordination, and Cushing is no exception: "On the very morning appointed for Cushing to sail on his perilous expedition an order came for the Navy Department to try him by court-martial for some infraction of international law towards an English vessel, which, according to Mr. Seward, had endangered the *entente cordiale* between England and the United States." The dashing "free lancer," "not disconcerted" by the possibility that he may have imperiled the diplomatic understanding most singularly important to the Union's success in the War, coolly proposes, "Let me go and blow up the 'Albemarle,' and try me afterward." The admiral, one man of action to another, agrees. There is then a comic interlude during which the incorrigibly boyish Cushing irritates his commander by regaling "numerous friends" on champagne and terrapin. After this the moment for action arrives, and Cushing sets out (296–98).

Now the hero shows his mettle. Assessing a desperate situation with "keen gray eyes," Cushing makes his move. Despite an alert and determined defense of the ironclad, "the child of fortune" manages an element of surprise. Luck and pluck—as Horatio Alger would have it—wins the day. Or sort of. Cushing sinks the *Albemarle* and escapes, but most of his command is killed or captured by the Confederates. "Cushing," however, escapes and "made himself famous" by achieving this "enterprise." He won the Union Army an advantage on the waterway and himself glory in the newspapers that nicknamed him "*Albemarle* Cushing." He received a field promotion and prize money of "sixty or seventy thousand dollars."[29] Admiral Porter, at a moment when military men appointed themselves the philosophers and guardians of American manhood, states his moral: "The success of Cushing shows that a man who makes up his mind to a certain thing and goes directly to the point, undeterred by obstacles, is almost sure to win, not only in blowing up ships, but in every-day affairs of life where great stakes are at risk. Here was a chance, and Cushing, 'seized the bull by the horns,' *voila tout"* (303). With such a man, Porter knows better than to stickle at details: "suffice it to say that I never tried Cushing by court-martial on Secretary Seward's charges of endangering the *entente cordiale* between England and the United States" (303). Diplomatic initiatives and international law, after all, are but empty forms. A man like Cushing is a vital force and answerable to higher laws.

This romantic and charming tale accords familiarly with much in popular imaginings of the American male and his commanding place in the world. Herman Melville, only slightly more reticent than Porter in his admiration of the young daredevil, cast his reaction to the *Albemarle* escapade into a poem called "At the Cannon's Mouth." Unlike Admiral Porter, however, Melville registers some misgivings. He writes of Cushing, "He has his fame; / But that mad dash at death, how name?" concluding:

> In Cushing's eager spirit was shown
> A spirit which brave poets own—
> That scorn of life which earns life's crown;
> Earns, but not always wins; but *he*—
> The star ascended in his nativity.[30]

Melville's suggestion of misgiving—his characteristic awareness of success's costs and failure's possibility—is not surprising. Cushing, in his ruthlessness and his lack of scruple, seems a more attractive but still recognizable avatar of Ahab. Melville knew to be wary of such men.

Remembering the Civil War allows Porter to proselytize a romantic version of militarized manhood: men of daring, of steely eyes, who wrest life's prize by acting in the face of desperate odds with defiant courage. Such romance occludes carnage and costs and devalues the more prosaic calculations of diplomacy. War affords opportunities to show, as Porter in his official commendation of Cushing put it, "heroic enterprise" in "hazardous" undertakings, a virtue fit for a risky, competitive, and hierarchical masculine world. "Enterprise" becomes such an important word in the imperial American lexicon that for Porter it merits nearly obsessive repetition.[31] He suggests, as part of the time's tone, that affairs of state and commerce be left to enterprising men of action, not to elder diplomats or State Department officials, not even to the newly emergent class of professionals and experts. Moreover, Porter's comparison of his young hero to Custer, whose self-assertive enterprise finally led him and his troop into needless catastrophe shortly after Cushing's quieter death in 1873, probably didn't trouble his readers. Custer's last stand became a central myth for imperial America in its ruthless and violent expansion across the continent and eventually beyond its limits.[32] The memories and myths of Custer and Cushing at the century's end help furnish a vision of the ruthless manhood imperial adventures require. Porter concludes, "In many respects Cushing and Custer were alike: . . . dashing, reckless, brave men, strangers to fear, who never thought of the consequences to themselves in any undertaking, no matter how desperate. . . . Their features were bold, the expression of their eye was the same, and both had lithe figures which seemed proof against fatigue. Put them side by side, and they would have passed for brothers. Perhaps nature fashions that kind of man alike, mentally and physically."[33] And Cushing might have added, in his Whitmanian exuberance about these lithe and vibrant male bodies, nature also entrusts to their vigor and vitality the fate of the nation and the expansion of its empire and influence. Should that require alienating allies and ignoring prudence and policy, exterminating Indians (to recall Custer's announced intention to extirpate the rebellious Sioux) and bullying neighbors, then so be it, for nature ordains it be so. This is no empire for old men; this is no world for diplomats. The prospects, in this environment, for a diplomat who was no longer young were slim; and in 1892 Douglass was no longer the embodiment of masculine vigor. He was, however, still black, and as minister to Haiti his color, as well as his gender, put him in an interesting position.

DOUGLASS'S WHITE MALE TROUBLE

Some familiar anxieties attached to white masculinity during the late nineteenth century manifest themselves in concurrently running stories in the New York newspapers during the spring of 1891 while negotiations around Mole St. Nicolas reached their crisis. To gauge the temper of the times in which Douglass worked and the brand of masculinity favored in the 1890s, consider the following. On May 18, 1891, while Douglass was struggling with Admiral Girardi in Haiti, the *World* ran a column promoting the efficacy of its own advertising on the front page under the headline: "Be Master or Slave: That's What Advertising Makes of a Business Man." The first sentence offers the following description of the manly virtues required to dominate in business: "There comes a 'hurry call' in every man's life. He has the chance to become a man of wealth, of position, of weight in the community. If he misses it he becomes practically a no body. When the call comes it is met either with the chariot of success or by the ambulance to take the poor unfortunate to the home for the helpless." The piece continues in this antithetical vein ("Drive or be driven, be master or slave"), recommending advertising in the *World* as the surest way to make sure that the reader ends up a master and not a slave, aggressively meeting the challenges of commerce rather than sinking beneath the chains of adversity.

Such racially inflected pieces were far from rare. The same paper a month later (June 26, 1891) carried a front page article with the sensational headline "Won by a Dusky Suitor: Good Ground L. I. Startled by a Sensational Elopement: . . . A White Girl Marries an Educated Colored Man." The article enumerates the physical comeliness of the suitor ("a figure like Herucles, brown skin, regular and not Negro features, and teeth like ivory"), his education (graduate of West Point and a civil engineer "who thoroughly knows his business"), and his excellent reputation. Nonetheless, the piece dwells on the pathetic state of the bride's mother ("nearly crazed with grief at the conduct of her daughter"); and while the article's overall tone is not unsympathetic to the handsome black man and his bride (who is "considered very pretty"), it was placed on the front page to set tongues clucking and to entertain the reader with a gossipy bit of interracial smut. More sensational is the bit of racist natural history that the newspaper had presented a few months before (February 8, 1891) in the form of a long, front page article titled "The 'Blue Gum Nigger': He Is Considered as Dangerous as a Mad Cur: Other Negroes in Terror of Him: His Bite Will Cause Blood Poisoning That Is Usually Fatal—Their Every Request Granted for Fear of Incurring Their Displeasure—How an Indian Died from the Effects of a Bite." This headline gives a pretty complete précis of the piece, which also contains useful information concerning how to identify these dangerous beings: "The blue gum can always be distinguished as soon as he opens his mouth and smiles. His gums will be seen to possess a hue which entitles him to the appellation by which he is known." The interested reader also finds instruction in treating these bites: "seek another blue gum who possesses the power to remove the deadly poison." Although (or perhaps because) these black men and women are said to be descendents of "royalty," they seem more like rabid beasts than members of the human family. A week later (February 15, 1891) the paper's Sunday edition carried a feature piece detailing how North Carolina had solved "the race problem" and placed the Negro "on the road to prosperity." Clever white men were set to laboring alongside black men so that the latter's naturally "imitative nature" might replace the "overseer's . . . huge, black snake whip" as a motive force. This ploy, the credit for which belongs "to the white man rather than to the black," succeeds brilliantly and the black man has "ceased singing and gone to hard work." The race problem has thus ceased to exist in North Carolina.

But of all these pieces culled from a casual survey of headlines in the *World,* none seemed more indicative of the terrors still attached to race than the large front page headline for May 18, 1891: "Born White; Died Black." The article has virtually nothing to say about the death apart from the remarkable alteration in the unlucky man's appearance and identity. His jaundice deepens until he appears like a "quadroon," then "like a mulatto," and finally "his entire skin was black." The article avoids any sympathetic identifications between the reader and the dying man to focus on the horrors of the racial change he undergoes. When his little children arrive for a final visit, readers are told only that they are "remarkably pretty" and "as white as the offspring of any white people." The terrors of dying black completely displaces the terrors of mortality. The children, conventional objects of sympathetic identification at such a moment, here serve only to emphasize, by their pretty whiteness, the uncanny transformation their dying father undergoes. The next day the newspaper noted on the front page that a similar case was unfolding in Indianapolis where a dying white man "is turning blacker every day and begins to look like a negro." Perhaps an epidemic of race shifting, of white men—members of an energetic and masterful race—turning the color of an indolent and servile people and dying was in the offing. The *World* finds this prospect infinitely more alarming than death itself.

Meanwhile, all through the spring all three newspapers carried extensive accounts of the protracted Sioux uprising in the Dakotas, the lynching of Italians in Louisiana, and the failure to bring the perpetrators to justice. Thus, national expansion and violent resistance, vigilante justice and nativist panic, the challenges of race and masculinity intertwine on the pages of the daily press, offering vivid indications of the ways in which Douglass, to paraphrase Fanon, found himself at the end of his long public career once again at war with his own racialized image.[34]

An example of the sorts of excoriation to which Douglass himself was subjected during his ministry to Haiti may be found in the *Sun*. On June 9, 1891, the *Sun* reported in a front page article, "Days of Blood in Hayti," that "the Mexican Consulate was forced and invaded by the troops, while the Consul himself [was] menaced" and appealed to the entire diplomatic corps to protest this violation of the principle of asylum. The article concluded with the simple statement that Minister Douglass had delayed his scheduled return to the United States because of Haiti's "unsettled condition." Ten days later, the *Sun* had much more to say about Hyppolite's suppression of the coup and his violation of the Mexican consulate in order to seize and execute several of the accused plotters who had sought asylum there. Hyppolite might well be insane and had been especially erratic during the protest visit by the diplomatic corps during which he stormed out of the room in a rage and then returned having, he said, given some orders. Douglass, present as the U.S. representative, was, readers were told, "ashen with fright," apparently believing that Hyppolite had ordered all the diplomats killed. The effect of the president's bullying on the other ministers present goes unreported. The article seems more intent on slandering Douglass than on reporting Haitian news. Purporting to quote an eyewitness who "evidently does not admire Minister Douglass," the article concludes:

> He says the white population accuses Mr. Douglass of siding with the Haytian Government in every instance where American citizens who have war claims against it have urged the payment of the claims; of being so absorbed in the contemplation of the experiment of black men governing themselves that he has forgotten his duties as the representative of his country; of seeking to impress the Haytians with his greatness by publishing in Port-au-Prince a French translation of his book "Forty Years a Slave" and of having said that if he had not been ignored in the negotiations for the possession of Mole St. Nicolas, our government would have acquired it. (*Sun,* June 19, 1891, 1)

Here in a nutshell are the charges to which Douglass would feel himself constrained to respond at the end of his career: insufficient enterprise in the pursuit of his duties, insufficient manliness in the face of opposition, and excessive identification with the black government of Haiti and its leader, once a U.S. ally and now a dangerously unstable despot.

By innuendo and suggestion, all these charges figured again in the *Sun*'s front page reporting of Douglass's return from Haiti to the United States on July 4. The article quotes Douglass's self-defense and thereby makes him repeat the descriptions of his own cowardice. He says, "'it was not true as reported that I had to flee for my life. . . . But we were at one time in great danger from the stray bullets that were flying around our house." Mr. Douglass, the article continues, "had received no official intimation that he had been recalled." It then goes on to make clear the nature of Douglass's true commitments and the reasons why his recall would be well advised: "Mr. Douglass evidently sympathized entirely with the Government of Hayti in the recent trouble and deprecates what he regarded as the sensational and unfair accounts of the affair published in the American papers. He referred sarcastically to the hanging of the Italians in New Orleans as an illustration of what might happen even in such a law abiding country as the United States." The article rehearses Douglass's dissatisfaction with Admiral Gherardi's "doings" in the negotiations concerning Mole St. Nicolas, and states that Douglass "thought himself competent to conduct the negotiations and denied that he had been timid or procrastinating in the matter." Asking for Haitian concessions as a reward for U.S. interference in the struggle between Hyppolite and Légitime was a poor strategy, Douglass is said to have claimed, and he is also said to have asserted that "he had endeavored to get the concession [of the port] simply through leading the Hyppolite Government to see that they should relinquish it to the United States in the interest of commerce and civilization" (*Sun,* July 4, 1891). One week later, the *Sun* allowed Douglass to sum up his views under these headlines: "Fred Douglass on Hayti. He says that Hyppolite is naturally humane and just. He thinks 'Hayti has shown that she cares no more for a white man than she does for a black proud of one of her color and not scared by anybody'" (*Sun,* July 10, 1891, 8). Readers might be expected to remember Douglass's reported blustering a few days later when an article titled "Dark Prospects of Hayti" stated that Douglass and his secretary had left Haiti "because they found the situation a little too hot for them" and implied that in their panic they left American commercial interests and American inhabitants of Haiti languishing in a perilous situation and praying for a squadron to come to their rescue (*Sun,* July 15, 1891, 7).

Douglass, who had made his career by adapting the models of dominant masculinity to his own identity as a black man, confronted once again, in the accusations leveled against him, the problem of race and the question of manliness. But this time he seems to encounter a limit to what he can claim from the dominant ideology as his own. In his first article for the *North American Review,* which he reprinted as one of the last chapters of his final autobiography, Douglass gave this account of the case against him:

> The charge is, that I have been the means of defeating the acquisition of an important United States naval station at the Mole St. Nicolas. It is said, in general terms, that I wasted the whole of my first year in Haiti in needless parley and delay, and finally reduced the chances of getting the Mole to such a narrow margin as to make it necessary for our government to appoint Rear-Admiral Gherardi as a special commissioner to Haiti to take the whole matter of negotiation for the Mole out of my hands. One of the charitable apologies they are pleased to make for my failure is my color; and the implication is that a white man would have succeeded where I failed.[35]

Central to these accusations is that he has failed to show the requisite degree of determined enterprise to accomplish the job and to win the prize. A white man, it is assumed, might have more ruthless Teutonic vigor and violent recklessness—more imperious impatience with parley, negotiation, and law, more ability to act without consideration of consequences, more, in short, enterprise—than this aging black diplomat could be expected to possess. Douglass's problem in Haiti involves the following contradiction: how can a black man show sufficient zeal in an enterprise whose goal it is to compromise the sovereignty of a black nation whose special significance Douglass himself described two years later in the Haitian Pavilion at the Chicago World's Fair when he said, "She was the first of all the cis-Atlantic world . . . in which the black man asserted his right to be free and was brave enough to fight for his freedom and fortunate enough to gain it."[36] During and immediately after his mission, Douglass failed to find an adequate solution to this problem.

From the first, the New York press and the financial interests behind it had been skeptical or hostile about Douglass's appointment, though the ministries to the black republics of Haiti and Liberia had been awarded to black ministers since the first Grant administration.[37] As Douglass said, "The color argument is not new. It besieged the White House before I was appointed." Ironically, several pundits asserted that receiving a black minister would be an insult to the black nation. Douglass continues, "They did not see that it would be shockingly inconsistent for Haiti to object to a black minister while she herself is black." "Prejudice," Douglass concludes, "sets all logic at defiance."[38] The logic at work here, however, is the militaristic logic of empire as a realm for the expression of violent and aggressive masculinity. Once a black republic like Haiti became a significant site for imperial ambition, the questions of race, gender, and power made the success of a black man, sure to have insufficient zeal and enterprise, doubtful. That Douglass would be accused of laggard zest in his pursuit of his nation's ends was foreordained from the start.

Douglass's own thinking on the issue of the mission's failure is more subtle. In his self-defense, written for the *North American Review* and reprinted in the final version of his last autobiography, race also plays a crucial part. The first item of his self-defense charges that the failure of America to solve its own racial problems at home compromises its ability to win the trust of black people abroad. Arguing that a white minister would have been unfitted for the post by "his American contempt for the colored race at home" and prevented thereby from winning "the respect and good will of colored people abroad," Douglass drives his point home:

> Haiti is no stranger to Americans or to American prejudice. Our white fellow-countrymen have taken little pains to conceal their sentiments. This objection to my color and this demand for a white man to succeed me spring from the very feeling which Haiti herself contradicts and detests. . . . This clamor for a white minister for Haiti is based upon the idea that a white man is held in higher esteem by her than is a black man, and that he could get more out of her than can one of her own color. It is not so, and the whole free history of Haiti proves it not to be so.[39]

A white minister, Douglass concludes, would be met by "the contempt and disgust of Haiti" (1028), not its approbation.

At this point, when Douglass has expressed his firm conviction that color matters, he adds to it an oddly qualifying proviso, one that asserts his understanding of American principles and his confusion considering their application. Even if it were true that Haitians were beset by an internalized racist logic that would lead them to respect the ministry of a white more than a black representative, the United States should defy such racist logic:

> It would be the height of meanness for a great nation like the United States to take advantage of such servility on the part of a weak nation. The American people are too great to be small, and they should ask nothing of Haiti on grounds less just and reasonable than those upon which they ask anything of France or England. . . . Are we to wring from it by dread of our power what we cannot obtain by appeals to its justice and reason? (1029)

This characteristic American appeal to America as the embodiment of equitable justice and self-evident reason enacts an odd and telling ambiguity, one that undermines the strength of Douglass's appeal to universal principles. The antecedent of the final crucial clause, "appeals to its justice and reason," is dangerously obscure. "Its" may refer to the justice and reason of Haiti or to the justice and reason of "our" own dreaded power. Everything depends on this distinction. The first refers to a moral absolute that by definition should be universally recognizable and self-evidently persuasive. The second extols the exercise of dreaded power in America's self-interest in accord with particular reasons of state and the demands of global competition. Either universal principles or imperial self-interest legitimates the threat of force, and in Douglass's account at this crucial moment it seems unclear to which he actually refers.

This is more than a grammatical quibble. Douglass quickly comes to the essential charge against him, that as a black man he was indifferent or hostile to American imperial interests, "unable to grasp the importance to American commerce and to American influence of such a [coaling] station in the Caribbean Sea."[40] Here one would have welcomed the acid contempt he would later heap on those in the United States who, as he would put it in his Chicago World's Fair speech on Haiti,

> to accomplish their personal and selfish ends, will fan the flame of passion between the factions in Haiti and will otherwise assist in setting revolutions afoot . . . if it give them a market for their worthless wares. . . . To them, the welfare of Haiti is nothing; the shedding of human blood is nothing; the

success of free institutions is nothing. And the ruin of a neighboring country is nothing. They are sharks, pirates and Shylocks, greedy for money, no matter at what cost of life and misery to mankind.[41]

One would have at least expected something of the sarcasm with which he reportedly attempted to deflate the sensationalized reporting of Hyppolite's atrocities by reminding U.S. readers that U.S. citizens were lynching other U.S. citizens with alarming frequency. None of this appears here. Instead, he rushes to present his own credentials as an enthusiastic agent of the nation's imperial self-interest, one who need apologize to no white man for his lack of zeal or even recklessness in the pursuit of the nation's goals:

> The fact is, that when some of these writers were in their petticoats, I had comprehended the value of such an acquisition, both in respect to American commerce and to American influence. The policy of obtaining such a station is not new. I supported Gen. Grant's ideas on this subject against the powerful opposition of my honored and revered friend Charles Sumner, more than twenty years ago, and proclaimed it on a hundred platforms and to thousands of my fellow-citizens. I said then that it was a shame to American statesmanship that, while almost every other great nation in the world had secured a foothold and had power in the Caribbean Sea, where it could anchor in its own bays and moor in its own harbors, we, who stood at the very gate of that sea, had there no anchoring ground anywhere. I was for the acquisition of Samana, and of Santo Domingo herself, if she wished to come to us. While slavery existed, I was opposed to all schemes for the extension of American power and influence. But since its abolition, I have gone with him who goes furthest for such extension.[42]

This is the note Douglass struck when he claimed, to reporters, that he would have convinced Hyppolite to cede sovereignty in the interests of "commerce and civilization." Nowhere does he sound more desperately and troublingly American. His support of President Grant's attempt to grab Santo Domingo remains clearly visible despite the fig leaf offered by the afterthought about popular will. "She" emphatically did not wish "to come to us," and her neighbor on the island of Hispaniola remained suspicious of American expansionism.[43] To Hyppolite and to other Haitians, commerce seemed to be not an agent of civilization but the motive force of U.S.

imperial demands, demands in which racism played an obvious and structuring role. Douglass's identification with America aligns him with a white nation's sense of entitlement to interfere at will in a black nation's affairs and sovereignty. Douglass's attempt to forget his color here makes him inevitably an agent of racist domination and a tool of a national policy whose imperialist injustices he should have denounced.

Douglass's probable reasons for not denouncing this imperialist land grab were, no doubt, also deeply American. He is performing a too familiar aspect of American identity as it disports itself on the global stage. He identifies the extension of American power and influence with the extension of American values—paradoxically universal values of justice, freedom, equality, the values of "commerce and civilization." The abolition of slavery has freed the United States to expand the sphere not merely of its interests and influence but of its liberal democratic virtues as far into the world as possible. How odd it is to read these sentiments in close proximity to Douglass's bitingly satirical observations concerning the precise manner in which American failures to honor these values—American injustice, oppression, and inequality at home—discredit the United States as a moral agent abroad. Moreover, he well knew that in Haiti the smokescreen of universalism hid the realities of all too specific U.S. interests—shipping magnates, militarists, and their apologists—whose stakes in U.S. dominance of the Caribbean basin were far from disinterested and whose machinations Douglass himself would denounce only a few months later. No one, least of all Douglass, would want to argue that democratic and enlightened principles would not have been welcome in Haiti where republican and revolutionary rhetoric was even then repeatedly made to mask brutal and oppressive dictatorships, a senseless and unjust racialized hierarchy of pigment, and a level of institutionalized incompetence stunning to behold. But Douglass turned a blind eye to the violent role that the United States, France, and other imperial powers had played in creating and maintaining this sad state of affairs. His strange inconsequence in urging American expansion, "commerce and civilization," as a prescription for its remedy rather than a manifestation of its root cause bespeaks his fullest achievement of a characteristically and disappointingly American national identity, one that fails to honor its own principles and fails to notice that failure.

Crucially, it is not Douglass's allegiance to particularity that compromises his moral and ethical vision, as recent champions of universalism suggest identity allegiances will do, but his subscription to an aggressive mascu-linity based on universal principles central to American national identity. Douglass's inability or unwillingness, at crucial moments, to distinguish between brutal self-interest and universal right, between the inequities of commerce and the promises of civilization, between America as it is and America as it promises to be, makes him in the fullest and most troubling sense an American representative. It has been characteristically American to believe that these things—American manhood, American interests, and universal justice—providentially coincide, even, or especially, when they are most at odds. In his willingness to become an agent for U.S. imperial-ist interests in the Caribbean, Douglass became, momentarily, the dupe of this hope and the fool of this belief. In his opposition to slavery, he judged his nation by its own criteria and found it wanting. In Haiti, at least momen-tarily, he fails to do so, failing to recognize that the gravest threat to the nation's values lies with those who attempt to cover violent and unjust prac-tices by false appeals to the nation's creed. In this sense, Douglass, during his failed ministry to Haiti, remains very much our troubling contempo-rary and compatriot. The failure of America becomes his own.

conclusion

American Identities and
Global Terror

The Western in the Middle East,
or American Identity Abroad

Beau Geste, William A. Wellman's 1939 cinematic romance of legionnaires besieged by Bedouins in a desert outpost, represents a version of Arab identity still familiar in the West. The orphaned Geste brothers, Beau (Gary Cooper), Digby (Robert Preston), and John (Ray Milland), described by their charming guardian (Susan Hayward) as "three little gentlemen of fortune," grow up and join the French Foreign Legion. Their incidental motivation involves a chivalrous desire to protect their guardian from a family scandal involving financial ruin and a purloined jewel, the Blue Water Sapphire. Their real motivation stems from their boyish desire for adventure. Their enlistment in the expeditionary forces of the French Empire continues their romantic childhood fantasies and games. Thus, the film imagines the armed conflicts of empire as the romantic projection of Western masculinity on the East, the expression of a boyish love of adventure on the territory and bodies of the natives. In one wonderful scene, recruits to the legion appear at a desert staging ground still in their civilian clothes, consisting of an assortment of easily recognizable central casting costumes. The burly American (Broderick Crawford) appears in a cowboy vest and a ten-gallon hat; the French counterfeiter (Harold Huber) sports a foulard and a beret; a stuffy Englishman wears a bowler hat and has, of course, a monocle. The film, like all romances, relentlessly reduces identity to type. Indeed, the genre makes its most effective appeals through such simplified and familiar identities. Romantic heroes should be iconic embodiments of masculine virtue; romantic heroines should be beautiful and resolute in adversity; romantic villains should be implacable avatars of evil. In the romantic mythology of the French Foreign Legion, the desert represents the place where European and American men go to forget who they were and what they did in more civilized climes. But what really gets forgotten in these oriental romances is that such fantastic simplifications of identity—extensions of romantic characterizations that reduce individuals to types—play a crucial part in the real expression of imperial power. The imposition of empire often depends on reductions of identity into a concise opposition between them and us, one that the long history of vicissitudes and conflicts in and among American identities traced in preceding chapters of this book both rehearses and contests.

The Geste boys run off to join the Legion after someone—perhaps one of them—steals the fantastically valuable Blue Water Sapphire, the mother of all sapphires and the basis of the family fortune. The stone, of course, originated in the East. The cursed gem is a favorite topos of the Orientalist romance in which purloined Eastern wealth frequently motivates conflicts and causes mayhem among Western antagonists. Percival Christopher Wren's novel and this film's adaptation of it share this trusty device with Wilkie Collins, A. C. Doyle, and many others. That these frequently ill-gotten gains usually bring death and destruction rather than wealth and ease seems wholly appropriate. They represent synecdochically the vast stolen human and material wealth of the Orient and the endless and costly skirmishes and wars among Western powers over the spoils of empire. They represent as well, one suspects, the bad conscience of the West, which, under the thin ideological cover of a civilizing mission and a romantic idea of identity, has long conducted the vicious subjection and plunder of colonized peoples it purported to uplift and protect. The West, like the United States itself, has often defined itself through its failure to live up to its own principles. The possibility that the American-led war in Iraq merely continues this tradition has haunted that enterprise from its inception.

Beau Geste indicates that the inception of the current Iraq war, and the war on terror of which it has sometimes been made a part, began long before the dreadful events of September 11, 2001. The film, at crucial moments, allows an attentive audience to read the history of the West's bad faith as it has expressed itself in America's struggles with identity. At the induction scene in which the legionnaires appear in their civilian costumes, they hear the villainous Sergeant Markoff (Brian Donlevy), a Russian martinet who has done time in Siberia (and who therefore represents a contemporary Eastern threat to American domestic and global interests), deliver an indoctrinating harangue. You are here, he tells the recruits, at the service of "twenty million natives," furnishing them the "protection and justice that is the tradition of the Foreign Legion." Yet, Markoff's sadism and greed, his abuse of his command, and his desire to steal the sapphire from Beau guarantee that the Westerners remain too embroiled in their own desires for wealth and struggles over plunder to pay much real attention to the Arabs they are supposed to be civilizing. In fact, Arabs surprisingly do not appear until the second half of the film and then only on the margins. The first Arabs we see, dressed in robes and head cloths like all the Arabs in the film, are two nameless "scouts"—like the Indian scouts standard to the film western—who guard the gateway to the desert, the place where white men cannot survive and that symbolizes the region's hostility to the invaders. When Markoff turns two would-be deserters out into the desert to die, these scouts furnish their implacable escorts and executioners. The desert, an almost instantly fatal environment to a white man, provides the natural habitat for these beings who are, of course, human but of a different order.

The desert denizens appear in numbers as the faceless hordes who besiege the fort at the film's climax. These Arabs serve primarily to disrupt the mutiny against Markoff's tyranny among the legionnaires, to suspend the struggle over the sapphire between Markoff and Beau, and to redirect all this internal strife outward. No explanation for the Arab attack seems necessary. The only motive the film attributes to them is predictably religious. Their "holy men," Markoff explains, are stirring them up. The film, especially interesting given current anxieties about Arab identity in Western lands, self-consciously presents the Arabs as figments of the Western imagination. Sergeant Markoff, his garrison reduced to just himself and one Geste brother (all the other mutineers and Beau himself have been killed in the attack), repulses the final Arab assault on the fort and chortles as the Bedouins retreat: "They come when I want them and leave when I don't need them any more. . . . They put down the mutiny for me and made me an officer and have given me the Legion of Honor." If the logic of romance reduces all identities to types, the Arabs appear as perfectly romantic characters, which is to say, not as characters at all. They are literally an undifferentiated mass of easily manipulated primitives or an implacable and motiveless menace. The film presents them exclusively from a distance as teeming crowds in identical robes and dying in great numbers that never merit counting, easy to intimidate, fool, and kill but dangerous nonetheless. No Arab is individualized, even within the narrow limits of romantic characterization or cinematic art. No Arab becomes a hero or a villain. No Arab's death throes require a close-up, because all Arabs, with their robes, their shrieks, and their holy wars, are all the same. They share a common identity that is absolutely different from the identities of the Westerners who have come to civilize or plunder them.

The ways in which this quaint Hollywood romance still seems contemporary hardly require enumeration. While American adventures in the Middle East have produced several fantastic Arab villains, it offers little place for individuated Arab identities and no audience for Arab complaints. As figments of the Western imagination, the Arab's romantic identity has been and continues to be terribly useful for the maintenance of power and for disguising the failure of Europeans and Americans to live up to the principles with which they identify themselves.

Simplified explanations of the links between identity and culture actually produce the impenetrable differences they pretend to describe. If Moslems attack then it must be an expression of their essential identity as religious fanatics hostile to the West. Their specific experiences of a world in which European and American expeditionary forces appear unbidden on Arab lands need not be considered. Meanwhile, European and American actions, and the actions of those with whom Westerners identify, are always more complicated and contingent even when they include the same barbarisms of torture or indiscriminate violence that supposedly express the identities of Arabs.

Identities, of course, are personal as well as public constructs. When I was a boy, my older brother and I were watching *Beau Geste* one Saturday afternoon. I was laughing because my brother had noticed that while the European defenders had names and at least rudimentary personalities, the Arabs had neither. And so he began to supply them with both by making up names for individual figures in the mounted hordes. What seemed especially funny to me is that he used the stock of Arabic words we shared with our parents and relatives from the "old country," almost exclusively names for the foods our mother cooked. "Ah, the attack of Sheik el Mahsi," he announced, singling out one warrior and naming him after the tasty stew of eggplant, onions, and tomatoes that was a household staple. "Retreat, O! Kibbi Nayii," addressing another swarthy menace as the dish of raw meat, cracked wheat, and spices that we ate some Sunday dinners and holidays. "I am wounded, Warak Dawali," one Arab falling from his horse cried to another, named for the grape leaves that we ate rolled with rice and onions with lemon and oil or lamb. I howled. And in later days this memory stayed with me, in part because such moments between brothers separated by many years in age are fairly rare but also because it was for me a moment of enlightenment.

When I remembered this episode, I would chuckle at what seemed to me an excellent joke. I would also come to wonder over what my brother had noticed. Why did the Arabs lack the names and identities that might differentiate them even within the crude characterizations of heroes and villains in a Hollywood romance? Why did they, like the Native Americans in the frontier romances that were my usual Saturday TV fare, require so little by way of motivation to explain their bloodthirsty shrieks and bloodcurdling menace? Why did their identity as Arabs explain in a single word everything we needed to know about them? In naming those Arabs with the names of our special food—and this is long before Levantine cuisine became popular in the United States—my brother was making an intimate if tenuous identification between us and those the film urged us to see as other than us, an identification involving as much ironic distance as sympathetic rapprochement and dependent on a determined moment of disidentification with the Western romance of the film's main narrative. We both understood—I realized this even at the age of eight—that we knew nearly as little about the Arabs on the screen as did the Europeans in the fort, as little as we knew about some of the old-country relatives who would sometimes visit or stay with us and from whom we were separated by our experience of America's peculiar modernity, by our failure to learn our parent's first language, and by our primary identification as American boys. But in Frank's joke our identities suddenly became more complex. We also knew—because we had been told—that we were Arabs too, related to those faceless menacing hordes, and that we were sitting in our quiet upstate New York living room having somehow already breached the defenses of the West.

There was something patently absurd in thinking of ourselves, first-generation native-born American boys, as identified with those screaming foreigners the film imagined Arabs to be, and that's one thing that made us laugh. We also knew—again from our parents, our relatives, and our own experience—that this projection of Arab identity was absurd, that Arabs were far from simple folk, that they had individual personalities, differentiated histories, and articulate motives for what they did, that they had separate and often conflicted allegiances to religions and regions, and that they (and by implication we as well) were, as I would say today, fully human subjects, however quirky and not so terribly different from our Italian, Polish, or Jewish American friends. Something in our sense of ourselves and of the world around us was becoming more complicated and less starkly simple than the wounding identity logic that film romance could allow us.

It took me a long time to think about identity in any systematic way or to realize Arab as an identity I might actually have to inhabit. But the process, I think, began with that boyish joke on that particular Saturday afternoon. My brother fulfilled, in the small public sphere of our parent's living room, the intellectual's function in a democratic society, for in a democratic society the intellectual is not a specialized profession but a particular role that any person at any given moment might play. By resisting an identification with a dishonest, Western-produced image to denigrate us Arabs and by recruiting my allegiance to a more complex version of ourselves, my brother was playing the intellectual's part in the formation and reformation of identities. He was pointing out a failure in America to do justice to our identity. In this special sense, I began to become an American at that moment.

So this is a story not about the organic roots of ethnic identity but about the frangible contingencies of group identifications and their complicated, often conflicted relationship to individual experience, public representation, and justice. It is not, however, a story that carries as its moral the lesson, heard with increasing frequency these days in the academy and among popular pundits, that ethnic or racial identity—the identities of groups— does not matter or can easily be forgotten.

The attitude toward Arabs and Arab identity that *Beau Geste* reflects, an attitude that denies to Arab identity any of the complexities and contingencies of identity formation evident in my experience of the movie, remains far too familiar today. Western discourse, on the popular and the professional level, continues to imagine Arabs as an undifferentiated mass without bothering to individuate very much among nations or peoples or individuals and without troubling very much to listen to what Arabs say on their own behalf. Thus, commentators as diverse as Bernard Lewis, Samuel Huntington, and Anne Coulter typically reduce Arab identity to Islam, and Islam to a religion of fanatical incitement. For these scholars, analysts, and pundits, all Arabs are the same Arab, the same religious fanatic, the same terrorist.[1] And when George W. Bush seeks rhetorically to reduce Saddam Hussein or Iraqi insurgents to romantic villains, implacable avatars of evil, in Western eyes, their Arab identity makes them merely manifestations of a familiar type and makes the president's job immeasurably easier. I do not mean to be facile here or to gloss over Saddam's ruthless tyranny or the indiscriminate terror of suicide bombers; I merely point out that neither tyranny nor violence belong uniquely or essentially to Arabs. The historical roots of Sadam's regime and the tactics of the Iraqi insurgency can barely be analyzed because demonizing "the" Arab remains an easy option for Western leaders like Bush, Blair, and Berlusconi.[2] The Arab as individual barely exists at all in the Western imagination, and the Arab as type remains linked to irrational or religious violence, opulence, sensuality, and evil. This useful fantasy of the Arab menace, like Markoff's Arabs, can be made to appear or disappear as needed. To see Saddam with his lavish palaces and dismal torture chambers as the latest recurrence of the eternal Arab eternally menacing the West, supported by the faceless, threatening hordes of the "Arab street" or the fanatical violence of the Iraqi insurgents, is far easier than to see Saddam as another modern despot like so many others and the Arab street as a realm of public opinion subject to the pressures of events and the distortions of local passions like other public spheres. America's part in the imposition of militarized violence and its own dismal record of torture have inflamed those passions. Hardest of all may be for Americans to honestly consider that their own failures to be just and to eschew unnecessary violence have bred the violence of Iraqi resistance that believes its terrible measures to be justified. Few Americans feel it necessary to consider how things might look were they to find themselves in the Iraqi's place.

A quarter of a century ago, Edward Said taught many of us to see Western representations of the East as a continuing tradition of Orientalism. At bottom, Orientalism is a discourse about identity, one in which all Orientals and especially all Arabs are essentially the same Arab. The discourse continues today, as the Bush administration pursues its Arab adventure and as a determining factor in American attitudes toward the Middle East generally and toward the Israeli occupation of Palestinian territories more specifically. Orientalists believe that the Arab mind and Islamic culture are different and therefore not to be understood according to Western habits of thought. This form of cultural relativism founds a reductive conceptual violence that legitimates even as it masks material and political injustices. In 1978 Said wrote:

> In practice this notion has meant that when Orientals struggle against colonial occupation, you must say . . . that Orientals have never understood the meaning of self-government the way "we" do. When some Orientals oppose racial discrimination while others practice it, you say "they're all Orientals at bottom" and class interest, political circumstances, economic factors are totally irrelevant. Or with Bernard Lewis, you say that if Arab Palestinians oppose Israeli settlement and occupation of their lands, then that is merely "the return of Islam," or, as a renowned contemporary Orientalist defines it, Islamic opposition to non-Islamic peoples, a principle of Islam enshrined in the seventh century. History, politics, and economics do not matter. Islam is Islam, the Orient is the Orient, and please take all your ideas about a left and a right wing, revolutions, and change back to Disneyland.[3]

The war on terror, the invasion of Iraq, and the tragic conflict between Israel and the Palestinians continue in their various ways the divisive logic of Orientalist ideas and identities. Orientalist ideas underpin Samuel Huntington's noxious and influential thesis of a clash among cultures, especially between Islam and the West, an idea that has disastrously reshaped the world it pretended to describe. Orientalist ideas have legitimated denunciations of Islam by Jerry Falwell and Andrew Sullivan, each of whom has claimed that the key to our current crises may be found in the errors of Islam rather than in understandable perceptions of Western policies (and understanding a perception does not mean that one necessarily finds oneself in accord with it), or in the mistakes of Arab leaders (and all leaders can make mistakes without becoming personifications of Satan), or in the pressures of modernization itself (which would make both Arabs and their leaders part of the world with which we are already familiar, a world in which the United States plays an enormous cultural, economic, and military part, rather than inhabitants of a desert locale removed from time and space as we know it).

The foundation of these professional and popular ideas is Orientalism, and Orientalism is an erroneous discourse of distorted identities. But, to paraphrase Nietzsche, identity may be an error without which we cannot live. So where does that leave us?

PRACTICAL DIFFERENCE:
THE REPORT OF THE ARAB INTELLECTUALS

Orientalist constructions of Arab identity and culture hold that since the Crusades Arabs have been increasingly impervious to ideas from outside the Moslem or Oriental world—wherever the boundaries of those imaginary realms are taken to be. According to Bernard Lewis, America's favorite authority on the Arab mind, this is precisely what went wrong as the Eastern sensibility, fed on a sense of humiliation and outrage as old as the Arabs' encounters with the superior military organization of the West, closed itself off from the developing world. Then as now, humiliation and resentment rather than reason and principle govern the Arab mind. As one Israeli of Sephardic origins put it, such ideas are not merely perversely romantic, they are essentially racist.[4] Such romantic and racist accounts of the Middle East and its peoples have gained new credence due to the sensational reporting on popular Islamic fundamentalist movements and intellectual leaders and the real terrors of suicide attacks in Israel, Iraq, Madrid, London, and New York.

But reading a recent UN-sponsored report on human development in the Arab World, written by other Arab intellectuals, belies the central identity claims underlying the Orientalist project, the dreams of Islamists, and the popular Western view of Arab identity. The cosmopolitanism of the report's outlook, its attention to specific situations in individual Middle Eastern states, and its heterogeneous intellectual underpinnings demonstrate a cast of mind far different from the inward-looking, self-obsessed, willfully ignorant Arab mindset that Lewis and others describe. Reading the report, its form as much as its content, challenges the assumptions of those in the West and in the East who have emphasized the essential imperviousness of Arab peoples to, and the fundamental incompatibility of Arab identity with, progressive ideas and modern concepts like democratic government, women's rights, and intellectual freedom.

For Bernard Lewis, the assumed imperviousness to Western ideas is the crucial component in the identity logic that makes Arabs and the West essentially different. Amin Maalouf understands the Arabs' position more in terms of historical contingency. He writes, "Throughout the Crusades, the Arabs refused to open their own society to ideas from the West. And this, in all likelihood, was the most disastrous effect of the aggression of which they were the victims. For an invader, it makes sense to learn the language of the conquered people; for the latter, to learn the language of the conqueror seems a surrender of principle, even a betrayal."[5] One lesson the colonial experience should have taught us in the West is that military force is a poor means with which to accomplish a civilizing mission or to implant democracy. In Lebanon during the first decades of the last century, my father was required to attend French schools, but later he made it a point to forget the French he was forced to learn. He was not an especially political man. Liberal apologists for a new American imperialism, whose watchwords, they claim, are not "colonies, conquest, and the white man's burden" but "an empire lite, a global hegemony whose grace notes are free markets, human rights and democracy, enforced by the most awesome military power the world has ever known," forget the essential incompatibility between violent imposition and political enlightenment. In doing so, they become the latest avatars of America's failure. These words are Michael Ignatieff's, from a *New York Times Magazine* cover piece printed the January before shock and awe began the Iraqi war and titled—ironically—"The Burden."[6] Ignatieff demonstrates a common enthusiasm for the oxymoronic union of liberal values and imperial domination. Two years later, he reaffirms that such a belief, while possibly dangerous or delusional (the words are his), is essentially and inevitably American, that is to say, part of who Americans think they are.[7] I would add that so is the American failure to live up to American principles part of the national identity Ignatieff celebrates.

But even Ignatieff finds himself constrained to admit that the barbed wire and bombs accompanying imperial projections of power, whatever may be their conscious intent, produce violent and incalculable reactions unlikely to further the cause of peace, democratization, or freedom. The dream of a war in the interests of civilization or to make the world safe for democracy always threatens to become a nightmare. Western media has generally shielded Americans and Europeans from actual images of the daily carnage in Iraq as military and civilian casualties continue to mount. But only glance at the incredibly gruesome black-and-white photos from the first Iraq war posted on the Digital Journalist Web site by photojournalist

Peter Turnley. "The Unseen Gulf War" presents images of death and mourning among Iraqi and Kurdish solders and civilians that should dispel the dangerous illusion that modern war is less savage and cruel than wars used to be, more like a video game won by surgical strikes with smart bombs than a wholesale slaughter of peoples and destruction of lives. War makes nothing better. The death and destruction on September 11, 2001, did nothing to improve Americans as a people or a society; the death and destruction Israel has rained down on the Palestinians has not made Israel more secure; the suicide attacks by Palestinians on Israel have not advanced the Palestinian cause. In view of all this carnage, the fantasy of war as a civilizing tool, shared by intellectuals like Ignatieff and policy officials like Paul Wolfowitz, seems especially pernicious. The fact that in Turnley's photos American soldiers in clean uniforms and pristine flak jackets coolly survey the charred and twisted corpses that their overwhelmingly superior technologies of death have produced reminds one that the aftermath for these American fighting men and women has often been rather grim even when they have not faced the daily terrors of injuries and death that have become Operation Iraqi Freedom's hallmark. War, which forces a stark confrontation with the identity logic of friend and foe, frequently forces terrified recognitions across that boundary. Such stark recognitions contribute to the difficulty of coming home to civilized life after being made into an instrument of death. Turnley's horrible images remind us of what Ignatieff and others would have us forget, that as long as the imperium's civilizing mission depends on an us-and-them identity logic, its wars and their aftermath will likely be a white man's burden on the West and on the rest of the world as well.

Even under the impact of war in the Middle East, the identity logic of absolute difference between them and us is difficult to sustain. It is precisely this identity logic and the supposed Arab hostility to Western thought that supports it that the form of the *Arab Human Development Report 2002* calls into question. Consider this citation, characteristic of the document as a whole:

> In the ultimate analysis, human development is development of the people, development for the people, and development by the people. Development of the people involves building human capabilities through the development of human resources. Development for the people implies that the benefits

of growth must be translated into the lives of people, and development by
the people emphasizes that people must be able to participate actively in
influencing the processes that shape their lives.[8]

To discuss the contents of this report far exceeds my competence. It seems
long on high ideals and a bit short on concrete, programmatic sugges-
tions—a failing to which intellectuals the world over are particularly prone.
But I do want to note the surprise I registered on discovering that Abraham
Lincoln's words, taken from a document that, in the United States, may
be second only to Jefferson's Declaration of Independence as a sacred inscription of national ideals, should furnish the rhetorical structure and conceptual grounding for a transnational group of Arab intellectuals considering
the problems of regional development in the Middle East. On the next few
pages of the report—which, by the way, makes excellent reading—the
authors cite "the great Arab historian and sociologist" from the fourteenth
century, Ibn Kahldoun, along with Antoine Lavoisier, Joseph Lagrange,
Adam Smith, David Ricardo, Robert Malthus, Karl Marx, and John Stuart
Mill (16–17). Elsewhere Khalil Gibran shares space with a host of Middle
Eastern, European, and American historians, sociologists, and economists.

Reading this report, one does not feel transported to a different world.
Rather, one recognizes an attempt by intellectuals from a conflicted region
to come to terms with the world as Americans and Europeans already know
it, a world, as these intellectuals from Arab countries put it, that represents
not a fated environment of clashing cultures but a set of choices. As the
authors see it, Arab states must choose "between remaining on the margins
of the modern world—and developing a new societal capacity, on both
the national and the pan-Arab levels, sufficient to ensure not only openness to the new world being shaped by globalization, a world in which
distance shrinks but geography and culture remain strongly present in all
spheres of human activity, but also a capacity for active participation in
shaping this new world from a position of capability and security."[9] The
content of the report calls repeatedly for democracy, secularization, education, equal rights for all women and minorities, the cherishing of local
identities and cultures, and the development of more global allegiances. It
represents, in short, an Arab project of progressive modernization engaged
with rather than resistant to the rest of the world.[10]

Despite the bellicose dreams of the new apologists for American empire, progressive modernization—whatever its internal problems and inherent failures—requires peace. These Arabs make clear that the greatest impediment to development comes from military strife in which internecine squabbles or foreign powers play a part, especially in Iraq and in the occupied territories of Palestine. In a sidebar, Hanan Ashrawi writes of the Palestinian plight:

> The tenacious pursuit and proclamation of our human-development agenda are rapidly being overpowered by the deafening din of the occupation's military onslaughts. Imprisoned on our own lands by a multiple and suffocating state of siege, our homes and institutions are being shelled and bombed on a daily basis, our activists and leaders assassinated while innocent children and adults are murdered in cold blood. Prevented from laying claim to our resources and rights, we witness our lands being confiscated and our crops and trees destroyed. Israeli military checkpoints fragment our human and territorial continuity and have become the most brutal expression of a discriminatory and pervasive system of willful humiliation and subjugation. All rights—including the right to shelter; to educational and health services; to work; to a clean and untainted environment; to a life free from war, fear, and coercion; to governance as an expression of the collective will for internal justice; and to gain access to the tools of information and knowledge— have been obliterated.[11]

And this sadly brings us to the central point of identity, justice, and terror in the Middle East: the war between Israel and the Palestinian people.

IDENTITY POLITICS WITH A VENGEANCE

In the aftermath of September 11, no image did more damage to the Palestinian cause in the United States than the video footage of a few youths celebrating the destruction and death just visited on America. American news outlets replayed the clip obsessively for days in what seemed like a determined attempt to discredit the Palestinian people and to demonstrate the true nature of the menace Israel faced from anti-Western Arab fanatics. Many of us remember that during what I'm afraid we must now call the first Gulf War in 1991 similar scenes of celebration came to represent, in Western and Israeli media, the Palestinian reaction to the Scud missiles Iraq launched at Israel. I must leave aside the question of whether this was the typical Palestinian response. It certainly was *a* Palestinian response. I am more interested in the mode in which these images were deployed as visible proof of Palestinian identity. In both cases, the images were meant to suggest that Palestinians specifically and Arabs more generally are not people with whom one can identify or negotiate. Their hatred is both savage and implacable. They celebrate the deaths of innocent people. We cannot understand or deal with them.

In Israel in 1991 several liberal writers, associated with the peace movement, signed a letter condemning the Palestinian response represented by those images and supporting the war against Iraq. But other Israeli intellectuals, like the writer Shimon Ballas, resisted identification with the terror around them in order to consider what, beyond a difference in identity, the response of these Palestinians might actually mean. In doing so, Ballas did not condone the violence celebrated by the Arabs, but he refused to yield to the consensus in his own society either:

> What disturbed me is the tendency of writers [in Israel] to be part of the consensus. And the consensus is a sacred cow. . . . I can understand the Palestinians. Those who were clapping when missiles fell on the Israelis, they did that after decades of repression. We destroy their houses, arrest them, torture them, kill them. And here, all of a sudden, the Jews are scared too, and their houses are being destroyed. Of course, I don't accept joy over affliction, but the Israeli peace camp felt "insulted." If they are for Sadaam, then we have nothing to talk about with such people. I don't agree with this position, and I think that it emerges from feelings of superiority over the Palestinians. A reaction like this is extremely grave, because it expresses a lack of will to maintain equality between the two sides.[12]

Such a statement seems to me both remarkably courageous and slightly masochistic. Of course, it was precisely such masochism, the painful refusal to identify unquestioningly with the terror of consensus on one's own "side," for which Christopher Hitchens and others condemned leftist intellectuals in the West who questioned the official account of and response to the terror attacks on September 11. Yet, such courageous masochism, the painful task of working across immediate identifications and against consensus to wider understandings, is what intellectuals who wish to help find a way out of this terribly dangerous moment must undertake. The alternative is a rhetoric of identity in which the essential character of the other is always evil. Note how often the American president uses terms like "evildoers," "axis of evil," "evil ones," preferring always the theological cadences of simple condemnation over the diplomatic complexities that might better represent the historical and situational complexities of the world. That theological rhetoric, and the actions it has helped legitimize, is now helping to destabilize the Middle East as well as Central and Southeast Asia.

Americans need a better model of the world, a better construction of themselves in their own complex and multifaceted experiences of their identities and allegiances. Americans cannot, as some have urged, think of themselves or the world without reference to identities. Identity marks the individual's sense of self and place in the world, and no one can make judgments or experience solidarity without it. Yet, identity should never be the final goal or arbiter of anyone's thoughts; identity should never be an excuse for injustice or the brutal exercise of power or the subjugation of peoples. Identity should be an opening to the world not a bulwark to hold the world at bay.

No more disheartening example of the failure to think identity in these terms may be found today than the ongoing, bloody conflict between Israel and the Palestinians, yet oddly or perhaps inevitably, within the crucible of that conflict a more encouraging sense of identity seems to be emerging. This is odd because it is a conflict predicated on the denial of any mutual identity, either regional or cultural, but it may be inevitable because there is evidence that such a mutual identity is already being forged. I must add that the denial is not symmetrical. Differentials of power and the reality of occupation separate Israel and the Palestinians in the territories. Moreover, many Ashkenazi Israelis resolutely reject the Middle East as a region and the Levant as a cultural site, preferring to identify with Europe or the United States. Ultimately, Israeli occupation of Palestinian territory and seizures of regional resources, practices made acceptable to Israelis by their belief in their superior Western identity, are, I believe, the crucial cause of the conflict. That Israel's actions have increasingly met with terrible acts of fanatical resistance by desperate peoples on the fringes of an increasingly disordered Palestinian society exacerbates the problem. And yet, those who play the role of intellectual in this moment of crisis without subscribing to the easy rigidity of us and them may ultimately point the way to new ways of thinking about identity for the region and for the rest of the world.

Intellectuals and activists on both sides of the Palestinian–Israeli identity divide work toward redrawing the lines not only of the political map but of identity itself. This goes on at a moment when Israeli military incursions and Palestinian missile attacks increase the conflict's terrors. In this light I would note the remarkable courage and persistence of the peace movements on both sides of the green line manifested in heroic joint Israeli–Palestinian demonstrations in Israel and in the occupied territories. Ayala Emmett has documented the existence and the persistence of these movements in *Our Sisters' Promised Land: Women, Politics, and Israeli–Palestinian Coexistence.* In her new introduction to a much needed reprint of that volume, Emmett writes, "Peace groups can be a model of and for cooperation and not just when things are easy but also in bad times, in the midst, and after the tragic, senseless violence is over."[13] The Israeli–Palestinian peace groups, whose female membership Emmett has been especially careful to chronicle, represent a different way of thinking about identity and justice, conflict and its resolution, a way that those who wish truly to serve the future should heed. And yet, as Emmett points out, their message and their very presence finds little place in U.S. media accounts of the Middle East, which prefer to emphasize the antagonists' supposedly eternal and irreconcilable differences.

One of the most comprehensive guides and strongest polemics in favor of new ways of thinking identity in times of terror is Ammiel Alcalay's fascinating book *After Jews and Arabs: Remaking Levantine Culture.* Perhaps only an American could have written such a book. Part impassioned polemic, part cultural survey, part political exploration, Alcalay's book registers the demographic and cultural tensions and the insistent heterogeneity of contemporary Israel. He challenges the consensus representation of Israeli identity and culture as European or Western and as resolutely separate from the Arab identities and cultures of the region. He portrays instead a more open, more regional, more multicultural identity in which both Israel's Sephardic and Ashkenazi Jews and the Palestinians themselves might find allies and allegiances among the other identities, religions, and cultures of the Middle East. For Alcalay this project is far from utopian. It recognizes and represents a situation that already demographically, culturally, and subjectively exists—it recognizes the region as teeming with nations within nations—a fact that only violence and terror can deny.

Alcalay offers no reassuring tales about the civilizing influence of culture or of cross-cultural understanding like other American multiculturalists love to tell. He notes, echoing George Steiner's dismay that cultural sophistication did not prevent the Holocaust, that "one can hum the tunes of Farid-al-Atrache, Umm Kulthum, or Muhammad Abdel Wahab one minute, and serve as an interrogator in which the Palestinian subject becomes an object of misplaced rage the next."[14] And yet, he turns to culture to demonstrate, as do the Israeli and Arab writers and intellectuals he cites, that the identity logic separating Jews and Arabs on which the legitimacy of this long bloody conflict rests will not bear scrutiny. To take one example, Alcalay quotes Ronny Someck's poem, "Jasmine: Poem on Sandpaper":

Fairuz raises her lips
to heaven
to let jasmine rain down
on those who once met
without knowing they were in love.
I'm listening to her in Muhammad's
Fiat at noon Ibn Gabirol St.
A Lebanese singer playing in an Italian car
that belongs to an Arab poet
from Baqa'al-Gharbiyye on a street named
after a Hebrew poet who lived in Spain.
And the jasmine?
If it falls from the sky at the end of days
it'll stay green for
just a second at
the next light.[15]

This is just a poem, but as a poem it notes, as many of the best poems do, the concrete, material, and cultural realities of the world on which it reflects and whose blindness it seeks to enlighten. If this be an Arab romance, unlike *Beau Geste* and the romantic notions of traditional Orientalists and current U.S. policies, it is one where the real complexities of lived identity find expression. Unlike *Beau Geste,* it is a romance of the real.[16]

No one can forget that such harmonious heterogeneities are easier to realize in a poet's song than in the lived experiences of prejudice, oppression, and injustice. Identity as a paradoxically univocal and conflicted construct emerges frequently in response to violence. Maalouf says, "People often see themselves in terms of whichever one of their allegiances is most under attack."[17] The result of such attacks is both and simultaneously the emergence of identity and the desire for vindication or revenge. The pressure of violence produces not only identity but the differentiation of identity groups into rigidified categories of us and them that can set the wheel of violence and identity turning. "The scene is now set and the war can begin." As Maalouf puts it, "Whatever happens 'the others' will have deserved it" (27). Thus identity solidifies and fractures under pressures from demands and desires of those to whom it stands opposed even when that opposition confuses the boundaries of subjectivity and the world.

If identity, as Maalouf remarks, "is in the first place a matter of symbols, even of appearances," then the disruption of the cycling of identity, terror, and violence may depend not only on the alleviation of material injustices and threats (though of course it depends on that) but also on people keeping their wits about them and recognizing the broad field of potential allegiances that already constitute them and their identities.[18] If an identity or sense of allegiance is a matter of symbols, then intellectuals and poets, those whose job it is to manipulate symbols and propagate allegiances, play a particularly important part in the formation of identities and in the harmonizing of heterogeneities. They help determine where the lines of identity get drawn and how the limits of allegiance are set. They can help mobilize terror or explore alternatives to violence. This does not mean that intellectuals or poets hold the keys to our current impasses over identity, but it does mean they have a real role to play in the exacerbation or assuagement of our fears and in the composition of our identities and our allegiances.

If identity and culture are in fact linked, as I believe they are, then honestly owning our identities requires keeping our terrors at bay and recognizing ourselves to be as impure, heterogeneous, conflicted, and generous as human cultures in their promiscuous interrelationships themselves tend to be. Consider the following remarkable figuration of culture in *The Muqaddimah,* Ibn Khaldun's speculative and scientific fourteenth-century philosophical treatise on history. Khaldun regards culture, under the affiliative institutions of dynasty or governance, to be an open market:

> Dynasty and government serve as the world's market-place, attracting to it the products of scholarship and craftsmanship alike. Wayward wisdom and

forgotten lore turn up there. In this market stories are told and items of historical information are delivered. Whatever is in demand on this market is in general demand everywhere else. Now, whenever the established dynasty avoids injustice, prejudice, weakness, and double-dealing, with determination keeping to the right path and never swerving from it, the wares on its market are as pure silver and fine gold. However, when it is influenced by selfish interests and rivalries, or swayed by vendors of tyranny and dishonesty, the wares of its market-place become as dross and debased metals. The intelligent critic must judge for himself as he looks around, examining this, admiring that, and choosing the other.[19]

The Arab historian offers a view of governance, allegiance, culture, and identity that remains open to the circulation of new ideas and new modes of thought through its territories. He also specifies a task for intellectual discrimination and intellectual actors in this marketplace of ideas. Yet, given the rigidity of ideas of culture and identity—both those championing and those attacking difference—currently fashionable in the United States, one is also struck how far we have strayed from this Arab ideal, an ideal we can also recognize as our own. Rectifying the errors of identity may not mean doing without identity's errors. Rather, it may suggest more painstaking effort in picking and maintaining the allegiances and identities that best serve us, our fellows, and our identifications with justice in the world by recognizing our openness and vulnerability to that world in ways that minimize rather than emphasize mayhem. Whether such a practice remains constitutive of identity or should be known by some other name seems to me still open to debate.

Orientalists will object that Islamic culture depends on reifications of identity that will resist new, more complex configurations. No more so, I would suggest, than the identities and religions of the West. We should also remember that it was Islam's universalism that changed the opinion of at least one American, raised in a more provincial faith, and taught him that his allegiances stretched beyond his own narrowly conceived identity group. I am thinking here of Malcolm X, whose experiences of Islam as a global religion during his pilgrimage to Mecca changed and broadened his views on racial identity and race relations in the United States. It may be the West itself, or at least the United States, that proves to be most resistant to the sorts of identity complexity with which both the Middle East and our domestic situations ask us to contend.

Part of the problem, I believe, is that a specific sort of identity politics remains in many ways the official policy of the U.S. government and the official story of the U.S. media. It remains at the root of America's failure. We prefer to see conflicts on the global stage as manifestations of ethnic, religious, or tribal differences. We seem, as a people, to identify too easily with the president's theological rhetoric of evil. This habit of mind distracts us from focusing on more rational questions of U.S. policy and reactions to it. For example, when polls consistently show that the world regards our policies and postures unfavorably, we tend to see this as an identity question—the "west against the rest," to borrow Samuel Huntington's formulation, or the New World against Old Europe to paraphrase Donald Rumsfeld—rather than a reasoned or at least comprehensible reaction by rational agents. Our vision of bin Laden is a dramatic case in point. This perverted prince of Saudi privilege is no one's idea of a rational actor, but our understanding of him has been impaired by too simple a rhetoric of good and evil and too great an eagerness to blame his actions on an unmotivated hatred of our values. Making no apologies for him or for his movement, Eqbal Ahmad writes, "Here is a man who was an ally of the United States, who saw America as a friend, then he sees his country being occupied by the United States and feels betrayal. Whether there is a sense of right and wrong is not what I'm saying. I'm describing what's behind this kind of extreme violence."[20] Eqbal Ahmad is speaking here before bin Laden's monstrous assault on American civilians, but, however painfully, I think his point still holds. His characterization of bin Laden and of terrorist violence generally offers needed nuances to the Bush administration's insistently theologized rhetoric of evil axes and rogue states and also to the hysterical promotion of culture conflicts and civilization wars that dominate U.S. media. That rhetoric has distorted all debates around the war in Iraq and threatens U.S. relations with the misnamed "Islamic" world. To say this is not to offer justifications for atrocity but merely to note that understanding, or even being able to identify, one's antagonists may be crucial in a world where, as horrific events in New York, Madrid, and London indicate, one's enemies can do terrible damage. The language of the "axis of evil," and the president's eagerness to use the theological weight of the idea of evil to characterize those who fight us, leaves no room for productive negotiation or progressive amelioration. One does not negotiate with evil; one simply, like Saint Michael stomping Satan, seeks to eradicate it. More of our intellectual and political leaders need to point out the limitations of such an approach.

In this light, some of the intellectuals I most admire these days are Palestinians and Israelis who, even at a moment when their people suffer horrendous violence and their society reaps the whirlwind brewed through decades of oppressive policies, find the courage to speak against the lies, treacheries, and violence by which Israel, abetted by the United States and assisted by colluding or incompetent Palestinian leaders, has maintained its illegal occupation of the Palestinian territories and its relentless oppression of the Palestinian people for the last thirty-six years.[21] That they also speak for more humane, generous, and just ways of understanding identity and responding to our need for belonging in the world makes them hopeful points of light on a darkening global scene. I claim them for the complicated tradition of identity and identification exemplified by American writers who, for better or worse and with degrees of success or failure, attempted to hold the nation to its own best and most universal principles of justice and freedom.

In Ibn Khaldun, one finds the following observations on identity and allegiances:

(Respect for) blood ties is something natural among men, with the rarest exceptions. It leads to affection for one's relations and blood relatives, (the feeling that) no harm ought to befall them nor any destruction come upon them. One feels shame when one's relatives are treated unjustly or attacked, and one wishes to intervene between them and whatever peril or destruction threatens them. This is a natural urge in man.

He then expands his observation:

Clients and allies belong in the same category. The affection everybody has for his clients and allies results from the feeling of shame that comes to a person when one of his neighbors, relatives, or a blood relation in any degree is humiliated. . . . It is in that sense that one must understand Muhammad's remark, "Learn as much of your pedigree as is necessary to establish your ties of kindred." It means that pedigrees are useful only in so far as they imply the close contact that is a consequence of blood ties and that eventually leads to mutual help and affection. Anything beyond that is superfluous. For a pedigree is something imaginary and devoid of reality. Its usefulness consists only in the resulting connection and close contact.[22]

There are at least two ways to read Khaldun's stricture. One asserts the organic unity of identity in the realm of actual blood descent or close personal contact. In this view, the world remains a tribal place and our sympathies do not extend, cannot extend, beyond what blood and culture preestablish for us. There is, however, another reading, which I prefer. Perhaps it is an American reading before America was ever imagined. Identity, like pedigree, is an act of the imagination, related to and sometimes in conflict with the world around it, but ultimately, like blood itself, an imaginary construct, one to which no limits may be set in advance. We are always, as my brother and I were as boys, looking at images of distant fanciful places and strange romantic people without names and learning our pedigrees. As Ammiel Alcalay put it:

> The crisis we have been brought to demands that we use our past to re-create new memories of our future, to reject versions of history that banish Arabs and Jews, Israelis and Palestinians, to separate realms, where there will be no intimacy or ambivalence, no love or jealousy, no respect or common destiny, where the full range of complex emotions, intentions, conscious and subconscious traces inherited through a long life lived in common will either simply be shelved in the name of some impersonal and polite forms of "co-operation" or, perhaps even worse, just be deemed unimaginable. . . . To make enemies of Arabs and Jews, to build layers of hatred through false assumptions, misrepresentations, propaganda presented as history, is to commit the most atrocious acts of self-destruction for we are all multiple and cannot pretend to be exclusively this or that.[23]

What is true for Arabs and Jews is true for everyone. The irreducible multiplicity of each identity means that no limit may be placed in advance on the allegiances, affiliations, or identifications one might form. As my brother and I learned, the other often turns out to be related to us both in his familiarity and in his strangeness. When Mohammed said, "Learn as much of your pedigree as is necessary to establish your ties of kindred," I take him to have meant something along these lines: we must learn to extend our ties to the world and to the various parts of ourselves, our cultures, and our identities that belong to it. That is certainly what I mean to suggest.

NOTES

INTRODUCTION

1. There are far too many works in this vein to mention here, but among the best known and most influential see, as examples, Nancy Frazer, *Unruly Practices: Power Discourse and Gender in Contemporary Social Theory* (Minneapolis: University of Minnesota Press, 1989); Gayatri Spivak, *In Other Worlds: Essays in Cultural Politics* (New York: Routledge, 1988); Gloria Anzaldúa, *Borderlands: The New Mestiza = La Frontera* (San Francisco: Aunt Lute Books, 1987); Toni Morrison, *Playing in the Dark: Whiteness and the Literary Imagination* (Cambridge, Mass.: Harvard University Press, 1992); Lisa Lowe, *Immigrant Acts: On Asian American Cultural Politics* (Durham, N.C.: Duke University Press, 1996).

2. See Dinesh D'Souza, *Illiberal Education: The Politics of Race and Sex on Campus* (New York: Free Press, 1991) and *The End of Racism: Principles for a Multicultural Society* (New York: Free Press, 1995); Arthur Schlesinger, *The Disuniting of America: Reflections on a Multicultural Society* (New York: Norton, 1992); and Todd Gitlin, *The Twilight of Common Dreams: Why America Is Wracked by Culture Wars* (New York: Henry Holt, 1995).

3. Hortense J. Spillers, *Black, White, and in Color: Essays on American Literature and Culture* (Chicago: University of Chicago Press, 2003); Dana D. Nelson, *National Manhood: Capitalist Citizenship and the Imagined Fraternity of White Men* (Durham, N.C.: Duke University Press, 1998); Robyn Wiegman, *American Anatomies: Theorizing Race and Gender* (Duke, N.C.: Duke University Press, 1995); Russ Castronovo, *Necro Citizenship: Death, Eroticism, and the Public Sphere in the Nineteenth-Century United States* (Durham, N.C.: Duke University Press, 2001).

4. The phrase, of course, is from Walter Benn Michaels; see *The Shape of the Signifier* (Princeton, N.J.: Princeton University Press, 2004), 19–81. See also Ross Posnock, *Color and Culture: Black Writers and the Making of the Modern Intellectual* (Cambridge,

Mass.: Harvard University Press, 1998); Paul Gilroy, *Against Race: Imagining Political Culture beyond the Color Line* (Cambridge, Mass.: Harvard University Press, 2000); and Philip Fisher, *Still the New World: American Literature in a Culture of Creative Destruction* (Cambridge, Mass.: Harvard University Press, 1999).

5. See Kwame Anthony Appiah, *In My Father's House: Africa in the Philosophy of Culture* (New York: Oxford University Press, 1992); Posnock, *Color and Culture;* Bruce Robbins, *Feeling Global: Internationalism in Distress* (New York: New York University Press, 1999); and Wai Chee Dimock, *Through Other Continents: American Literature across Deep Time* (Princeton, N.J.: Princeton University Press, 2006).

6. Quoted in Arthur M. Schlesinger, *The Disuniting of America,* 27. Interestingly, for Schlesinger, the struggle for America's soul involves defending the predominantly "white" coloration of American culture. Samuel Huntington makes an even more passionate appeal for American exclusiveness in *Who Are We? The Challenges to America's Identity* (New York: Simon and Schuster, 2004), where returning to the nation's exclusively Anglo-Saxon and Protestant culture seems the best way to meet the challenges of its increasing heterogeneity. So the tension between inclusive principles and exclusive practices continues today.

7. The jeremiad, as Sacvan Bercovitch's indispensable work demonstrates, remains part of the ritual of consensus in the United States. Yet, dissensus and terror seem much more typical aspects of life in the United States than consensus and resolution. See Sacvan Bercovitch, *The Rites of Assent: Transformations in the Symbolic Construction of America* (New York: Routledge, 1993).

8. Unless otherwise noted, all italics in quotations are from the original. Kwame Anthony Appiah, *The Ethics of Identity* (Princeton, N.J.: Princeton University Press, 2005), xiv.

9. I have in mind here Amy Gutmann's analysis of what she calls the good, bad, and ugly aspects of identity's necessary relationship to democracy. See her *Identity and Democracy* (Princeton, N.J.: Princeton University Press, 2003), 1–37. See as well Richard Rorty, *Achieving Our Country: Leftist Thought in Twentieth-Century America* (Cambridge, Mass.: Harvard University Press, 1998).

10. Fisher, *Still the New World,* 163–64.

11. Walter Michaels offers similar advice to his fellow Americans in *The Trouble with Diversity: How We Learned to Love Identity and Ignore Inequality* (New York: Henry Holt, 2006). He argues quite cogently that the real oppressive differences in the United States are economic, not religious, racial, gendered, or sexual. To do so he must downplay both the experience of identity and the material ways in which oppression and identity have been melded in the United States, both past and present.

12. In work that lies just beyond the scope of interest of this book but that has still helped shape my thinking, criticism of what Judith Butler calls identity regimes in queer theory manifest a similar dissatisfaction with identity categories and a similar concern with their persistant importance. See, for example, Eve Sedgwick, *Epistemology of the Closet* (Berkeley: University of California Press, 1990); Judith Butler, *Gender*

Trouble: Feminism and the Subversion of Identity (New York: Routledge, 1990) and *Bodies That Matter: On the Discursive Limits of "Sex"* (New York: Routledge, 1993); and Wendy Brown, *States of Injury: Power and Freedom in Late Modernity* (Princeton, N.J.: Princeton University Press, 1995). See as well Diana Fuss, *Essentially Speaking: Feminism, Nature, and Difference* (New York: Routledge, 1989).

13. Such issues in the twenty-first century occupy the attention of many in Europe and the United States. Derrida has recently reminded us that for Kant, cosmopolitanism involves specific questions of hospitalities and a conflicted interplay of identities between "we" who are at "home" and those "others" who demand accommodation. In the United States such questions have been part of the national discourse and a focus for its anxieties at least since, as we will see in chapter 1, Jefferson warned of the dangers to republican values of too rapid immigration. See Jacques Derrida, *On Cosmopolitanism and Forgiveness,* trans. Mark Dooley and Michael Hughes (London: Routledge, 2002); and his "The Right to Philosophy from the Cosmopolitan Point of View (the Example of an International Institution)," in *Ethics, Institutions, and the Right to Philosophy,* trans. and ed. Peter Pericles Trifones (Lanham, Md.: Rowman and Littlefield, 2002). Michael Hardt and Antonio Negri find in the universal expansiveness of America's constitutional principles the problematic origin of an emergent cosmopolitan global order. See *Empire* (Cambridge, Mass.: Harvard University Press, 2000), xiv–xv, 166–72.

14. For an incisive account of the sometimes nearly utopian hopes and the productive limitations of American cosmopolitanism, see Bruce Robbins, *Feeling Global: Internationalism in Distress* (New York: New York University Press, 1999), especially 11–59. Robbins argues, "There can be no American-style or American-situated internationalism that will not reflect, on some level, American assumptions and interests" (40). I would add that there is unlikely to be any American internationalism that does not reflect American failures as well. Like Robbins, I too do not find this necessarily damning.

15. Dimock, *Through Other Continents,* 3. Dimock's book seems to respond to the challenges posed by Peter Carifiol's polemic against the Americanist obsession with America in *The American Ideal: Literary History as a Worldly Activity* (New York: Oxford University Press, 1991).

16. Wai Chee Dimock, *Residues of Justice: Literature, Law, Philosophy* (Berkeley: University of California Press, 1996), 9. Dimock's critique of justice and her specification of literature have been very influential on my thinking here.

17. Kwame Anthony Appiah, *The Ethics of Identity,* xiv.

18. I here disagree with Michael Lind's assertion that "a nation may be dedicated to a proposition, but it cannot be a proposition—this is the central insight of American nationalism," for in America the terms of that liberal nation's creed, justice and freedom for all, give meaning to market capitalism and commodities—to the baseball, apple pie, Chevy cars, and shopping malls associated with freedom of association and of choice—and to the family, neighborhoods, and schools that Lind believes root us affectively to the nation. These become American as they are felt to express the nation's

ideal commitment to liberty, to choice, to equality, and to justice. Michael Lind, *The Next American Nation: The New Nationalism and the Fourth American Revolution* (New York: Free Press, 1995), 4–5. For a critique of the ways in which Lind's liberal nationalist argument lapses back into an identity logic of its own, see Michaels, *The Shape of the Signifier,* 41–43. Here my point will be that logical inconsistency never can loosen the hold of identity and that if identity is an error, it is one—like many another affective state—that we cannot (at least yet) do (or think) without.

19. John Rawls, *A Theory of Justice,* rev. ed. (Cambridge, Mass.: Harvard University Press, 1999).

20. As Michaels notes, this appeal for the primacy of class in considerations of justice is an old and well-respected, though recently largely neglected, position in American political and cultural life. See Michaels, *The Trouble with Diversity.*

21. For Rawls as for Russ Castronovo, imagining the American citizen as a liberal subject entails a figurative death of the body and of the particularities associated with it. See Castronovo, *Necro Citizenship.*

22. Rawls, *A Theory of Justice,* 103, 118.

23. Ralph Waldo Emerson, *Nature,* in *Essays and Lectures,* ed. Joel Porte (New York: Library of America, 1983), 10.

24. Ibid., 104, 105.

25. There is nothing otherworldly or even unfamiliar about the original position Rawls describes. It should be imagined not so much as a unique origin in space or time (like aspects of Hobbes's or Locke's contending versions of states of nature) but as a sort of imaginative or rhetorical commonplace into which contestants can always enter—should always enter—"by deliberately following the constraints it expresses to simulate the reflections of the parties"—to undertake deliberations about justice, what Stanley Cavell calls the ongoing and ordinary "conversation of justice." Stanley Cavell, *Conditions Handsome and Unhandsome: The Constitution of Emersonian Perfectionism* (Chicago: University of Chicago Press, 1990), 101–26. As Rawls restates his idea in *Justice as Fairness:* "We must specify a point of view from which a fair agreement between free and equal persons can be reached." John Rawls, *Justice as Fairness: A Restatement* (Cambridge, Mass.: Belknap Press, Harvard University Press, 2001), 15. The veil of ignorance describes the imaginative requirement to register others as equals and as equally entitled to justice. It marks the distance each one must take from personal desires and fears for conversations about justice to occur.

26. See Michael Sandel, *Liberalism and the Limits of Justice* (New York: Cambridge University Press, 1982), 40–46.

27. See Gutmann, *Identity and Democracy,* 13–15.

28. On the conflicts within the subject in both Kant and Rawls's revision of Kant, see Randall Halle, *Queer Social Philosophy: Critical Readings from Kant to Adorno* (Urbana: University of Illinois Press, 2004), 25–62, especially 55–56.

29. Identity, in this context, expresses what Wendy Brown has analyzed and criticized in *States of Injury.* I fully acknowledge the limitations of identity as a grounds for politics

or ethics, but I believe that identity remains part of imaginative deliberations and self-recognitions, even when it is identity we are resisting. See Wendy Brown, *States of Injury: Power and Freedom in Late Modernity* (Princeton, N.J.: Princeton University Press, 1995), and her *Regulating Aversion: Tolerance in the Age of Identity and Empire* (Princeton, N.J.: Princeton University Press, 2006).

30. Emerson, "History," in *Essays and Lectures,* 238.

31. Grant F. Scott, ed., *Selected Letters of John Keats* (Cambridge, Mass.: Harvard University Press, 2002), 195.

32. Kateb quotes Keats's letter to Richard Woodhouse of October 27, 1818, which reads: "The Sun, the Moon, the Sea and Men and Women who are creatures of impulse are poetical and have about them an unchangeable attribute—the poet has none; no identity. . . . When I am in a room with People if I ever am free from speculating on creations of my own brain, then not myself goes home to myself: but the identity of every one in the room begins . . . to press upon me that, I am in a very little an[ni]hilated." Quoted in George Kateb, *Emerson and Self-Reliance* (Thousand Oaks, Calif.: Sage, 1995), 30.

33. Rawls, *Theory of Justice,* 218.

34. Du Bois, "Dusk of Dawn: An Essay toward an Autobiography of a Race Concept," in *W. E. B. Du Bois: Writings,* ed. Nathan Huggins (New York: Library of America, 1999), 651.

35. See especially Posnock's discussion of Du Bois's relationship to Crummell in *Color and Culture,* 17–20. Among the many things Du Bois seems to have begun, whiteness studies should thus be included. This endeavor is continued in Noel Ignatiev, *How the Irish Became White* (New York: Routledge, 1995); Toni Morrison, *Playing in the Dark;* Theodore W. Allen, *The Invention of the White Race,* vol. 2, *The Origin of Racial Oppression in Anglo-America* (New York: Verso, 1997); and more theoretically, Thomas DiPiero, *White Men Aren't* (Durham, N.C.: Duke University Press, 2002).

36. Du Bois, "Dusk of Dawn," 673.

37. Ibid., 649–50.

38. Herman Melville, *Moby-Dick, or The Whale* (Chicago: Newberry Library, 1988), 167–68.

39. Emerson, "Experience," in *Essays and Lectures.*

40. On the polarity between literature and justice, embodiment and abstraction, see again Wai Chee Dimock, *Residues of Justice,* whose influence on these pages should be evident.

41. Melville, *Moby-Dick,* 52.

42. Martha C. Nussbaum, *Cultivating Humanity: A Classical Defense of Reform in Liberal Education* (Cambridge, Mass.: Harvard University Press, 1997). Tolerance, of course, has become a watch word of contemporary politics and administrative initiatives. For a thorough critique of the limits (and continued utility) of tolerance as social, political, and governmental discourse and the ways in which it can serve to obscure more material questions of justice and maintain problematic regimes of power, see

Wendy Brown, *Regulating Aversion: Tolerance in the Age of Identity and Empire* (Princeton, N.J.: Princeton University Press, 2006). For a related analysis of race thinking, see K. Anthony Appiah and Amy Gutmann, *Color Consciousness: The Political Morality of Race* (Princeton, N.J.: Princeton University Press), especially Appiah's contribution, "Race, Culture, Identity: Misunderstood Connections," 30–105.

43. Samuel Huntington, *The Clash of Civilizations and the Remaking of World Order* (New York: Simon and Schuster, 1996). I have written at some length on Huntington's version of a right-wing cultural studies in *Anxious Intellects: Academic Professionals, Public Intellectuals, and Enlightenment Values* (Durham, N.C.: Duke University Press, 2000), 89–107.

44. Nussbaum, *Cultivating Humanity,* 115.

45. Amin Maalouf, *In the Name of Identity: Violence and the Need to Belong,* trans. Barbara Bray (New York: Arcade, 2001), 66.

46. Ibid., 72.

47. Thus a progressive observer like Tariq Ali can describe contemporary global crises as a "clash of fundamentalisms" (the dig at Huntington is obvious), and a conservative commentator like Dinesh D'Souza can identify a natural affinity between the complaints of Islamic fundamentalists and the beliefs of American Christian conservatives, both of whom identify modernity with secularization and resist it. See Tariq Ali, *The Clash of Fundamentalisms: Crusades, Jihads, and Modernity* (London: Verso, 2002); and Dinesh D'Souza, *The Enemy at Home: The Cultural Left and Its Responsibility for 9/11* (New York: Doubleday, 2007).

48. Maalouf, *In the Name of Identity,* 25.

49. Michaels, *The Trouble with Diversity,* 14–15.

50. Michaels does sometimes write as if he believes the ideal world has arrived but escaped notice. Writing of Du Bois's definition of a black man as one who must ride in the Jim Crow car, Michaels asserts, "Now that no one has to ride Jim Crow, there is no such thing as a black man. Or a white man either" (Michaels, *The Trouble with Diversity,* 47–48).

51. The fact, as Michaels himself notes, that racism has become something to be apologized for rather than something to be celebrated in public certainly represents a shift in the official definition of society, but the effects of that shift on an individual's lived experiences confronted by the racism Michaels also admits "we" probably still share may be more rather than less easy to endure or calculate. Moreover, the conflation of identity and ideology—the attribution of subversive or dangerous ideologies to specific identities—has a long and continuing history in U.S. anxieties about immigration (dating at least to Jefferson and everywhere evident in recent works by Huntington and others) as many Arab and Moslem Americans have recently discovered.

52. Michaels, of course, wants to shift the discussion from identity to class, but his own rhetoric demonstrates how difficult it is to stabilize the differences between race and class on which his argument is staked. "More generally," he concludes his introduction, "the trick is to think of inequality as a consequence of our prejudices rather

than as a consequence of our social system and thus to turn the project of creating a more egalitarian society into the project of getting people (ourselves and, especially, others) to stop being racist, sexist, classist homophobes" (*The Trouble with Diversity,* 20). Surely Michaels meant to attribute economic injustice not to our social but to our economic system, not to prejudice but to capitalism. The grotesque and iniquitous distribution of wealth that Michaels deplores (and I do, too) is the result, he has been claiming, of economic policy—regressive taxation, underfunded social services, unequally supported schools—not of social pathologies—sexism, racism, homophobia, class prejudice. Why then at this crucial moment does the social system take the place of economics? Why does Michaels have so little to say about economics or about capitalism's notorious tendency to concentrate money in fewer and fewer hands? Why does he repeatedly make the error of conflating the categories "working class" and "poor" without explanation or justification (see 201)? More than a simple mistake, this seems a revealing symptom of how continuously difficult it is in American history and in the American present to separate justice and identity, the economic and the social.

1. JEFFERSON'S HEADACHE

1. Joseph J. Ellis, *American Sphinx: The Character of Thomas Jefferson* (New York: Vintage Books, 1998), 52.

2. Andrew Burstein, *The Inner Jefferson: Portrait of a Grieving Optimist* (Charlottesville: University Press of Virginia, 1995), xii–xiii. See as well Merrill D. Peterson, *The Jefferson Image in the American Mind* (New York: Oxford University Press, 1960).

3. Peterson, *The Jefferson Image in the American Mind,* 443. Joseph Ellis writes, "Lots of Americans cared deeply about the meaning of his memory. He had become the Great Sphinx of American history, the enigmatic and elusive touchstone for the most cherished and contested convictions, and contested truths in American culture." Ellis, *American Sphinx: The Character of Thomas Jefferson* (New York: Vintage Books, 1998), 12.

4. The best exploration of Jefferson's attitudes toward race as a complex expression of his culture's conflicts on the issue and his own psychological response to them is still found in Winthrop Jordan, *White over Black: American Attitudes toward the Negro, 1550–1812* (Chapel Hill: University of North Carolina Press, 1968), 469–81.

5. Edmund S. Morgan, *American Slavery, American Freedom* (New York: Norton, 1975), 380.

6. Ibid., 381. As Morgan notes, "The seeming inconsistency, not to say hypocrisy, of slaveholders devoting themselves to freedom was not peculiar to . . . Jefferson or to Washington. Nor was it peculiar to Virginia. The men who came together to found an independent United States, dedicated to freedom and equality, either held slaves or were willing to join hands with those who did. None of them felt entirely comfortable about the fact, but neither did they feel responsible for it" (4).

7. Scholars who have dealt extensively with the Jefferson-Hemings relationship or the scandal surrounding it include Jordan, *White over Black;* Fawn Brodie, *Thomas*

Jefferson: An Intimate History (New York: W. W. Norton, 1974); John Chester Miller, *The Wolf by the Ears: Thomas Jefferson and Slavery* (New York: Free Press, 1977); Virginia Dabney, *The Jefferson Scandals* (New York: Dodd, Mean, 1981); Burstein, *The Inner Jefferson;* Roger Wilkins, *Jefferson's Pillow: The Founding Fathers and the Dilemma of Black Patriotism* (Boston: Beacon Press, 2001); and most thoroughly, Annette Gordon-Reed, *Thomas Jefferson and Sally Hemings: An American Controversy* (Charlottesville: University of Virginia Press, 1997).

8. Wilkins, *Jefferson's Pillow,* 9.

9. Ibid., 134.

10. Peterson, *Jefferson Image in the American Mind,* vii.

11. Gordon-Reed, *Thomas Jefferson and Sally Hemings,* xiii.

12. Unless otherwise noted, all italics in quotations are from the original. Wilkins, *Jefferson's Pillow,* 101.

13. Gordon-Reed, *Thomas Jefferson and Sally Hemings,* 113.

14. J. Miller, *The Wolf by the Ears,* 176.

15. Gordon-Reed extensively documents such defenses and persuasively demonstrates their peculiarities and their flaws. See *Thomas Jefferson and Sally Hemings,* 116–57.

16. Brodie, *Thomas Jefferson,* 22–23. Charles Miller says, "His initial step was to accumulate data, nearly any data. Unfortunately, the collection of data was also the most important and at time the only step in Jefferson's studies. At this task of collection, however, he was compulsive." Charles A. Miller, *Jefferson and Nature* (Baltimore, Md.: Johns Hopkins University Press, 1988), 41. Miller adds, "Jefferson was unquestionably more comfortable collecting and exchanging information than he was working out ideas explaining the data he had acquired" (43). William J. Scheick argues that Jefferson's *Notes* represents, in significant part, Jefferson's reaction to the chaos of the American Revolution, the grief engendered by the deaths of his daughter and wife in 1781 and 1782, and the humiliation of his term as governor of Virginia. See "Chaos and Imaginative Order in Thomas Jefferson's *Notes on the State of Virginia,*" in *Essays in Early Virginia Literature Honoring Richard Beale Davis,* ed. J. A. Leo Lemay (New York: Burt Franklin, 1977), 221–34.

17. Leo Marx, *The Machine in the Garden: Technology and the Pastoral Ideal in America* (New York: Oxford University Press, 1964), 118.

18. C. Miller, *Jefferson and Nature,* 43.

19. Thomas Jefferson, *Notes on the State of Virginia,* ed. Frank Shuffelton (New York: Penguin Books, 1999), 55. Subsequent references to this edition appear in parentheses in the text.

20. C. Miller, *Jefferson and Nature,* 48–55. See also Marx, *The Machine in the Garden;* Robert A. Ferguson, "Mysterious Obligation: Jefferson's *Notes on the State of Virginia,*" *American Literature* 52 (1980): 381–406; and Robert A. Ferguson, *Law and Letters in American Culture* (Cambridge, Mass.: Harvard University Press, 1984), 34–58. In addition, see Floyd O. Ogburn, "Structure and Meaning in Thomas Jefferson's *Notes on the State of Virginia,*" *Early American Literature* 15 (1980): 141–50; and Harold Hellenbrand,

"Roads to Happiness: Rhetorical and Philosophical Design in Jefferson's *Notes on the State of Virginia*," *Early American Literature* 20 (1985): 3–23.

21. In *White Men Aren't* (Durham, N.C.: Duke University Press, 2002), Thomas Dipiero traces the emergent identification of reasonable discourse and white identity in eighteenth-century science, especially natural history (52–150). See also Dana Nelson, *National Manhood: Capitalist Citizenship and the Imagined Fraternity of White Men* (Durham, N.C.: Duke University Press, 1998), especially 102–34.

22. In Jared Gardner's account of the emergence in the 1780s of a "master plot" of American culture, Jefferson's *Notes on the State of Virginia* provides one key in the coalescence of American subjectivity around a set of anxieties involving relationships to Europe and to race. *Master Plots: Race and the Founding of an American Literature, 1787–1845* (Baltimore, Md.: Johns Hopkins University Press, 1998).

23. Pamela Regis, *Describing Early America: Bartram, Jefferson, Crevecoeur, and the Rhetoric of Natural History* (DeKalb: Northern Illinois University Press, 1992), 104. See also Merrill D. Peterson, *Thomas Jefferson and the New Nation* (New York: Oxford University Press, 1970), 247–48; and Christopher Looby, "The Constitution of Nature: Taxonomy as Politics in Jefferson, Peale, and Bartram," *Early American Literature* 22 (1987): 252–73.

24. Of course, the book is not merely an encyclopedia but also a polemical text. See George Alan Davy, "Argumentation and Unified Structure in *Notes on the State of Virginia*," *Eighteenth-Century Studies* 26 (1993): 581–93. Regis concludes her chapter on Jefferson's *Notes:* "But disquiet enters the static array of the natural historical objects when Jefferson examines the department of man. Blacks elude both natural historical and legal classification. The American Indians, in one section of the book, are mere natural historical objects, their history unspoken, supposed not to exist. . . . A consequence of its natural historical framework, Jefferson's book obscures the representation of white history, omits the history of blacks, and flattens the telling of a single story about one native American." Regis, *Describing Early America*, 105. William J. Scheick argues that the paradoxical tension between order and chaos structures the whole of Jefferson's book. "Chaos and Imaginative Order in Thomas Jefferson's *Notes on the State of Virginia*," 221–34.

25. See, for example, Brodie, *Thomas Jefferson*, 144–45; Burstein, *The Inner Jefferson*, 60–61. See also Gisela Tauber, who ingeniously but not altogether convincingly reads Jefferson's book as an autobiography in code in "*Notes on the State of Virginia:* Thomas Jefferson's Unintended Self-Portrait," *Eighteenth-Century Studies* 26 (1993): 635–48.

26. Quoted in Burstein, *The Inner Jefferson*, 61–62. See also Peterson, *Thomas Jefferson and the New Nation*, 246–47.

27. By the end of the eighteenth century, the idea of the Native American as "a memento mori" was in several registers—Puritan sermons, Filson's retailing of the Boone legend, the scientific discourses of Europe—already well established and figures in Jefferson's treatment of their remains here. See Richard Slotkin, *Regeneration through Violence: The Mythology of the American Frontier, 1600–1860* (Norman: University of Oklahoma Press, 1973), 275.

28. C. Miller, *Jefferson and Nature*, 7.

29. Of Ossian, Jefferson wrote: "Ossian's poems . . . have been and will, I think, during my life, continue to be to me the sources of daily pleasures. The tender and the sublime emotions of the mind were never before so wrought up by the human hand. I am not ashamed to own that I think this rude bard of the North the greatest poet that has ever existed." Quoted in Eleanor D. Berman, *Thomas Jefferson among the Arts* (New York: Philosophical Library, 1947), 47. Though Macpherson's inventions were extraordinarily influential in England, France, Italy, and especially Germany, they perhaps nowhere had broader or longer-lasting influence than they had in North America. Cooper, Emerson, Thoreau, Whitman, and Melville were all admirers of Macpherson's Celtic bard and the joys of grief with which he was associated. Among his earliest and most devoted admirers was Thomas Jefferson. See Paul J. Degategno, "'The Source of Daily and Exalted Pleasure': Jefferson Reads the Poems of Ossian," in *Ossian Revisited*, ed. Howard Gaskill (Edinburgh: Edinburgh University Press, 1991), 73–93; Burstein, *The Inner Jefferson*, 31–41; and Paul J. Degategno, *James Macpherson* (Boston: Twayne, 1989), 129–34.

30. Malcolm Kelsall, *Jefferson and the Iconography of Romanticism: Folk, Land, Culture and the Romantic Nation* (New York: St. Martin's Press, 1999), 97. Kelsall writes, "The idea of an originary people is directly derived from eighteenth-century British romantic nationalism in general, and from Jefferson's favourite poet Ossian in particular" (96). See also Jack McLaughlin, "Jefferson, Poe, and Ossian," *Eighteenth-Century Studies* 26 (1993): 627–34. On manly grief as a crucial component of the eighteenth-century political imagination, see Julie Ellison, *Cato's Tears and the Making of Anglo-American Emotion* (Chicago: University of Chicago Press, 1999).

31. Lee Quinby, *Freedom, Foucault, and the Subject of America* (Boston: Northeastern Press, 1991), 18.

32. Jean M. Yarbrough, *American Virtues: Thomas Jefferson and the Character of a Free People* (Lawrence: University Press of Kansas, 1998), 20–21. Charles Miller remarks, "One implication of moral-sense reasoning is that there can be no genuine, or at least no widespread, evil in the world." *Jefferson and Nature*, 92.

33. Cited in Yarbrough, *American Virtues*, 17.

34. Cited in C. Miller, *Jefferson and Nature*, 98.

35. Yarbrough, *American Virtues*, 18–19.

36. Jefferson has a definite fondness for grotesque bodily metaphors when describing ills in the body politic, as when he says of the "mobs of great cities" that they "add just so much to the strength of pure government, as sores do to the strength of the human body. It is the manners and spirit of a people which preserve a republic in vigour. A degeneracy in these is a canker which soon eats to the heart of its laws and constitution" (171). Russ Castronovo notes that slavery was often associated with moral and sexual incontinence; see *Necro Citizenship: Death, Eroticism, and the Public Sphere in the Nineteenth-Century United States* (Durham, N.C.: Duke University Press, 2001), 62–100.

37. Letter to John Holmes, April 22, 1820, in *Thomas Jefferson: Writings,* ed. Merrill D. Peterson (New York: Library of America, 1984), 1433–35.

38. Henry Homes, Lord Kames, *Elements of Criticism,* 2nd ed., 2 vols. (Philadelphia: M. Carey, 1816), 1: 118.

39. Ibid., 1: 137.

40. Merrill Peterson, Jefferson's extremely sympathetic biographer, wrote that Jefferson's racial opinions were "a product of frivolous and tortuous reasoning, of preconception, prejudice, ignorance, contradiction, and bewildering confusion of principles." Peterson, *Thomas Jefferson and the New Nation,* 262. John Chester Miller, though equally sympathetic, remarks: "Manifestly, Jefferson was under powerful psychological compulsion to believe that the blacks were innately inferior." *The Wolf by the Ears,* 52. See also Jordan, *White over Black,* 440–69.

41. For Jefferson's relationship to eighteenth-century aesthetics and the sublime, see Quinby, *Freedom, Foucault, and the Subject of America* (Boston: Northeastern Press, 1991), 10; Scheick, "Chaos and Imaginative Order in Thomas Jefferson's *Notes on the State of Virginia*"; and Berman, *Thomas Jefferson among the Arts,* 32.

42. Christopher Looby, "The Constitution of Nature," 254. For Jefferson's fear of corruption and decay in republics where disharmony and change rule, see Drew R. McCoy, *The Elusive Republic: Political Economy in Jeffersonian America* (New York: Norton, 1982).

43. Scheik, "Chaos and Imaginative Order in the Thomas Jefferson's *Notes on the State of Virginia,*" 232. On Jefferson and the Hudson River School, see as well C. Miller, *Jefferson and Nature,* 260; Kelsall, *Jefferson and the Iconography of Romanticism,* 80–81; and Howard Mumford Jones, *O Strange New World: American Culture, The Formative Years* (New York: Viking Press, 1964), 358–66. Slotkin discusses the mixed nature of Jefferson's deployment of the sublime and the pastoral to suggest the movement from a threatened present to a peaceful future in *Regeneration through Violence,* 245–47.

44. See C. Miller, *Jefferson and Nature,* 50.

45. Malcolm Kelsall, *Jefferson and the Iconography of Romanticism,* 88–89. Like the passage describing Natural Bridge, the passage on the rivers also disrupts the book's order. It might better have appeared in answer to Query II, "Rivers, Rivulets, and how far they are Navigable" rather than in Query IV, "A Notice of Its Mountains," for the passage's force derives from Jefferson's impassioned description of the rivers rending the mountain asunder and passing off to sea.

46. Immanuel Kant, *The Critique of Judgement,* trans. James Creed Meredith (Oxford: Clarendon Press, 1980), 115. Gayatri Spivak has recently analyzed the racial and global implication of Kant's association of an ability to appreciate sublimity with the capacity to become a political subject in *A Critique of Postcolonial Reason: Toward a History of the Vanishing Present* (Cambridge, Mass.: Harvard University Press, 1999), 26–36. See also Bruce Robbins's discussion of both Kant and Spivak in "The Sweat Shop Sublime," *PMLA* 117 (January 2002) 1: 84–97, especially 95–96.

47. Kelsall, *Jefferson and the Iconography of Romanticism,* 89.

48. Frank Shuffelton, "Thomas Jefferson: Race, Culture, and the Failure of Anthropological Method," in *A Mixed Race: Ethnicity in Early America,* ed. Frank Shuffelton (New York: Oxford, 1993), 258; see also Ferguson, "'Mysterious Obligation'"; Ferguson, *Law and Letters in American Culture,* 34–58; and Jordan, *White over Black,* 477–80, 482–511.

49. Or as Pamela Regis put it, "In Jefferson's Baconian division of knowledge, natural history relied on the mental faculty of memory. Moral philosophy, which included ethics and law, was a function of reason." Regis, *Describing Early America,* 84–85. See also C. Miller, *Jefferson and Nature,* 18–19.

50. Robert Ferguson concludes, "Slavery exists but outside of law; it becomes in consequence a structural incongruity in *Notes* spilling between and among sections," which accounts for why, as Ferguson says, the "prevailing mood of *Notes* as a text is one of profound Anxiety." Ferguson, "'Mysterious Obligation,'" 401, 400.

51. J. Miller, *The Wolf by the Ears,* 67. That Jefferson did not fear the Indians seems more surprising given the diplomatic and military problems they represented. During the Revolution Virginia was menaced by hostile indigenes from the west and the south. See, for example, Peterson, *Thomas Jefferson and the New Nation,* 156.

52. Peterson, *Thomas Jefferson and the New Nation,* 259.

53. Lewis P. Simpson, *The Dispossessed Garden: Pastoral and History in Southern Literature* (Athens: University of Georgia Press, 1975). As Jordan puts it, this sense of a hierarchy of humans "gave vent to the deep social sense that society was, like nature, properly and naturally a harmonious hierarchical structure with each element set fixedly in its appointed place." Jordan, *White over Black,* 491.

54. Other contemporary commentators, including Benjamin Rush in his "Address upon Slave Keeping" and Samuel Stanhope Smith in his "An Essay on the Causes of the Variety of Complexion and Figure in the Human Species," made the point that whatever defaults of intellect or ambition enslaved Africans seemed to manifest were the result of their condition and not their character. See Jordan, *White over Black,* 281–94, 445–57.

55. Shuffelton, "Thomas Jefferson: Race, Culture, and the Failure of Anthropological Method," 269.

56. Mitchell Robert Breitwieser, "Jefferson's Prospect," *Prospects: An Annual of American Cultural Studies* (University of Cambridge Press) 10 (1985): 317.

57. As Jordan characterized this attitude, "We, therefore, do not lust and destroy, it is someone else. . . . Either chain him or expel his black shape from our midst, before we realize that he is ourselves." *White over Black,* 579. See also Paul Gilroy, *Against Race: Imagining a Political Culture beyond the Color Line* (Cambridge, Mass.: Harvard University Press, 2000), 44–45.

58. On the participation of blacks in the American Revolution, see, for example, Wilkins, *Jefferson's Pillow,* 44–45. The standard work is still Benjamin Quarles, *The Negro in the American Revolution* (Chapel Hill: University of North Carolina Press, 1961,

1996), 68–110. See also Sidney Kaplan and Emma Nogrady Kaplan, *The Black Presence in the Era of the American Revolution* (Amherst: University of Massachusetts Press, 1989), 6–89.

59. David Walker, *David Walker's Appeal to the Coloured Citizens of the World*, ed. Peter P. Hinks (University Park: Pennsylvania State University Press, 2000), 63; emphasis in original.

60. Ferguson, "Mysterious Obligation," 404.

2. AHAB'S CANNIBALS

1. William V. Spanos, *The Errant Art of Moby-Dick: The Canon, the Cold War, and the Struggle for American Studies* (Durham, N.C.: Duke University Press, 1995).

2. Herman Melville, *Moby-Dick, or The Whale* (Chicago: Newberry Library, 1988), 145. All references in the text are to this edition.

3. Samuel Otter, *Melville's Anatomies* (Berkeley: University of California Press, 1999), 164–65. See, as well, Geoffrey Sanborn, *The Sign of the Cannibal: Melville and the Making of a Postcolonial Reader* (Durham, N.C.: Duke University Press, 1998). For "cold war" readings, see, among others, F. O. Matthiessen, *American Renaissance: Art and Expression in the Age of Emerson and Whitman* (London: Oxford University Press, 1941); R. W. B. Lewis, *American Adam: Innocence, Tragedy, and Tradition in the Nineteenth Century* (Chicago: University of Chicago Press, 1955); Walter Bezanson, "*Moby-Dick:* Work of Art," in *Moby-Dick: Centennial Essays,* ed. Tyrus Hillway and Luther S. Mansfield (Dallas: Southern Methodist University Press, 1953). For a reading of the novel that identifies Ahab as a type of modern totalitarian but does not see Ishmael as the hero of freedom, see C. L. R. James, *Mariners, Renegades, and Castaways* (New York: Allison & Busby, 1953).

4. Of course, an entire range of possible Ahabs have paced the decks since the Melville revival in the 1920s. Ahab has served as a tragic embodiment of America's Adamic freedom, as a presentiment of tyrannical threats to American democracy, as a rhetorical pyrotechnician of America's imperialist ideology. See Lewis Mumford, *Herman Melville: A Study of His Life and Vision* (New York: Harcourt, Brace, and World, 1929, 1962); R. W. B. Lewis, *American Adam;* Wai-Chee Dimock, *Empire for Liberty: Melville and the Poetics of Individualism* (Princeton, N.J.: Princeton University Press, 1988); and Donald Pease, *Visionary Compacts: American Renaissance Writing in Cultural Context* (Madison: University of Wisconsin Press, 1987). Some critics have attempted to reclaim a more positive reading of his struggle. See, for example, Toni Morrison, "Unspeakable Things Unspoken," *Michigan Quarterly Review* 28, no. 1 (Winter 1989): 1–34; William Spanos, *The Errant Art of Moby-Dick;* Clare Spark, *Hunting Captain Ahab: Psychological Warfare and the Melville Revival* (Kent, Ohio: Kent State University Press, 2001).

5. Matthiessen, *American Renaissance,* 459. As William Cain points out, *Moby Dick* was important to Matthiessen and to us "because of what it reveals to readers about democracy in America." William E. Cain, *F. O. Matthiessen and the Politics of Criticism* (Madison: University of Wisconsin Press, 1988), 178–79.

6. Spanos, *The Errant Art of Moby-Dick,* 184.

7. Edward Said, "Islam and the West Are Inadequate Banners," *Observer,* September 16, 2001.

8. Russell Banks, in his successful novel about Brown, makes precisely this comparison. See Banks, *Cloudsplitter: A Novel* (New York: Vintage, 1999).

9. Harold Bloom, introduction to *Ahab* (New York: Chelsea House, 1991), 4.

10. It is precisely this relationship between history and trauma that Cathy Caruth makes available as "the possibility of a history that is no longer straightforwardly referential (that is, no longer based on simple models of experience and reference) . . . permitting *history* to arise where *immediate understanding* may not." Cathy Caruth, *Unclaimed Experience: Trauma, Narrative, and History* (Baltimore, Md.: Johns Hopkins University Press, 1996), 11; emphasis in original.

11. Pease, *Visionary Compacts,* 273. Wai-Chee Dimock, in *Empire for Liberty,* actually sees Ishmael, not Ahab, as the character whose obfuscation of real relationship performs an incipient logic of U.S. imperialism. Spanos, in *The Errant Art of Moby-Dick,* and Spark, in *Hunting Captain Ahab,* defend Ishmael and Ahab respectively against these various critiques.

12. That dread, as Geoffrey Sanborn's reading suggests, is more precisely a dread that the play of surfaces that renders all knowledge incomplete might stop rather than it might continue. The other for Ishmael remains, as does Queequeg, a virtual image rather than a knowable essence. Sanborn, *The Sign of the Cannibal,* 157–69.

13. David Leverenz, *Manhood and the American Renaissance* (Ithaca, N.Y.: Cornell University Press, 1989), 279.

14. See Marvin Meyers, *The Jacksonian Persuasion: Politics and Belief* (Stanford, Calif.: Stanford University Press, 1957), 10; Pease, *Visionary Compacts,* 275. Pease easily adapts the common assumptions of sociological discourse originating in and continuous with the cold war moment and mood he claims conditioned *Moby Dick's* reception. These assumptions and anxieties were formulated in the forties and fifties by historians like Marvin Meyers, by literary critics like F. O. Matthiessen, by sociologists like David Riesman in *The Lonely Crowd,* and by public intellectuals like Paul Goodman in *Growing Up Absurd* and focused on the failures of American character, and especially of American men, to fulfill America's covenants with justice and with freedom. Pease's reading of Ishmael's flight from freedom thus props itself on the sort of cold war anxiety to which he wishes to offer a plausible and persuasive alternative. The anxiety itself finds ample support in Melville's novel and in nineteenth-century American literature more generally.

15. Spark, *Hunting Captain Ahab,* 12; Sacvan Bercovitch, *Rites of Assent* (New York: Routledge, 1993), 359. While mounting his own critique of imperialist ideology in American literature, John Carlos Rowe has expressed some impatience with the univocity of "recent recital judgments of Melville" and appealed for "more varied standards of political and thus aesthetic judgment." See his *Literary Culture and U.S. Imperialism: From the Revolution to World War II* (New York: Oxford University Press, 2000), 79.

16. James, *Mariners, Renegades, and Castaways,* 121.

17. "The disciplinary division of labor renders them docile material, as pliant to the materialistic purposes of the corporate owners of the means of production, who would exploit them and the earth ruthlessly for the sake of capital gain, as to the grotesquely vindictive purposes of the 'idealistic' monomaniac, who would wreck vengeance against the uncentered be-ing of being for the sake of justifying the anthropological Adamic *logos,* the integrity of the absolute (American) Self." Spanos, *Errant Art of Moby-Dick,* 217.

18. C. L. R. James, *American Civilization* (Cambridge, Mass.: Blackwell, 1993), 75–76.

19. James, *Mariners, Renegades, and Castaways,* 187.

20. Ibid.

21. John Carlos Rowe, arguing against the simple identification of Melville with imperial individualism, notes that "Melville incorporates in many of his narratives a searching critique of the very 'individualism'" that he is accused of embodying. Rowe, *Literary Culture and U.S. Imperialism,* 95.

22. James, *Mariners, Renegades, and Castaways,* 65.

23. Ibid., 112, 84.

24. Ibid., 112.

25. Matthiessen, *American Renaissance,* 447. For an ingenious reading of the significance of Queequeg's withdrawal from Ishmael's narrative in terms of the complexities of cross-cultural comprehension, see Sanborn, *Sign of the Cannibal,* especially 118–69.

26. Cain, *F. O. Matthiessen and the Politics of Criticism,* 179.

27. Pease, *Visionary Compacts,* 269.

28. Mumford, *Herman Melville,* 125–26. I would note that in Mumford's own terms the labeling of Moby Dick as an embodiment of "accident" and "the vacant external powers in the universe" (126) seems to be an instance of a critic falling under Ahab's persuasive spell, for there is no necessary or self-evident reason why accident or the universe should be "evil." The terrible logic by which the West recognizes whatever opposes its will as evil reveals itself here along with the Western virtues.

29. James, *American Civilization,* 76.

30. On individualism contrasted to individuality, see Bercovitch, *Rites of Assent,* 307–18.

31. Unlike Lauren Berlant's reading of the prosthetics of gender, Ahab's reliance on prostheses makes him more vulnerable rather than furnishing him with an "apotropaic shield." See Berlant, "National Brands/National Bodies: *Imitation of Life,*" in *Comparative American Identities: Race, Sex, and Nationalities in the Modern Text,* ed. Hortense Spillers (New York: Routledge, 1991), 133.

32. At least since Fredrick Pattee coined the phrase the "feminine fifties," American critics have recognized a vast alteration in gender relations taking shape in the decade before the Civil War. See Fred Pattee, *The Feminine Fifties* (New York: D. Appleton-Century, 1940); Barbara Welter, *Dimity Convictions: The American Woman*

in the Nineteenth Century (Athens: Ohio University Press, 1976); Ann Douglas, *The Feminization of American Culture* (New York: Knopf, 1977); Leland S. Person Jr. *Aesthetic Headaches: Women and a Masculine Poetics in Poe, Melville, and Hawthorne* (Athens: University of Georgia Press, 1988); David Leverenz, *Manhood and the American Renaissance;* Michael Kimmel, *Manhood in America: A Cultural History* (New York: Free Press, 1996), especially 13–80; G. J. Barker-Benfield, *The Horrors of the Half-Known Life,* 2nd ed. (New York: Routledge, 2000). For the best discussion of the general impossibility of white masculinity, see Thomas DiPiero, *White Men Aren't* (Durham, N.C.: Duke University Press, 2002).

33. Barker-Benfield, *Horrors of the Half-Known Life,* 6; Leverenz, *Manhood and the American Renaissance.*

34. Alexis de Tocqueville, "Fortnight in the Wilderness," in George Wilson Pierson, *Tocqueville and Beaumont in America* (New York: Oxford University Press, 1938), 243.

35. Barker-Benfield, *Horrors of the Half-Known Life,* 17.

36. Edward Jarvis, "On the Supposed Increase of Insanity," *American Journal of Insanity* 8 (1852): 360.

37. When Pip goes mad from his exposure to isolation, his readily apparent insanity differs markedly from Ahab's more difficult to distinguish *manie sans delire,* the sane application of reasonable means to crazed ends, which occurs because of his exposure to other men. For contemporary accounts of insanity's links to civilization, see Barker-Benfield, *Horrors of the Half-Known Life,* 50–53.

38. Leverenz, *Manhood and the American Renaissance,* 279–306.

39. Ibid., 292, 295.

40. Ibid., 305.

41. Sanborn, *The Sign of the Cannibal,* 155. On Melville and cannibals, see, for example, Gorman Beauchamp, "Montaigne, Melville, and the Cannibals," *Arizona Quarterly* 37, no. 4 (Winter 1981): 293; and Rowe, *Literary Culture and U.S. Imperialism,* 95.

42. I cite from a late nineteenth-century edition of the translation Melville used, *The Essays of Michel de Montaigne,* trans. Charles Cotton, ed. W. Carew Hazlitt (New York: A. L. Burt, 1892), 207. Further references to this addition of Montaigne appear in parentheses in the text.

43. Though my terms and my final point differ in emphasis from Sanborn's, I have found his reading of Melville generally and *Moby Dick* in particular extremely illuminating. See Sanborn, *Sign of the Cannibal,* especially 118–69.

44. René Girard makes the largest claims for the origins of violence and of civilization in acts of ritual violence that establish hierarchies of difference. He works out this problematic of identity in violence most explicitly in *Violence and the Sacred* (Baltimore, Md.: Johns Hopkins University Press, 1977). I, however, am not proposing a theory of universal history. Rather, I propose to examine specific anxieties shaped by the intellectual and political moments in which Melville and Montaigne wrote.

45. Sanborn, *Sign of the Cannibal,* 163.

46. Sigmund Freud, *Group Psychology and the Analysis of the Ego,* trans. James Strachey (New York: Norton, 1959), 37; emphasis in original.

47. Christopher Newfield's brilliant reading of Freud's *Group Psychology and the Analysis of the Ego* as the culmination of an antidemocratic fear of homoerotic bonding that he traces through Emerson and others restates Newfield's commendable faith in democratic association and in an incorporated self that might serve egalitarian and democratic ends. Freud, surveying the wreckage wrought by the barbarity of incorporated groups, especially the conjunction of church and state, might be forgiven for taking a more dismal view of male associations. Religious fanaticism and nationalistic militarism are two possible outcomes of incorporated societies, and democratic principles cannot, in themselves, guarantee that a group will not elect to move in those directions. Real groups, unlike anarchosyndicalist utopias, tend to generate hierarchies. Without principles incorporated with the group and defended by the group's members from the group itself, hierarchies become expressions of pure power, and such expressions, because they can never be pure, are always doomed and spread that doom outward. The difficulty for each individual is to choose and for intellectuals to choose to make the choice as clear as possible. See Newfield, *The Emerson Effect: Individualism and Submission in America* (Chicago: University of Chicago Press, 1996), 91–128.

48. Leverenz, *Manhood and the American Renaissance,* 281.

49. Freud, *Group Psychology and the Analysis of the Ego,* 59.

50. Ibid., 55–56.

51. Newfield, *The Emerson Effect,* 64.

52. Sharon Cameron, *The Corporeal Self: Allegories of the Body in Melville and Hawthorne* (Baltimore, Md.: Johns Hopkins University Press, 1981), 58.

3. LYDIA MARIA CHILD'S ROMANCE

1. I take these words and point from Philip Gould's *Covenant and Republic: Historical Romance and the Politics of Puritanism* (New York: Cambridge University Press, 1996), 5 and 92–93.

2. As Heather Roberts puts it, analyzing Child's Christian cosmopolitanism in her "Letters from New York," "Child's narrative persona embodies the public heart, forging sympathetic connections with passing strangers and with her newspaper audience as a means of strengthening the communal bonds necessary to enable progressive social change." Roberts, "'The Public Heart': Urban Life and the Politics of Sympathy in Lydia Maria Child's Letters from New York," *American Literature* 76, no. 4 (2004): 749–75, 754. See, as well, Debra J. Rosenthal, "Floral Counterdiscourse: Miscegenation, Ecofeminism, and Hybridity in Lydia Maria Child's *A Romance of the Republic,*" *Women's Studies* 31 (March–April 2002): 221–45; and Mark G. Vasquez, "Your Sister Cannot Speak to You and Understand You As I Do": Native American Culture and Female Subjectivity in Lydia Maria Child and Catharine Maria Sedgwick," *ATQ* 15, no. 3 (September 2001): 173–90.

3. See, for example, Dana Nelson, introduction to Lydia Maria Child, *A Romance of the Republic,* ed. Dana Nelson (1867; Lexington: University of Kentucky Press, 1997); and Nelson, *The Word in Black and White: Reading Race in American Culture, 1638–1867* (New York: Oxford University Press, 1992); Carolyn Karcher, *The First Woman in the Republic: A Cultural Biography of Lydia Maria Child* (Durham, N.C.: Duke University Press, 1994) and introduction to Lydia Maria Child, *Hobomok and Other Writings about Indians,* ed. Carolyn Karcher (New Brunswick, N.J.: Rutgers University Press, 1992); Bruce Mills, *Cultural Reformation and the Literature of Reform* (Athens: University of Georgia Press, 1994); and Karsten Piep, "Liberal Visions of Reconstruction: Lydia Maria Child's *A Romance of the Republic* and George Washington Cable's *The Grandissimes,*" *Studies in American Fiction* 31, no. 2 (Autumn 2003): 165–90. For a different take on identity fixations among Child's critics, see Julie Cary Nerad, "Slippery Language and False Dilemmas: The Passing Novels of Child, Howells, and Harper," *American Literature* 75, no. 4 (2003): 813–41.

4. Child's "Letters from New York" were written between 1841 and 1843 for the *National Anti-Slavery Standard* and published in book form in 1843.

5. Remember, of course, Thomas Jefferson, who balanced feminized Indians against hypermasculine Africans in *Notes on the State of Virginia.*

6. Carolyn Karcher, introduction to Child, *Hobomok and Other Writings on Indians,* xv. On the importance of historical fiction in the early republic, see Gould, *Covenant and Republic,* especially 1–19.

7. Child possessed a respect for other religions rare among Christian apologists. See, as well, Lydia Maria Child, *The Progress of Religious Ideas,* 3 vols. (New York: C. S. Francis, 1855).

8. Gould, *Covenant and Republic,* 63.

9. As Thomas Wentworth Higgenson comments in his biographical sketch of Child, "In judging of this little book, it is to be remembered that it appeared in the very dawn of American literature." Higgenson found such special pleading essential to any appreciation of this book. Especially, he seems to have found the plot twist revolving around Mary's desperate marriage to Hobomok and the Indian's final noble act renouncing Mary and his child to be "the least artistic things in the book." However artistically problematic, they are ideologically very suggestive. Higginson, "Lydia Maria Child," in *Eminent Women of the Age* (Hartford, Conn.: S. M. Betts, 1869), reprinted in *Philothea, or Plato against Epicurus: A Novel of the Transcendental Movement in New England by Lydia Maria Child* (Hartford, Conn.: Transcendental Books, 1975).

10. Patricia Holland, for example, offers the following: "In Child's version the young white woman makes *two* forbidden marriages, to the Indian first and then to the outcast Anglican, similarly the victim of oppression. All three characters suffer from the father's dictates, and as Karcher points out, *Hobomok* twists the usual point of view in American writings by *pairing* rather than contrasting the Indian and the Anglican: both are condemned by her father; both fulfill spiritual aspirations that Puritanism denies her; both embody the sexuality Puritanism tries to repress. In the young woman

is a figure who asserts her right to decide her own life, choose her own religion, re-claim her sexuality, and declare her own worth." Holland, "Legacy Profile: Lydia Maria Child (1802–1880)," *Legacy* 5 (Fall 1988): 49; emphasis in original.

11. As Mary tells her friend Sally, three years after her marriage and just before Brown's surprising return sends Hobomok packing, "I am sure I am happier than I ever expected to be after Charles's death, which is more than I deserve, considering I broke my promise to my dying mother, and deserted my father in his old age" (138).

12. At crucial moments in *Hobomok,* the Puritan women act to soften the exces-sive dogmatism or violence of their men. Mary's dying mother says to her husband, "If Brown comes back, you must remember our own thwarted love, and deal kindly with Mary," to which Conant replies, "Your dying request shall be obeyed" (108). Hobomok will play a similar role as a model of a softened form of masculinity. Indeed, as Dana Nelson and Julie Ellison have reminded contemporary readers, a cer-tain masochism is integral to traditional ideals of republican male virtue that stand in contrast to an emergent, more aggressive articulation of modern masculinity. Dana Nelson quotes Benjamin Rush's program for republican education: "Let our pupil be taught that he does not belong to himself, but that he is public property. Let him be taught to love his family, but let him be taught at the same time, that he must forsake and even forget them, when the welfare of his country requires it." Rush, "Of the Mode of Education Proper in a Republic," quoted in Dana Nelson, *National Manhood: Cap-italist Citizenship and the Imagined Fraternity of White Men* (Durham, N.C.: Duke Uni-versity Press, 1998), 12. See, as well, Nelson's discussion of republican self-management, 11–15. It is, of course, just such a lesson in self-management that Hobomok's maso-chism is meant to deliver through the complexities of the Early Republic's emergent gender realignment. See also Julie Ellison, *Cato's Tears and the Making of Anglo-American Emotion* (Chicago: University of Chicago Press, 1999). For the tension between persis-tent republican values and emergent capitalist liberalism in *Hobomok* and *Hope Leslie,* see Gould, *Covenant and Republic,* 91–132.

13. Karcher, *The First Woman in the Republic,* 236. Karcher is particularly critical of Child's philosophical romance *Philothea, or Plato against Epicurus* (1836) in which Child responded to the skeptical conservatism of Francis Wright's *A Few Days in Athens* (1822). Child set out to rescue both religious and moral sentiment by championing transcendental ideas and universal principles as the necessary basis for moral and ethical reform. Both novels are available in *Philothea, or Plato against Epicurus* (see note 8).

14. "The Black Saxons," in *A Lydia Maria Child Reader,* ed. Carolyn Karcher (Dur-ham, N.C.: Duke University Press, 1997), 182–83.

15. Ibid., 191; emphasis in original.

16. Ibid. Scott Peeples explores the complexities of such antiracist racial mimicry in Child in his fascinating extension of Eric Lott's analysis of black face to the histor-ical specificities of Sullivan's Island, the setting for "The Black Saxons," in "Love and Theft in the Carolina Lowcountry," *Arizona Quarterly* 60, no. 2 (Summer 2004): 33–56. Much of the story, as Peeples points out, occupies the reader with the eloquent

debate about justice and vengeance among the slaves, who are represented as "neither bloodthirsty nor docile, but rational," and the education by them of Mr. Duncan. The failure of that education to complete itself in emancipation demonstrates, according to Peebles, the shortcomings of love and the necessity, in Child's view, of violence.

17. "To Abolitionists," in *A Lydia Maria Child Reader*, 192.

18. Ibid., 197.

19. Carolyn L. Karcher, "Introduction: Journalism and Social Critique," in *A Lydia Maria Child Reader*, 298.

20. Ibid., 303; emphasis in original.

21. Scott Pratt, "Rebuilding Babylon: The Pluralism of Lydia Maria Child," *Hypatia: A Journal of Feminist Philosophy* 19, no. 2 (Spring 2004): 92–104, 100; emphasis in original. Pratt makes a persuasive case for Child, and other pluralistic feminists, as originators of an American tradition of attempting to embrace difference that includes the pragmatists, especially John Dewey.

22. Child, *A Lydia Maria Child Reader*, 320.

23. Ibid., 315; emphasis in original. In another letter Child makes a similar point comparing the imagined careers of a wealthy and unscrupulous real estate speculator who purposely bankrupts and dispossesses his debtor and a desperate clerk who embezzles from his firm. The first enjoys social prestige and a reputation as a "shrewd business man" while the latter ends on Blackwell's Island. "Society made both these men thieves; but punished the one, while she rewarded the other" (322). Even more surprisingly, Child adds the following evidence for her theory of the social origin and social utility of crimes and criminals: "That criminals so universally *feel* themselves the victims of injustice, is one strong proof that it is true; for impressions entirely without foundation are not apt to become universal" (322; emphasis in original). To realize this, however, one must imaginatively identify with and adopt the perspective of the criminal and thereby compromise the very basis of respectability.

24. Ibid., 318. It is worth noting that Child's advocacy of cosmopolitanism, here manifest in her sympathetic identification with these foreign graves—one inscribed "Mutter"—had its limits. In 1866, in "A High Flying Letter," provoked by balloon travel, she worries not about poor foreigners but about affluent Americans seeking education in Europe away from their national culture and republican ideals. These Americans return, she frets, with a commitment to aristocratic society and a failure to identify with equal rights and the American people (ibid., 330–31). Sounding a bit like Jefferson, but fearing the influence of foreign education more than the presence of foreigners, Child argues that "men who are to assume the immense responsibilities and perform the sublime duties of American citizens should be educated in America, under the influence of our republican institutions, breathing an atmosphere of equal rights, and habitually feeling themselves, to all intents and purposes, a portion of the people" (331). Clearly for Child the failure of those republican institutions to realize the principles of equality and the identification of citizens with society did not ultimately compromise the potentialities of the principles she hoped to reinvigorate or of the identifications she hoped to renew.

25. Child, *A Lydia Maria Child Reader*, 325; emphases in original.

26. Child, *The Progress of Religious Ideas*, 1: vii; emphasis in original.

27. This applies to specific practices as well, as when Child writes, "The old Braminical idea that every sin must have its prescribed amount of punishment, and that the gods would accept the life of one person as atonement for the sins of others, prevailed also in Greece and Rome; but there it mainly took the form of heroic self-sacrifice for the public good" (ibid., 1: 303). Child's debts to Hegel are everywhere apparent as in the following passage on the emergence of Greek philosophy: "The spirit of freedom, conspicuous in poetry and the arts, manifested itself in all forms of thought. Theories of God and the soul escaped from the locks and keys of priests into the minds of philosophers, who lectured upon them openly, excited other minds to investigation, and led the way to general discussion. The world was beginning to pass out of the age of childhood, which receives unquestioning all it is taught. It was entering the age of youthful, inquiring intellect, poetic, erratic, allured by castles in the air, but eager, buoyant, and free" (1: 330). Thus, the ideas of old Bramins and "Hindu rationalists" find themselves rearticulated at the origins of Western metaphysics.

28. Carolyn Karcher, *The First Woman in the Republic*, 510. On Child's view of America's future, see Carolyn Karcher, "Lydia Maria Child's *A Romance of the Republic*: An Abolitionist Vision of America's Racial Destiny," in *Slavery and the Literary Imagination*, ed. Deborah McDowall and Arnold Rampersad (Baltimore, Md.: Johns Hopkins University Press, 1989); and also Karcher, *The First Woman in the Republic*, 510–31.

29. Karcher writes that "ultimately, Child's allegiance to an ideal of assimilation that remained white dominated prevented her from imagining satisfactory alternatives to the social order she had so trenchantly anatomized. . . . Child found it impossible to envision a truly egalitarian, multicultural society." (*The First Woman in the Republic*, 527). Karcher is right, but that Child cannot quite imagine what the final end of amalgamation might be seems less important than her presentation of the means by which the republic's failures might be rectified.

30. Child, *A Romance of the Republic*, 7. Subsequent references to this edition appear in parentheses in the text.

31. Shirley Samuels describes a similar reversal later in the novel involving Gerald Fitzgerald's son Gerald. She contends that such characters discover themselves to be not heirs of property but the property of heirs. Samuels, *Romances of the Republic: Women, the Family, and Violence in the Literature of the Early American Nation* (New York: Oxford University Press, 1996), 126. Samuels discusses the distortions of identity under slavery and especially in Child's romance; see 113–28.

32. Gerald's desire to emulate the "Grand Bashaw" imports an orientalized despotism to the heartland of the American republic. Here Child deploys prejudice against the East to make apparent to her readers how foreign to American national identity the passions and practices of slavery are.

33. Despite its resemblance to Bellini's *Norma*, frequently referenced within the novel itself, Child insisted that she based her plot on personal knowledge of actual

events. She has one of the fugitive slaves in her romance remark, "Judging by my own experience . . . the most fertile imagination could invent nothing more strange and romantic than many of the incidents which grow out of slavery." The link of Child's knowledge to the escaped slave's experience bespeaks an identification that is close to the romance's moral heart. Child, *A Romance of the Republic*, 361. See Karcher, *The First Woman in the Republic*, 512.

34. In this, the novel differs from both contemporary and later representations of racial mixture. See, for example, Karcher's summary of treatments of racial mixture contemporary with Child's in *The First Woman in the Republic*, 527–31.

4. JOHN BROWN'S IDENTITIES

1. "Reply of Mrs. Child [to Mrs. Mason]" from *Correspondence between Lydia Maria Child and Gov. Wise and Mrs. Mason of Virginia* (1860), 18–28, in *A Lydia Maria Child Reader*, ed. Carolyn L. Karcher (Durham, N.C.: Duke University Press, 1997), 250–51; emphasis in original. For an account of Brown's legend as hero or scourge, martyr or madman, see Zoe Trodd and John Stauffer, introduction to *Meteor of War: The John Brown Story*, ed. Zoe Trodd and John Stauffer (Maplecrest, N.Y.: Brandywine Press, 2004); David S. Reynolds, *John Brown, Abolitionist: The Man Who Killed Slavery, Sparked the Civil War, and Seeded Civil Rights* (New York: Knopf, 2005), especially 3–13 and 480–506; and most extensively, Merrill D. Peterson, *John Brown: The Legend Revisited* (Charlottesville: University of Virginia Press, 2002).

2. David W. Blight, *Race and Reunion: The Civil War in American Memory* (Cambridge, Mass.: Harvard University Press, 2001), 39.

3. John Brown, "Provisional Constitution and Ordinances for the People of the United States, May 8, 1858," in *Meteor of War*, ed. Trodd and Stauffer, 110.

4. Curry, along with contemporaries Thomas Hart Benton, Grant Wood, and Frederic Remington, created a visual language and repertoire of images that continue to structure national ideas and idealizations of the Midwest as America's heartland. See, for example, the images and essays in *John Steuart Curry: Inventing the Middle West*, ed. Patricia Junker (New York: Hudson Hills Press, 1998); and M. Sue Kendall, *Rethinking Regionalism: John Steuart Curry and the Kansas Mural Controversy* (Washington, D.C.: Smithsonian Institution Press, 1986).

5. M. Sue Kendall sees both Curry's ambiguous murals and the controversies that they provoked and that disrupted their completion as expressions of a social climate that included the resurgence, in Kansas and nationally, of the KKK as well as Curry's own reservations about zealous reformers. See Kendall, "Alien Corn," in *John Steuart Curry*, ed. Junker, 176–77; and Kendall, *Rethinking Regionalism*, 86–88. It is Curry's interpretation of Brown that Hollywood, in Merle Curtis's *Santa Fe Trail* (1940), depended on both pictorially and thematically. The film, like Curry's mural, reflects attitudes toward Brown made popular in Robert Penn Warren's tendentious attempt to portray Brown as a demagogue and charlatan in *John Brown: The Making of a Martyr* (1929). In the film, two young cavalry officers—Jeb Stuart (Errol Flynn) and

George Armstrong Custard (Ronald Reagan), representing the interests and views of the South and the North, combine forces to pursue Brown through Kansas and finally to capture him at Harpers Ferry. Raymond Massey's Brown, equal parts prophet and lunatic, could have stepped out of Curry's mural and into the movie's frame, wind-torn beard and all. Brown, however, wore that iconic beard only briefly after his escape from Kansas. When Russell Banks reworks Brown's figure and story in his brilliant historical novel *Cloudsplitter,* he makes his narrator, Owen Brown, explicitly state that his father was usually clean shaven in part to distance his figure from the figure represented in Curry's mural.

6. For Turner and other black insurrectionists as historical precedents from whom Brown drew appropriate lessons, see Reynolds, *John Brown, Abolitionist,* 105–10. For Turner's legend, see Scot French, *Rebellious Slave: Nat Turner in American Memory* (Boston: Houghton Mifflin, 2004).

7. Lerone Bennett, "Tea and Sympathy: Liberals and Other White Hopes," in *The Negro Mood and Other Essays* (Chicago: Johnson, 1964), 100–101; emphasis in original. On Brown's cross-racial identification, see John Stauffer, *The Black Hearts of Men: Radical Abolitionists and the Transformation of Race* (Cambridge, Mass.: Harvard University Press, 2001); and Reynolds, *John Brown, Abolitionist.*

8. For the influence of both Turner and Denmark Vesey on Stowe's conception of Dred, see Robert S. Levine, *Martin Delaney, Frederick Douglass, and the Politics of Representative Identity* (Chapel Hill: University of North Carolina Press, 1997), 160–65.

9. See Robert B. Stepto, "Sharing the Thunder: The Literary Exchanges of Harriet Beecher Stowe, Henry Bibb, and Frederick Douglass," in *New Essays on "Uncle Tom's Cabin,"* ed. Eric J. Sundquist (New York: Cambridge University Press, 1986); and Levine, *Martin Delany, Frederick Douglass, and the Politics of Representative Identity,* 144–76.

10. Stowe, at the end of *Uncle Tom's Cabin,* requires the "mothers of America" to be sure that they feel right, seemingly sure herself that right feeling will lead them to oppose slavery. As Leonard Tennenhouse recently put it, she "rests her case . . . with a revolution of the heart that insists on emotions that cross lines of both race and gender. At best, then, her novel arrives at an emotional resolution to a political problem, a feeling of family that cannot translate into a household capable of containing racial difference, at least not within the boundaries of the United States." Tennenhouse, "Libertine America," *Differences: A Journal of Feminist Cultural Studies* 11, no. 3 (1999/2000): 1–28, 22. Elizabeth Barnes argues that Stowe's emphasis on sympathetic identification reduces the other to another version of the same. This is, of course, a danger inherent in any attempt to understand or to act across divides in society and between people, but without some belief in sameness, difference easily lapses into lax gestures of incomprehensibility that can lend themselves to defenses of injustices, like slavery, as a peculiar institution impenetrable to outsiders. See Elizabeth Barnes, *States of Sympathy: Seduction and Democracy in the American Novel* (New York: Columbia University Press, 1997). See as well Christopher Diller, "Sentimental Types and Social Reform in

Uncle Tom's Cabin," *Studies in American Fiction* 32, no. 1 (Spring 2004): 21–48; and Jeanine Marie Delombard, "Representing the Slave: White Advocacy and Black Testimony in Harriet Beecher Stowe's *Dred,"* *New England Quarterly* 75, no. 1 (March 2002): 80–106.

11. Richard Brodhead suggests that the ethos of love in *Uncle Tom's Cabin* represents a disciplinary regime. One might actually wish that this were so, but the problem with literature from an aesthetic or a political point of view is its incapacity to discipline or master its own reception. See Brodhead, *Cultures of Letters: Scenes of Reading and Writing in Nineteenth-Century America* (Chicago: University of Chicago Press, 1993), 35. The ethics of masochism is as vulnerable as the politics of right feeling to misreading. For readings of the varied and contradictory receptions of Stowe's novel, see Jim O'Laughlin, "Articulating *Uncle Tom's Cabin,"* *New Literary History* 31 (2000): 573–97. Marianne K. Noble argues that suffering in sentimental literature may subvert sexual norms and express feminine desire. See "Masochistic Eroticism in *Uncle Tom's Cabin:* Feminist and Reader-Response Approaches," in *Approaches to Teaching Stowe's "Uncle Tom's Cabin,"* ed. Elizabeth Ammons and Susan Belasco (New York: Modern Language Association of America, 2000), 150–61; and Nobel, *The Masochistic Pleasures of Sentimental Literature* (Princeton, N.J.: Princeton University Press, 2000). One of the strongest readings of *Uncle Tom's Cabin* across its own grain remains Hortense Spillers's "Changing the Letter: The Yokes, the Jokes of Discourse, or Mrs. Stowe, Mr. Reed," in *Slavery and the Literary Imagination,* ed. Deborah McDowal and Arnold Rampersad (Baltimore, Md.: Johns Hopkins University Press, 1989), 26–61. See as well Lauren Berlant, "Poor Liza," *American Literature* 70, no. 3 (September 1998): 635–68. Gregg D. Crane analyzes Stowe's own discomfort with the "moral-emotional dissonance" produced by the nation's crisis over slavery. See *Race, Citizenship, and Law in American Literature* (Cambridge University Press, 2002), 70–86.

12. Sympathy sometimes fails in *Uncle Tom's Cabin* as well, where, for example, Simon Legree's failure to sympathize with Tom at the final moment of Tom's martyrdom marks the white man as the novel's villain.

13. Harriet Beecher Stowe, *Dred: A Tale of the Dismal Swamp,* ed. Robert S. Levine (Harmondsworth, England: Penguin Books, 2000), 98. Subsequent references to this edition appear in parentheses in the text.

14. As Robert Levine and others have noted, *Dred,* in its representational strategies and its moral vision, goes considerably beyond the sentimental romance and the Garrisonian ethics of *Uncle Tom's Cabin.* On the limits of sympathy and patience as represented by Tiff's rebellion, see Levine, *Martin Delany, Frederick Douglass, and the Politics of Representative Identity,* 166–67. Polly is only one of several white women whose failure to sympathize the novel judges. For example, Aunt Nesbit, the relative of the novel's romantic heroine, Nina (whose own good death while she nurses cholera victims will be the sentimental and ethical climax of the main narrative), appears to be a monster of insensibility. Informed that Mrs. Cripps has died, she observes to Nina: "O, these low families don't mind such things much . . . ; they never have much feeling. There's

no use doing for them—they are miserable poor creatures" (103). The good death sometimes fails to humanize those who witness it. Mrs. Cripps's death makes visible the inhumanity bred by failures of sympathy among men and women who own slaves.

15. Jeanine Marie Delombard points out that Stowe's increasing emphasis on slavery as a legal rather than a sentimental problem reflects shifts in white abolitionist discourse in the 1850s. See "Representing the Slave," 80–106. She sees Edward Clayton, however, still playing the part of patriarchal apologist for nonviolent resistance. I am more interested in the ways in which Stowe repeatedly stages her hero's imaginative and moral inadequacy to the enormity of the situation he confronts.

16. Robert S. Levine argues that the very lateness of Dred's introduction into the novel, and the surprising ways in which he eventually seems familiarly linked to all the novel's black characters, forms part of Stowe's representational strategy to remind her readers of the limitations of even a sympathetic white person's point of view on the realities of black life and resistance. Levine, *Martin Delany, Frederick Douglass, and the Politics of Representative Identity*, 160.

17. Racial condescension remains a comfortable strategy for Stowe, even in *Dred* where one can encounter such bits of racist wisdom as the following: "The African race have large ideality and veneration; . . . The negro race, with many of the faults of children, unite many of their most admirable qualities, in the simplicity and confidingness with which they yield themselves up in admiration of a superior friend" (306). Thus, thoughtless typification exists in the same novel with so much that is more compelling and complex in treating "the African race."

18. I have borrowed from Levine's excellent notes to his edition of *Dred* for these biblical texts.

19. Levine points out that "Stowe rhetorically participates in the political terror inspired by the prophetic tradition of the black heroic deliverer as embodied both by Turner and her fictional creation Dred." Levine, *Martin Delaney, Frederick Douglass, and the Politics of Representative Identity*, 174.

20. For an excellent reading of Styron's novel and a compelling reconstruction of its reception, see Albert E. Stone, *The Return of Nat Turner: History, Literature, and Cultural Politics in Sixties America* (Athens: University of Georgia Press, 1992).

21. William Styron, "This Quiet Dust," *Harpers*, April 1965, 136.

22. Ibid.; Styron, *The Confessions of Nat Turner* (New York: Vintage, 1992), 133.

23. See Eric J. Sundquist, *To Wake the Nations: Race in the Making of American Literature* (Cambridge, Mass.: Harvard University Press, 1993), 37–83.

24. *The Confessions of Nat Turner and Related Documents*, ed. Kenneth S. Greenberg (Boston: Bedford/St. Martin's, 1996), 41. For a speculative analysis of the interplay between Gray's terror and Turner's manipulation, see Sundquist, *To Wake the Nations*, 38–55.

25. The violence was terrible. Approximately sixty whites, including one infant and more than twenty insurrectionists, were killed in battle or hanged. Over one hundred black bystanders were victimized by white panic and lynch law in the raid's aftermath.

26. *The Confessions of Nat Turner,* ed. Greenberg, 41–42; emphasis in original.

27. Styron, Stone notes, accepts Gray's central contention that Turner's actions were the result of mental confusion and religious insanity. See Stone, *The Return of Nat Turner,* 34.

28. Ibid., 88.

29. *William Styron's Nat Turner: Ten Black Writers Respond,* ed. John Henrik Clarke (Boston: Beacon Press, 1968), vii. Styron's detractors, white and black, frequently charged him with distortions of the historical record, but the record itself, as noted above, is so fragmentary and distorted at its origin, and the novel as a form so notoriously ruthless in its manipulation of "fact" to support "theme," that such historical inaccuracies, if they do exist, do little to explain the controversy's heat. For this reason, attempts to defend Styron's responsible use of historical sources, like Henry Irving Tragle, "Styron and His Sources," *Massachesetts Review* 11 (Winter 1970): 134–53; and Arthur D. Casciato and James L. W. West, "William Styron and the Southampton Insurrection," *American Literature: A Journal of Literary History, Criticism, Bibliography* 52, no. 4 (January 1981): 564–77, seem largely beside the point. Positions on the novel did not always divide along the color line. Saunders Redding liked it, John Hope Franklin admired its take on slavery, and some white critics like Wilfred Sheed panned it. But the controversy, for its participants, was saliently about perspectival issues associated with racial identity and community.

30. Styron reviewed both Stanley Elkin's *Slavery: A Problem in American Institutional and Intellectual Life* and Frank Tannenbaum's *Slave and Citizen* in the *New York Review of Books* in 1963. For him history clearly told a story in which blacks were psychologically wrecked by a slave system they failed to resist, and they continued to bear the scars into the present day. His acceptance of an easy association between black identity and social pathology was evident and troubling to his black critics. See Stone, *The Return of Nat Turner,* 50.

31. See, for example, Shaun O'Connell, "Styron's Nat Turner," *Nation,* October 16, 1967, 373–74; *Newsweek,* October 16, 1967, cover story; Eliot Fremont Smith, *New York Times,* October 3–4, 1967, two-part all-out rave; and C. Van Woodward in the *New Republic,* October 7, 1967. Herbert Aptheker took on himself the thankless task of pointing out the novel's historical misconceptions. See his article in *Political Affairs,* October 1967, and "A Note on History," *Nation,* October 16, 1967.

32. Ernest Kaiser, "The Failure of William Styron," in *William Styron's Nat Turner,* 57, 58; emphasis in original.

33. Loyle Hairston, "William Styron's Nat Turner—Rogue Nigger," in *William Styron's Nat Turner,* 67.

34. Charles V. Hamilton, "Our Nat Turner and William Styron's Creation," in *William Styron's Nat Turner,* 74; emphasis in original.

35. Mike Thelwell, in *William Styron's Nat Turner,* 82–83.

36. Albert Murray, "A Troublesome Property," *New Leader,* December 4, 1967, 18–21, 18.

37. Murray quotes the following "old song": "Well you can be milk-white / And just as rich as cream / And buy a solid gold carriage / With a four horse team / But you cain't keep the world / From movering round / Or stop old Nat Turner from gaining ground" (ibid., 18–19).

38. Murray, like many of Styron's black critics, correctly traces the sources of Styron's characterization back to the widely influential holocaust thesis popularized by Stanley Elkin, rendering a Nat Turner who has been "emasculated and reduced to fit snugly into a personality structure based on highly questionable and essentially irrelevant conjectures about servility, to which Styron has added a neo-Reichean hypothesis about the corrolation [sic] between sex repression and revolutionary leadership. Instead of the man of meditation who fasted and prayed to become the Moses of his people, instead of the good shepherd who bequeathed a heritage of activism to American ministers (never more active than at present), both black and white men of the gospel will find here a black man who really wants to marry someone's white sister— a man with a sex hang-up who goes out into the wilderness to meditate only to get a simple thing like freedom hopelessly confused with masturbation while having fantasies about white women" (ibid., 19). See also, for example, Loyle Hairston, "William Styron's Dilemma," *Freedomways,* Winter 1968, 7–11. As Hairston sees it, the answer to the question "Why then does the slave revolt?" should require no elaborate psychosexual speculation. If Nat Turner were not black, and the slavery he rebelled against were not American slavery, such elaborations would be considered irrelevant (7). For many white writers, the motives of black rebellion remained mysterious indeed. See, for example, James Lowell McPherson, "America's Slave Revolt," *Dissent,* January–February 1968, 86–89; and Robert Coles, "Backlash: The Confessions of Nat Turner," *Partisan Review,* Winter 1968, 128–33.

39. William Styron, "Afterword to the Vintage Edition: Nat Turner Revisited," in *The Confessions of Nat Turner,* 433–34, 435.

40. John Oliver Killens, "The Confessions of Willie Styron," in *William Styron's Nat Turner,* 43.

41. Styron, "Afterword," in *The Confessions of Nat Turner,* 448; emphasis in original.

42. Thelwell, in *William Styron's Nat Turner,* 91.

43. Styron, "Afterword," in *The Confessions of Nat Turner,* 449.

44. Ibid., 436.

45. Russell Banks, *Cloudsplitter: A Novel* (New York: Harper Collins, 1999), 414. All references in the text are to this edition.

46. In scholarly work on Brown, this refiguring of identity, race, and agency has been proceeding apace. See, most notably, Stauffer, *The Black Hearts of Men,* and Reynolds, *John Brown, Abolitionist.*

47. Perhaps Banks borrows the comparison between Brown and Ahab from Richard O. Boyer's *The Legend of John Brown: A Biography and a History* (New York: Knopf, 1973), which, in the words of Merrill Peterson, found that "Brown stands at the center

of American history. He is Ahab, who loses his life in pursuit of the Leviathan, slavery." See Peterson, *John Brown: The Legend Revisted,* 159–60.

48. For the ways in which Brown's Puritanism was part of his ambiguous public persona during as well as after his lifetime, see Reynolds, *John Brown, Abolitionist,* 14–28.

5. EMERSON'S ACTIVISM

1. The position Warren takes in his first book regarding Brown and slavery, race and regionalism, continues to shape his contribution to the Southern agrarian manifestos collected in *I'll Take My Stand: The South and the Agrarian Tradition by Twelve Southerners* (New York: Harper, 1930).

2. John Brown, "Provisional Constitution and Ordinances for the People of the United States, May 8, 1858," in *Meteor of War: The John Brown Story,* ed. Zoe Trodd and John Stauffer (Maplecrest, N.Y.: Brandywine Press, 2004), 110.

3. Robert Penn Warren, *John Brown: The Making of a Martyr* (1929; repr., Nashville, Tenn.: J. S. Sanders, 1993), 245.

4. Ibid., 245–46.

5. Peter S. Field, *Ralph Waldo Emerson: The Making of a Democratic Intellectual* (New York: Rowman and Littlefield, 2002). For the evolution of Emerson's thinking about race and his emergent commitment to abolitionism, see especially 167–208.

6. Charles Chesnutt cites both Douglass's experiences of oppression and their characterization by white abolitionists: "He had often been introduced to audiences as 'a graduate from slavery with his diploma written upon his back': from [a mob in] Indiana he received the distinction of a post-graduate degree." Charles W. Chesnutt, *Frederick Douglass* (Boston: Small, Maynard, 1899), 43. Emerson expressed his distaste for professional reformers and his sense of their limitations as partial men engaged in important work that their own partialities threatened in "New England Reformers," a speech that he delivered in Boston the same year he himself lent his unprofessional energies to the abolition movement. While this may express Emerson's hovering between "confusion and commitment," as Len Gougeon suggests, it may also express his refusal to confuse the expression of what he regarded as his true calling and the demands of occasions to which he felt it necessary to lend his voice. Gougeon, *Virtue's Hero: Emerson, Antislavery, and Reform* (Athens: University of Georgia Press, 1990), 70.

7. "The Fugitive Slave Law," in *Emerson's Antislavery Writings,* ed. Len Gougeon and Joel Meyerson (New Haven, Conn.: Yale University Press, 1995), 74. All references to Emerson's antislavery writings unless otherwise noted refer to this edition and appear in the text.

8. Habermas, describing the intellectual as an "educated person acting without a 'political mandate,'" remarks that the intellectual "acquires a *specific* role only when he is able to address a public opinion formed by the press and the struggle between political parties. Only in a constitutional state does the political public sphere become the medium of, and serve to reinforce, the process of democratic will formation" (emphasis in original). Moreover, Habermas also notes, the public sphere is the realm of a certain crucial nonprofessional professionalism. In a nice definition, he notes (paraphrasing

Anatole France) that "the intellectual is one who makes use of the means of his [or her] profession outside the sphere of his [or her] profession—that is, in the political public sphere." Jürgen Habermas, "Heinrich Heine and the Role of the Intellectual in Germany," in *The New Conservatism: Cultural Criticism and the Historians' Debate,* trans. Shierry Nicholsen (Cambridge, Mass.: MIT Press, 1989), 73. Emerson noted the expansion of the public sphere during his time to include "all classes" in his 1854 address "The Fugitive Slave Law."

9. Habermas, "Heinrich Heine and the Role of the Intellectual in Germany," in *The New Conservatism,* 73–74. A similar doubleness characterizes recent critical estimations of Emerson. As T. Gregory Garvey writes, "The detranscendentalizing of Emerson has given him unexpected purchase in a wide range of critical debates. Thus far, though, the debate is also characterized by a kind of dual image—Emerson is portrayed as a philosopher of independence, spiritual autonomy, and psychological power, and he is represented as an ardent family man and a reformer zealous enough to help finance John Brown's guerrilla war in Kansas. The coexistence, often within the same text, of these two representations—Emerson the Transcendentalist and Emerson the reformer—is sustaining a unique dynamism within Emerson Studies." Such a doubleness may be less Emerson's personal dilemma than the intellectual's general dilemma. See Garvey, introduction to *The Emerson Dilemma: Essays on Emerson and Social Reform* (Athens: University of Georgia Press, 2001), xxi.

10. Cornel West, John Carlos Rowe, and Christopher Newfield have each offered distinguished, nuanced, and compelling readings of Emerson's failings that proceed along and develop these lines of criticism, which, of course, are strangely reminiscent of Warren's Southern populist stigmatization of Emerson's antidemocratic, woolly-headed transcendentalism. Michael Lopez analyzes the long-standing critical discontent with and "scholarly condescension" to Emerson's thought as the "anti-Emerson tradition" in American criticism. This tradition finds the writer "worthy of preservation . . . but inherently objectionable or uninteresting." Lopez, *Emerson and Power: Creative Antagonism in the Nineteenth Century* (DeKalb: Northern Illinois University Press, 1996), 22. See Cornel West, *The American Evasion of Philosophy* (Madison: University of Wisconsin Press, 1989); John Carlos Rowe, *At Emerson's Tomb: The Politics of Classic American Literature* (New York: Columbia University Press, 1997); and Christopher Newfield, *The Emerson Effect: Individualism and Submission in America* (Chicago: University of Chicago Press, 1996). More recently Kerry Larson has explored Emerson's complicated and sometimes paradoxical thoughts about justice in "Justice to Emerson," *Raritan* 21, no. 3 (Winter 2002): 46–47, and "Illiberal Emerson," *Nineteenth-Century Prose* 33, no. 1 (Spring 2006): 28–72. I have been deeply impressed by Gregg D. Crane's more developed reading of Emerson's reliance on doctrines of higher law in his political activism. I agree with Crane's response to Emerson's critics, and I here retrace what Crane himself calls the protopragmatist aspects of Emerson's evocation of higher principles to focus on Emerson's relationship to the nation's failure. See *Race, Citizenship, and Law in American Literature* (Cambridge: Cambridge University Press, 2002), 104–30.

11. West, *The American Evasion of Philosophy,* 27; Rowe, *At Emerson's Tomb,* 18.

12. *Emerson in His Journals,* ed. Joel Porte (Cambridge, Mass.: Harvard University Press, 1982), 338. Cited in West, *The American Evasion of Philosophy,* 28.

13. West, *The American Evasion of Philosophy,* 40.

14. For the anxieties bred in Emerson's thought by the specter of the Jacksonian mob, see, for example, Eric Cheyfitz, *The Trans-Parent: Sexual Politics in the Language of Emerson* (Baltimore, Md.: Johns Hopkins University Press, 1981); and his "A Common Emerson: Ralph Waldo Emerson in an Ethnohistorical Context," *Nineteenth-Century Prose* 30, no. 12 (Spring/Fall 2003): 250–81. See also Joel Porte, "Emerson and the Refounding of America," *Nineteenth-Century Prose* 30, no. 12 (Spring/Fall 2003): 227–49, where Porte describes Emerson's struggle with democratically corrupted language to encompass an American ideal; and David M. Robinson, "Emerson, American Democracy, and 'Progress of Culture,'" *Nineteenth-Century Prose* 30, no. 12 (Spring/Fall 2003): 282–99. For Emerson's dedication to an American ideal everywhere betrayed, see Eduardo Cadava, *Emerson and the Climates of History* (Stanford, Calif.: Stanford University Press, 1997), especially 149–201.

15. For the view that emancipation must be a moral rather than merely an expedient act, Cadava cites the passage from Child's piece in the January 17, 1862, *Liberator.* Cadava, *Emerson and the Climates of History,* 169.

16. Emerson, "New England Reformers," in *Essays and Lectures,* ed. Joel Porte (New York: Library of America, 1983), 605.

17. Garvey, "Emerson's Political Spirit and the Problem of Language," in *The Emerson Dilemma,* 14–15.

18. The shift from content to context that David Robinson has noted informs Emerson's sense of the reformer's mission from the very first. See Robinson, *Emerson and Conduct of Life: Pragmatism and Ethical Purpose in the Later Work* (New York: Cambridge University Press, 1993).

19. This conflicted negotiation between speaker and audience is a great theme of Emerson's entire career. In "Self-Reliance" he notes that for nonconformity "the world whips you with its displeasure." But the truth he would speak to power requires he judge and sometimes defy the power of a disapproving populace: "A man must know how to estimate a sour face. . . . When the ignorant and the poor are aroused, when the unintelligent brute force that lies at the bottom of society is made to growl and mow, it needs the habit of magnanimity and religion to treat it godlike as a trifle of no concernment." Emerson, "Self-Reliance," in *Essays and Lectures,* 264–65.

20. Emerson, "The Uses of Great Men," in *Essays and Lectures,* 619.

21. George Kateb, *Emerson and Self-Reliance* (Thousand Oaks, Calif.: Sage, 1995), 25.

22. Rowe, *At Emerson's Tomb,* 1–41.

23. Rowe addresses the seminal argument that Bercovitch develops in *Rites of Assent: Transformations in the Symbolic Construction of America* (New York: Routledge, 1993), 307–51.

24. Andrew Ross, *No Respect: Intellectuals and Popular Culture* (New York: Routledge, 1989), 207.

25. Habermas, "Heinrich Heine and the Role of the Intellectual in Germany," in *The New Conservatism*, 73.

26. Len Gougeon describes Emerson's self-education on these and related issues as well as the general importance of these books to the abolition movement in *Virtue's Hero*, 70–79.

27. *Journals and Miscellaneous Notebooks of Ralph Waldo Emerson*, ed. William H. Gilman, 16 vols. (Cambridge: Belknap Press, Harvard University Press, 1960–82), 9: 98.

28. Terry Eagleton, *The Ideology of the Aesthetic* (Oxford, England: Basil Blackwell, 1990), 27.

29. Harriet Beecher Stowe, *Uncle Tom's Cabin, or Life among the Lowly* (New York: Signet, 1998), 480; emphasis in original.

30. See Jane Tompkins, *Sensational Designs: The Cultural Work of American Fiction, 1760–1860* (New York: Oxford University Press, 1985). For the transgendering of sentiment crucial to an emergent, bourgeois republican ideology, see Julie Ellison, *Cato's Tears and the Making of Anglo-American Emotion* (Chicago: University of Chicago Press, 1999).

31. Eagleton, *The Ideology of the Aesthetic*, 27.

32. Quoted in Robert Richardson, *Emerson: The Mind on Fire* (Berkeley: University of California Press, 1995), 382.

33. In "The Work of Art in the Age of Mechanical Reproduction," Benjamin wrote: "This is the situation of politics which Fascism is rendering aesthetic. Communism responds by politicizing art." In Walter Benjamin, *Illuminations*, trans. Harry Zohn (New York: Schocken Books, 1969), 242.

34. Newfield, *The Emerson Effect*. Other writers have attempted to reevaluate Emerson's individualism. As Sam McGuire Worley puts it, "So reminded of the continual, collective responsibility for our institutions at the heart of Emerson's understanding of politics, we can better see the reasoning behind his emphasis on individuals." Worley, *Emerson, Thoreau, and the Role of the Cultural Critic* (Albany: State University of New York Press, 2001), 20. See also Kateb, in *Emerson and Self-Reliance*, who sees self-reliance as a mode of engaging rather than withdrawing from the world; and Michael Lopez, who in *Emerson and Power* reaffirms Emerson's affiliation with Dewey and West as a cultural critic for whom the unsettling potential of personal power is fundamental to his engagement with democracy. See as well John Michael, *Emerson and Skepticism: The Cipher of the World* (Baltimore, Md.: Johns Hopkins University Press, 1988); and Stanley Cavell, *Conditions Handsome and Unhandsome: The Constitution of Emersonian Perfectionism* (Chicago: University of Chicago Press, 1990).

35. Newfield, *The Emerson Effect*, 19, 23.

36. David F. Ericson demonstrates, once more, the enormously problematic productivity of liberal ideology in American debates over slavery in which both abolitionists and apologists made reference to liberal values of individualism, equity, freedom, and progress to justify their positions and to rally support to their opposed causes.

Ericson, *The Debate over Slavery: Antislavery and Proslavery Liberalism in Antebellum America* (New York: New York University Press, 2000).

37. See Garvey, *The Emerson Dilemma:* "The Spirit offered Emerson a nonsectarian locus of faith that held out the possibility of reconciling belief in the divinity of the individual with the desire to facilitate social harmony in the nation as a whole. . . . Spirit represents a set of core values that he believed able to provide the ideological foundation of a consensus society" (15). The status of those core values remains questionable and is one thing the intellectual's speech seeks to assay in his appeals to their power.

38. On the centrality of *Representative Men,* see, for example, David Jacobson, *Emerson's Pragmatic Vision: The Dance of the Eye* (University Park: Pennsylvania State University Press, 1993); David Robinson, *Emerson and the Conduct of Life: Pragmatism and Ethical Purpose in the Later Work* (Cambridge, England: Cambridge University Press, 1993); Mark Patterson, "Emerson, Napoleon, and the Concept of the Representative," *ESQ* 31, no. 4 (1985): 230–42.

39. See T. Gregory Garvey, "Emerson's Political Spirit," in *The Emerson Dilemma,* especially 28–32.

40. *Nature,* in Emerson, *Essays and Lectures,* 22.

41. Regarding Emerson's rhetorical demolition of Daniel Webster after the compromise of 1850, Sam McQuire Worley posits Emerson's engagement with cultural criticism in the following terms: "We can now see more clearly the role Emerson assigns the cultural leader. The need for constant interpretation of culture places significant responsibility on the man of letters. The figure of the transcendentalist minister as guardian and watch dog of values seen in Parker gives way to Emerson's cultural interpreter whose interpretive authority comes from his position within, not above, society." Worley, *Emerson, Thoreau, and the Role of the Cultural Critic,* 71.

42. Of course, what Emerson speaks of here is what Tocqueville described as the tyranny of the majority. For Emerson's relation to Tocqueville, see Cheyfitz, *The Trans-Parent* and "A Common Emerson."

6. DOUGLASS'S COSMOPOLITANISM

1. For Douglass's designation as "Representative Colored Man in the United States," see Peter F. Walker, *Moral Choices: Memory, Desire, and Imagination in Nineteenth-Century American Abolition* (Baton Rouge: Louisiana State University Press, 1978), 210. As Waldo F. Martin puts it, in a chapter titled "A Composite National Identity," "Douglass's assimilationism embodied this pivotal conflict" between "Afro-American race pride" and "an Anglo-American vision." *The Mind of Frederick Douglass* (Chapel Hill: University of North Carolina Press, 1984), 213. Sacvan Bercovitch reminds us that Douglass's investments in the dominant culture's vision of freedom as self-possession furnishes him a powerful trope in his abolitionist writings. *Rites of Assent: Transformations in the Symbolic Construction of America* (New York: Routledge, 1993), 370–71. Gregg D. Crane identifies Douglass's creative reinterpretation of the nation's founding document, the Constitution, as a freedom text, as the theoretical grounding of his

"cosmopolitan constitutionalism" in his opposition to slavery. The problems of cosmopolitanism grounded in higher law will come to the fore in this chapter's second half. See *Race, Citizenship, and Law in American Literature* (Cambridge: Cambridge University Press 2002), 104–30.

2. Female African-American intellectuals from Julia Cooper through Michelle Wallace and Hazel Carby have charged black male leaders with sexism. See, for example, Anna Julia Cooper, "Womanhood: A Vital Element in the Regeneration and Progress of a Race," in *A Voice from the South,* ed. Mary Helen Washington (1892; repr., New York: Oxford University Press, 1988), 31–32; bell hooks, *Ain't I a Woman: Black Women and Feminism* (Boston: South End Press, 1981), 90; Deborah E. McDowell, "The First Place: Making Frederick Douglass and the Afro-American Narrative Tradition," in *Critical Essays on Frederick Douglass,* ed. William L. Andrews (Boston: G. K. Hall, 1991), 208; Hortense J. Spillers, "The Crisis of the Negro Intellectual, a Post Date," in Spillers, *Black, White, and in Color: Essays on American Literature and Culture* (Chicago: University of Chicago Press, 2003), especially 468–69; Michele Wallace, *Black Macho and the Myth of the Superwoman* (New York: Dial Press, 1979); Hazel Carby, *Race Men* (Cambridge, Mass.: Harvard University Press, 1998). Maurice O. Wallace has recently argued that such centrality given to the black male figure has disabled careful study of the paradoxes and imbrications of black masculinity, and he pays particular attention to the ways in which an especially militarized version of masculinity has been as crucial for African Americans as it has been for American culture more generally. See *Constructing the Black Masculine: Identity and Ideality in African American Men's Literature and Culture, 1775–1995* (Durham, N.C.: Duke University Press, 2002), in which he discusses Douglass, Delaney, and Washington at some length. See also Marlon B. Ross, *Manning the Race: Reforming Black Men in the Jim Crow Era* (New York: New York University Press, 2004).

3. Ross Posnock, *Color and Culture: Black Writers and the Making of the Modern Intellectual* (Cambridge, Mass.: Harvard University Press, 1998), 52; Posnock cites James Baldwin, *The Price of the Ticket: Collected Non-Fiction, 1948–1985* (New York: St. Martins, 1985), 66, 181. Robert S. Levine's analysis of Douglass's professional struggle with Martin Delaney and other black intellectuals for attention and influence foregrounds Douglass's self-creation as a representative man in ways that emphasize his situation as a working black intellectual. See Robert S. Levine, *Frederick Douglass and Martin Delaney and the Politics of Representative Identity* (Chapel Hill: University of North Carolina Press, 1997).

4. Posnock, *Color and Culture,* 53.

5. Frederick Douglass, "Men of Color, To Arms!" in *The Oxford Frederick Douglass Reader,* ed. William L. Andrews (New York: Oxford University Press, 1996), 224.

6. "The Claims of the Negro Ethnologically Considered: An Address Delivered in Hudson, Ohio, on 12 July 1854," in *The Frederick Douglass Papers,* Series 1, *Speeches, Debates, and Interviews* (New Haven, Conn.: Yale University Press, 1991), 2: 506. Subsequent references to this edition appear in parentheses in the text.

7. Frederick Douglass, *Autobiographies* (New York: Library of America, 1994), 125.

8. Francis Smith Foster, *Witnessing Slavery: The Development of Ante-Bellum Slave Narratives,* 2nd ed. (Madison: University of Wisconsin Press, 1994), 71.

9. Borrowing from José Muñoz's work, Maurice O. Wallace refers to the dynamics of such a situation as a reassertion of identity that transforms identity through "disidentificatory means." In Muñoz's terms, this involves "recycling and rethinking encoded meaning." Muñoz, *Disidentifications: Queers of Color and the Performance of Politics* (Minneapolis: University of Minnesota Press, 1999), 31; cited, along with Richard Majors and Janet Mancini Billson, *Cool Pose: The Dilemmas of Black Manhood in America* (New York: Lexington Books, 1992), in Wallace, *Constructing the Black Masculine,* 46–47. On the problem of sympathizers, see Dwight A. McBride's discussion of Margaret Fuller's sympathetic appropriation of Douglass's first narrative in her review that stresses, explicitly, that "whiteness" is the standard of humanity and justice even as she argues that Douglass gives ample proof of deserving inclusion within, so to speak, the pale. See McBride, *Impossible Witness: Truth, Abolitionism, and Slave Testimony* (New York: New York University Press, 2001), 75–78.

10. Smith, introduction to Douglass, *My Bondage and My Freedom,* in *Autobiographies,* 132.

11. As Eric Sundquist notes, even literacy for Douglass assumed its power "less for any inherent reason than because . . . [it] was a weapon of resistance frequently forbidden to slaves." Sundquist, *To Wake the Nations: Race in the Making of American Literature* (Cambridge, Mass.: Belknap Press, Harvard University Press, 1993), 105.

12. Douglass, *Autobiographies,* 96. See Henry Louis Gates's discussion of this passage and the revision of it in *Figures in Black: Words, Signs, and the "Racial" Self* (New York: Oxford University Press, 1987), 120.

13. Douglass, *Autobiographies,* 366.

14. As John Ernest has recently remarked, "By 1855 he works to emphasize not the divine roots of but rather the cultural battles over identity." Ernest, *Resistance and Reformation in Nineteenth-Century African-American Literature: Brown, Wilson, Jacobs, Delany, Douglass, and Harper* (Jackson: University Press of Mississippi, 1995), 155.

15. Douglass, *Life and Times,* in *Autobiographies,* 939–40. Later in the book Douglass gives this question a more pointed formulation: "No man, perhaps, had ever more offended popular prejudice than I had then lately done. I had married a wife. People who had remained silent over the unlawful relations of the white slave masters with their colored slave women loudly condemn me for marrying a wife a few shades lighter than myself. They would have had no objection to my marrying a person much darker in complexion than myself, but to marry one much lighter, and of the complexion of my father rather than of that of my mother, was, in the popular eye, a shocking offense, and one for which I was to be ostracized by white and black alike" (961).

16. See James M'Cune Smith's remark on Douglass's attribution of his genius to his Anglo-Saxon blood, in the introduction to *My Bondage and My Freedom,* 136.

17. Douglass, *My Bondage and My Freedom,* in *Autobiographies,* 155.

18. Joyce Middleton argues that Douglass's rhetorical power derives from the oral culture of his mother's people. See Middleton, "Oral Memory and the Teaching of Literacy: Some Implications from Toni Morrison's Song of Solomon," in *Rhetorical Memory and Delivery: Classical Concepts for Contemporary Composition and Communication,* ed. John Frederick Reynolds (Hillsdale, N.J.: Lawrence Erlbaum Assoc., 1993), 117–20.

19. McFeely suggests that Douglass's identification of this image with his mother played a part in his later fascination with Egypt. William S. McFeely, *Frederick Douglass* (New York: Norton, 1991), 331–32.

20. Much of the nineteenth-century debate concerning the racially composite character of the ancient world, especially Egypt, sounds remarkably familiar a century and a half later. See Waldo E. Martin Jr., *The Mind of Frederick Douglass* (Chapel Hill: University of North Carolina Press, 1984), 204–5.

21. Jenny Franchot, "The Punishment of Esther: Frederick Douglass and the Construction of the Feminine," in *Frederick Douglass: New Literary and Historical Essays,* ed. Eric J. Sundquist (Cambridge: Cambridge University Press, 1990), 159. For "hermaphrodite" as a term of invective, see Phillip Foner, ed., *Frederick Douglass on Women's Rights* (Westport, Conn.: Greenwood Press, 1976), 3.

22. Cited in Martin, *The Mind of Frederick Douglass,* 206. For the "ethnological purpose" of this trip, see McFeely, *Frederick Douglass,* 330–32.

23. Douglass, "Our Composite Nationality," in *The Frederick Douglass Papers,* Series 1, 5 vols. (New Haven, Conn.: Yale University Press, 1991), 4: 241, 4: 254.

24. Frantz Fanon, *Black Skin, White Masks* (New York: Grove Press, 1967), 194; Posnock, *Color and Culture,* 238–39.

25. "Haiti," as Douglass would put it in 1893, has long "been very much in the thoughts of the American People." "Haiti and the Haitian People," in *The Frederick Douglass Papers,* 5: 520. For how Haiti has occupied American imaginings, see, for example, Joan Dayan, *Haiti, History, and the Gods* (Berkeley: University of California Press, 1995); Anna Brickhouse, "The Writing of Haiti: Pierre Faubert, Harriet Beecher Stowe, and Beyond," *American Literary History* 13, no. 3 (2001): 407–44; and Sean Goudie, *Creole America: The West Indies and the Formation of Literature and Culture in the New Republic* (Philadelphia: University of Pennsylvania Press, 2007. See as well David Scott, *Conscripts of Modernity: The Tragedy of Colonial Enlightenment* (Durham, N.C.: Duke University Press, 2004).

26. For the particulars of this episode I have relied on Douglass's own account in his last autobiography; on McFeely, *Frederick Douglass,* 334–58; and on Douglass's own diplomatic correspondence collected in *A Black Diplomat in Haiti: The Diplomatic Correspondence of U.S. Minister Frederick Douglass from Haiti, 1889–1891,* ed. Norma Brown, 2 vols. (Salisbury, N.C.: Documentary Publications, 1977), especially 1: 58, 149, 218, and 2: 61, 72, 94, 96, 101, 107, 130, 133, 136, 150, 243, 244.

27. McFeely, *Frederick Douglass,* 346.

28. Porter, "A Famous Naval Exploit," *North American Review,* September 1891, 296–304, 296.

29. Ibid., 303. In addition to "*Ablemarle* Cushing," he also received the sobriquets the "Hero of the War," "Lincoln's Raider," and "Lincoln's Commando." See Ralph J. Roske and Charles Van Doren, *Lincoln's Commando: The Biography of Commander W. B. Cushing, U.S.N.* (New York: Harpers, 1957), 193–252. Only a few years later, Charles Van Doren would show his own daring and enterprise during the quiz show scandals.

30. "At the Cannon's Mouth," in *Battle Pieces and Aspects of the War: Civil War Poems* (New York: Prometheus Books, 2001), 135–36, cited in Roske and Van Doren, *Lincoln's Commando*, 254; emphasis in original.

31. It gave Porter "pleasure to inform the officers and men of the squadron under my command that the rebel ram *Albemarle* . . . has been destroyed by Lieutenant William B. Cushing, who, in this hazardous enterprise, has displayed a heroic enterprise seldom equaled and never excelled." Roske and Van Doren, *Lincoln's Commando*, 248.

32. On the mythologizing of Custer, the best source is still Richard Slotkin, *The Fatal Environment: The Myth of the Frontier in the Age of Industrialization, 1800–1890* (Middletown, Conn.: Wesleyan University Press, 1985), 433–532.

33. Porter, "A Famous Naval Exploit," 303.

34. See *World*, February 8, March 3, and May 19, 1891; *Herald*, May 6, May 7, and May 9, 1891.

35. Douglass, *Life and Times*, in *Autobiographies*, 1027.

36. "Haiti and the Haitian People," in *The Frederick Douglass Papers*, 5: 521.

37. McFeely, *Frederick Douglass*, 335.

38. Douglass, *Life and Times*, in *Autobiographies*, 1027, 1028.

39. Ibid., 1028.

40. Ibid., 1029.

41. Douglass, "Haiti and the Haitian People," in *The Frederick Douglass Papers*, 5: 517.

42. Douglass, *Life and Times*, in *Autobiographies*, 1029.

43. In Haiti, as McFeely notes, the new minister had to overcome not his color but his known sympathies for President Grant's imperial adventure into neighboring Santo Domingo to which he here refers. McFeely, *Frederick Douglass*, 336. As Millery Polyne points out, Douglass also finds himself caught between two agonistic models of pan-Americanism, a North American sense of the term used as a shield for U.S. imperial designs in the hemisphere and a Caribbean sense of the term signifying intraregional cooperation and identification based on a shared history of colonization and race-based slavery. Polyne, "An (Un)Profitable Servant: Haiti, 'Santo Domingo,' and Frederick Douglass as Pan-Americanist," presented to the Frederick Douglass Institute for African and African-American Studies, University of Rochester, November 2005.

CONCLUSION

1. The tragic events in Iraq have forced a rudimentary distinction between branches of Islam on the American consciousness and a half-hearted distinction between moderates and extremists, but that is about as far as it goes.

2. This is even truer of American reluctance to consider that their imperialism

may be less pure than appeals to democratization, the current name for America's civilizing mission, could admit. Notable exceptions remain on the fringes of public discourse. See Ellen Meiksins Wood, *Empire of Capital* (New York: Verson, 2003); David Harvey, *The New Imperialism* (London: Oxford University Press, 2003); Chalmers Johnson, *The Sorrows of Empire* (New York: Henry Holt, 2004); and Paul Smith, *Primitive America* (Minneapolis: University of Minnesota Press, 2007). Such occluded purposes and internationalized violence have long played a part in shaping American identity. See also Amy Kaplan, *The Anarchy of Empire in the Making of U.S. Culture* (Cambridge, Mass.: Harvard University Press, 2002); and Eric Cheyfitz, *The Poetics of Imperialism: Translation and Colonization from "The Tempest" to Tarzan* (Philadelphia: University of Pennsylvania Press, 1997).

3. Edward W. Said, *Orientalism* (New York: Vintage Books, 1978), 107.

4. Bernard Lewis, *What Went Wrong? Western Impact and Middle Eastern Response* (New York: Oxford University Press, 2002). I will have more to say about the complexities of Israeli society, but for now I would note that within Israeli society such Orientalist attitudes seem to characterize relations, even on the left, between European or Ashkenazi Jews and their Oriental or Sephardic counterparts. Faced with the opinion of a prominent Ashkenazi critic that his sympathy for the situation of Arabs and Palestinians was born from his own sense of humiliation bred through contact with the superior European culture of the dominant group, Shimon Ballas, a Sephardic novelist, voiced this frustration as well as any Arab could have when he said, "In other words, there is no reason to relate to me—as a writer or as a human being—as to someone having principles or a world-view. One should only see my political positions as a reaction to the humiliation that I supposedly suffered. But what about the pure Ashkenazi who also felt solidarity with the Arabs and fought along with me? They didn't struggle because of degradation but because they had principles. But I, at least according to Shaked, couldn't possibly develop any principles but only react as a result of my humiliation. Such a claim is not only perverse, but racist." Quoted in Ammiel Alcalay, "Exploding Identities," in *Memories of Our Future: Selected Essays, 1982–1999* (San Francisco: City Lights Books, 1999), 228.

5. Amin Maalouf, *The Crusades through Arab Eyes* (New York: Schocken Books, 1984), 264.

6. Michael Ignatieff, "The Burden," *New York Times Magazine,* January 5, 2003, 22–27, 50–55, 24. For a book-length celebration of liberal empire, see Niall Ferguson, *Colossus: The Price of America's Empire* (New York: Penguin Press, 2004). Such accounts can ill afford to assess the relationship of new modes of domination to the requirements of capitalist economic relationships and the exploitation of markets and resources. See Harvey, *The New Imperialism,* and Smith, *Primitive America.*

7. Michael Ignatieff, "Who Are Americans to Think That Freedom Is Theirs to Spread?" *New York Times Magazine,* June 26, 2005, 42–47.

8. *The Arab Human Development Report 2002,* sponsored by the United Nations

Development Programme, Regional Bureau for Arab States (UNDB/RBAS) (New York: United Nations Publications, 2002), 16.

9. Ibid., 32–33.

10. Ironically, the bruited result of a 2002 poll of worldwide opinion suggests that inwardness, self-obsession, and ignorance are attributes that much of the world attributes to the United States as the Bush administration's foreign policy represents it. See, for example, Richard Morin, "Poll Finds World Doubts U.S. Motives in Iraq (*Washington Post,* December 4, 2002), a journalistic account of the poll conducted by the Pew Research Center of the People and the Press that surveyed public attitudes toward the United States in forty-four countries, which demonstrated a "strong global consensus that the United States disregards the views of others in carrying out its foreign policy" and that the Bush administration's motives for pursuing Saddam are questionable.

11. *The Arab Human Development Report 2002,* 32.

12. Quoted in Ammiel Alcalay, *After Jews and Arabs: Remaking Levantine Culture* (Minneapolis: University of Minnesota Press, 1993), 243–44.

13. See Ayala Emmett, *Our Sisters' Promised Land: Women, Politics, and Israeli–Palestinian Coexistence* (Ann Arbor: University of Michigan Press, 2003), xviii.

14. Ammiel, *After Jews and Arabs,* 254.

15. Ibid., 266.

16. Others on both sides of the Palestinian–Israeli divide have undertaken to question the salience of reified identities. See, for example, Edward Said's afterword to the republication of *Orientalism* (New York: Vintage Books, 1994) and the essays collected in *Mapping Jewish Identities,* ed. Laurence J. Silberstein (New York: New York University Press, 2000).

17. Amin Maalouf, *In the Name of Identity* (New York: Arcade, 2001), 26.

18. Ibid., 120.

19. Ibn Khaldun, *The Muqaddimah: An Introduction to History,* trans. Franz Rosenthal, 2nd ed. (Princeton, N.J.: Princeton University Press, 1967), 23–24.

20. Eqbal Ahmad, *Terrorism Theirs and Ours,* foreword and interview by David Barsamian (New York: Seven Stories Press, 2001), 219–20.

21. See, to take only two examples, Tanya Reinhart, *Israel/Palestine: How to End the War of 1948* (New York: Seven Stories Press, 2002); and Norman G. Finkelstein, *Image and Reality of the Israel–Palestine Conflict* (New York: Verso, 1995).

22. Khaldun, *The Muqaddimah,* 98–99.

23. Alcalay, "Why Israel," in *Memories of Our Future,* 208.

INDEX

John Michael is professor of English and of visual and cultural studies at the University of Rochester.